McMINN COUNTY, TENNESSEE

MARRIAGES

1820-1870

Researched, Compiled, and Edited

by

REBA BAYLESS BOYER

This volume was reproduced from
an 1964 edition located in the
publishers private library,
Greenville, South Carolina

Please direct all Correspondence & Orders to:

Southern Historical Press, Inc.
P.O. Box 1267
375 W Broad Street
Greenville, S.C. 29602-1267

Originally published: Tennessee 1964
Copyright Transferred: Southern Historical
Press, Inc. 1983
ISBN: 978-0-89308-330-4
Printed in the United States of America

ABBOT, A. T. to Mary Harmon   20 July 1867
   m. 21 July by Wm. Thompson, M.G.
   Reference: Marriage Book G Page 18

ADAMS, Henry S. to Catherine Carter   25 August 1864
   m. 25 August by Rev. L. W. Crouch
   Reference: County Archives; Marriage Book F
   Page 6

ADAMS, John to Sely Goltonney   13 November 1829
   Daniel Kelly, Security
   Reference: County Archives

ADAMS, W. C. to Malissa B. Crawford   25 March 1846
   Reference: Marriage Book C Page 136

ADARE, Wm. C. to Martha Reed   4 March 1856
   m. 6 March by H. M. Sloop, M.G.
   Reference: Marriage Book D Page 108

AGEMAN, William S. to Martha Hardy   20 September 1849
   m. 21 September by M. Southard, M.G.
   Reference: County Archives; Marriage Book D
   Page 18

AHL, Daniel W. to Emaline Wilson   15 March 1843
   m. 15 March by John Jenkins, J.P.
   Reference: Marriage Book C Page 76

AIKEN, Thomas to Eliza Dempsey   23 July 1864
   m. 24 July by A. D. Briant, J.P.
   Reference: County Archives; Marriage Book F
   Page 5

AILEY - see also ALY

AIRHEART, Nicholas to Clarinda Eden   8 February 1843
   m. 9 February by A. Haren, M. G.
   Reference: Marriage Book C Page 73

AKIN, Thomas to Nancy Roark   Not Dated
   m. 21 February 1867 by D. Carpenter, M.G.
   Reference: Marriage Book G Page 10

AKINS, Zechariah to Mary Ann Anderson   30 June 1838
   m. 1 July by Larkins Taylor, J.P.
   Reference: County Archives: Marriage Book C
   Page 4

ALDEHOFF, H. W. v. to Ellen M. McCallie   20 September 1841
   m. 21 September by M. C. Hawk,
   Minister of M. E. Church
   Reference: Marriage Book C Page 47

ALEXANDER, Alex F. C. to Martha A. Pearce   11 August 1860
   m. 13 August by L. W. Crouch, M.G.
   Reference: Marriage Book E Page 10

ALEXANDER, John to Dialpha Turner   24 October 1855
   m. 24 October by A. D. Bryant, J.P.
   Reference: Marriage Book D Page 104

ALEXANDER, Wiley to Sarah Jane Wilson   25 October 1866
   m. 25 October by Jno. N. Moore, M.G.
   Reference: County Archives: Marriage Book G
   Page 2

ALISON, William F. to M. J. Scarborough   5 August 1851
   Reference: Marriage Book D Page 42

ALLEN, Byrum to Nancy M. Black   13 September 1870
    m. 13 September by J. S. Russel, M.G.
    Reference: Marriage Book F Page 47

ALLEN, James to Lethey L. Myres   1 September 1845
    Reference: Marriage Book C Page 125

ALLEN, John to Mary Perry   15 January 1845
    m. 15 January by Tapley Gregory, J.P.
    Reference: County Archives;
    Marriage Book C Page 116

ALLEN, Spartan to Rachel Stephenson   18 February 1841
    m. 18 February by John Tate, M.G.
    Reference: Marriage Book C Page 38

ALLISON - see also ALISON

ALLRED, Frances to Miss Serena Dorherty   20 December 1849
    m. 20 December 1850 /sic/ by J. Jack, M.G.
Reference: Marriage Book D Page 23

ALVY, Henry to Susanah Gunter   2 May 1849
    m. 3 May by E. Newton, M.G.
    Reference: Marriage Book D Page 14

ALY, Benjamin J. to Nancy J. Prichard   8 July 1865
    m. July 11 by Elihu Kelly, J.P.
    Reference: Marriage Book F Page 21

AMES, Henry to Easter C. Cate   24 September 1865
    m. 24 September by Wm. C. Owen, J.P.
    Reference: Marriage Book F Page 26
    County Archives

AMINERINE, /AMARINE?/, Henry to Jane Porter   30 July 1820
    m. 5 August by Jno. Walker, Jr., M.G.
    Reference: County Archives
    /Note: See PORTER, Robert W./

AMONS, H. S. to Nancy Thompson   15 January 1859
    Elisha Monroe, Security
    m. 16 January by James Henderson, J.P.
    Reference: County Archives;
    Marriage Book D Page 155

ANDERSON, Alexander to Nancy Ann Harris   2 September 1851
    Reference: Marriage Book D Page 42

ANDERSON, John to Luamey Shell   24 January 1867
    m. 24 January by A. G. Small, M.G.
    Reference: County Archives;
    Marriage Book G Page 9

ANDERSON, John M. to Sarah Jane Ware   9 November 1848
    m. 9 November by Robert Gregory, M.G.
    Reference: Marriage Book D Page 7

ANDERSON, Peter to Sarah Mathews   6 February 1839
    m. 7 February by George W. Mayo, J.P.
    Reference: Marriage Book C Page 14

ANDERSON, Robert A. to Martha A. Templeton   25 November 1847
    Reference: Marriage Book C Page 163

ANDERSON, W. H. to Sarah M. Crow   2 November 1858
    m. by T. Sullens, M.G.
    Reference: Marriage Book D Page 149

ANDERSON, William W. to Mrs. Louisa P. Smith   13 December 1842
   /Daughter of Thomas J. Campbell/
   m. 13 December by L. R. Morrison, V.D.M.
   Reference: Marriage Book C Page 69 and
   McMinn Chancery Suit No. 179

ANDES, Adam W. to Malinda Swaggerty   18 November 1865
   m. 18 November by Daniel McPhail, J.P.
   Reference: Marriage Book F Page 30

ANDREWS, William to Susan A. D. Hughes   28 July 1853
   m. 28 July by Wm. H. Ballew, J.P.
   Reference: County Archives; Marriage
   Book D Page 68

ARIC - see also ARRIC & ORRICK

ARMSTRONG, Cary A. to Sarah Farmer   30 December 1828
   m. 2 January 1829 by D. Cantrell, Esq.
   Reference: County Archives

ARMSTRONG, James to Meldridge Goode   12 October 1836
   m. 13 October by Thos. Wakefield, J.P.
   Reference: County Archives

ARMSTRONG, James A. to Susan C. Kimbrough   12 January 1865
   m. 12 January by W. A. Nelson, M.G.
   Reference: County Archives;
   Marriage Book F Page 14

ARMSTRONG, James Madison to Celinda Baker   13 June 1838
   m. 14 June by Ralph E. Tedford, M.G.
   Reference: County Archives
   Marriage Book C Page 4

ARMSTRONG, John to Malinda James   21 December 1847
   m. 21 December by E. P. Bloom, J.P.
   Reference: Marriage Book C Page 22

ARMSTRONG, Patrick to Martha Owens   25 January 1838
   Reference: Marriage Book C Page 1

ARMSTRONG, Patrick to Martha Vinson   31 January 1842
   m. 31 January by J. H. Benton, J.P.
   Reference: Marriage Book C Page 52

ARMSTRONG, T. J. to Maryann Baker   17 August 1844
   Reference: Marriage Book C Page 106

ARMSTRONG, William to Elizabeth White   2 January 1839
   m. 3 January by David Cantrell, J.P.
   Reference: Marriage Book C Page 13

ARMSTRONG, Wm. to Margret Newman   24 January 1867
   m. 24 January by C. R. Hoyl, M.G.
   References: Marriage Book G Page 9

ARMSTRONG, Wm. B. to Malinda C. Blankenship   16 January 1866
   m. 16 January by Elihu Kelly, J.P.
   Reference: County Archives; Marriage Book F
   Page 36

ARNOLD, Bennet to Darcas Wiseman   27 October 1829
   James M. Howell, Security
   Reference: County Archives

ARNOLD, Henry to Mary Housley   17 April 1841
   Reference: Marriage Book C Page 40

                              3

ARNWINE - see also ARWINE

ARRIC, James to Jenney Struhton   27 September 1866
   "Marriage Contract forfited by Jinny Struton
   Returned 13th day October 1866 - James Arric"
   Reference: Marriage Book G Page 1

ARRICK, James to Elizabeth Hix   31 December 1866
   m. 6 January 1867 by A. D. Bryant, J.P.
   Reference: Marriage Book G Page 8

ARRICK - see also ARIC, ORRICK

ARTHER, Felix to Mary Allen   22 January 1870
   m. 23 January by James Parkison, J.P.
   Reference: Marriage Book G Page 57

ARWINE, Marshal to Angeline Thomas   21 August 1856
   m. 22 August by T. B. Waller, M.G.
   Reference: Marriage Book D Page 113

ARWOOD, Lea to Mrs. Virginia Dennis   27 April 1867
   m. 20 /sic/ April by G. M. Hutsell, J.P.
   Reference: Marriage Book G Page 14

ASH, Hugh B. to Nancy Jones   5 May 1824
   m. 6 May by Robert W. McClary, J.P.
   Reference: County Archives

ASH, James R. to Margaret Rebecca Martin   28 May 1839
   m. 28 May by T. B. Love, J.P.
   Reference: Marriage Book C Page 17

ASH, James R. to Mrs. Elizabeth Walton   8 March 1849
   m. 8 March by Samuel Snoddy, J.P.
   Reference: Marriage Book D Page 13

ASH, W. B. to Mary A. Culpepper   10 June 1856
   m. 15 September by Wm. R. Long, M.G.
   Reference: Marriage Book D Page 110

ASHLEY, Howell to Darcus Melton   11 March 1865
   m. 16 March by P. M. Long, J.P.
   Reference: Marriage Book F Page 16

ASHLEY, James to Sarah Washam   7 May 1849
   m. 3 /sic/ May by A. L. Dugan, J.P.
   Reference: Marriage Book D Page 14

ASHLY, William to Elizabeth Cook   6 April 1841
   m. 6 April by C. Sanders, M.G.
   Reference: Marriage Book C Page 40

ASHLEY, William to Sarah Mayriod   18 March 1848
   Reference: W. P. A.
   /Page missing in Book C/

ATCHLEY, Robert to Nacy M. Butler   30 August 1845
   m. 11 September by Jonathan Thomas, J.P.
   Reference: Marriage Book C Page 125

ATCHLY, Pleasant to Malisy A. Williams 19 February 1868
   m. 20 February by Levi Fitzgerald, M.G.
   Reference: Marriage Book G Page 28

ATKINS, Allin to Eveline Shelton   29 January 1866
   m. 30 January by S. M. Thomas, J.P.
   Reference: Marriage Book F Page 37

ATKINS, B. F. to Jane B. Smith   21 February 1868
    m. 23 February by J. A. Wiggins, M.G.
    Reference: County Archives;
    Marriage Book G Page 28

ATKINS, E. D. to Rebecca Melton   13 December 1850
    Reference: Marriage Book D Page 35

ATKINS, Joseph W. to Mrs. Mary J. Witt   6 May 1868
    m. 6 May by W. H. Morrison, M.G.
    Reference: Marriage Book G Page 32

ATKINS, Madison to Maryan Thomas   2 October 1847
    m. 3 October by John Gaston, M.G.
    Reference: Marriage Book C Page 160

ATKINS, Wade H. to Elizabeth Melvin   29 June 1827
    m. 1 July by John Miller, J.P.
    Reference: County Archives

ATKINSON, Camel to Dorcas Newbury   7 October 1840
    Reference: Marriage Book C Page 32

ATKINSON, James G. to Mary C. Watkins   12 August 1867
    m. 18 August by James A. Cass, J.P.
    Reference: Marriage Book G Page 19

ATKINSON, W. L. to Darcus E. Loughmiller   1 October 1850
    m. by T. L. Hoyl, M.G.
    Reference: Marriage Book D Page 33

ATKINSON, Wm. T. to Manerva Smith   11 February 1864
    m. 11 February by A. H. Wilson
    Reference: Marrige Book E Page 12

ATLEE, B. G. to Nora Sehorn   18 May 1870
    m. 19 May by J. J. Manker, M.G.
    Reference: Marriage Book G Page 60

ATLEE, John L. to Sarah Humphreys   22 May 1856
    m. 22 May by S. Philips, M.G.
    Reference: County Archives;
    Marriage Book D Page 110

AULFORD, Mathew to Martha C. Young   2 July 1848
    m. 2 July by Wm. H. Ballew, J.P.
    Reference: Marriage Book D Page 3

AUSBORN, N. L. to Harret C. Godard   27 September 1855
    m. 27 September by J. Cunningham, M.G.
    Reference: Marriage Book D Page 102

AUSTIN, B. P. to Elizabeth Taylor   15 December 1870
    m. 18 December by Wm. C. Barnett, J.P.
    Reference: Marriage Book G Page 71

AVANS, Wesley to Artilessa Brock   27 December 1848
    Reference: Marriage Book D Page 9

AXLEY, J. W. to Miss M. A. Smith   6 August 1860
    m. 7 August by John H. Brewer, M.G.
    Reference: Marriage Book E Page 16

AYRES, N. Tandy of Hillsborough, Ohio to   8 July 1867
    Mary P. Atlee
    m. 9 July by R. A. Black, M.G.
    Reference: Marriage Book G Page 17;
    "Athens Republican" 12 July 1867 Vol. 1, No.1

AYTSE, Alfred C. to Loretta Reed   10 March 1864
    m. 17 March by Rev. D. Carpenter
    Reference: Marriage Book E Page 14 and
    Marriage Book F Page 1

BAILES, James K. to Lear Jane Templeton   11 April 1846
    Reference: Marriage Book C Page 137

BAILEY, Severe to Nancy Officer   15 August 1827
    James Officer, Security
    m. 17 August by E. H. Randolph
    Reference: County Archives

BAILEY, Wiley to Adaline Hayes   15 July 1865
    m. 15 July by A. J. Mathis, M.G.
    Reference: Marriage Book F Page 21

BAIN, J. V. to Rebecca Newman   10 June 1859
    m. 12 June by W. M. Newman, J. P.
    Reference: Marriage Book E Page 2

BAIN, Samuel R. to Amanda E. Patty   1 October 1850
    m. 1 October by Wilson Chapman, M. G.
    Reference: Marriage Book D Page 33

BAINE, Jas. C. to Louiza E. MCaffey   13 November 1858
    m. 14 November by Robert Cochran, J. P.
    Reference: Marriage Book D Page 150

BAKER, A. J. to Mary Henderson   1 January 1840
    m. 3 January by A. N. Harris, M. G.
    Reference: Marriage Book C Page 25

BAKER, Alexander to Mrs. Prudence Womack   31 October 1843
    m. 14 November by Jonathan Thomas, J. P.
    Reference: Marriage Book C Page 89

BAKER, Calaway to Mrs. Eliza J. Johnson   11 March 1865
    m. 12 March by Jos. Janeway, M. G.
    Reference: County Archives; Marriage Book F
    Page 16

BAKER, Calloway to Delila Peters   30 March 1839
    m. 30 March by John McGaughy, J. P.
    Reference: Marriage Book C Page 16

BAKER, Eli D. to Louisa Rose   7 March 1855
    m. 8 March by L. B. Waller, M. G.
    Reference: Marriage Book D Page 96

BAKER, J. A. to Elizabeth M. Derrick   10 December 1844
    m. 12 December by E. P. Bloom, J. P.
    Reference: Marriage Book C Page 114

BAKER, James to Louisa Bayless   21 August 1841
    Reference: Marriage Book C Page 45

BAKER, James to Scyntha Lawson   18 November 1864
    John Price, Security
    m. 22 November by Rev. Dan Carpenter
    Reference: County Archives; Marriage Book F
    Page 10

BAKER, James T. to Mary E. Grubbs   5 May 1866
    John A. Blanton, Security
    m. 10 May by C. R. Hoyl, M. G.
    Reference: County Archives;
    Marriage Book F Page 41

BAKER, Jas. T. to Margrett E. Frady   30 December 1870
    Thomas Crabtree, Security
    m. 1 January 1871 by W. H. Stephenson, J. P.
    Reference: County Archives;
    Marriage Book G Page 71

BAKER, John to Mrs. Elizabeth Hudgens   4 December 1849
    R. F. Braden, Security
    Reference: County Archives;
    Marriage Book D Page 22

BAKER, John Jr. to Pemela Davis   12 June 1858
    James H. Hornsby, Security
    Reference: County Archives;
    Marriage Book D Page 141

BAKER, John R. to Emma R. Duff   20 March 1867
    Daniel E. Case, Security
    m. 21 March by J. S. Russell, M. G.
    Reference: County Archives;
    Marriage Book G Page 12

BAKER, Joseph to Nancy Emelina Hickey   19 September 1845
    m. 21 September by T. S. Rice, J. P.
    Reference: County Archives;
    Marriage Book C Page 127

BAKER, William S. to Adilla Bailey   1 September 1828
    William Shamblin, Security
    Reference: County Archives

BALES, Hugh M. to Dorthula Hoback   12 February 1851
    m. 13 February by Stephen Sharetts, M. G.
    Reference: Marriage Book D Page 38

BALES, James K. to Abigale Benton   18 January 1849
    m. 18 January by R. A. McAdoo, J. P.
    Reference: Marriage Book D Page 10

BALES - see also BAILES, BAYLES

BALL, G. T. to Miss S. A. Qualls   1 September 1869
    m. 2 September by G. W. Morton, J. P.
    Reference: Marriage Book G Page 50

BALL, L. L. to Lucinda Pearce   12 March 1857
    m. 12 March by S. V. Philips, M. G.
    Reference: Marriage Book D Page 124

BALL, Thomas T. to Nancy A. Shipley   12 February 1868
    m. 13 February by A. D. Briant, J. P.
    Reference: Marriage Book G Page 28

BALL, Wm. S. to Sarah J. Ball   5 May 1859
    m. 14 May by D. W. Beaver, M. G.
    Reference: Marriage Book E Page 10

BALLARD, Jefferson to Sarah Camp   5 June 1868
    Reference: Marriage Book G Page 32

BALLEW, David D. to Celia D. Sparks   4 February 1843
    m. 9 February by E. P. Bloom, J. P.
    Reference: Marriage Book C Page 72

BALLEW, Stephen to Ann Everton   8 October 1842
    m. 3 November by A. Carlock, J. P.
    Reference: Marriage Book C Page 63

BALLEW - see also BELLEW

BANDY, Thos. J. to Mary A. Lewis   1 October 1864
  Reference: Marriage Book F Page 8

BANKS, John to Rebecca Raper   1 April 1866
  m. 1 April by Joseph Hamilton, J. P.
  Reference: Marriage Book F Page 40

BARB, Francis M. to Sarah Bedford   6 January 1853
  m. 6 January by S. Sharrets, M. G.
  Reference: Marriage Book D Page 61

BARGER, William to Elizabeth Rutledge   28 November 1865
  m. 29 November by Z. Rose, Regular M. O.Gospel
  Reference: County Archives:
  Marriage Book F Page 31

BARKER, A. H. to Elizabeth Melton   25 August 1858
  m. 25 August by C. Long, M. G.
  Reference: Marriage Book D Page 145

BARKER, Burrell B. to Sarah A. Wilky   3 December 1867
  Martin McKinny, Security
  m. 3 December by G. W. Coleman, M. G.
  Reference: County Archives;
  Marriage Book G Page 24

BARKER, J. S. to Mahala H. Caldwell   4 December 1856
  m. 4 December by Robert Reynolds, J. P.
  Reference: Marriage Book D Page 120

BARKER, James to Permelia Glaze   1 September 1868
  m. 1 September by E. Z. Williams, J. P.
  Reference: Marriage Book G Page 35

BARKER, James A. to Elizabeth J. Love   6 January 1841
  m. 7 January by Lewis Brewer, M. G.
  Reference: Marriage Book C Page 36

BARKER, W. G. to Margaret Ann Barker   10 March 1847
  m. 11 March by Wm. H. Ballew, J. P.
  Reference: Marriage Book C Page 154

BARKSDALE, Alfred to Winny Yancy   4 November 1842
  m. 4 November by A. Carlock, J. P.
  Reference: Marriage Book C Page 67

BARKSDALE, George to Martha Green   10 May 1842
  m. 10 May by A. Carlock, J.P.
  Reference: Marriage Book C Page 57

BARKSDALE, James to Katherine Webb   1 April 1840
  m. by H. C. Cook, J.P.
  Reference: Marriage Book C Page 28

BARKSDALE, Sherrod to Eliza Owens   1 July 1839
  m. 4 July by T. L. Hoyl, J. P.
  Reference: Marriage Book C Page 20

BARNARD, James of Athens to Ann Elizabeth Lea,
  daughter of Luke Lea, Esq. of Cleveland
  m. in Cleveland 9 December 1840 by
  Rev. James Tedford
  Reference: "the Hiwassee Patroit" December 15, 1840
  Vol. II, No. 40

BARNES, James C. to Elizabeth Hatford /or Flatford7 17 August 1847
  Reference: Marriage Book C Page 159

BARNES, Moses to Rebecca Benton
   Abraham Barnes, Security
   Reference: County Archives
        1 January 1825

BARNET, James R. to Sarah A. Thornton
   m. 29 July by John Scruggs, Minister
   Reference: Marriage Book C Page 44
        28 July 1841

BARNETT, Charles C. to Lucindy McGoss
   m. 7 November by Daniel McPhail, J. P.
   Reference: Marriage Book D Page 34
        6 November 1850

BARNETT, James to Sarah Harmond
   m. 21 February by W. Gettys, J. P.
   Reference: Marriage Book G Page 58
        21 February 1870

BARNETT, John W. to Martha Katharine McGinty
   Reference: Marriage Book D Page 3
        26 July 1848

BARNETT, Joseph H. to M. A. Smith
   m. 13 March by Saml. Wilson, J. P.
   Reference: Marriage Book D Page 13
        10 March 1849

BARNETT, Nathaniel to Martha Patty
   m. 10 August by Robert Gregory, M. G.
   Reference: County Archives
        3 August 1837

BARNETT, Saml. to Anna Cultan
   m. 24 November by Fielding Pope, M. G.
   Reference: County Archives
        23 November 1829

BARNETT, Stephen L. to Mary E. Cochran
   m. 17 November by Joseph Peller, M. G.
   Reference: Marriage Book G Page 69
        16 November 1870

BARNETT, Thomas J. to Mary S. West
   m. 7 April by James Forrest, J. P.
   Reference: County Archives;
   Marriage Book F Page 1
        7 April 1864

BARNETT, W. C. to Mary E. Lee
   m. 21 October by W. L. Burn, J. P.
   Reference: County Archives;
   Marriage Book G Page 2
        20 October 1866

BARNETTE, Charles A. to Louisa Armstrong
   m. 9 December by George A. Caldwell, M. G.
   Reference: Marriage Book D Page 121
        9 December 1856

BASINGER, H. C. to Miss M. K. Elliott
   Reference: Marriage Book D Page 8
        30 November 1848

BASINGER, H. K. to Julia N. Melton
   m. 15 June by W. H. Stephenson, J. P.
   Reference: Marriage Book F Page 19
        8 June 1865

BASINGER - see also BASSINGER, BAYSINGER

BASKET, Charles R. to Susan Spearman
   m. 8 April by William McKamy, J. P.
   Reference: Marriage Book D Page 51
        8 April 1852

BASSELL, Wm. to Amanda M. Sallee
   m. 16 October by C. Godbey, M. G.
   Reference: Marriage Book D Page 103
        16 October 1855

BASSHE, Gottlich to Eliza C. Gilbert
   m. 31 October by J. M. Kelly, M. G.
   Reference: Marriage Book C Page 110
        31 October 1844

BASSINGER, L. P. to Rosamond Bunch   17 November 1844
    m. 18 November by John Jenkins, J. P.
    Reference: Marriage Book C Page 112

BASSINGER - see also BASINGER, BAYSINGER

BATES, Ezekiel of Bradley Co. to Elizabeth Jane   16 May 1847
    Douglass, daughter of John Douglass
    m. 17 May by Leander Wilson, M. G.
    Reference: County Archives: Marriage Book C
    Page 156: "Knoxville Register" Volume 7 #337,
    2 June 1847

BATES, Dr. S of Kentucky to Sarah Hogan,
    Second daughter of Col. Wm. Hogan of Athens
    m. in Athens 20 March 1834
    Reference: Knoxville Register Volume 18 #923
    2 April 1834

BATES, William to MAlinda J. Erwin   16 August 1865
    m. 20 August by W. A. Nelson, M. G.
    Reference: Marriage Book F Page 24

BAXTER, Barnet (Barney) J. to Sally Billingsly   10 February 1839
    Edmund R. Hendly, Security
    Reference: County Archives;
    Marriage Book C Page 15

BAYLES, Donnel M. to Hannah Benton   5 February 1846
    m. 7 February by R. A. McAdoo, J. P.   /sic/
    Reference: Marriage Book C Page 152

BAYLESS, A. T. to Margarett Hemphill   10 August 1870
    m. 16 August by C. Denton, M. G.
    Reference: Marriage Book G Page 63

BAYLESS, John P. to Martha Jane Franklin   30 October 1845
    m. 30 October by A. Slover, M. G.
    Reference: Marriage Book C Page 129

BAYLESS, John T. to Ann A. Haynie   3 January 1855
    m. 3 January by T. T. Russell, M. G.
    Reference: Marriage Book D Page 92

BAYSINGER - see also BASINGER, BASSINGER

BEAM, Ezekiel to Jane Loyd   11 October 1842
    m. 11 October by M. D. Anderson, J. P.
    Reference: Marriage Book C Page 64

BEAN, Stokely to Mira Brandon   24 September 1856
    m. 25 September by Robert Reynolds, J. P.
    Reference: Marriage Book D Page 115

BEAN, Wm. H. to Mirah Thornton   3 February 1849
    m. 4 February by John Scruggs, M. G.
    Reference: Marriage Book D Page 11

BEANE, Wm. M. to Sarah E. Beard   20 November 1856
    m. 20 November by James Parkerson, J. P.
    Reference: Marriage Book D Page 119

BEAVER, David W. to Anna Thomas   8 November 1838
    m. 8 November by George W. Mayo, J. P.
    Reference: Marriage Book C Page 10

BEAVER, James to Eliza E. Acre   26 December 1864
    Reference: Marriage Book F Page 12

BEAVER - see also BEEVER

BEAVERS, Spencer to Mrs. Mary Cobbs   11 February 1841
    m. 11 February by J. McGaughy, J. P.
    Reference: Marriage Book C Page 38

BEAVERS, Sterling C. to Ann Eliza Beavers   12 July 1842
    m. 12 July by Hiram Ingram, M. G.
    Reference: Marriage Book C Page 59

BECK, Ephrem to Caty Bunch   22 November 1869
    m. 24 November by S. M. Thomas, J. P.
    Reference: County Archives;
    Marriage Book G Page 54

BECK, Israel to Miss Christian P. McKenzie   26 February 1851
    m. 27 February by William Walker
    Reference: Marriage Book D Page 39

BECKET, Thos. R. to Jane C. Wingo   22 January 1856
    Reference: Marriage Book D Page 107

BEDWELL, Plesant to Mary E. Roads   7 October 1868
    m. 8 October by James Parkenson, J. P.
    Reference: Marriage Book G Page 37

BEENE, Aron to Sarah A. Cabe   25 July 1866
    m. 25 July by A. J. Kirksey, J. P.
    Reference: Marriage Book F Page 44

BEEVERS, James S. to Nancy M. McPhail   14 August 1867
    m. 14 August by Hiel Buttram. M. G.
    Reference: Marriage Book G Page 19

BEFARNER, Abram to Matilda A. Crawford   22 December 1858
    m. 22 December by Joseph Neil, J. P.
    Reference: Marriage Book D Page 153

BELL, F. M. to Elizabeth Stephenson   24 April 1867
    m. 25 April by W. A. Nelson, M. G.
    Reference: Marriage Book G Page 14

BELL, W. S. to Elizabeth D. Keith   23 October 1851
    m. "on the evening of the 23d October 1851
    in the presence of Chas. McClung, E. G. Peal,
    Wm. F. Keith, and others" by James Park, M. V. D.
    Reference: Marriage Book D Page 45

BELL, William F. to Mrs. Francis Rose   20 May 1866
    m. 20 May by W. G. Horton, J. P.
    Reference: Marriage Book F Page 41

BELLEW, George W. to Mary Ann Caywood   15 October 1829
    Thomas C. Ripley, Security
    Reference: County Archives

BELLOWS, Mathias R. to Sarah Jane Clementson   18 September 1838
    m. 18 September by L. R. Morrison, V. D. M.
    Reference: Marriage Book C Page 7

BENCH, James H. to Avy E. Bench   29 January 1846
    m. 29 January by Justus Steed, J. P.
    Reference: Marriage Book C Page 132

BENNETT, William J. Y. to Mary E. Only   18 July 1849
    W. E. Hickey, Security
    m. 19 July by William Walker, J. P.
    Reference: County Archives:
    Marriage Book D Page 16

BENSON, Isaac to Jane Collier   22 March 1842
    m. 22 March
    Reference: Marriage Book C Page 55

BENSON, Isaac to Angeline Cobb   12 January 1857
    m. 13 January by J. Atkins, M. G.
    Reference: Marriage Book D Page 122

BENTON, A. M. to Mary A. Firestone   Not Dated
    m. 30 March 1859 by Robert Reynolds, J. P.
    Reference: Marriage Book D Page 159

BENTON, Elijah to Sarah Pearce   15 September 1839
    m. 15 September by J. McGaughy, J. P.
    Reference: Marriage Book C Page 22:
    Marriage Book C Page 24

BENTON, James to Matilda Wood   20 November 1839
    m. 21 November by Robert Gregory,
    Minister of the Baptist Church
    Reference: Marriage Book C Page 26

BENTON, James F. to Narcessa White   20 December 1843
    m. 21 December by Moses A. Cass, J. P.
    Reference: Marriage Book C Page 94

BENTON, John to Sarah Davis   2 October 1845
    m. 2 October by R. A. McAdoo, J. P.
    Reference: Marriage Book C Page 127

BENTON, John to Matilda C. Bolding   January 1847
    m. 27 January by E. P. Bloom, J. P.
    Reference: Marriage Book C Page 151

BENTON, T. L. to Mary Shipley   20 October 1854
    Daniel Bales, Security
    Reference: County Archives:
    Marriage Book D Page 89

BERRY, Samuel A. to Sarah Ann Moore or Morrow   11 May 1854
    Absolom Hill, Security
    m. 11 May by M. R. Ware, J. P.
    Reference: County Archives:
    Marriage Book D Page 83
    Note: In original bond and original license
      last name of bride is Moore, but in Marriage
      Record Book the Moore has been crossed over
      and Morrow written above.

BIGGS, Allen C. to Margrate L. Joyce   13 October 1868
    m. 25 November by C. Long, M. G.
    Reference: Marriage Book G Page 38

BIGGS, James M. to Sarah M. Hambright   8 October 1855
    m. 10 October by J. M. Blackburn, M. G.
    Reference: Marriage Book D Page 103

BIGGS, Thomas to A. E. Kimbrough   16 May 1864
    George W. Boyd, Security
    m. 17 May by W. A. Nelson, M. G.
    Reference: County Archives;
    Marriage Book F Page 3

BIGHAM, Asbury to Nancy J. Carver   22 June 1864
    David Bowerman, Security
    m. 23 June by W. H. Stepheson, J. P.
    Reference: County Archives:
    Marriage Book F Page 4

BILLINGSLEY, James to Sarah McCollum   26 March 1855
    m. 27 March by D. W. Beaver, M. G.
    Reference: Marriage Book D Page 97

BINGHAM (BIGHAM), Isaac M. to Charity Temple Doss   28 March 1849
    James Allen, Security
    m. 28 March by John Jenkins, J. P.
    Reference: County Archives: Marriage Book D
    Page 13

BISHOP, J. M. to Miss M. E. Clark   13 January 1870
    m. 14 January by G. M. Miller, M. G.
    Reference: Marriage Book G Page 57

BISHOP, Joseph to Mary Ivy   27 November 1834
    m. 30 November by Jonathan Thomas, J. P.
    Reference: County Archives

BISHOP, Robert to Sarah I. Dewitt   15 November 1865
    Reference: Marriage Book F Page 30

BISHOP, Sylvester to Martha A. Givens   27 July 1864
    m. 27 July by Wm. G. Wilson, M. G.
    Reference: County Archives: Marriage Book F
    Page 6

BISHOP, Thomas to Nancy Wright   1 December 1852
    m. 2 December by O. M. Liner, J. P.
    Reference: Marriage Book D Page 59

BISHOP, Washington to Lucinda Boyd   26 July 1865
    m. 26 July by James Parkison, J. P.
    Reference: County Archives: Marriage Book F
    Page 22

BLACKBURN, James to Mary Carter   25 March 1852
    Alfred Casteller, Security
    Reference: County Archives: Marriage Book D
    Page 49

BLACKBURN, Milton E. to Margaret Griffith   25 October 1864
    m. 25 October by Jas. Parkison, J. P.
    Reference: County Archives: Marriage Book F
    Page 9

BLACKWELL, J. R. to Anna Gregg   19 June 1839
    m. 20 June by Thomas Hoyl, J. P.
    Reference: Marriage Book C Page 18

BLAIN, M. V. to Mary Fields   21 January 1846
    m. 29 January by Daniel McPhail, J. P.
    Reference: Marriage Book C Page 132

BLAIN - see also BLANE

BLAIR, A. T. to Eliza Ann Reynolds   21 May 1846
    m. 21 May by Green L. Reynolds, J. P.
    Reference: Marriage Book C Page 138

BLANE, Mordecai G. to Mary A. Buttram   27 September 1850
    m. 28 September by Hiel Buttram, M. G.
    Reference: Marriage Book D Page 32

BLANE - see also BLAIN

BLANKINGSHIP, J. to Miss M. E. Ware   23 April 1868
    m. 23 April by Calvin Denton, M. G.
    Reference: Marriage Book G Page 30

BLANKINSHIP, I. H. to Miss M. M. Coldwell   22 October 1868
    m. 22 October by Calvin Denton, M. G.
    Reference: County Archives: Marriage Book
    G Page 38

BLANTON, Hezekiah to Bedience Young   4 October 1848
    m. 5 October by Taply Gregory, J. P.
    Reference: Marriage Book D Page 5

BLANTON, John to Matilda Armstrong   1 March 1828
    Isham Amarine, Security
    Reference: County Archives

BLEDSOE, Daniel to Peggy Cagle
    m. 17 September 1850 by John Gaston, M. G.
    Reference: Marriage Book D Page 32

BLEVINS, Argyle to Sarah E. Graves   1 June 1869
    Reference: Marriage Book G Page 46

BLEVINS, Charles H. to Mahala J. Picring   21 January 1869
    m. 21 January by J. Janeway, M. G.
    Reference: Marriage Book G Page 43

BLIZARD, Leonidas to Sallie A. Gibson   29 September 1870
    John F. Slover, Sr., Security
    m. 29 September by J. S. M. French, M. G.
    Reference: County Archives: Marriage Book G
    Page 66

BLOOM, P. D. K. to Marthy A. Newman   9 March 1867
    W. R. Watts, Security
    m. 17 March by Morgan Miller, J. P.
    Reference: County Archives: Marriage Book G
    Page 12

BOGART, George W. to Nancy L. Barnett   12 February 1852
    m. 12 February by Jona. Lyons, M. G.
    Reference: Marriage Book D Page 48

BOGART, S. to Mary A. Baker   7 January 1856
    m. 10 January by Wm. Newman, J. P.
    Reference: County Archives: Marriage Book D
    Page 106

BOGGESS, S. M. to Martha M. McKehan   11 May 1855
    m. 13 May by Hiel Buttram, M. G.
    Reference: Marriage Book D Page 98

BOLDING, William to Talitha Brower   10 April 1845
    m. 10 April by R. A. McAdoo, J. P.
    Reference: Marriage Book C Page 119

BOLIN, William to Elvira Robison   14 April 1864
    m. 14 April by Wm. G. Wilson, M. G.
    Reference: County Archives: Marriage Book F
    Page 1

BOLING - see also BOULDING

BOLLEN, Samuel to Claressa Moss   4 October 1849
    W. L. Smith, Security
    m. 4 September /sic/ by A. L. Dugan, J. P.
    Reference: County Archives: Marriage Book D
    Page 19

BONINE, Andrew J. to Catherine Wyatt   8 April 1851
    Reference: Marriage Book D Page 40

BONINE, Andrew J. to Eliza Kelly   **19 April 1852**
   m. 21 April by J. Jack, M. G.
   Reference: Marriage Book D Page 51

BONINE, Jacob to Cathrine Daugherty   12 March 1869
   m. 18 March by John Davis, M. G.
   Reference: Marriage Book G Page 45

BONINE, John to Caroline Rue   13 January 1858
   Elihu Kelley, Security
   m. 3 /sic/ January by J. J. Elliott, J. P.
   Reference: County Archives: Marriage Book D
   Page 135

BONINE, William to Lucinda Raburn   11 November 1852
   m. 11 November by Stephen Sharits, M. G.
   Reference: County Archives:
   Marriage Book D Page 58

BONNER, C. L. to Maranda McNabb   5 August 1867
   James Grigeron, Security
   m. 7 August by Stephen Hill, J. P.
   Reference: County Archives: Marriage Book G
   Page 18

BONNER, J. B. to Miss M. L. Dodson   10 December 1866
   m. 27 December by S. M. Thomas, J. P.
   Reference: County Archives: Marriage Book G
   Page 6

BOOFER (endorsed BOOHER), John to Mary Wassom   **18 September 1844**
   m. 19 September by G. W. Wallis, J. P.
   Reference: Marriage Book C Page 109

BOOFFHER, John to Catharine McCan   31 July 1858
   Reference: Marriage Book D Page 143

BOOHER - see BOOFER

BOOKER, Abraham to M. C. Nelson   12 February 1855
   Reference: Marriage Book D Page 94

BOOKOUT, James H. to Mary M. Cox   23 October 1867
   John A. Bookout, Security
   m. 23 October by E. Z. Williams, J. P.
   Reference: County Archives: Marriage Book G
   Page 22

BOOKOUT, John to Celia Massingell   8 February 1840
   m. 8 February by J. C. Carlock, J. P.
   Reference: Marriage Book C Page 24

BOOKOUT, John to Rebecah Davis   16 May 1866
   m. 16 May by E. Z. Williams
   Reference: Marriage Book F Page 41

BOON, Allen to Anna Hardy   15 September 1838
   m. 16 September by D. Cantrell, J. P.
   Reference: Marriage Book C Page 7

BORDEN, W. J. to Eliza J. Pierce   2 July 1857
   m. 2 July by J. M. Gibson, J. P.
   Reference: Marriage Book D Page 127

BOREN, Russell to Nancy Rhea   9 July 1844
   m. 11 July by Moses A. Cass, J. P.
   Reference: Marriage Book C Page 104

BOREN - see also BOWREN

BOULDING, John R. to Nancy A. Barnett   16 September 1844
    m. 17 September by Robert Gregory, Min.
    Reference: Marriage Book C Page 108

BOWER, Hosa H. to Anna Haney   25 September 1854
    Martin Pain, Security
    m. 25 September by David W. Beaver, M. G.
    Reference: County Archives: Marriage Book D
    Page 87

BOWERMAN, Michael to Mary Ann Smith   22 February 1842
    Silas Smith, Security
    m. 22 February by John Jenkins, J. P.
    Reference: County Archives: Marriage Book C
    Page 53

BOWMAN, Divid to Sarah Shamblain   9 November 1856
    m. 9 November by Joel Culpepper, J. P.
    Reference: Marriage Book D Page 118

BOWMAN, Milburn to Mrs. Martha Shook France   9 May 1867
    William H. Howard, Security
    m. 9 May by W. G. Horton, J. P.
    Reference: County Archives: Marriage Book G
    Page 15

BOWMAN - see also BOMAN

BOWRY, Joseph to Mattie E. Williams   24 November 1864
    m. 25 November by A. T. Brooks, M. G.
    Reference: County Archives: Marriage Book F
    Page 11

BOYD, Andrew to Martha Phillips   25 November 1847
    m. 25 November by Wm. Rucker, J. P.
    Reference: Marriage Book C Page 163

BOYD, David L. to Sarah E. Barb   26 June 1845
    m. 26 June by Jonathan Thomas, J. P.
    Reference: Marriage Book C Page 121

BOYD, Henry to Mary Carter (Colored)   28 October 1869
    Reference: Marriage Book G Page 53

BOYD, John K. to L. Bark   21 November 1840
    m. 26 November by Jonathan Thomas, J. P.
    Reference: Marriage Book C Page 34

BOYD, Jordan to Dialtha Morris   5 July 1865
    Sylvester Bishop, Security
    m. 6 July by D. B. Cunnungham, M. G.
    Reference: Marriage Book F Page 20

BOYD, Robert of Polk County to Miss Bar_____ Dauls   15 April 1865
    of McMinn County
    m. 15 April 1858 by W. O. Cameron Esq.
    Reference: Athens Post X(502, of May 1858)

BOYD, Robert to Judieth C. Coffee   18 February 1858
    m. 18 February by E. L. Miller, J. P.
    Reference: Marriage Book D Page 137

BOYDE, John T. to Mollie T. Eldridge   10 February 1869
    m. 11 February by A. Maxwell, J. P.
    Reference: Marriage Book G Page 44

BOYDE, Martin to Sarah Dearmond   30 September 1868
    Reference: Marriage Book G Page 37

BRABSON, R. B. to Sarah M. Keith   24 September 1844
    m. 24 September by John Scruggs, M. G.
    Reference: Marriage Book C Page 109

BRACKET, Albert to Elizabeth Neill   5 March 1855
    m. 5 March by James Baker, J. P.
    Reference: Marriage Book D Page 95

BRADEN, E. W. to Nancy Jane Smith   24 May 1850
    m. 24 May by John Key, M. G.
    Reference: Marriage Book D Page 28

BRADEN, James to Susan Derrick   25 July 1842
    m. 26 July by E. P. Bloom, J. P.
    Reference: Marriage Book C Page 59

BRADFORD, Alexander to Martha Wear   4 May 1867
    Wm. C. Hawk, Security
    m. 8 May by L. W. Crouch, M. G.
    Reference: County Archives: Marriage Book G
    Page 15

BRADFORD, Daivd to Sarah Dougherty   25 October 1842
    m. 25 October by John Jenkins, J. P.
    Reference: Marriage Book C Page 66

BRADFORD, Henry C. Esq. Attorney at Law of
    Bedford County, Tenn. to Mrs. Elizabeth Hord
    of McMinn County, daughter of Wm. Armstrong of
    Hawkins County
    m. 28 October 1828
    Reference: "Knoxville Enquirer" Volume 1 #36
    5 November 1828

BRADFORD, James F. Esq., Attorney at Law to Nancy
    Kinder, daughter of Peter Kinder
    m. 16 March 1831 by Rev. George Horn
    Reference: "Knoxville Register" Volume 15 #766
    6 April 1831

BRADFORD, Patton A. to Miss Amanda C. Stawk, all of   25 April 1861
    McMinn County
    m. 25 April 1861
    Reference: Athens Post Volume XIII #658, Friday
    3 May 1861

BRADOCK, Asahel to Nancey Seay   26 December 1827
    William T. Grisham, Security
    Reference: County Archives

BRADY, J. F. to Miss Elvery Castell   26 September 1866
    m. 26 September by Wm. G. Horton, J. P.
    Reference: County Archives: Marriage Book F
    Page 47

BRANAM (BRANUM), Edward to Margaret Shook   12 September 1852
    Thos. Rogers, Security
    Reference: County Archives: Marriage Book D
    Page 56

BRANAM - see also BRANUM

BRANDON, E. J. to Miss A. J. Hollis   17 April 1868
    m. 19 April by Wm. Thompson, M. G.
    Reference: Marriage Book G Page 29 and
    Marriage Book G Page 31

BRANDON, H. B. to Louisa Waide   1 September 1845
    m. 1 September by Heil Buttram, M. G.
    Reference: Marriage Book C Page 126

BRANDON, John to Tilathea Q. Firestone   9 July 1857
   m. 23 August by R. Reynolds, J. P.
   Reference: Marriage Book D Page 127

BRANDON, John to Mrs. Susan Mee   24 November 1868
   m. 29 November by D. W. Beaver, M. G.
   Reference: Marraige Book G Page 40

BRANDON, Wm. to M. A. F. Landers   8 December 1863
   m. 17 December by W. R. Long
   Reference: Marriage Book E Page 10

BRANHAM, Parmer to Susannah Howard   22 November 1842
   m. 22 November by J. H. Benton, J. P.
   Reference: Marriage Book C Page 68

BRANON, James to Susan Taylor   8 February 1851
   m. 13 December by Jas. Douglass, M. G.
   Reference: Marriage Book D Page 38

BRANUM - see also BRANAM

BREAZEALE, H. W. to Catharine Foster   25 February 1846
   m. 26 February by G. W. Wallis, J. P.
   Reference: Marriage Book C Page 134

BREEDLOVE, John to Sarah Ann Breedlove   20 April 1839
   Reference: Marriage Book C Page 16

BREEDWELL, Washington to Phany Callahan   14 June 1839
   Reference: Marriage Book C Page 18

BREWER, G. W. to Mrs. Jennie Roberts   15 November 1864
   m. 15 November by John McGaughey, J. P.
   Reference: County Archives: Marriage Book F
   Page 10

BREWER, James S. to Alice H. Cantrell   6 December 1865
   Wm. A. Warren, Security
   Reference: County Archives: Marriage Book F
   Page 32

BREWER, James S. to M. A. Hawk   30 July 1868
   John Peters, Security
   Reference: County Archives: Marriage Book G
   Page 34

BREWER, P. W. to Algeline Barker   9 December 1840
   m. 10 December by T. B. Love, J. P.
   Reference: Marriage Book C Page 34

BRIANT (BRYANT), Gameliel to Rebecca Dobkins   1 August 1854
   Wm. Dobkins, Security
   m. 1 August by Reuben Deavers, M. G.
   Reference: County Archives: Marriage Book D
   Page 85

BRIANT, James A. to Armena Williams   25 April 1848
   m. 25 April by John Jenkins, J. P.
   Reference: W. P. A.

BRIANT, Mathew S. to Fanney S. Lane   3 July 1867
   A. C. Roberson, Security
   m. 3 July by W. A. Nelson, M. G.
   Reference: County Archives: Marriage Book G
   Page 17

BRIANT - see also BRYANT

BRIDGES, Geo. W. to Margaret D. Gettys   27 April 1848
   m. 27 April by John B. Meek, M. G.
   Reference: W. P. A.

BRIDGES, Jas. H. to Eliza Dyer   30 June 1849
   J. M. Lambert, Security
   m. 1 July by John Spears, J. P.
   Reference: County Archives: Marrige Book D
   Page 16

BRIDGES, John L. to Hellen E. Blackwell   20 April 1841
   Reference: Marriage Book C Page 41

BRIDGES, John L. to Eliza J. Gettys   2 November 1853
   George A. Caldwell, Security
   m. 2 November by George A. Caldwell, M. G.
   Reference: County Archives: Marriage Book D
   Page 73

BRIDGES, John L. to Margaretta Amanda Deadrick 9 December 1856
   m. 9 December by Geo. A. Caldwell, M. G.
   Reference: Marriage Book D Page 121

BRIDGES, William H. to Rebeckah O. St. John 30 December 1852
   m. 30 December by J. Cunningham, M. G.
   Reference: County Archives: Marriage Book D
   Page 61

BRIGHAM, F. to Virginia Owens   5 October 1866
   m. 7 October 1866 by J. W. Mann, M. G.
   Reference: County Archives: Marriage Book G
   Page 1

BRITT, A. J. to Nancy Jane Land   29 April 1869
   m. 2 May by G. M. Bloom, J. P.
   Reference: Marriage Book G Page 46

BRITTAIN, W. C. to Jane Robeson   26 November 1844
   Reference: Marriage Book C Page 113

BRITTON, William C. to Jane Robison   25 November 1847
   m. 25 November by William H. Ballew, J. P.
   Reference: Marriage Book C Page 163

BROCK, A. B. to Hariet Smith   10 July 1869
   Reference: Marriage Book G Page 47

BROCK, Andrew J. to Emeline Jack   10 October 1853
   Lawrence Brock, Security
   m. 15 October 1853 by B. E. Cass, J. P.
   Reference: County Archives: Marriage Book D
   Page 72

BROCK, Benjamin to Mary Baker   16 November 1862
   m. 17 November by John Jack, M. G.
   Reference: Marriage Book E Page 6

BROCK, Benjamin T. to Rheda Mannery   28 December 1847
   m. 30 December by J. Jack, M. G.
   Reference: Marriage Book C Page 165

BROCK, Blasingale to Mary Rogers   17 September 1867
   Wm. B. Johnson, Security
   Reference: County Archives: Marriage Book G
   Page 21

BROCK, Blassingame to Mary Morgan   14 July 1843
   Reference: Marriage Book C Page 81

BROCK, David to Ann Stout   27 November 1852
    m. 28 November by A. Swafford, J. P.
    Reference: County Archives: Marriage Book D
    Page 59

BROCK, Elmore to Mary Bonner   2 January 1850
    m. 3 January by Wm. McKamy, J. P.
    Reference: Marriage Book D Page 24

BROCK, Henry J. to Sarah Cloud   11 May 1838
    m. 21 May by Barney Castell, Elder
    in C. Church
    Reference: Marriage Book C Page 3

BROCK, Isaac to Mary Jane Sanders   10 April 1848
    m. 10 April by J. Jack, M. G.
    Reference: McMinn County Chancery Court Case
    No. 233 and W. P. A.

BROCK, J. W. to Delilah T. Coffee   20 October 1866
    Reference: Marriage Book G Page 2

BROCK, Jordan L. to Malvina Thompson   17 October 1866
    m. 18 October by Elihue Kelley, J. P.
    Reference: Marriage Book G Page 2

BROCK, Lawrence P. to Polly Cloud   24 May 1838
    m. 29 May by Barney Castell, Elder
    Reference: Marriage Book C Page 3

BROCK, Martin to Nancy Johnson   16 January 1860
    m. 17 January by C. R. Hoyl, M. G.
    Reference: Marriage Book E Page 6

BROCK, Michail to Elizabeth Harmon`   8 March 1865
    m. 9 March by S. W. Royston, J. P.
    Reference: County Archives: Marriage Book F
    Page 16

BROCK, Perry G. to Mary A. E. Lafferty   21 April 1852
    m. 22 April by William R. Walker, J. P.
    Reference: County Archives: Marriage Book D
    Page 52

BROCK, T. J. to Maria C. Newman   26 December 1865
    m. 28 December by J. S. Russell, M. G.
    Reference: Marriage Book F Page 34

BROCK, Terry to Elizabeth Walker   11 September 1843
    Reference: Marriage Book C Page 85

BROCK, W. J. to Martha M. Hibberts   18 October 1870
    Reference: Marriage Book G Page 67

BROCK, William to Nancy Nacion   17 December 1870
    m. 18 December by L. W. Crouch, M. G.
    Reference: Marriage Book G Page 71

BROCK, Wm. M. to Eliza J. Rabourn   13 August 1858
    m. 12 /sic7 August by J. J. Elliott, J. P.
    Reference: Marriage Book D Page 144

BROOKSHIRE, V. (Vardra) to Mary Brookshire   20 December 1849
    m. 20 December by Wm. McKany, J. P.
    Reference: County Archives: Marriage Book D
    Page 23

BROOKSHIRE, William to Rebecca C. Brookshire   11 July 1849
    C. P. Gollahon, Security
    m. 17 July 1849 by Wm. Makamy, J. P.
    Reference: County Archives: Marriage Book D
    Page 16

BROWDER, Calvin to Mary Ann Nance   12 October 1853
    Morris C. Sullins, Security
    m. 13 October by M. A. Cass, M. G.
    Reference: County Archives: Marriage Book D
    Page 72

BROWDER, J. W. to Miss J. A. Tunel   11 March 1868
    m. 12 March by C. R. Hoyle, M. G.
    Reference: Marriage Book G Page 30

BROWDER, Robert F. to Arminda C. Erwin   31 December 1845
    m. 1 January 1846 by M. C. Hawk
    Reference: Marriage Book C Page 131

BROWDER, Samuel D. to Nancy Triplet   10 September 1846
    m. 10 September by C. D. Smith, M. G.
    Reference: County Archives: Marriage Book C
    Page 143

BROWN, A. B. to Mary Newland   16 August 1841
    m. 19 January 1842 by Robert Frazier, M. G.
    Reference: Marriage Book C Page 45

BROWN, Andrew J. to Elizabeth Sanders   26 January 1856
    Reference: Marriage Book C Page 14

BROWN, Andrew Jackson to Rebecca Jane Mize   16 February 1856
    m. 18 February by Robert Reynolds, J. P.
    Reference: Marriage Book D Page 108

BROWN, Columbus to Abigale Sivil   5 June 1849
    Joseph Anderson, Security
    "Returned no property fould by C. Brown
    the intend Bride's Groom"
    Reference: County Archvies: Marriage Book D
    Page 15

BROWN, David to Polly Swinford   18 September 1838
    m. 23 September by Wm. McKamy, J. P.
    Reference: Marriage Book C Page 7

BROWN, David to Elizabeth A. McKenzie   15 November 1849
    Jo C. Weir, Security
    m. 15 November by William Walker, J. P.
    Reference: County Archives: Marriage Book D
    Page 21

BROWN, E. G. to Lucy Whetsell   12 September 1858
    m. 12 September by Geo. A. Caldwell, M. G.
    Reference: Marriage Book D Page 146

BROWN, G. F. to Mary J. Brown   28 December 1864
    m. 29 December by A. R. Wilson, M. G.
    Reference: County Archives: Marriage Book F
    Page 12

BROWN, G. W. to Elizabeth Herald   28 July 1845
    m. 28 July by J. W. Barnett, J. P.
    Reference: Marriage Book C Page 123

BROWN, G. W. to Mary Ann Thompson   9 December 1852
    m. 9 December by W. C. Daily, M. of M. E. Church
    South, Holston Conf.
    Reference: County Archives: Marriage Book D
    Page 60

BROWN, George to Susan Barker   3 April 1856
    m. 3 April by R. Reynolds, J. P.
    Reference: Marriage Book D Page 109

BROWN, H. R. to Elizabeth Tomson   10 July 1858
    m. 13 July by C. Long, M. G.
    Reference: Marriage Book D Page 143

BROWN, Henry to Reuhama Shoemaker   4 February 1841
    m. by Wm. Dodson, J. P.
    Reference: Marriage Book C Page 37

BROWN, Hiram J. to Elizabeth J. Castell   17 May 1853
    John Cate, Security
    m. 19 May by W. C. Daily, M. G.
    Reference: County Archives: Marriage Book D
    Page 66

BROWN, James to Nancy George   13 May 1848
    m. 17 May by Jas. C. Bryan, J. P.
    Reference: W. P. A.

BROWN, James to Mary Carroll   5 October 1848
    m. 5 October by A. Slover, M. G.
    Reference: Marriage Book D Page 5

BROWN, James to Mrs. Susan Douglass   19 April 1852
    m. by J. Jenkins, J. P.
    Reference: Marriage Book D Page 51

BROWN, James R. to Thuney Barnett   27 August 1838
    m. 27 August by Thos. L. Hoyle, J. P.
    Reference: Marriage Book C Page 6

BROWN, Major Joel K. of Calhoun to Miss Betsey
    Colville, daughter of George Colville, Esq. of
    McMinn County
    m. 15 June 1824 by Rev. John Walker
    Reference: "Knoxville Register" Volume VIII
    Number 411 25 June 1824

BROWN, Joel K. to Mrs. Hester Ann Brown   5 June 1840
    m. 5 June by John Tate, M. G.
    Reference: Marriage Book C Page 30

BROWN, John M. to Emaline Small   23 March 1868
    A. G. Small, Security
    m. 31 March by Samuel B. West, M. G.
    Reference: County Archives: Marriage Book G
    Page 30

BROWN, John W. of Roane County to Sarah Jane Matlock
    m. 11 March 1852 by Rev. Wm. F. Forrest
    Reference: Marriage Book D Page 49 and
    "The Athens Post", Volume IV, Number 182, 19 March
    1852

BROWN, Joseph to Matilda Hicks   12 December 1848
    m. 12 December by Thomas T. Russell, M. G.
    Reference: Marriage Book D Page 8

BROWN, Joseph H. to Huldy Logan   9 January 1828
    Sidna Bolden, Security
    Reference: Marriage Book D Page 8

BROWN, M. A. to Sarah Louisa Baker   30 November 1870
    m. 30 November by E. L. Miller, M. G.
    Reference: Marriage Book G Page 70

BROWN, Ritchard to Mary Presley   17 April 1857
    m. 16 /sic/ April by James Bonner, J. P.
    Reference: Marriage Book D Page 125

BROWN, Samuel to Frances E. Harris   25 July 1864
    William R. Jones, Security
    Reference: Marriage Book F Page 5

BROWN, Thos. W. to Amanda Hamelton   10 April 1869
    m. 11 April by James Parkerson, J. P.
    Reference: Marriage Book G Page 46

BROWN, W. C. to Suzanah J. Right   9 July 1867
    m. 12 July by Stephen Hill, J. P.
    Reference: Marriage Book G Page 17

BROWN, William to Mary Grady   11 March 1833
    Joseph Brown, Security
    Reference: County Archives

BROWN, Wm. to Lucinda Cooper   22 February 1842
    m. 22 February by Robert Gregory, Minister
    of Baptist Church
    Reference: Marriage Book C Page 53

BROWN, Wm. to Mary Weatherly   27 January 1859
    m. 27 January by R. Reynolds Esq. J. P.
    Reference: County Archives: Marriage Book D
    Page 156 and Marriage Book E Page 6

BROWN, Wm. to Mrs. Elizabeth Scott   20 December 1865
    George E. Whitaker, Security
    Reference: County Archives: Marriage Book F
    Page 33

BROWN, Wm. to Sallie Cate   30 January 1868
    m. 1 February by Wm. Thompson, J. P.
    Reference: Marriage Book G Page 27

BROWN, William F. to Manda M. Rentfro   5 July 1838
    m. 5 July by John Tate, M. G.
    Reference: Marriage Book C Page 4

BROWN, Wm. H. to Mary L. Baysinger   11 November 1868
    Reference: Marriage Book G Page 39

BROWN, Wm. S. to Martha Smith   6 November 1869
    Reference: Marriage Book G Page 53

BRUDEN, George to Marry Lowry   18 December 1829
    Coonrod Stanner, Security
    Reference: County Archives

BRUMET, A. H. to Mrs. Martha Burn   17 December 1866
    C. R. Hoyl, Security
    m. 23 December by C. R. Hoyl, M. G.
    Reference: County Archives: Marriage Book G
    Page 6

BRUMIT, S. C. to Leona A. Rogers   2 August 1856
    m. 3 August by Jas. Parkerson, J. P.
    Reference: Marriage Book D Page 112

BRUMITT, J. F. to Miss S. A. McCrary   24 February 1869
    Reference: Marriage Book G Page 44

BRUMMET, J. F. to Letty Barnes   15 February 1853
    A. J. Wingo, Security
    m. 20 February by O. M. Liner, J. P.
    Reference: County Archives: Marriage Book D
    Page 63

BRUNNER, David to Nancy J. Witt   2 March 1867
    m. 3 March by Charles Cate, J. P.
    Reference: Marriage Book G Page 12

BRYAN, Robert to Elza J. Harless   21 December 1844
    m. 22 December by Justice Steed, J. P.
    Reference: Marriage Book C Page 114

BRYAN, William to Mary L. Cate   7 May 1853
    Robert E. Cate, Security
    m. 8 May by W. C. Daily, M. G. M. E. Church South
    Reference: County Archives: Marriage Book D
    Page 66

BRYAN - see also BYRAN

BRYANT, James to Sarah Ann Gulliage   25 November 1839
    Reference: Marriage Book C Page 8 and Page 25

BRYANT, Lewis F. to L. C. Pennington   9 February 1867
    m. 14 February by A. G. Small, M. G.
    REference: County Archives: Marriage Book G
    Page 11

BRYANT, Pleasant to Polly Rucker   18 September 1841
    Reference: Marriage Book C Page 46

BRYANT, Robert to Ann Eliza Brown   1 September 1856
    m. 1 September by Joseph Neil, J. P.
    Reference: Marriage Book D Page 113

BRYANT - see also BRIANT

BUCHANAN, Joseph to Margaret Dolen   11 December 1848
    m. 13 December by J. W. Thompson, M. G.
    Reference: Marriage Book D Page 8

BUCHANAN, Marshall to Sarah Hudgins   22 January 1865
    m. 22 January by Wm. C. Owen, J. P.
    Reference: County Archives: Marriage Book F
    Page 15

BUCHANNON, Elias to Scyntha Lewis   4 March 1844
    Reference: Marriage Book C Page 98

BUCHANNON, John to Mary Grigsby   14 October 1865
    m. 15 October by Charles Cate, J. P.
    Reference: County Archives: Marriage Book F
    Page 28

BUCK, John C. R. to Talitha Q. Williams   10 January 1866
    J. W. Hamilton, Security
    m. 11 January by Morgan Miller, J. P.
    Reference: County Archives: Marriage Book F
    Page 35

BUCKANON, George to Martha Dunn   4 November 1867
    m. 4 November by J. M. Workman, J. P.
    Reference: Marriage Book G Page 24

BUCKER, Robert to Lavista Mitchell   4 February 1857
    m. 7 February by M. R. Wear, J. P.
    Reference: Marriage Book D Page 123

BUCKNER, G. W. D. to Miss S. E. Owens   30 August 1858
    m. 1 September by G. W. Rentfro, M. G.
    Reference: Marriage Book D **Page 145**

BUCKNER, J. S. to Matilda Beaver   31 August 1853
    Jacob M. Womack, Security
    m. 31 August by A. John, M. G.
    Reference: County Archives: **Marriage Book D**
    Page 69

BUCKNER, James to Susanah Stephenson   25 February 1838
    m. 25 February by Robert Gregory, M. G.
    Reference: County Archives: **Marriage Book C**
    Page 2

BUCKNER, James to Elizabeth Jemison (Jamison) 15 November 1866
    Rufus Buckner, Security
    m. 18 November by Elihu Kelly, J. P.
    Reference: County Archives: **Marriage Book G**
    Page 4

BUCKNER, James W. to Eliza Porter   25 March 1854
    Lewis Beaver, Security
    m. 29 March by A. John, M. G.
    Reference: County Archives: **Marriage Book D**
    Page 82

BUCKNER, Rufus to Mary Yonce   24 November 1865
    m. 24 November by Elihu Kelly, J. P.
    Reference: Marriage Book F Page 31

BUCKNER, W. A. to Mary J. Owen   23 September 1858
    m. 24 September 1861 /sic7 by H. Rice, M. G.
    Reference: Marriage Book D **Page 147**

BUCKNER, William to Rachel V. McKiney   24 July 1866
    m. 24 July by W. A. Nelson, M. G.
    Reference: County Archives: **Marriage Book F**
    Page 44

BULLINGTON, W. J. to Sarah Boon   13 January 1858
    m. 13 January by Thos. Russell, M. G.
    Reference: Marriage Book D **Page 135**

BUNCH, Anderson to Louisa Kinsor   5 March 1858
    m. 6 March by Wm. H. Newman, M. G.
    Reference: Marriage Book D Page 137

BUNCH, DANIEL to Rachel Bennett   29 October 1849
    Wm. Forrest, Security
    Reference: County Archives: **Marriage Book D**
    Page 20

BUNCH, Joseph to Mary Pugh   2 January 1839
    m. 5 January by John Walker, M. G.
    Reference: Marriage Book C **Page 16**

BUNCH, Joseph to Judith Massey   6 March 1855
    m. 8 March by M. R. Wear, Esq.
    Reference: Marriage Book D Page 96

BUNCH, Lambert to Sarah Willis   27 March 1841
    m. 30 March by Richard A. McAdoo, J. P.
    Reference: Marriage Book C **Page 39**

BURGAR, G. E. to Mary Hamilton   2 March 1859
    Reference: Marriage Book D Page 157

BURGER, Adam to Mary Hawkins   22 September 1837
    m. 24 September by Robert Randolph, M. G.
    Reference: County Archives

BURGER, Eli to Letty Daugherty   27 September 1865
    m. 8 October 1866 /sic/ by Elihu Kelley, J. P.
    Reference: Marriage Book F Page 26

BURGER, George E. to Hannah R. Everton   11 June 1857
    m. 11 June by J. Jack, M. G.
    Reference: Marriage Book D Page 127

BURGER, John M. to Manda Caves   30 July 1846
    m. 30 July by M. A. Cass, J. P.
    Reference: Marriage Book C Page 141

BURGER, Michael D. to Lotty Ann Clark   19 November 1853
    m. 19 November by J. Jack, M. G.
    Reference: Marriage Book D Page 75

BURGER, W. S. to Mary C. Dickerson   26 November 1870
    John W. Gilbert, Security
    m. 27 November by J. S. Petty, M. G.
    Reference: County Archives: Marriage Book G
    Page 70

BURK, Andrew to Emily Gibbs   30 December 1856
    m. 6 January 1857 by George A. Caldwell, M. G.
    Reference: Marriage Book D Page 122

BURK, H. H. to Sarah C. Rucker   15 November 1854
    m. 15 November by Joseph A. Ziegler, J. P.
    Reference: Marriage Book D Page 89

BURK, John to Rebecca Pew   7 October 1856
    Reference: Marriage Book D Page 116

BURK, Roswell P. to Catharine J. Wilson   10 January 1844
    m. 10 January by M. D. Anderson, J. P.
    Reference: Marriage Book C Page 96

BURK, Samuel to Elizabeth J. Riggins   4 October 1860
    m. 4 October by Thos. Grisham, J. P.
    Reference: Marriage Book E Page 16

BURK, W. A. to Miss S. L. Hill   3 March 1866
    W. M. Cunningham, Security
    m. 4 March by E. Z. Williams, J. P.
    Reference: County Archives: Marriage Book F
    Page 38

BURK, Wm. to Mrs. Elenor Gregory   30 November 1857
    m. 31 /sic/ November by Joseph Gibson, J. P.
    Reference: Marriage Book D Page 132 and Deed
    Book N. Page 190

BURK, William P. to Margaret A. Wilson   20 August 1850
    m. 20 August by John C. Gaston, M. G.
    Reference: Marriage Book D Page 31

BURK, William T. to Adaline Amanda Carter   14 February 1838
    m. 15 February by Wm. Shamblin, J. P.
    Reference: Marriage Book C Page 1

BURKS, Allen to Tenesse Roberts   4 July 1829
    Edmund Roberts, Security
    Reference: County Archives

BURN, Harison B. to Margaret E. Barnett   16 September 1865
    Thomas J. Lowry, Security
    m. 17 September by Thomas J. Lowry, J. P.
    Reference: County Archives: Marriage Book F
    Page 26

BURNET, John H. to Franky L. McCray
    (Fanny McCrary)
    m. 28 October by A. Slover, G. M.
    Reference: Marriage Book C 162: "Knoxville
    Register" Volume 7 No. 360 November 10, 1847

BURNETT, Lewis to Charity Swinford   31 May 1839
    Reference: Marriage Book C Page 17

BURNETT, Wm. P. to Sarah S. Shults   20 February 1861
    m. 20 February by Joseph Neil, J. P.
    Reference: Marriage Book E Page 12

BURNS, Arthur to Mrs. Eliza Cooke   27 April 1855
    m. 27 April by B. A. Prophet, M. G.
    Reference: Marriage Book D Page 98

BURNS, J. F. to Jane Baker   19 November 1870
    m. 20 November by W. C. Barnett, J. P.
    Reference: Marriage Book G Page 69

BURNS, W. D. to Eliza J. Land   31 January 1865
    m. 2 February by J. Jack, M. G.
    Reference: Marriage Book F Page 15

BURRIS, William to Mahala Rudd
    m. 27 December 1849 by Samuel Snoddy, J. P.
    Reference: Marriage Book D Page 23

BURSELL, Wm. B. to Caroline Sallee   22 November 1849
    P. L. Gamble, Security
    m. 22 November by Wm. H. Ballew, J. P.
    Reference: County Archives: Marriage Book D
    Page 21

BUSH, George to Catharine Prince   11 April 1846
    m. 12 April by S. H. Jordan, J. P.
    Reference: Marriage Book C Page 137

BUTLER, G. W. to Elizabeth Catharine Porter   3 April 1855
    m. 5 April by A. Vance, M. G.
    Reference: Marriage Book D Page 97

BUTLER, Isaac to Marha /sic/ Price   11 January 1854
    m. 12 January by A. Barb, J. P.
    Reference: Marriage Book D Page 77

BUTLER, John to Prissilla Atchley   7 August 1846
    m. 10 August by J. Thomas, J. P.
    Reference: Marriage Book C Page 141

BUTTRAM, Embre to Sarah Wattenbarger   12 October 1846
    m. 15 October by Heil Buttram, M. G.
    Reference: Marriage Book C Page 145

BUTTRAM, Jacob to Josephine Wilson   30 September 1850
    m. 1 October by D. Carpenter, M. G.
    Reference: Marriage Book D Page 33

BUTTRAM. Jas. to Jane Rothwell   3 August 1844
    m. 8 August by Lewis Carter, M. G.
    Reference: Marriage Book C Page 106

BUTTRAM, John G. to Sarah J. Foster   14 February 1854
    m. 15 February by Heil Buttram, M. G.
    Reference: Marriage Book D Page 80

BUTTRAM, Moses to Mary Ann Foster   31 August 1850
    m. 5 September by E. E. Gillenwater, M. G.
    Reference: Marriage Book D Page 31

BUTTRAM. William to Elizabeth Ann Foster   6 October 1851
    m. 9 October by Heil Buttram, M. G.
    Reference: Marriage Book D Page 44

BYERS, Goodman H. to Marthy C. Jackson   4 May 1867
    C. C. Crumley, Security
    m. 5 May by M. A. Cass, M. G.
    Reference: County Archives: Marriage Book G
    Page 15

BYINGTON, A. R. to Miss F. C. Johens   28 July 1868
    m. 28 July by J. W. Mann, M. G.
    Reference: Marriage Book G Page 33

BYINGTON, Alfred R. to Elizabeth C. Guffey   25 June 1850
    Reference: Marriage Book D Page 28

BYINGTON, Alfred R. to Mrs. Mary Jane Grisham   4 January 1853
    Joseph Erwin, Security
    m. 6 January by William R. Walker, J. P.
    Reference: County Archives: Marriage Book D
    Page 61

BYRAN, Peter L. to Anna Horton   13 July 1846
    m. 14 July by Wm. Rucker, J. P.
    Reference: Marriage Book C Page 140

CAGLE, Ignatious W. to Nancy Lemmons   18 October 1848
    m. 20 October by James C. Bryan, J. P.
    Reference: Marriage Book D Page 6

CAGLE, Matthew to Keziah J. Morgan   26 April 1842
    m. 28 April by Thos. Camp, J. P.
    Reference: Marriage Book C Page 57

CAGLE - see also KEGGAL, KEGGLE

CAHILL - see KAHILL

CAIN, Jacob to Fany Ogle   21 February 1842
    Reference: Marriage Book C Page 53

CAIN - see also CANE

CALAHAN, William to Martha Browder   3 November 1842
    Reference: Marriage Book C Page 67

CALDWELL, J. G. to Miss M. E. Hyden   26 October 1867
    m. 29 October by Jacob Brillhart, M. G.
    Reference: Marriage Book G Page 22

CALDWELL, Jessee B. to Martha J. Frizzell   4 July 1850
    m. 4 July by Robert Gregory, M. G.
    Reference: Marriage Book D Page 29

CALDWELL, Oliver P. H. to Lucinda J. Johnson   12 December 1843
    m. 11 /sic/ December by Joseph Peller, M. G.
    Reference: Marriage Book C Page 92

CALDWELL, Thomas to Mrs. Mary Ann Logan   1 September 1842
    Reference: Marriage Book C Page 61

CALDWELL - see also CAULDWELL, COLDWELL, COLWELL

CALHOUN, James C. to Mary E. George   23 August 1855
    m. 23 August by George A. Caldwell, M. G.
    Reference: Marriage Book D Page 102

CALHOUN, Jordon to Jane Mattocks   1 March 1845
    m. 3 March by H. Ingram, M. G.
    Reference: Marriage Book C Page 118

CALLAHAN - see also CALAHAN

CALLAWAY, Dr. Thomas F. M. of Monroe County to
    Grace S. Meigs, daughter of Mrs. Elizabeth Meigs
    of McMinn County
    m. 31 May 1825 by Rev. James Axley
    Reference: "Knoxville Register" Volume IX #461
    10 June 1825

CALLAWAY, Williams S. of Madisonville to Sarah Ann
    Hurst, daughter of Elijah Hurst of McMinn County
    m. 8 November 1832 by Rev. Danil Buckner
    Reference: "Knoxville Register" Volume 17 #852
    21 November 1832

CAMBELL, Landon to Nancy Guinn   31 January 1867
    m. 31 January by W. H. Newman, M. G.
    Reference: County Archives: Marriage Book G
    Page 10

CAMEL, Galloway to Mary Thompson   2 January 1843
    m. 3 January by R. A. McAdoo, J. P.
    Reference: Marriage Book C Page 70

CAMERON, Edward D. to Caroline Madux   23 July 1839
    m. 25 July by H. C. Cook, J. P.
    Reference: Marriage Book C Page 21

CAMERON, James D. to Marry E. Pickens   19 January 1869
    m. 19 January by Jno. M. Moore, M. G.
    Reference: Marriage Book G Page 43

CAMERON - see also CAMRON

CAMP, Ansrulies D. E. to Elizabeth F. Bogard   4 July 1866
    m. 4 July by W. W. Thorpe
    Reference: Marriage Book F Page 43

CAMP, John to Polly Parkison   16 February 1829
    m. 18 February by J. W. McMillin, J. P.
    Reference: W. P. A.

CAMP, John B. to Mary D. Bridges   13 January 1870
    m. 13 January by J. H. Martin, M. G.
    Reference: Marriage Book G Page 57

CAMP, William F. H. to Margret N. Dugan   8 July 1866
    m. 12 July by Elihu Kelley, J. P.
    Reference: Marriage Book F Page 43

CAMP - see also KEMP

CAMPBELL, D. L. to Miss Judiah McAdoo   16 December 1851
    m. 18 December by A. Barb, J. P.
    Reference: Marriage Book D Page 46

CAMPBELL, James F. to Sallie Blizsard   5 September 1866
    m. 5 September by J. Walerman, M. G.
    Reference: Marriage Book F Page 46

CAMPBELL, Malchiah to Margaret McCalley   16 February 1848
    m. 17 February by David F. Jamison, J. P.
    Reference: Marriage Book C Page 167

CAMPBELL, Richard B. to Isabella S. Bridges   23 May 1843
    m. 23 May by L. R. Morrison, V. D. M.
    Reference: Marriage Book C Page 79

CAMPBELL, T. J. to Miss Frances E. Bridges   11 June 1846
    m. 11 June by L. R. Morrison, V. D. M.
    Reference: Marriage Book C Page 139

CAMPBELL, Thomas to Dolly Snow   6 November 1828
    Reference: W. P. A.

CAMPBELL, William to Elizabeth Ballard   14 December 1846
    m. 14 December by David F. Jamison, J. P.
    Reference: Marriage Book C Page 148

CAMPBELL - see also CAMBELL, CAMEL

CAMRON, A. M. to Eliza Jane Rodden   12 December 1866
    m. 13 December by C. R. Hoyl, M. G.
    Reference: County Archives: Marriage Book G
    Page 6

CAMRON, Henry to Margaret A. Stephens   10 May 1842
    m. 12 May by L. L. Ball, J. P.
    Reference: Marriage Book C Page 66

CANNON, G. M. to Miss A. E. L. Netherland   23 February 1870
    m. 23 February by J. Albert Hyden, M. G.
    Reference: County Archives: Marriage Book G
    Page 58

CANNON, Isaac to Rufrey Kibble   17 November 1838
    m. 18 November by L. L. Ball, J. P.
    Reference: Marriage Book C Page 10

CANNON, Richard to Delila Gilbert   30 December 1852
    m. 30 December by William McKamy, J. P.
    Reference: Marriage Book D Page 61

CANNON, William to Matilda Crawford   12 July 1844
    m. 14 July by Daniel McPhail, J. P.
    Reference: Marriage Book C Page 104

CANNON, William to Mary Doss   16 February 1846
    m. 16 February by A. Swafford, J. P.
    Reference: Marriage Book C Page 133

CANNON, William to Catherine Roggers   5 July 1866
    m. 4 /sic/ July by Elder F. M. Avins
    Reference: Marriage Book F Page 43

CANNON, William A. to Mary C. Elkins   7 June 1865
    m. 7 June by Z. Rose, M. G.
    Reference: Marriage Book F Page 19

CANSELLER, Israel to Ellen Luvine Cunningham   10 February 1847
    m. 11 February by Samuel Wilson, J. P.
    Reference: Marriage book C Page 152

CANSLER, N. H. to Hannah Reynolds   28 December 1841
    m. 30 December by John Scruggs, Minister
    Reference: Marriage Book C Page 51

CANTERLL, M. D. L. to Nancy E. Vaughn   27 October 1855
    m. 1 November by T. T. Russell, M. G.
    Reference: Marriage Book D Page 104

CANTRELL, David to Sarah Derrick   11 February 1841
    m. 11 February by Bynum Jarnagin, J. P.
    Reference: Marriage Book C Page 38

CANTRELL, David to Rebecca Crocket   17 October 1851
    m. 19 October by C. R. Hoyl, M. G.
    Reference: Marriage Book D Page 44

CANTRELL, F. M. to Martha M. Sellers   4 December 1849
    m. 27 December by C. R. Hoyl, M. G.
    Reference: Marriage Book D Page 22

CANTRELL, Gabriel to Miss Alzira McMinn   4 October 1842
    m. 4 October by Green L. Reynolds, J. P.
    Reference: Marriage Book C Page 63

CANTRELL, L. E. to Sarah Firestone   12 January 1852
    Reference: Marriage Book D Page 47

CANTRELL, Malcomb to Margaret A. Cooke   30 November 1864
    m. 1 December by C. R. Hoyl, M. G.
    Reference: Marriage Book F Page 11

CANTRELL, Noah C. to Mary Derrick   25 July 1846
    m. 26 July by E. P. Bloom, J. P.
    Reference: Marriage Book C Page 141

CANTRELL, Reynolds to Sarah A. E. Vaughan   14 February 1849
    m. 14 February by W. F. Forrest, M. G.
    Reference: Marriage Book D Page 12

CANTRELL, Robert C. to Esther J. Stansbury   22 October 1844
    m. 24 October by Moses A. Cass, J. P.
    Reference: Marriage Book C Page 110

CANTRELL, Terrell to Maranda J. Manery   21 July 1845
    m. 24 July by M. A. Cass, J. P.
    Reference: Marriage Book C Page 123

CANTRELL, Thomas C. to Louisa Lawson   1 March 1843
    m. 9 March by Hiram Ingram, M. G.
    Reference: Marriage Book C Page 75

CANTRELL, Thomas K. to Sarah Riggs   24 February 1846
    m. 5 March by M. A. Cass, J. P.
    Reference: Marriage Book C Page 134

CANTRELL, William to Margret Cooke   29 /November/ 1851
    m. 30 November by G. W. Kirksey, J. P.
    Reference: Marriage Book D Page 46

CAPENTER, John C. to Mary Wood   29 June 1868
    m. 29 June by D. Carpenter, M. G.
    Reference: Marriage Book G Page 32

CAPS, Columbous to Mary E. Beaver   15 November 1855
    m. 12 November 1856 /sic/ by Hile Buttram, M. G.
    Reference: Marriage Book D Page 104

CARDEN, James to Sarah Malone   16 April 1839
    m. 18 April by A. Barb, J. P.
    Reference: Marriage Book C Page 16

CARDEN, W. J. to Miss E. L. White   1 August 1868
     m. 1 August by A. D. Briant, J. P.
     Reference: Marriage Book G Page 34

CARDIN, L. F. to Julia A. Richerson   31 January 1866
     m. 4 February by Joseph Hamilton, J. P.
     Reference: Marriage Book F Page 37

CARDIN, William to Martha Hays   23 December 1869
     m. 23 December by J. W. Gilbert, J. P.
     Reference: Marriage Book G Page 55

CARDWELL, A. to Mary Ann McElwee   3 May 1869
     m. 4 May by T. Sullins, M. G.
     Reference: Marriage Book G Page 46

CARDWELL, James H. of Knoxville to Mrs. Hazy   8 December 1840
     Mitchell, daughter of Nathan Sullens
     m. 8 December by Rev. Hiram Ingram
     Reference: Marriage Book C Page 34 and
     "Hitwassee Patriot" 15 December 1840
     Volume II Number 40

CARLE, W. H. to Elizabeth Lane   5 August 1865
     m. 5 August by William C. Owen, J. P.
     Reference: Marriage Book F Page 22

CARLE - see also CORLEY

CARLOCK, Asahel to Mary Douglass   24 January 1842
     Reference: Marriage Book C Page 52

CARLOCK, E. W. to Mary J. Wells   12 October 1858
     m. 14 October by S. J. Philips, M. G.
     Reference: Marriage Book D Page 148

CARLOCK, Isaac D. to Harriate Owen   7 January 1869
     m. 7 January by N. B. Goforth, M. G.
     Reference: Marriage Book G Page 42

CARLOCK, L. L. H. to Nancy C. Cass   22 December 1866
     m. 26 December by Jacob Brillhart, M. G.
     Reference: Marriage Book G Page 7

CARMICHAEL, J. G. to Sarah E. Lasater   21 December 1865
     m. 21 December by J. B. Bumbraugh, M. G.
     Reference: Marriage Book F Page 33

CARMICHAEL, J. L. to Ruth K. Prigmore   12 March 1844
     m. 24 April 1845 /sic/ by Thos. H. Small,
     M. G. C. P. C.
     Reference: Marriage Book C Page 99

CARNEY, G. W. to Charity Biggs   10 July 1866
     m. 12 July by E. B. Cass, J. P.
     Reference: Marriage Book F Page 43

CARNEY, Joshua to Patience Lewis   14 July 1838
     m. 11 /sic/ July by C. Sanders, M. G.
     Reference: Marriage Book C Page 4

CARNEY, Madison to Martha Jane Helms   22 June 1847
     m. 24 June by J. C. Weir, J. P.
     Reference: Marriage Book C Page 156

CARPENTER, Moses M. C. to Margaret M. McKeehen   7 December 1865
     m. 7 December by Rev. Dan Carpenter, M. G.
     Reference: County Archives: Marriage Book F
     Page 32

CARPENTER, Wm. F. to Permelia E. Wood   26 December 1866
    m. 3 January 1867 by D. Carpenter, M. G.
    Reference: Marriage Book G Page 8

CARPENTER - see also CAPENTER

CARR, William to Nancy Gorden   7 September 1838
    m. 9 September by R. E. Teadford, M. G.
    Reference: Marriage Book C Page 7

CARR, Williaz B. to Clarrinda Linor   2 November 1846
    m. 3 November by William Newton, M. G.
    Reference: Marriage Book C Page 146

CARREL - see also CAMEL

CARRELL, John to Luesie Wattenbarger   14 January 1868
    m. 16 January by E. S. Miller, M. G.
    Reference: Marriage Book G Page 26

CARRIGIN, Charles H. to Mary Elvira Benton   30 December 1843
    m. 31 December by C. Sanders, M. G.
    Reference: Marriage Book C Page 95

CARRIGIN, James M. to Martha Ann Head   21 February 1847
    m. 21 February by Joseph Cobbs, J. P.
    Reference: Marriage Book C Page 153

CARRIGIN, John C. to Minerva Harris   23 March 1853
    m. 24 March by Joseph Cobb, J. P.
    Reference: Marriage Book D Page 65

CARROL, James A. to Jane Lawson   24 October 1849
    m. 25 October by J. W. Miller, M. G.
    Reference: Marriage Book D Page 20

CARROLL, Alfred to Vincy Buttram   18 October 1841
    m. 19 October by William Dotson, J. P.
    Reference: Marriage Book C Page 48

CARROLL, Heil to Betsy Jane Hurt   20 November 1866
    m. 20 November by Heil Buttram, M. G.
    Reference: County Archives: Marriage Book G
    Page 4

CARROLL, Jas. H. to Nancy J. Fields   22 November 1865
    m. 23 November by Heil Buttram, M. G.
    Reference: Marriage Book F Page 31

CARROLL, James M. to Mahala Kelley   6 October 1859
    m. 7 October by J. Jack, M. G.
    Reference: Marriage Book E Page 10

CARROLL - see also CARRELL

CARSON, Alfred to Caroline Lower   25 May 1848
    m. 28 May by J. Jack, M. G.
    Reference: Marriage Book D Page 2

CARTER, O. C. to Miss Addie C. Hoback   10 July 1869
    m. 13 July by John N. Stamper, M. G.
    Reference: Marriage Book G Page 48

CARTER, Peter to Miss Jarusha Dobbs   2 March 1842
    m. 3 March by Joseph Minzes, J. P.
    Reference: Marriage Book C Page 54

CARTER, Robert A. to Catharine Gilley   24 September 1856
    m. 28 September by Wm. MCamy, J. P.
    Reference: Marriage Book D Page 114

CARTER, W. M. to Elizabeth Crabtree   4 July 1867
    Reference: Marriage Book G Page 17:
    Marriage Book G Page 23

CARTER, William to Elizabeth Crews   12 January 1843
    m. 12 January by W. H. Ballew, J. P.
    Reference: Marriage Book C Page 71

CARTER, Wm. M. to Elizabeth Couch   4 August 1845
    m. 7 August by Wm. Rucker, J. P.
    Reference: Marriage Book C Page 123

CARTRIGHT, E. D. to Jane Haggard   30 April 1857
    m. 30 April by Wm. Newman, J. P.
    Reference: Marriage Book D Page 126

CARTRIGHT, Jas. to Martha C. E. Smith   15 January 1859
    m. 16 January by Robert Cochran, J. P.
    Reference: Marriage Book D Page 155

CARTRIGHT, Wm. A. to Mary Ann Jones   13 November 1858
    Reference: Marriage Book D Page 151:
    W. P. A.

CARTRIGHT - see also CARRIGHT

CARVER, Andrew to Sarah Brown   9 August 1870
    m. 11 August by P. M. Long, J. P.
    Reference: Marriage Book G Page 63

CARVER, Campbell to Mary Simpson   9 April 1870
    m. 14 April by P. M. Long, J. P.
    Reference: Marriage Book G Page 60

CARVER, Camul to Miss Thursey C. Walsh   29 August 1866
    m. 29 August by P. M. Long, J. P.
    Reference: Marriage Book F Page 46

CASAD, John C. to Nancy J. McAmis   21 July 1842
    m. 21 July by R. W. Patty, Minister M. E.
    Church
    Reference: Marriage Book C Page 59

CASADA, James M. to Minerva J. Nelson   13 June 1842
    m. 21 June by R. W. Patty, M. M. E. Church
    Reference: Marriage Book C Page 58

CASADA, Wesly to Elizabeth Gaston   6 May 1840
    m. 7 May by H. Ingram, M. G.
    Reference: Marriage Book C Page 29

CASADA, William to Nancy Manerva Crisp   16 April 1846
    Reference: Marriage Book C Page 137

CASADA - see also CASIDA, CASSADA

CASEY, J. A. to Miss M. R. Forester   16 July 1870
    "The license in this case returned endorsed
    by both parties forfeiting and rescinding
    the contracts of marriage, witnessed by A. S.
    Robeson, (Blacksmith)"
    Reference: Marriage Book G Page 62

34

CASEY, J. A. to Miss N. T. Matthews   23 July 1870
    m. 23 July by J. W. Gilbert, J. P.
    Reference: Marriage Book G Page 63

CASEY, Moses to Elizabeth Coe   19 May 1829
    James Ellison, Security
    m. 27 May by Wm. Dotson, J. P.
    Reference: W. P. A.

CASEY - see also CAZY

CASH, Bogan to Elizabeth A. King   21 December 1841
    m. by William Dotson, J. P.
    Reference: Marriage Book C Page 50

CASH, Bogan to Mary Riddle   7 October 1867
    A. D. Briant, Security
    m. 10 October by D. W. Bevers, M. G.
    Reference: County Archives: Marriage Book G
    Page 21

CASH, James I. to Elizabeth J. Eakin   4 February 1856
    m. 4 February by David W. Beaver, M. G.
    Reference: Marriage Book D Page 107

CASIDA, James to Mary J. Bradford   29 January 1868
    John Long, Security
    m. 29 January by G. W. Coleman, M. G.
    Reference: County Archives: Marriage Book G
    Page 27

CASLANE, Jamez to Sarah Runnelz   9 November 1846
    m. 12 November by Wm. Newton, M. G.
    Reference: Marriage Book C Page 146

CASS, James W. to Sarah Ann Riggs   4 June 1866
    "I Sary An Riggs do certify that all contracts
    existing betwene me and J. W. Cass is forferted
    by my concente & reqeste you take them back-
    Sary Ann Riggs"
    Reference: Marriage Book F Page 42

CASS, T. A. to Susan A. Blackburn   18 April 1854
    m. 18 April by W. Witcher, M. G.
    Reference: Marriage Book D Page 83

CASS, William M. to Julia A. Douglas   31 December 1856
    m. 1 January 1857 by C. Long, M. G.
    Reference: Marriage Book D Page 122

CASS - see also CASST

CASSADA, John W. to Rebeccah Davis   4 October 1853
    m. 6 October by Daniel McPhail, J. P.
    Reference: Marriage Book D Page 72

CASSADY, John W. to Mary Jane Bales   24 October 1868
    m. 26 October by A. J. Shelton, J. P.
    Reference: Marriage Book G Page 39

CASSADY, John W. to Louisa J. Smith   6 October 1870
    m. 9 October by Wm. Thompson, M. G.
    Reference: Marriage Book G Page 66

CASSIDY - see also CASADA, CASIDA

CASTELL, Benjamin to Martha Madison   12 October 1856
    m. 12 October by G. W. Rentfro, M. G.
    Reference: Marriage Book D Page 116

CASTELL, D. L. to Amanda Anderson   7 October 1865
   m. 8 October by Wm. C. Owen, J. P.
   Reference: Marriage Book F Page 27

CASTELL, Elijah to Patience Taber   24 March 1827
   m. 24 March by Merrimon
   Reference: W. P. A.

CASTEEL, George to Mary Ann Malone   8 June 1867
   m. 9 June by W. G. Horton, J. P.
   Reference: Marriage Book G Page 16

CASTEEL, Joseph to Ruthey Ann Grisham   13 June 1867
   Reference: Marriage Book G Page 16

CASTEEL, M. H. to Mary N. Elbert   1 January 1850
   m. January by J. C. Pendergrass, M. G.
   Reference: Marriage Book D Page 23

CASTEEL, Plesant B. to Mary M. Garrelt   24 May 1869
   m. 24 May by Elihu Kelley, J. P.
   Reference: Marriage Book G Page 46

CASTEEL, Washington to Hetty Malone   1 May 1839
   m. 1 May by A. Barb, J. P.
   Reference: Marriage Book C Page 17

CASTEEL, Willis to Elizabeth Elliot   16 August 1839
   Reference: Marriage Book C Page 22

CATE, Alfred W. to Mary Gregory   7 November 1846
   m. 12 November by Wm. Rucker, J. P.
   Reference: Marriage Book C Page 146

CATE, C. C. to Miss L. C. Russell   12 June 1858
   m. 13 June by John Scruggs, M. G.
   Reference: Marriage Book D Page 41

CATE, Charles to Narcessa McMillan   1 December 1828
   John H. Porter, Security
   Reference: W. P. A.

CATE, Charles to Mary P. Baker   8 August 1839
   m. 8 August by J. M. Kelley, M. G.
   Reference: Marriage Book C Page 21

CATE, Charles to Elizabeth Overby   10 January 1865
   m. 10 January by Jas. Baker, J. P.
   Reference: County Archives: Marriage Book F
   Page 14

CATE, David to Serelsey McCrary   21 March 1857
   m. 22 March by Jas. Baker, J. P.
   Reference: Marriage Book D Page 125

CATE, G. C. to Miss Elin V. Reynolds   13 April 1867
   m. 18 April by J. A. Hyden, M. G.
   Reference: Marriage Book G Page 13

CATE, Greenberry to Magdalena Cate   20 September 1843
   m. 21 September by Z. Rose, M. G.
   Reference: Marriage Book C Page 85

CATE, Henry to Tennie Miller   30 June 1869
   Reference: Marriage Book G Page 47

CATE, Jacob C. to Sarah C. Bales   27 January 1869
   m. 28 January by S. H. Cate, M. G.
   Reference: Marriage Book G Page 43

CATE, John to Harriet Errickson   7 August 1850
   Reference: Marriage Book D Page 29

CATE, John to Sarah J. Witt   4 October 1855
   m. 4 October by Janes A. Zigler, J. P.
   Reference: Marriage Book D Page 103

CATE, Col. Jonathan N., merchant of Dalton, Ga.   11 September 1849
   to Martha M. Maples, daughter of Wm. Maples
   m. 13 September by Hiram Douglass, M. G.
   Reference: Marriage Book D Page 18:
   "Knoxville Register" Volume 34 #1691
   6 October 1849

CATE, Noah to Mahala Isham   21 December 1854
   m. 21 December by J. Thomas, J. P.
   Reference: Marriage Book D Page 92

CATE, Peter B. to Gemima Womack   26 December 1850
   m. 26 December by William R. Walker
   Reference: Marriage Book D Page 36

CATE, R. E. to Arminda Stephenson   15 November 1858
   m. 16 October /sic/ by J. S. Russell, M. G.
   Reference: Marriage Book D Page 151

CATE, Robert to Elizabeth Brown   15 December 1843
   m. 15 December by R. A. McAdoo, J. P.
   Reference: Marriage Book C Page 93

CATE, Robert to Mary J. Hardin   3 August 1857
   m. 4 August by C. Long, M. G.
   Reference: Marriage Book D Page 128

CATE, Robert C. to Sarah E. Cooper   30 October 1866
   m. 1 November by C. R. Hoyl, M. G.
   Reference: Marriage Book G Page 3

CATE, Robert E. to Rachel E. Denniss   29 October 1857
   m. 29 October by H. M. Roberts, J. P.
   Reference: Marriage Book D Page 131

CATE, Solomon to Eliza McCariel   19 November 1846
   m. 19 November by J. Jack, M. G.
   Reference: Marriage Book C Page 147

CATE, Thos. J. to Mary Horton   28 December 1869
   m. 28 December by A. Templeton, M. G.
   Reference: Marriage Book G Page 55

CATE, W. P. to Mary Wolf   19 November 1858
   m. 20 November by F. M. Houer, M. G.
   Reference: Marriage Book D Page 151

CAULDWELL, Thomas to Lusey Long   25 February 1852
   m. 26 February by Robert Gregory, M. G.
   Reference: Marriage Book D Page 48

CAVILL, Wm. to Elizabeth Renfrow   6 October 1855
   m. 7 October by James Forest, J. P.
   Reference: Marriage Book D Page 103

CAVILL - see also COVEAL

CAZY, John A. to Mary J. Filio   6 January 1858
   m. 7 January by Joseph W. Gibson, J. P.
   Reference: Marriage Book D Page 134

CESIL - see also CICILL

CECILL, Joseph M. to Sarah Brazeal   10 February 1853
    m. 10 February by D. Carpenter, M. G.
    Reference: Marriage Book D Page 63

CENTER - see also SENTER

CHAMBERS, Abner to Rachel M. Thornhill   23 April 1857
    m. 23 April by J. A. Zigler, J. P.
    Reference: Marriage Book D Page 126

CHAMBERS, Edmond to Elizabeth Taylor   20 April 1829
    Wm. Caves, Security
    Reference: W. P. A.

CHAMBERS, John to Frances Carney   22 April 1844
    m. 24 April by M. A. Cass, J. P.
    Reference: Marriage Book C Page 101

CHAMBERS, John J. to Mariah Swinford   14 November 1849
    m. 14 November by John J. Robison, M. G.
    Reference: Marriage Book D Page 21

CHAMBERS, McConnell to Rebecca Sivils   1 September 1865
    m. 2 September by S. M. Thomas, J. P.
    Reference: Marriage Book F Page 24

CHAMBERS, Richard to Milla Melton   23 October 1866
    m. 26 October by S. M. Thom, J. P.
    Reference: Marriage Book G Page 2

CHAMBERS, Robert E. to Susan J. Meghee   30 September 1852
    m. 30 September by Wm. Burns, J. P.
    Reference: Marriage Book D Page 57

CHAMLEE, Adnisom Judson to Eliza Thalch   27 December 1850
    m. 29 December by T. S. Rice, J. P.
    Reference: Marriage Book D Page 36

CHAMLEE, Thos: A. Louisa I. Johnson   22 March 1866
    m. 22 March by T. R. Bradshaw
    Reference: Marriage Book F Page 39

CHAMLEE, William to Elizabeth Fair   13 December 1843
    m. 19 December by T. S. Rice, J. P.
    Reference: Marriage Book C Page 92

CHAMLEE - see also SHAMLEE

CHAPMAN, Madison to Zilpha Lee   24 December 1844
    Reference: Marriage Book C Page 115

CHAPMON, Coleman W. to Ann Forguson   20 October 1838
    Reference: Marriage Book C Page 9

CHAPMON - see also SHAPMAN

CHARLES, James M. to Eliza Jane Dodson   23 August 1849
    m. 23 August 1850 /sic/ by Wm. F. Forest, M. G.
    Reference: Marriage Book D Page 17

CHATTIN, J. D. to Susan Cooke   12 April 1847
    Reference: Marriage Book C Page 155

CHESNUT, Wm. S. to Martha E. Furgerson   19 December 1857
    m. 24 December by C. R. Hoyl, M. G.
    Reference: Marriage Book D Page 133

CHESNUTT, Saml. G. to Mary J. Hoyl   10 January 1865
    m. 11 January by I. R. Chesnutt, M. G.
    Reference: County Archives: Marriage Book F
    Page 13

CHESTNUTT, J. W. to Elmira Benton   4 November 1868
    A. J. Armstrong, Security
    m. 5 November by N. B. Goforth, M. G.
    Reference: County Archives: Marriage Book G
    Page 39

CHILDERS, George W. to Catharine Robertson   14 July 1846
    m. 16 July by David F. Jamerson, J. P.
    Reference: Marriage Book C Page 140

CHILDERS, J. W. to Mrs. Lodicy Grant   11 August 1865
    m. 13 August by Wm. L. McKnight, J. P.
    Reference: Marriage Book F Page 23

CHILDRES, Josiah to Anna Shelton   21 April 1838
    m. 5 June by R. J. Moore, J. P.
    Reference: Marriage Book C Page 3

CHOATE, Emery to Elizabeth Bottoms   24 November 1846
    m. 24 November by J. C. Weir, J. P.
    Reference: Marriage Book C Page 148

CHRISMAN, A. J. to Elizabeth Foster   10 December 1853
    E. N. Dunlap, Security
    m. 10 December by E. L. Miller, J. P.
    Reference: County Archives: Marriage Book D
    Page 75

CHRISMAN, Isaac to Sarah Foster   16 August 1852
    m. 17 August by Wm. R. Elder, M. G.
    Reference: Marriage Book D Page 55

CHRISTIAN, Allen to Martha Jane Lile   10 July 1847
    m. 10 July by T. S. Rice, J. P.
    Reference: Marriage Book C Page 157

CLARK, A. J. to Marry Ann Shook   25 March 1858
    m. 28 March by Thos. Rogers, J. P.
    Reference: Marriage Book D Page 138

CLARK, Andrew J. to Sarah J. Swafford   27 September 1853
    Reference: Marriage Book D Page 71

CLARK, Charles I. to Nancy Smith   25 July 1864
    Reference: Marriage Book F Page 6

CLARK, D. C. to Caroline Foster   29 December 1868
    m. 30 December by Wm. L. McKnight, J. P.
    Reference: County Archives: Marriage Book G
    Page 42

CLARK, David to Sarah A. Coats   17 November 1870
    m. 17 November by A. Hawn, M. G.
    Reference: Marriage Book G Page 69

CLARK, Gabril to Elizabeth M. Swaffer   5 December 1855
    m. 6 December by Joel Culpeper, J. P.
    Reference: Marriage Book D Page 105

CLARK, H. R. to Nancy Swaffore   20 April 1870
    m. 21 April by O. M. Liner, J. P.
    Reference: Marriage Book G Page 60

CLARK, James M. to Susan Hoback   30 March 1864
    m. 8 April by Rev. D. Carpenter
    Reference: Marriage Book E Page 14

CLARK, John to Nancy Hampton   10 July 1844
    m. 10 July by John Jinkins, J. P.
    Reference: Marriage Book C Page 104

CLARK, John F. to Drucilla Amos   26 June 1829
    Elihu S. Barclay, Security
    m. 29 June by Obediah Bolding
    Reference: W. P. A.

CLARK, John W. to Amanda Rains   3 June 1852
    m. 4 June
    Reference: Marriage Book D Page 53

CLARK, Joseph P. to Mary Swafford   7 January 1868
    m. 9 January by F. A. Dixon, J. P.
    Reference: Marriage Book G Page 26:
    Marriage Book G Page 29   .

CLARK, Peter to Crata Humphrey   18 February 1829
    Edmond Casteel, Security
    Reference: W. P. A.

CLARK, W. B. to Mary Farmer   23 July 1870
    m. 24 July by J. M. Miller, M. G.
    Reference: County Archives: Marriage Book G
    Page 63

CLARK, William B. to Abigail Humphrey   12 January 1853
    m. 13 January by O. M. Liner, J. P.
    Reference: County Archives: Marriage Book D
    Page 62

CLATON, Wm. S. E. to Mary H. Stallcup   24 August 1867
    m. 25 August by G. M. Bloom, J. P.
    Reference: Marriage Book G Page 19

CLAYTON, G. W. to Elvira Crockett   18 October 1865
    m. 19 October by J. S. Russell, M. G.
    Reference: Marriage Book F Page 28

CLEAG, Alexander, of Athens, to Jemima Hurst,
    daughter of Elijah Hurst of McMinn County
    m. 22 November 1832 by Benjamin Isbell, Esq.
    Reference: "Knoxville Register" Vol. 17
    #855 12 December 1832

CLEAGE, Thos. A. to Penelope S. Vandyke   15 September 1856
    m. 15 September by George A Caldwell, M. G.
    Reference: Marriage Book D Page 114

CLEMENTSON, John to Mary Steed   17 February 1853
    m. 17 February by Wm. C. Daily, M. G.
    Reference: County Archives: Marriage Book D
    Page 63

CLEVELAND, E. L. to Miss L. L. Marshal   3 December 1868
    m. 23 December by A. Templeton, M. G.
    Reference: Marriage Book G Page 40

CLEVELAND, Presley to Millie (Mollie) B. Briant   4 July 1867
    m. 4 July by W. A. Nelson, M. G.
    Reference: Marriage Book G Page 17 and
    "Athens Republican" 12 July 1867 Vol. I, #1

CLINE, Joseph to Martha Jack   27 September 1865
    m. 20 September 1866 /sic/ by Elihu Kelley, J.P.
    Reference: Marriage Book F Page 27

CLONTS. John to Caroline Emery   6 March 1850
    m. 6 March by James Bonner, J. P.
    Reference: Marriage Book D Page 26

COATS, Albia to Miss Polly Senter   23 May 1828
    Robert Scott, Security
    Reference: W. P. A.

COATS, Jasper to Elizabeth Grigsby   3 January 1859
    m. 3 January by Johnathan Thomas, J. P.
    Reference: Marriage Book D Page 154

COATS, Thomas to Caroline Rose   14 March 1855
    m. 14 March 1859 /sic/ by Johnathan Thomas, J.P.
    Reference: Marriage Book D Page 96

COATS, Wm. A. to Viney Keeten   26 October 1866
    m. 28 October by Rev. Dan Carpenter
    Reference: County Archives: Marriage Book
    G Page 3

COBB, Andrew to Manday Cate   4 July 1868
    m. 23 July by G. M. Hutsell, J. P.
    Reference: Marriage Book G Page 34

COBB, George to Susan Amos   12 August 1829
    William C. L. Adams, Security
    Reference: W. P. A.

COBB, Jesse M. to Mary V. Cooper   23 August 1853
    m. 8 September by C. R. Hoyl, M. G.
    Reference: Marriage Book D Page 69

COBB, Joseph to Caroline Lattimore   17 November 1844
    m. 18 November by F. McGonigal, M. G.
    Reference: County Archives: Marriage Book C
    Page 112

COBB, R. B. to Catharine J. Baker   7 August 1844
    Reference: Marriage Book C Page 106

COBBEL, G. M. to Miss N. A. Shamlee   13 January 1870
    m. 20 January by J. S. Russell, M. G.
    Reference: Marriage Book G Page 57

COBBS, C. W. to Elizabeth Reynolds   23 July 1846
    m. 28 July by A. Templeton, M. G.
    Reference: Marriage Book C Page 140

COBBS, J. B. to Miss S. C. Thompson   1 March 1852
    m. 2 March by T. L. Hoyl
    Reference: Marriage Book D Page 49

COCHRAN, James A. to Mrs. Mary J. Patty   19 November 1865
    m. 19 November by W. C. Owen, J. P.
    Reference: Marriage Book F Page 31

COCHRAN, R. P. to Mary Laseter   27 September 1867
    m. 27 September by J. B. Kimbrough, M. G.
    Reference: Marriage Book G Page 21

COCHRAN, Robert E. to Sarah W. Dodson   27 September 1841
    m. 5 October by Robert Gregory, M. G.
    of Baptist Church
    Reference: Marriage Book C Page 47

COFFEE, James O. to Eliza Ann Grady   8 January 1851
   m. 8 January by J. C. Bryant, J. P.
   Reference: Marriage Book D Page 36

COFFEY, Asbury M. to Mary G. Bradford   22 July 1828
   Jonathan Allen, Security
   Reference: W. P. A.

COFFEY, Robert to Louisa Kinchelo   27 October 1853
   m. 28 October by James C. Bryan, J. P.
   Reference: Marriage Book D Page 73

COFFMAN, Abner L. to Sarah Couch   20 July 1843
   Reference: Marriage Book C Page 81

COFFMAN, Albert to Elizabeth Kinser   20 August 1845
   m. 24 August by Justus Steed, J. P.
   Reference: Marriage Book C·Page 125

COFFMAN, Anderson to Louisa J. Campbell   28 July 1843
   m. 30 July by Rev. B. Buckner
   Reference: Marriage Book C Page 82

COFFMAN, David H. to Mary C. Sterns   17 September 1846
   m. 17 September by Wm. Rucker, J. P.
   Reference: Marriage Book C Page 143

COFFMAN, G. P. F. to Elizabeth A. Wear   10 April 1841
   m. 13 April by Robert Mansell, M. G.
   Reference: Marriage Book C Page 41

COLE, J. H. to Miss M. E. Standifer   4 May 1868
   Reference: Marriage Book G Page 32

COLE, John to Polly Ann Dean   7 October 1848
   Reference: Marriage Book D Page 6

COLE, Joseph to Glaphrey Heard   28 February 1842
   m. 1 March by T. S. Rice, J. P.
   Reference: Marriage Book C Page 54

COLE, Lafait to Catherine Hanks   23 November 1866
   m. 23 November by F. A. Dixon, J. P.
   Reference: County Archives: Marriage Book
   G Page 5

COLE, Philip to Eliza Smith   8 November 1843
   Reference: Marriage Book C Page 90

COLE, Solomon to Harriet Emory   27 July 1843
   m. 27 July by Asahil Carlock, J. P.
   Reference: Marriage Book C Page 82

COLEMAN, Charles F. to Sarah Wray   27 September 1842
   m. 28 September by Jonathan Thomas, J. P.
   Reference: Marriage Book C Page 62

COLEMAN, J. D. to Amy Williams   3 March 1859
   m. 9 March by William Newman, J. P.
   Reference: Marriage Book D Page 158

COLEMAN, James M. to Elizabeth G. Walker   29 October 1840
   Reference: Marriage Book C Page 33

COLEMAN, William to Cornelia Crawford   26 December 1865
   m. 26 December by A. Haun, M. G.
   Reference: Marriage Book F Page 34

COLIER, Banister to Polly Armstrong   19 February 1838
 m. 19 February by Saml. H. Jordan, J. P.
 Reference: Marriage Book C Page 1

COLIER, James M. to Mary Douglass   23 March 1850
 m. 24 March by J. C. Carlock, J. P.
 Reference: Marriage Book D Page 27

COLLIER - see also COLEIR

COLLINS, A. M. to Sarah Burns   21 September 1856
 m. 25 September by J. G. Swisher, M. G.
 Reference: Marriage Book D Page 114

COLLINS, Alfred M. to Sarah Melton   12 November 1846
 m. 13 November by John Jenkins, J. P.
 Reference: Marriage Book C Page 147

COLLINS, J. B. to Elizabeth Jane McCarty   12 December 1849
 m. 15 December by Henry Price, M. G.
 Reference: Marriage Book D Page 23

COLLINS, Jacob M. to Catherine Franklin   16 January 1847
 m. 17 January by J. H. Benton, J. P.
 Reference: Marriage Book C Page 151

COLLINS, Larkin to Nancy Newkirk   27 April 1846
 m. 3 May by Edwin A. Atlee
 Reference: Marriage Book C Page 137

COLLINS, Robert to Miss Lile Pike   2 August 1865
 m. 3 August by W. H. Stephenson, J. P.
 Reference: Marriage Book F Page 22

COLLINS, W. W. to Louisa E. Culberson   3 October 1865
 m. 3 October by Wm. C. Owen, J. P.
 Reference: Marriage Book F Page 27

COLLINS, William to Mary E. Ady   31 July 1838
 m. 31 July by A. Slover, M. G.
 Reference: Marriage Book C Page 5

COLTHARP, A. J. to Harriet M. Lowery   5 November 1856
 m. 6 November by George A. Caldwell, M. G.
 Reference: Marriage Book D Page 119

COLTHARP, A. J. to Jane Russell   14 November 1864
 m. 17 November by John Scruggs, M. G.
 Reference: Marriage Book F Page 10

COLTHARP, G. H. to Mrs. Ada L. Russell   28 February 1866
 m. 1 March by N. B. Goforth, M. G.
 Reference: Marriage Book F Page 38

COLTHARP, J. H. to Jane Fain   21 February 1866
 m. 21 February by Thomas J. Russell, M. G.
 Reference: Marriage Book F Page 38

COLTHARP, O. R. to Miss Z. L. Lee   31 January 1870
 m. 1 February 1870 by J. S. Russell, M. G.
 Reference: Marriage Book G Page 58

COLTHARP, G. H. to Martha A. Denton   27 June 1860
 m. 28 June by C. R. Hoyl, M. G.
 Reference: Marriage Book E Page 6

COLVILLE, John to Martha Jarnagin   20 August 1841
 m. 20 August by L. R. Morrison, V. D. M.
 Reference: Marriage Book C Page 45

COLVILLE, John H. to Jennette V. Lide   6 June 1843
    m. 6 June by A. Slover, M. G.
    Reference: Marriage Book C Page 79

COMB, J. C. to Miss M. E. Web   12 January 1870
    m. 13 January by Stephen Hill, J. P.
    Reference: Marriage Book G Page 57

COMB, Jackson to Malinda Walker   24 March 1866
    m. 1 April by S. M. Thomas, J. P.
    Reference: Marriage Book F Page 39

COMBS, Gideon to Elizabeth Hammer   24 August 1841
    m. 24 August by L. R. Morrison, V. D. M.
    Reference: Marriage Book C Page 45

COOK, Martin to Eliza Jane Eddington   21 October 1847
    m. 22 October by G. C. Metcalfe, Esq.
    Reference: Marriage Book C Page 161

COOK, Samuel to Jane Young   25 March 1848
    Reference: W. P. A.

COOK, Thomas J. to Sarah M. Moss   17 February 1864
    m. 18 February by C. R. Hoyl, M. G.
    Reference: Marriage Book E Page 18

COOK, Wm. H. to Mary A. Kantz   22 July 1857
    m. 23 July by J. M. Miller, M. G.
    Reference: Marriage Book D Page 127

COOKE, George W. to Sarah J. Gilbreath   21 October 1840
    m. 22 October by Wilson Chapman
    Reference: Marriage Book C Page 33

COOKSTON, Isaac to Mary Ann Miller   29 July 1869
    m. 29 July by W. W. Neal, M. G.
    Reference: Marriage Book G Page 48

COOLEY, Andrew to Lidia Cooley   5 February 1846
    m. 5 February by Mc. Atchley, Minister
    Reference: Marriage Book C Page 133

COOPER, B. M. to Miss M. C. Boyd   25 August 1868
    m. 27 August by C. R. Hoyl, M. G.
    Reference: Marriage Book G Page 35

COOPER, Bennett to Mary Robinson   10 October 1860
    m. 10 October by John McGaughey, J. P.
    Reference: Marriage Book E Page 16

COOPER, Francis M. to Sarah Ann Manis   27 February 1854
    m. 28 February by G. W. Wallace, J. P.
    Reference: Marriage Book D Page 80

COOPER, James to Margret Armstrong   21 May 1866
    R. C. Cate, Security
    m. 22 May by C. R. Hoyl, J. P.
    Reference: County Archives: Marriage Book
    F Page 42

COPELAND, Charles P. to Eliza Ann Thompson   5 August 1840
    m. 6 August by Bynum Jarnagan, J. P.
    Reference: Marriage Book C Page 30

COPELAND, John L. to Sarah Katharine Rily   29 January 1847
    m. 29 January by J. C. Gaston, M. G.
    Reference: Marriage Book C Page 151

COPELAND (COURTNEY), Wm. P. to Evaline Curd   18 January 1841
   m. 19 January by Bynum Jarnigan, J. P.
   Reference: Marriage Book C Page 36

COPPET, Alfred to Mary Ann Shaw   19 April 1853
   m. 18 /sic7 April by Wm. Walker, J. P.
   Reference: Marriage Book D Page 65

CORLEY, W. M. to Miss S. I. Ware   11 October 1869
   m. 21 October by N. B. Goforth, M. G.
   Reference: Marriage Book G Page 52

CORLEY - see also CARLE

CORN, Hamilton to Nancy J. Thompson   16 January 1866
   Reference: Marriage Book F Page 36

CORNAG, Edward H. to Matilda Worley   3 February 1942
   m. 3 February by Robert Frazier, M. G.
   Reference: Marriage Book C Page 53

COUCH, G. W. to Elizabeth A. Land   31 January 1866
   m. 31 January by J. S. Russell, M. G.
   Reference: Marriage Book F Page 37

COUCH, Joseph to Mary Ware   17 March 1841
   Reference: Marriage Book C Page 39

COURTNEY, John M. to Katharine S. Neal   20 January 1841
   m. 21 January by G. E. Mountcastle
   Reference: Marriage Book C Page 36

COURTNEY, Wm. P. - see COPELAND, Wm. P.

COVEAL, Andrew to Rebeca A. Perry   1 September 1870
   m. 3 September by Stephen Hill, J. P.
   Reference: Marriage Book G Page 64

COVEAL - see also CAVILL

COVING, Joseph to Miss E. S. West   20 November 1854
   m. 24 November by D. Carpenter, M. G.
   Reference: Marriage Book D Page 89

COWAN, Andrew to Margaret Fisher   11 January 1858
   m. 12 January 1859 /sic7 by Johnathan Thomas,
   J. P.
   Reference: Marriage Book D Page 134

COWAN, David to Matilda Templeton   13 August 1829
   David Barden, Security
   Reference: W. P. A.

COX, Alexander F. to Amelia V. Atlee   1 May 1850
   m. 1 May by J. W. Miller, M. G.
   Reference: Marriage Book D Page 27

COX, Benjamin to Jane Hawkins   16 November 1827
   m. 18 November by _____ Couch, J. P.
   Reference: W. P. A.

COX, Elisha to Isabella Dickson   3 February 1841
   m. 4 February by Bynum Jarnagin, J. P.
   Reference: Marriage Book C Page 37

COX, Hiram to Luzireene Senter   1 August 1844
   m. 2 August by John Jenkins, J. P.
   Reference: Marriage Book C Page 105

COX, Isam H. to Sallie A. Benson   19 April 1859
   m. 20 April by I. Atkins, M. G.
   Reference: County Archives
   Note: This license was not entered on
   Marriage Record Books

COX, J. J. to Sarah A. Shugart   10 May 1865
   m. 11 May by M. Paine, M. G.
   Reference: Marriage Book F Page 18

COXEY, John to Letty Lawson   25 August 1849
   m. 25 August by Nat. Barnett, M. G.
   Reference: Marriage Book D Page 17

COXEY, John to Mary Orton   21 January 1851
   m. 21 January by B. A. John, M. G.
   Reference: Marriage Book D Page 37

CRABTREE, Rice to Celia Ward   9 March 1859
   m. 10 March by Jas. H. Melton, J. P.
   Reference: Marriage Book D Page 158

CRABTREE, Thomas to Easter Green   27 January 1841
   m. 29 January by John Jenkins, J. P.
   Reference: Marriage Book C Page 37

CRADDICK, David to Texas A. Fleming   29 June 1864
   m. 1 July by J. M. Miller, M. G.
   Reference: Marriage Book F Page 4

CRAEG, John N. to Nancy L. Rogers   16 October 1843
   m. 17 October by M. D. Anderson, J. P.
   Reference: Marriage Book C Page 88

CRANE - see CRAYN

CRAWFOR, Thomas to Amanda Higdon   27 June 1839
   m. 7 July by Hamilton Bradfor, J. P.
   Reference: Marriage Book C page 20

CRAWFORD, James to Susan Crawford   6 November 1848
   m. 6 November by Daniel McPhail, J. P.
   Reference: Marriage Book D Page 7

CRAWFORD, John to Libbie J. Tompkins   6 March 1860
   m. 6 March by Geo. A. Caldwell, M. G.
   Reference: Marriage Book E Page 6

CRAWFORD, John C. to Elizabeth E. Pain   31 May 1847
   m. 3 June by David F. Jameson, J. P.
   Reference: Marriage Book C Page 156

CRAWFORD, Solomon K. to Susanah Hackler   24 January 1840
   m. 26 January by J. M. Melton, M. G.
   Reference: Marriage Book C Page 26

CRAWLEY, Elisha to Sarah D. Dorsey   16 May 1848
   m. 16 May by Uriah Johnston, J. P.
   Reference: Marriage Book D Page 2

CRAWLEY - see CROWLEY

CREASMAN, James M. to Nancy Haymes   2 May 1849
   m. 3 May by J. C. Bryan, J. P.
   Reference: Marriage Book D Page 14

CREASMAN, Joseph H. to Francis J. Guffey   17 February 1855
   Reference: Marriage Book D Page 95

CREASMAN, Samuel D. to Mary E. Dugger   25 July 1854
    m. 27 July by J. A. Wilson J. P.
    Reference: Marriage Book D Page 85

CREASMAN - see also CRISMAN

CREWS - see also CRUSE

CREWSE, Johnson to Mary McGuire   20 March 1843
    m. 23 March by W. H. Ballew, J. P.
    Reference: Marriage Book C Page 77

CRISMAN, Wilbert to Elizabeth Smith   11 January 1848
    m. 13 January by B. E. Blain, J. P.
    Reference: Marriage Book C Page 165

CRISP, John to Polly Bond   18 March 1840
    m. 19 March by M. W. Cunningham, J. P.
    Reference: Marriage Book C Page 27:
Marriage Book C Page 28

CRITENDON, James to Nancy J. Colvell   27 September 1854
    m. 28 September by Robert Gregory, M. G.
    Reference: Marriage Book D Page 87

CRITTENDEN, George W. to Lucinda Caldwell   11 February 1843
    m. 12 February by M. D. Anderson, J. P.
    Reference: Marriage Book C Page 74

CRITTENDEN, James H. to Samantha Ellis
    m. 2 October 1851 by Nathaniel Barnett, M. G.
    Reference: Marriage Book D Page 44

CRITTENDEN, Jasper N. to Eliza C. Willson   10 Janaury 1865
    m. 12 January by W. T. Russell, M. G.
    Reference: Marriage Book F Page 14

CRITTENDEN, Nathaniel to Saprina Beckett   17 December 1823
    John Gee, Security
    m. by Jesse Dodson, M. G.
    Reference: W. P. A.

CRITTENDEN, Wm. to Mrs. Barbara B. Gibson   24 November 1864
    m. 24 November by P. M. Long, J. P.
    Reference: Marriage Book F Page 11

CRITTENDEN, Wm. R. to Sarah Ann Miller   21 May 1855
    m. 22 May by H. M. Roberts, J. P.
    Reference: Marriage Book D Page 98

CROCKET, John to Sarah Carney   26 May 1866
    m. 28 May by A. J. Kirksey, J. P.
    Reference: County Archives: Marriage Book F
Page 42

CROCKETT, J. H. to Caroline Martin   3 February 1859
    m. 6 February by Robert Cochran, J. P.
    Reference: Marriage Book D Page 156

CROCKETT, Josiah H. to Iwanona Derrick   27 November 1851
    m. 27 November by C. R. Hoyl, M. G.
    Reference: Marriage Book D Page 46

CROCKETT, Nelson M. to Mrs. Edith Patty   1 March 1855
    m. 1 March by Robert Gregory, M. G.
    Reference: Marriage Book D Page 95

CROCKETT, Thos. J. to L. V. Taylor   27 March 1869
    m. 28 March by Morgan Miller, J. P.
    Reference: Marriage Book G Page 45

CROCKETT, William H. to Mary Thornton   6 October 1840
    m. 8 October by John Scruggs
    Reference: Marriage Book C Page 32

CROMWELL, James S. to Margaret Shields   4 March 1829
    John B. Cromwell, Security
    Reference: W. P. A.

CROSS, John to Amanda Porter   21 December 1865
    m. 21 December by Robert Mansell, M. G.
    Reference: Marriage Book F Page 33

CROSS, Wm. W. to Nancy C. Miller   15 May 1857
    m. 24 May by H. M. Roberts, J. P.
    Reference: Marriage Book D Page 126

CROSSLAND, John to Elizabeth Adams   10 November 1825
    m. 10 November by James McKamy, J. P.
    Reference: W. P. A.

CROUCH, L. W. to Mary E. Varnell   15 October 1858
    m. 19 October by J. Atkins, M. G.
    Reference: Marriage Book D Page 148

CROW, Adolphus H. to Emeline Glaze   8 February 1844
    m. 8 February by A. Slover, M. G.
    Reference: Marriage Book C Page 97

CROW, C. C. to Jane E. Atlee   24 December 1867
    m. 24 December by R. D. Black, M. G.
    Reference: Marriage Book G Page 25

CROW, James L. to Corrie Turner   29 June 1869
    m. 29 June by J. C. Barb, M. G.
    Reference: Marriage Book G Page 47

CROWDER, R. P. to Miss H. M. Magill   23 June 1860
    m. 28 June by A. H. Barkley, M. G.
    Reference: Marriage Book E Page 12

CROWELL, Izerael E. to Sarah Tate   22 November 1828
    m. 22 November by John S. Wilson, J. P.
    Reference: W. P. A.

CROXTON, G. R. to Rebecca Crewman   1 January 1868
    m. 2 January
    Reference: Marriage Book G Page 25

CRUMLEY, C. C. to Sarah A. Jackson   9 June 1867
    m. 9 June by J. W. Gilbert, J. P.
    Reference: Marriage Book G Page 16

CRUSE, John to Eliza Ann Cate   7 February 1844
    m. 7 February by J. H. Benton, J. P.
    Reference: Marriage Book C Page 97

CRUTCHFIELD, Hiram to Martha Witt   25 February 1864
    m. 25 February by Rev. D. Carpenter
    Reference: Marriage Book E Page 18

CULPEPER, Houston to Sarah Smith   17 March 1870
    m. 17 March by J. D. Lyle, J. P.
    Reference: Marriage Book G Page 59

CULPEPER, W. to Sally Armstrong   19 October 1848
    m. 22 October by A. Swafford, J. P.
    Reference: Marriage Book D Page 6

CULPEPPER, F. M. to Miss P. M. Lemmons   20 August 1860
    m. 23 August by Calvin Denton, M. G.
    Reference: Marriage Book E Page 10

CULPEPPER, G. W. to Sarah Forgy   4 December 1839
    m. 5 December by E. Newton, M. G.
    Reference: Marriage Book C Page 19

CULPEPPER, J. A. to Elizabeth A. Benton   4 November 1856
    m. 6 November by T. L. Hoyl, M. G.
    Reference: Marriage Book D Page 118

CULPEPPER, J. T. to Nancy J. Evans   26 November 1853
    m. 27 November by H. C. Cooke, M. G.
    Reference: Marriage Book D Page 75

CULPEPPER, Joel to Mrs. Elizia Jenkins   19 April 1866
    m. 19 April by J. M. Miller, M. G.
    Reference: Marriage Book F Page 39

CULPEPPER, Joseph J. to Polly Ann Wallin   30 April 1846
    m. 30 April by Alfird Swafford, J. P.
    Reference: Marriage Book C Page 137

CULTON, Alexander to Sarah F. Newman   27 July 1841
    m. 27 July by John Scruggs, Minister
    Reference: Marriage Book C Page 44

CUNNINGHAM, David B. to Mary Henderson   25 December 1850
    m. 25 December by Wm. H. Ballew, J. P.
    Reference: Marriage Book D Page 36

CUNNINGHAM, John to Margaret Sallee   27 October 1855
    m. 28 October by C. Gadley, M. G.
    Reference: Marriage Book D Page 104

CUNNINGHAM, Moses to Mrs. Margaret A. Graves   14 February 1850
    m. 14 February by John Robinson, M. G.
    Reference: Marriage Book D Page 25

CUNNINGHAM, Thos. to Dicy Wilson   17 November 1842
    m. 17 November by W. F. Forest, M. G.
    Reference: Marriage Book C Page 67

CUPP, Lewis to Clara Ratledge   23 September 1864
    Reference: Marriage Book F Page 7

CURD, James H. to Miss D. A. Cooper   13 May 1870
    m. 17 May 1871 /sic7 by C. R. Hoyl, M. G.
    Reference: Marriage Book G Page 60

CURD - see also KIRD

CURTIS, Moses to Elizabeth Ann Grubb   1 June 1866
    m. 3 June by G. M. Coleman, M. G.
    Reference: Marriage Book F Page 42

CURTIS, William to Parthena Green   2 April 1868
    m. 2 April by J. S. Russell, M. G.
    Reference: County Archives: Marriage Book
    G Page 29

DACUS, P. H. C. to Mary E. Hammonds   16 January 1869
    m. 17 January by A. Marshman, J. P.
    Reference: Marriage Book G Page 42

DAKE, Henry J. to Lidia Lucindy Knox   16 August 1848
    m. 17 August by Thomas B. Weller, M. G.
    Reference: Marriage Book D Page 4

DAKE, Jackson G. to Ann Riddle   22 December 1840
    m. 24 by George Yost, Minister of Methidest
    Protest. Church
    Reference: Marriage Book C Page 35

DAKE, Joseph M. to Margarette Desham   17 August 1824
    m. 17 August by Henry Price, J. P.
    Reference: W. P. A.

DANIELS, Mount to Elizabeth Jane Fillpots   25 July 1866
    m. 30 July by Uriah Payne
    Reference: Marriage Book F Page 44

DARLING, Charles P. to Melissa McFarland   21 August 1865
    m. 21 August by J. H. Magill, J. P.
    Reference: Marriage Book F Page 24

DAUGHERTY, Charles R. to Susan E. Queener   14 June 1865
    Reference: Marriage Book F Page 19

DAUGHERTY, Chas. R. to Sally C. Derrick   1 August 1865
    m. 2 August by Elihu Kelley, J. P.
    Reference: Marriage Book F Page 22

DAUGHERTY, Dennis H. to Eliza A.
    m. 2 September 1860
    Reference: McMinn County Chancery Case #605

DAUGHERTY, Jas. M. to Martha E. Riggs   19 January 1858
    m. 21 January by J. J. Elliott, J. P.
    Reference: Marriage Book D Page 135

DAUGHERTY, John to Harriet E. Randolph   13 January 1858
    m. 12 /sic7 January by J. J. Elliott, J. P.
    Reference: Marriage Book D Page 135

DAUGHERTY, William to Nancy Riggs   5 November 1846
    m. 5 November by M. A. Cass, J. P.
    Reference: Marriage Book C Page 146

DAUGHERTY - see also DOPHERTY, DORHERTY, DOUGHERTY

DAUNY - see also DAWNEY

DAVENPORT - see also DEAVENPORT

DAVIS, Andrew S. to Miss Francis E. Shell   8 March 1868
    m. 8 March by A. Barb, J. P.
    Reference: Marriage Book G Page 30

DAVIS, Arthur to Mrs. Ann Graham   19 January 1865
    m. 22 January by Uriah Payne, M. G.
    Reference: Marriage Book F Page 41

DAVIS, Benjamin C. to Rachel Davis   10 December 1840
    Reference: Marriage Book C Page 34

DAVIS, Campbell to Elizabeth Vaughan   17 October 1853
    m. 20 October by David W. Beaver, M. G.
    Reference: Marriage Book D Page 73

DAVIS, G. C. to Miss Ataline Dotherroe   12 February 1856
    m. 14 February by J. H. Melton, J. P.
    Reference: Marriage Book D Page 107

DAVIS, George N. to Martha L. Hale   30 January 1851
    Reference: Marriage Book D Page 38

DAVIS, H. M. to Jane T. Wasson   10 April 1845
    m. 10 April by Wm. Rucker, J. P.
    Reference: Marriage Book C Page 119

DAVIS, Henry B. to Nancy Pickens   30 November 1838
    m. 30 November by Obadiah Bolding, M. G.
    Reference: Marriage Book C Page 11

DAVIS, Huiston to Elizabeth Davis   13 September 1858
    m. 13 September by Joseph Neel, J. P.
    Reference: Marriage Book D Page 146

DAVIS, J. Z. to Catharine Hinkle   12 January 1846
    m. 13 January by W. F. Forrest, M. G.
    Reference: Marriage Book C Page 132

DAVIS, James (Jeremiah) W. to Sarah Spearman   17 April 1852
    m. 20 April by Wm. McKamy, J. P.
    Reference: Marriage Book D Page 53 & 54

DAVIS, John W. to Nancy A. Young   27 January 1841
    m. 27 January by Richard A. McAdoo, J. P.
    Reference: Marriage Book C Page 37

DAVIS, John W. to Mary E. St. John   15 December 1853
    m. 15 December by George A. Caldwell, M. G.
    Reference: Marriage Book D Page 76

DAVIS, Marien to Miss Sallie M. Slaughter   3 August 1866
    m. 5 August by E. G. Randolph, M. G.
    Reference: County Archives: Marriage
    Book F Page 45

DAVIS, Martin to Sarah Stephenson   5 April 1867
    m. 7 April by Wm. Erixon, M. G.
    Reference: Marriage Book G Page 13

DAVIS, Rector to Miss Lieu Anna Lemmons   29 November 1850
    m. by J. Jenkins, J. P.
    Reference: Marriage Book D Page 35

DAVIS, Robert to Elizabeth Morris   20 March 1839
    Reference: Marriage Book C Page 15

DAVIS, T. W. to Miss M. S. T. Davis   19 November 1869
    m. 20 November by E. Z. Williams, J. P.
    Reference: Marriage Book G Page 54

DAVIS, Thomas W. to Lorene Dethro   10 April 1852
    m. by J. Jenkins, J. P.
    Reference: Marriage Book D Page 51

DAVIS, W. C. to Mollie Ivins   5 July 1864
    m. 5 July by E. Rowley, M. G.
    Reference: Marriage Book F Page 4

DAVIS, W. O. to Nancy J. Tunnell   24 May 1864
    m. 24 May by E. Z. Williams, J. P.
    Reference: Marriage Book F Page 3

DAVIS, William to Caroline Blackwell   12 February 1849
    m. 13 February by John Jenkins, J. P.
    Reference: Marriage Book D Page 11

DAVIS, William Y. to Elizabeth A. McCammon   28 January 1854
    Reference: Marriage Book D Page 78

DAWNY - see also DAUNY

DAWSEN, James M. to Susanah Knox   4 April 1839
 Reference: Marriage Book C Page 16

DAY, Hiram to Rhoda Strutton   20 April 1842
 Reference: Marriage Book C Page 56

DEADRICK, Lon to Amanda Cleage, daughter of
 Clinton Cleage (colored)
 m. April 1865
 Reference: McMinn Circuit Court Case #995
 Filed 17 July 1867

DEAL, Jordan to Eliza Edmonson   18 July 1864
 Reference: Marriage Book F Page 5

DEAN, Aron to Miss Charlotta Ward   /97 January 1849
 Reference: Marriage Book D Page 10

DEAN, D. D. to Caroline Prewit   15 September 1869
 m. 16 September by A. D. Briant, J. P.
 Reference: Marriage Book G Page 51

DEAN, Decatur W. to Nancy M. Woody 28 December 1865
 m. 28 December by A. D. Briant, J. P.
 Reference: Marriage Book F Page 34

DEAN, James A. to Clarissa Griffith 18 September 1849
 m. 18 September by J. Atkins, Minister
 Reference: Marriage Book D Page 18

DEAN, Russell to Louisa Minerva Gamble 7 July 1854
 m. 7 July by M. Southard, M. G.
 Reference: Marriage Book D Page 85

DEAN, William S. to Elizabeth Woody 6 March 1865
 m. 7 March by Rev. William Thompson
 Reference: County Archives: Marriage
 Book F Page 16

DEARMAN, Thos. E. to Sarah Clark 28 March 1848
 Reference: W. P. A.

DEARMON, William B. to Mary Cook 10 August 1841
 m. 10 August by Moses A. Cass, J. P.
 Reference: Marriage Book C Page 44

DEATON, Lery to Elizabeth MCulhany 2 January 1858
 m. 2 January by Wm. H. Ballew, J. P.
 Reference: Marriage Book D Page 133

DEATON, William to Sarah McGuire 16 December 1846
 m. 18 December by Wm. H. Ballew, J. P.
 Reference: Marriage Book C Page 149

DEAVENPORT, George to Salie H. Mitchel 22 December 1857
 m. 22 December by George A. Caldwell, M. G.
 Reference: Marriage Book D Page 133

DEAVERS, H. B. to Elizabeth Swatzell 16 October 1865
 m. 17 October by T. J. Russell, M. G.
 Reference: Marriage Book F Page 28

DECKER, Geo. to Jane McMillon 12 November 1854
 m. 12 November by A. D. Bryant, J. P.
 Reference: Marriage Book D Page 89

DECKER, Wm. to Emaline Turner   11 February 1858
    m. 11 February by Joseph Neil, J. P.
    Reference: Marriage Book D Page 136

DELANEY, John to Elizabeth Gooley   26 January 1865
    m. 26 January by Wm. C. Owen, J. P.
    Reference: Marriage Book F Page 15

DELZELL, John N. to Nancy J. Lowry   31 August 1841
    m. 31 August by L. R. Morrison, V. D. M.
    Reference: Marriage Book C Page 46

DEMENT, Thos. J. to Miss Zoe L. Ickes   6 October 1870
    m. 6 October by R. A. Cobb, Rector
    St. Pauls Church
    Reference: County Archives: Marriage
    Book G Page 66

DENNIS, Allen to Sallie E. Lane   15 April 1865
    m. 16 April by Z. Rose, M. G.
    Reference: Marriage Book F Page 17

DENNIS, Charles to Nancy Dennis   23 December 1843
    m. 24 December by Tapley Gregory, M. G.
    Reference: W. P. A.

Note: Lower half of page 94, Book C, missing

DENNIS, Isaac to Mary Dennis   9 February 1857
    Reference: Marriage Book D Page 123

DENNIS, I. Sham to Rebecca Thompson   25 September 1856
    m. 25 September by H. M. Roberts, J. P.
    Reference: Marriage Book D Page 115

DENNIS, James D. to Malinda Green   26 August 1840
    m. 27 August by Richard A. McAdoo, J. P.
    Reference: Marriage Book C Page 31

DENNIS, Joel to Sarahan Robberts   11 December 1848
    m. 12 December by Thomas B. Weller, M. G.
    Reference: Marriage Book D Page 8

DENNIS, John to Martha M. Hackler   8 April 1865
    m. 13 April by B. Frazier, M. G.
    Reference: County Archives: Marriage
    Book F Page 17

DENNIS, Mark to Rachel Mathews   23 September 1854
    m. 24 September by J. A. Zeigler, J. P.
    Reference: Marriage Book D Page 87

DENNIS, Mark to Mary W. Elder   29 November 1855
    m. 2 December by H. M. Roberts, J. P.
    Reference: Marriage Book D Page 105

DENNIS, Orrin to Virginia Cate
    m. 22 December 1861 (McMinn County residents
    but marriage may have been performed elsewhere)
    Reference: McMinn Chancery Case #57

DENNIS, Samuel to Mary Blankenship   28 September 1852
    m. 28 September by A. Barb, J. P.
    Reference: Marriage Book D Page 56

DENNIS, Tilman to Martha Amos   28 February 1838
    Reference: Marriage Book C Page 2

DENNIS, William to Sophia Moore   16 December 1846
  m. 17 December by Thomas B. Willis, M. G.
  Reference: Marriage Book C Page 149

DENSON, John to Martha Ivans   19 January 1856
  Reference: Marriage Book D Page 107

DENSON, Thos. to Margaret Collins   11 January 1856
  Reference: Marriage Book D Page 106

DENTON, G. H. to Amanda E. Magill   5 September 1870
  m. 5 September by W. H. Crawford, M. G.
  Reference: Marriage Book G Page 64

DENTON, Isaac to M. E. Vinzant   7 May 1869
  m. 9 May by J. B. Kimbrough, M. G.
  Reference: Marriage Book G Page 46

DENTON, John to Narcissa Womack   4 December 1856
  m. 4 December by H. M. Roberts, J. P.
  Reference: Marriage Book D Page 120

DENTON, Patton to Sarah Womack   22 December 1856
  m. 25 December by H. M. Roberts, J. P.
  Reference: Marriage Book D Page 121

DENTON, Thomas to Mary Newman   3 September 1868
  m. 15 September by J. S. Russell, M. G.
· Reference: Marriage Book G Page 35

DEPUTY, James to Peggy Hardin   26 February 1829
  Saml. Wheeler, Security
  Reference: W. P. A.

DERICK, A. C. to Sallie A. Riggs   13 June 1868
  m. 14 June by C. Cate, J. P.
  Reference: Marriage Book G Page 33

DERICK, Wm. to Sarah J. Hamel   11 September 1867
  m. 11 September by C. Cate, J. P.
  Reference: Marriage Book G Page 20

DERRICK, A. G. to Sarah A. Smith   22 November 1844
  m. 25 November by Green L. Reynolds, J. P.
  Reference: Marriage Book C Page 113

DERRICK, Erastus L. to Louisa Stansberry   17 May 1854
  m. 28 May by J. J. Elliott, J. P.
  Reference: Marriage Book D Page 83

DERRICK, J. M. B. to Harriett S. Allen   22 October 1870
  Reference: Marriage Book G Page 68

DETHEROW, Jacob to Elizabeth Gibson   16 December 1847
  m. 23 December by John Jenkins, J. P.
  Reference: Marriage Book C Page 163

DETHEROW - see also DERTHEROW, DOTHERROE

DEVANEY, Thomas W. to Frances Davis   20 April 1864
  m. 20 April by E. Rowley, M. G.
  Reference: Marriage Book F Page 1

DEVAULT, William to Louisa Pearson   21 September 1839
  Reference: Marriage Book C Page 23

DICKEY, W. H. H. to Mary A. Hyden   10 January 1866
  m. 11 January by J. Albert Hyden, M. G.
  Reference: Marriage Book F Page 35

DILL, Harrison to Nancy Rogers
    m. 20 April 1849 by James Scarbrough, M. G.
    Reference: Marriage Book D Page 14

DILLARD, John to Rebecca Hellums   22 December 1838
    m. 25 December by John Courtney, M. G.
    Reference: Marriage Book C Page 11

DILLARD, John A. to Catharine Hackler   23 September 1865
    m. 25 September by H. M. Sloop, M. G.
    Reference: Marriage Book F Page 26

DILLICK, David N. to Amanda Allen   10 August 1869
    Reference: Marriage Book G Page 49

DILPIRT, James J. to Mrs. Clearinda Wilka   3 October 1868
    m. 4 October by W. W. Haymes, M. G.
    Reference: Marriage Book G Page 37

DIMMITT, Calvin M. to Nancy L. Marcum   30 July 1864
    m. 30 July by E. Z. Williams, J. P.
    Note: This entry is on November 1864 page
    and numbered in sequence with the November
    entries but reads July.
    Reference: Marriage Book F Page 11

DITMORE, C. S. to Mrs. Elizabeth Stansbury   13 September 1865
    m. 14 September by Elihu Kelley, J. P.
    Reference: Marriage Book F Page 25

DITMORE, Edwin to Rhoda Riggs   8 December 1829
    Reference: W. P. A.

DITMORE, John to Amanda Bolding (Bowling)   2 September 1839
    m. 12 September by C. Sanders, M. G.
    Reference: Marriage Book C Page 22

DITMORE, Vincent G. to Mary Mannery   24 March 1838
    m. 24 March by Jas. Barnett, J. P.
    Reference: Marriage Book C Page 3

DIXON, Edom to Melissa E. Slaughter   12 November 1852
    m. 14 November by Dimmon Dorsey, Esq.
    Reference: Marriage Book D Page 58

DIXON, Eli to Mary Couch   14 October 1842
    m. 15 October by Robert Gregory, Minister
    of Baptist Church
    Reference: Marriage Book C Page 65

DIXON, Eli to Malessa Randolph   18 January 1847
    m. 21 January by W. F. Forrest, M. G.
    Reference: Marriage Book C Page 151

DIXON, Franklin A. to Elizabeth Studdard   12 August 1852
    m. 12 August by A. Swafford, J. P.
    Reference: Marriage Book D Page 54

DIXON, J. W. to Mary Ann T. Tanner   17 February 1868
    m. 20 February by Wm. McKnight, J. P.
    Reference: Marriage Book G Page 28

DIXON, James A. to Martha C. Swaffer   7 January 1868
    m. 9 January by F. A. Dixon, J. P.
    Reference: Marriage Book G Page 26

DIXON, James H. to Sarah E. Newman   4 August 1855
    m. 9 July /sic7 by Robert Gregory, M. G.
    Reference: Marriage Book D Page 101

DIXON, John to Martha Riddle   11 February 1847
    m. 11 February by B. E. Blain, J. P.
    Reference: Marriage Book C Page 152

DIXON, John to Mrs. Mary McCallie   23 January 1851
    m. 23 January by A. Swafford
    Reference: Marriage Book D Page 37

DIXON, John D. to Miss C. M. Curtis   29 March 1869
    m. 4 April by J. S. Russell, M. G.
    Reference: Marriage Book G Page 45

DIXON, John G. to Lucinda Hampton   16 February 1859
    m. 17 February by Joel Culpepper, J. P.
    Reference: Marriage Book D Page 157

DIXON, John J. to Elvira Bird   16 January 1845
    m. 16 January by Samuel Wilson, J. P.
    Reference: Marriage Book C Page 116

DIXON, S. W. to Nancy A. E. Howell   27 September 1855
    m. 27 September by J. Cunningham, M. G.
    Reference: Marriage Book D Page 102

DIXON, Thomas to Emeline Riddle   3 February 1848
    m. 3 February by Heil Buttram, M. G.
    Reference: Marriage Book C Page 167

DIXON, William to Nancy Cannon   26 August 1840
    Reference: Marriage Book C Page 31

DIXON, Wm. M. to Margaret C. Kahill   16 June 1860
    m. 1 July by Morgan Miller, J. P.
    Reference: Marriage Book E Page 12

DOAN, Absolom H. to Sarah L. Brown   7 February 1843
    Reference: Marriage Book C Page 73

DOBB, Pryor to Miss A. J. Manis   29 December 1868
    m. 29 December by Wm. Thompson, M. G.
    Reference: Marriage Book G Page 41

DOBBS, Daniel to Miss Bartheny Watz   13 January 1847
    m. 14 January by G. W. Wallis, J. P.
    Reference: Marriage Book C Page 151

DOBBS, Lide W. to Catharine Monroe   1 November 1843
    m. 2 November by G. W. Wallis, J. P.
    Reference: Marriage Book C Page 89

DOBBS, Parris L. to Lucinda Fields   10 October 1846
    m. 11 October by G. W. Wallis, J. P.
    Reference: Marriage Book C Page 144

DOBBS, Prior to Jane Dotson   29 January 1864
    m. 29 January by Z. Rose, M. G.
    Reference: Marriage Book E Page 10

DOBBS, William W. to Sarah J. Sellers   23 November 1846
    m. 26 November by G. Wallis, J. P.
    Reference: Marriage Book C Page 148

DOCKERY, William to Sarah Dockery   15 July 1848
    m. 16 July by G. W. Kirksey, J. P.
    Reference: Marriage Book D Page 3

DODD, Berry to Sarah Rutherford   19 March 1840
    m. 19 March by H. C. Cook, J. P.
    Reference: Marriage Book C Page 28

DODD, Lang R. to Virginia A. Ensminger   11 October 1855
    m. 11 October by S. Sharets, M. G.
    Reference: Marriage Book D Page 103

DODD, William to Eliza Ann Fry   2 September 1846
    m. 3 September by G. W. Wallis, J. P.
    Reference: Marriage Book C Page 143

DODD, William R. to Martha D. Lock   11 April 1868
    m. 12 April by T. Sullins, M. G.
    Reference: Marriage Book G Page 31

DODSON, A. J. to Mrs. S. B. Henderson   5 July 1870
    m. 5 July by N. B. Goforth, M. G.
    Reference: Marriage Book G Page 62

DODSON, E. A. to Rachel C. Forrest   19 July 1845
    m. 22 July by Wm. F. Forrest, M. G.
    Reference: Marriage Book C Page 122

DODSON, Jefferson to Sarah Smith   28 July 1829
    John Dodson, Security
    Reference: W. P. A.

DODSON, Jesse B. to Sarah Newton   22 October 1842
    m. 22 October by N. Harrison, M. G.
    Reference: Marriage Book C Page 65

DODSON, Jesse W. to Elizabeth J. McKamy   1 February 1850
    m. 5 February by Wm. F. Forrest, M. G.
    Reference: Marriage Book D Page 25

DODSON, Jessee to Miss Ailsey M. Newman   7 November 1848
    daughter of Wm. Newman
    m. 9 November by Wilson Chapman, M. G.
    Reference: Marriage Book D Page 7; "Knoxville
    Register" Vol. 8 #414 29 November 1848

DODSON, John to Elizabeth Fields   28 August 1829
    James Smith, Security
    Reference: W. P. A.

DODSON, John B. to Rebecca C. Epperson   14 August 1865
    m. 15 August
    Reference: Marriage Book F Page 23

DODSON, L. B. to Mary Ann Anderson   9 January 1854
    Reference: Marriage Book D Page 77

DODSON, Lazarus to Rebecca L. Sullins   5 June 1849
    m. 4 /sic/ June by Thos. H. Small, M. G.
    Reference: Marriage Book D Page 15

DODSON, Marcellus M. to Susan Hardy   16 February 1843
    m. 16 February by L. R. Morrison, V. D. M.
    Reference: Marriage Book C Page 74

DODSON, McMillan (McMinn) to Sarah D. Cunningham   9 May 1848
    m. 9 May by G. W. Alexander, M. G.
    Reference: W. P. A.: Oregon Donation Land Claim
    Number 4727

DODSON, Nimrod to Mrs. Margaret Ann Grigsby   5 June 1843
    m. 6 June by W. F. Forest, M. G.
    Reference: Marriage Book C Page 79

DODSON, Oliver M. to Miss Angeline Kelley   26 October 1865
    m. 26 October by J. W. Mann, M. G.
    Reference: Marriage Book F Page 29

57

DODSON, P. L. to Amanda Pew   22 September 1869
    m. 23 September by S. M. Thomas, J. P.
    Reference: Marriage Book G Page 51

DODSON, Willford to Miss Lusena J. Porter   24 January 1854
    m. 24 January by S. A. Spofford,
    Presbyterian Minister
    Reference: Marriage Book D Page 78

DODSON, William L. to Mary Craig, daughter of
    Wm. Craig and Sally Woods
    m. 2 September 1823
    Place of marriage not known
    Reference: Wm. Dodson Bible in possession
    of Earl Dixon, Englewood, Tenn. and copy in
    files of compiler.
    (Note: This was a pioneer family of McMinn
    County and the marriage could have been here)

DONAHOO, Irvan to Nancy Napier   29 April 1828
    Reference: W. P. A.

DORSEY, Dimmon to Elizabeth Newman   22 August 1838
    m. 23 August by L. Morison, M. G.
    Reference: Marriage Book C Page 6

DORSEY, Jonathan to Pegyann Jackson   27 September 1849
    Reference: Marriage Book D Page 19

DORSEY, McCamy W. to Rebecca Newman   15 March 1843
    m. 16 March by John Scruggs, Minister
    Reference: Marriage Book C Page 76

DORSEY, McKamy W. to Laura S. Newman   14 April 1858
    m. 15 April by George A. Caldwell, M. G.
    Reference: Marriage Book D Page 138

DORSEY, Micaijah to Emaline Pertileo   14 January 1839
    m. January by A. Slover, M. G.
    Reference: Marriage Book C Page 13

DORSEY - see also DOSSY

DOSS, James L. to Nancy Gage   23 July 1850
    m. 23 July by A. Swafford, J. P.
    Reference: Marriage Book D Page 29

DOSS, John to Sarah Walling   12 February 1847
    m. 14 February by A. Swafford, J. P.
    Reference: Marriage Book C Page 152

DOSS, William to Jane (Mary Jane) Cannon   1 January 1848
    m. 2 January 1849 by Alfred Swafford, J. P.   /1849/
    Reference: Marriage Book D Page 9

DOSSY /DORSEY?/, J. A. to Rebecky A. Richardson 29 September 1868
    m. 1 October by J. A. Higgens, M. G.
    Reference: Marriage Book G Page 37

DOTSON, Alfred to Elizabeth Patty   31 December 1839
    m. 2 January 1840 by Robert Gregory,
    Minister of Baptist Church
    Reference: Marriage Book C Page 26

DODSON, Allen to Martha Arnwine   15 October 1840
    m. 15 October by John Foster, J. P.
    Reference: Marriage Book C Page 32

DOTSON, Edmand to Susanah Casey   13 February 1840
    Reference: Marriage Book C Page 25

DOUGLASS, John to Susan Barker   6 February 1846
    m. 9 February by E. Newton, M. G.
    Reference: Marriage Book C Page 133

DOUGLASS, Oliver C. to Rebecca Johnson   12 April 1864
    m. 14 April by J. Jack, M. G.
    Reference: Marriage Book F Page 1

DOUGLASS - see also DUGLASS

DOUTHIT, Samuel to Mrs. Gincy Turk   21 June 1845
    m. 22 June by M. C. Hawk, M. G.
    Reference: Marriage Book C Page 121;
    McMinn Will Book D, Page 314

DRAKE, John to Rachel Baldwin   20 January 1842
    m. 20 January by A. C. Robison, J. P.
    Reference: Marriage Book C Page 52

DUCKWORTH, G. W. to Susan A. Rose   15 August 1865
    m. 16 August by William Thompson, M. G.
    Reference: Marriage Book F Page 24

DUCKWORTH, L. J. to Nancy A. Bracket   16 October 1858
    m. 16 October by M. A. Cass, M. G.
    Reference: Marriage Book D Page 148

DUCKWORTH, Thos. N. to Mary Simons   16 March 1857
    m. 17 March by Geo. W. Rentfro, M. G.
    Reference: Marriage Book D Page 124

DUCKWORTH, W. A. to Mary C. Boon   4 April 1867
    m. 4 April by J. S. Russell, M. G.
    Reference: Marriage Book G Page 13

DUCKWORTH, Wailstill to Miss Abigail S. Stanton   13 September 1856
    m. 14 September by G. W. Rentfro, M. G.
    Reference: Marriage Book D Page 114

DUCKWORTH, William to Nancy Versha   22 May 1852
    m. 23 May by Dan Carpenter, M. G.
    Reference: Marriage Book D Page 52

DUGAN, James H. to Mary E. Barnett   9 May 1843
    m. 25 May by Wilson Chapman, M. G.
    Reference: Marriage Book C Page 78

DUGAN, Robert to Louisa Aerington   30 April 1828
    m. James Allison, Security
    Reference: W. P. A.

DUGAN, William A. to Elmira Cooper   14 September 1853
    m. 15 September by H. C. Cook, M. G.
    Reference: Marriage Book D Page 71

DUGAN, Wilson to Miss Casander Long   30 October 1838
    m. 30 October by J. C. Carlock, J. P.
    Reference: Marriage Book C Page 8

DUGGAN, A. M. to Margaret L. Burnett   27 January 1855
    m. 28 January by Wm. R. Elder, M. G.
    Reference: Marriage Book D Page 94

DUGGAN, D. C. to Susan T. Patty   8 October 1868
    m. 22 October by C. R. Hoyl, M. G.
    Reference: Marriage Book G Page 38

DUGGAN, Guilford C. to Malinda E. Blackburn   3 May 1865
     m. 3 May by J. L. Mann, M. G.
     Reference: Marriage Book F Page 18

DUGGAN, Thos. P. to Sarah F. J. Patty   9 October 1865
     m. 12 October by C. R. Hoyl, M. G.
     Reference: Marriage Book F Page 27

DUGGAN - see also GANDD

DUGGER, James to Lucinda Largin   9 December 1840
     Reference: Marriage Book C Page 34

DUGGER, Joseph to Nancy Fairbanks   5 October 1865
     Reference: Marriage Book F Page 27

DUGGER, Thomas to Miss Francis Griffitts   31 October 1868
     m. 1 November by Elihu Kelley, J. P.
     Reference: Marriage Book G Page 39

DUGLASS, James to Elizabeth Firestone   8 October 1829
     David Firestone, Security
     Reference: W. P. A.

DUKE, William to Nancy Killingsworth   23 March 1842
     m. 24 March by C. W. Rice, J. P.
     Reference: Marriage Book C Page 55

DULA, Franklin to Elizabeth Russell   20 January 1866
     Reference: Marriage Book F Page 36

DUNCAN, John to Eliza Wyatt   1 December 1865
     m. 2 December 1866 /sic/ by Elihu Kelley, J. P.
     Reference: Marriage Book F Page 32

DUNN, Col. John N. of Cleveland to Miss Saliva   1 October 1862
     Alexander
     m. 1 October 1862 at residence of bride's
     father near Athens by Rev. Geo. A. Caldwell
     Reference: Athens Post Volume XV No. 732
     3 October 1862

DURHAM, Dr. A. P. of Penfield, Georgia to Miss   1 May 1860
     Sallie L. Calloway
     m. 1 May 1860 at residence of bride's father
     near Riceville, Tenn.
     Reference: Athens Post Volume XII No. 607,
     11 May 1860

DURHAM. William D. to Ann Faulkner   23 June 1842
     Reference: Marriage Book C Page 59

DYE, Thos. to Judy Dye   29 June 1847
     m. 1 July by Tapley Gregory, J. P.
     Reference: Marriage Book C Page 157

DYER, James to Miss Florantha Vaughan   18 January 1838
     m. 4 June by Wm. Dotson, J. P.
     Reference: Marriage Book C Page 1

DYER, Robert to Mary Harkrider   28 April 1849
     m. 29 April by John Spears, J. P.
     Reference: Marriage Book D Page 14

DYRE, Elijah to Sarah C. Beaver   13 June 1865
     m. 15 June by D. Carpenter, M. G.
     Reference: Marriage Book F Page 19

EADENS - see also EDENS

EAKINS, Allen to Susan Cash   21 July 1852
    m. 22 July by David W. Beaver, M. G.
    Reference: Marriage Book D Page 54

EATON, Charles H. to Rebecca Cate   22 June 1848
    m. 22 June by James D. Henley, J. P.
    Reference: Marriage Book D Page 3

EATON, Eli A. to Nancy M. Tunull   7 February 1846
    m. 8 February by M. Swenney, Esq.
    Reference: Marriage Book C Page 133

EATON, Henery J. to Sarah L. Jarnagan   24 February 1848
    m. 24 February by Wm. H. Ballew, J. P.
    Reference: Marriage Book C Page 168:
    W. P. A.

EATON, James L. to Jane Wingwood   20 January 1844
    m. 21 January by B. C. Blain, J. P.
    Reference: Marriage Book C Page 96

EATON, John to Mary E. McGrue   21 February 1869
    m. 21 February by Hamelton Pearce, J. P.
    Reference: Marriage Book G Page 44

EATON, John A. to Mary E. McGrew   10 December 1864
    Reference: Marriage Book F Page 12

EATON, William to Jane Robison   27 December 1842
    m. 28 December by Moses Swenny, J. P.
    Reference: Marriage Book C Page 70

EATON, Z. T. to Rebecky Davis   4 September 1867
    m. 5 September by D. B. Cunningham, M. G.
    Reference: Marriage Book G Page 20

EATON - see also EADAN, EADEN, EADENS

EATONS, James to Celia Hambrick   October 1855
    m. 12 October by James A. Zigler, J. P.
    Reference: Marriage Book D Page 103

EAVES - see EVES

EAVEZ (EAVENS) /EAVES7, James to Mary Fowler   17 August 1850
    m. 18 August by J. M. Scarbrough
    Reference: Marriage Book D Page 30

EDLEN, Henry to Mary Duckworth   29 August 1866
    m. 29 August by J. S. Russell, M. G.
    Reference: Marriage Book F Page 46

EBLEN, Wm. C. to Mrs. E. L. McElrath   14 November 1865
    m. 14 November by J. G. Swisher, M. G.
    Reference: Marriage Book F Page 30

EDDINGTON - see also EDINGTON, HEDDINGTON

EDENS, F. M. to Elisabeth Bedford   27 December 1845
    m. 1 January 1846 by W. Rucker, J. P.
    Reference: Marriage Book C Page 130

EDENS, Jame /James7 M. to Catherine Bedford   26 December 1846
    m. 31 December by R. A. McAdoo, J. P.
    Reference: Marriage Book C Page 150

EDENS, Seth to Miss S. C. Thompson   18 August 1870
    m. 18 September by James T. Smith, M. G.
    Reference: Marriage Book G Page 64

EDGEMAN, Samuel to Jane Allen   29 July 1843
  m. 30 July by J. W. Barnett, J. P.
  Reference: Marriage Book C Page 82

EDGEMON - see also AGEMAN

EDGMON, J. J. to Rachel L. Ferrell   17 July 1865
  m. 26 July by J. B. McCallan, M. G.
  Reference: Marriage Book F Page 21

EDGMON, Simon G. to Sarah R. Browder   12 August 1868
  m. 13 August by T. Sullins, M. G.
  Reference: Marriage Book G Page 34

EDGWORTH, F. E. to Marget A. Aric   7 September 1868
  m. 11 September 1869 /sic7 by Daniel McPhail,
  J. P.
  Reference: Marriage Book G Page 35

EDMINTEN, Peter to Margaret Chavis   29 April 1852
  m. 29 April by Jonathan Lyons, M. G.
  Reference: Marriage Book D Page 52

EDMONDS, Robert to Catharine Pardon   27 November 1869
  m. 27 November by J. H. Magill, J. P.
  Reference: Marriage Book G Page 54

EDMONDS, Wm. to Betsey Dye   18 January 1869
  m. 18 January by J. H. Magill, J. P.
  Reference: Marriage Book G Page 42

EDMONDSON, Samuel to Rachel Madox   23 February 1838
  m. 29 February by Wm. Shamblin, J. P.
  Reference: Marriage Book C Page 2

EDWARDS, Fletcher to Betsy Black   4 February 1829
  Frederick Crysock, Security
  m. 9 February by J. W. McMillin, Security
  Reference: County Archives: W. P. A.

EDWARDS, John to Elizabeth Evans   19 July 1827
  Reference: W. P. A.

EDWARDS, William to Charlotte Young   24 December 1839
  Reference: Marriage Book C Page 19
  Note: See next entry

EDWARDS, William to Charlotte Young   24 December 1840
  m. 25 December 1839 by Ezekiel Ward, M. G. /sic7
  Reference: Marriage Book C Page 27

EFFERT, J. H. to Mrs. M. A. W. Hanks   7 June 1848
  m. 8 June by M. C. Hawk, M. G.
  Reference: Marriage Book D Page 2

ELDER, Jacob to Ellen C. Ware   31 October 1866
  m. 1 November by Stephen Hill, J. P.
  Reference: Marriage Book G Page 3

ELDER, James to Mrs. Mary White   11 April 1864
  m. 14 April by T. B. Waller, M. G.
  Reference: Marriage Book F Page 1

ELDER, Robert to Mrs. Mary Witt   8 January 1841
  m. 14 January by Ezekiel Ward, J. P.
  Reference: Marriage Book C Page 36

ELDER, Robert to Eliza Coldwell
m. 20 January by L. B. Waller, M. G.
Reference: Marriage Book D Page 10

19 January 1849

ELDER, Saml. H. to Sarah J. White
Reference: Marriage Book F Page 9

29 October 1864

ELDREDGE, Joseph to Susan Rice
m. 15 October by A. Slover, M. G.
Reference: Marriage Book C Page 145

15 October 1846

ELDRIDGE, James F. to Malissa Hambright
m. 20 November by Henry Price, M. G.
Reference: Marriage Book C Page 112

19 November 1844

ELDRIGE, Benjamin to Rebecca Middleton
m. 16 September by Samuel Wilson, J. P.
Reference: Marriage Book C Page 159

14 September 1847

ELISON, Wm. A. to Elizabeth Reynolds
Thomas Gaston, Security
m. 15 September by N. B. Goforth, M. G.
Reference: County Archives: Marriage Book
G Page 21

14 September 1867

ELLIOT, F. M. to Eliza J. Crocket
m. 16 September by H. M. Sloop, M. G.
Reference: Marriage Book D Page 146

15 September 1858

ELLIOT, Jessee to Elizabeth Nation
m. 2 July by Robert Henderson, M. G.
Reference: Marriage Book D Page 3

24 June 1848

ELLIOTT, James J. to Evvie M. Preswood
m. 8 November 1866 /sic7 by Elihu Kelly, J. P.
Reference: Marriage Book F Page 29

26 October 1865

ELLIOTT, John to Sarah Carney
Reference: Marriage Book C Page 74

11 February 1843

ELLIOTT, P. B. to Emelin Kelly
m. 20 June by M. A. Cass, J. P.
Reference: Marriage Book C Page 103

20 June 1844

ELLIOTT, Thomas to Mary J. Rutherford
m. 11 February by M. A. Cass, J. P.
Reference: Marriage Book C Page 152

10 February 1847

ELLIOTT, Thomas W. to Amy Thompson
m. 18 February by M. A. Cass, J. P.
Reference: Marriage Book C Page 153

17 February 1847

ELLIS, A. B. to Matilda Lawson
m. 25 March by Jonathan Thomas, J. P.
Reference: Marriage Book C Page 28

25 March 1840

ELLIS, Allen to Malinda Foster
m. 3 August by David F. Jamison, J. P.
Reference: Marriage Book D Page 4

1 August 1848

ELLIS, Benjamin A. to Mary Ann Maples
m. 8 August by William W. Haymes, J. P.
Reference: Marriage Book D Page 4

7 August 1848

ELLIS, James to Nancy Pearson
m. 23 August by Daniel McPhail, J. P.
Reference: Marriage Book C Page 142

19 August 1846

ELLIS, Jeremiah B. to Sarah Thompson   10 September 1850
    m. 10 September by Robert Gregory, M. G.
    Reference: Marriage Book D Page 32

ELLIS, John M. to Hannah Maples   21 December 1842
    Reference: Marriage Book C Page 70

ELLIS, M. L. to Mary F. Barker   22 October 1869
    m. 22 October by E. Z. Williams, J. P.
    Reference: Marriage Book G Page 52

ELLIS, Phillip to Louisa Harden   7 January 1839
    m. 8 January by Andrew Crawford, J. P.
    Reference: Marriage Book C Page 12

ELLIS, Robert H. to Clarissa Randolph   2 December 1864
    m. 4 December by A. F. Brooks, M. G.
    Reference: Marriage Book F Page 11

ELLISON - see also ELISON

ELMORE, William to Nancy L. Dixo /Dixon7   7 April 1849
    m. 10 April by Thomas T. Russell, M. G.
    Reference: Marriage Book D Page 14

EMBREE (HEMBREE), Jonathan H. to Lina Kelley   25 January 1849
    m. 16 /sic7 January by A. L. Dugan, J. P.
    Reference: Marriage Book D Page 10

EMERSON, A. J. to Martha Coats   3 January 1868
    Carel Emerson, Security
    m. 5 January by G. W. Morton, J. P.
    Reference: County Archives: Marriage Book
    G Page 26 and Book G Page 29

EMERSON, Henry to Minerva Pearce   18 February 1843
    m. 22 February by Edward Newton, M. G.
    Reference: Marriage Book C Page 74

EMERSON, J. W. to Sarah Jane Bayless   24 December 1847
    m. 24 December by W. F. Forrest, M. G.
    Reference: Marriage Book C Page 164

EMERSON, William to Lidia Long   16 July 1849
    m. 17 July by W. F. Forrest, M. G.
    Reference: Marriage Book D Page 16

EMERSON, Wm. to Mrs. Josephine (Isophene) Haggard   26 May 1856
    m. 26 May by Robert Gregory, M. G.
    Reference: County Archives: Marriage Book D
    Page 110: McMinn Chancery Case #80

EMERSON - see also EMMERROSON, EMMERSON

EMERY, James to Sarah Graves   9 January 1849
    Reference: Marriage Book D Page 10

EMERY - see also EMORY, EMRY

EMRY, Silas to Margaret Sulivan   8 February 1842
    Reference: Marriage Book C Page 54

ENGLAND, Edward to Elizabeth A. Owens   1 September 1851
    Reference: Marriage Book D Page 42

ENGLEDOW, Richard T. to Elizabeth Sehorn   31 August 1842
    m. 31 August by J. Cunningham, M. G.
    Reference: Marriage Book C Page 61

ENSLEY, John to Mary E. Buck
    m. 14 February by Morgan Miller, J. P.
    Reference: Marriage Book G Page 44
                                    13 February 1869

ENSMINGER, Charles to Sarah J. Benton
    m. 28 December by S. W. Royston, J. P.
    Reference: Marriage Book F Page 12
                                    27 December 1864

EPLEY, David W. to Ester E. Fite
    m. 7 October by W. H. Cate, J. P.
    Reference: Marriage Book G Page 66
                                    6 October 1870

EPPERSON, J. B. to Miss M. E. Brown
    m. 24 August by C. J. Wright, M. G.
    Reference: Marriage Book G Page 35
                                    24 August 1868

EPPERSON, John L. to Melinda J. Borlison
    m. 29 August by Jas. Parkison, J. P.
    Reference: Marriage Book D Page 86
                                    29 August 1854

EPPERSON, Thomas N. to Malinda J. Calloway
    m. 8 December by W. A. Nelson, M. G.
    Reference: Marriage Book G Page 40
                                    8 December 1868

ERECKSON, Robert M. to Lizzie Dennis
    m. 21 January by Wm. Ereckson, M. G.
    Reference: Marriage Book G Page 43
                                    20 January 1869

ERECKSON, Williamson to Elizabeth Mansell
    Reference: Marriage Book C Page 63
                                    30 September 1842

ERICKSON, Jacob K. to Martha Mansel
    m. 15 April by Wm. Stewart, M. G.
    Reference: Marriage Book C Page 40
                                    14 April 1841

ERRICKSON, Johnson to Edy Melton
    m. 28 November by Jas. C. Bryan, J. P.
    Reference: Marriage Book D Page 21
                                    28 November 1849

ERRICKSON, J. J. to Miss Parthena J. Johns
    m. 26 February 1863 by Rev. M. A. Cass
    all of McMinn County
    Reference: Athens Post Volume XV, #754
    6 March 1863
                                    26 February 1863

ERVIN, A. J. to Mrs. Eliza Brown
    m. 7 September by W. C. Owens, J. P.
    Reference: Marriage Book G Page 50
                                    7 September 1869

ERVIN, Isaac N. to Phebe R. Trim
    Reference: Marriage Book C Page 23
                                    5 September 1839

ERVIN, W. H. to Elizabeth Boman
    m. 9 June by W. C. Owen, J. P.
    Reference: Marriage Book G Page 16
                                    9 June 1867

ERWIN, Benjamin to Catharine Erwin
    m. 20 December by Abner Lawson, J. P.
    Reference: W. P. A.
                                  20 December 1825

ERWIN, Carrol to Susan M. Derrick
    m. 29 September by H. C. Reynolds, J. P.
    Reference: Marriage Book G Page 65
                               26 September 1870

ERWIN, J. R. to Mary J. Myers
    m. 5 October by J. M. Miller, M. G.
    Reference: Marriage Book F Page 27
                                    2 October 1865

ERWIN, John to Malinda Atkinson   29 July 1829
    m. 30 July by John Courtney
    Reference: W. P. A.

ERWIN, John A. to Sarah Ann Williams   20 January 1869
    m. 22 January by Levi Fitzgerald, M. G.
    Reference: Marriage Book G Page 43

ERWIN, John R. to Debara A. Duly   14 October 1856
    m. 15 October by James Parkerson
    Reference: Marriage Book D Page 116

ERWIN, Joseph D. to Allamarinda Erkerson   17 December 1855
    m. 18 December by M. A. Cass, M. G.
    Reference: Marriage Book D Page 105

ERWIN, Lewis to Barbay Ellison   8 August 1845
    m. by M. C. Atchley, Minister
    Reference: Marriage Book C Page 124

ERWIN, Lewis S. to Sarah A. Casteel   10 September 1857
    m. 10 September by T. Sullins, M. G.
    Reference: Marriage Book D Page 129

ERWIN, Wm. B. to Sarah Gregory   22 March 1856
    m. 29 March by H. M. Roberts, J. P.
    Reference: Marriage Book D Page 108

ESCEX, John to Sarah Jane Sesrett   26 January 1867
    m. 31 January by A. Barb, J. P.
    Reference: Marriage Book G Page 9

ETTER, Lemuel to Josephine Brown   28 November 1868
    m. 10 December by Jno. N. Moore, M. G.
    Reference: Marriage Book G Page 40

ETTER, Martin Luther to Lourena Long   3 May 1851
    Reference: Marriage Book D Page 40

ETTER, Valentine to Cintha P. Willhite   19 November 1856
    m. 20 November by M. A. Cass, M. G.
    Reference: Marriage Book D Page 119

EUBANKS - see UBANKS

EVANS, Harris to Martha J. Gibbs   4 February 1854
    Reference: Marriage Book D Page 79

EVANS, R. M. to Eliza J. Lowry   9 September 1857
    m. 10 September by John Scruggs, M. G.
    Reference: Marriage Book D Page 129

EVANS - see also AVANS, AVENS, EAVEZ

EVERETT, John W. D. to Eliza Jane Brock   6 March 1854
    m. 7 March by Samuel W. Woods, M. G.
    Reference: Marriage Book D Page 81

EVERHART, John to Fany Grogan   27 October 1866
    m. 11 November by John P. Greens, J. P.
    Reference: Marriage Book G Page 3

EVERTON, Alexander to Caroline Jack   4 July 1853
    m. 7 July by B. E. Cass, J. P.
    Reference: Marriage Book D Page 67

EVES, Wm. H. to Nancy E. Moss   26 October 1868
    m. 27 October by J. M. Miller, M. G.
    Reference: Marriage Book G Page 39

FAGAN, William S. to Eliza Sattefield   16 October 1838
    m. 16 October by Thos. L. Hoyl, J. P.
    Reference: Marriage Book C Page 9

FAIN - see also FANE

FALKNER, James to Susan Crow   16 January 1850
    m. 17 January by Hiel Buttram, P. G.
    Reference: Marriage Book D Page 24

FANNON, Nathaniel to Mary Emaline Chanley   24 June 1838
    m. 24 June by A. Slover, M. G.
    Reference: Marriage Book C Page 4

FARLESS, Samuel to Polly Grisham   6 January 1851
    m. 6 January by A. John, M. G.
    Reference: Marriage Book D Page 36

FARMER, Carrol D. to Elizabeth A. Montgomery   22 March 1866
    m. 22 March by Hiel Buttram, M. G.
    Reference: Marriage Book F Page 39

FARMER, Isham W. to Mary Bedford   9 December 1841
    m. 9 December by R. A. McAdoo, J. P.
    Reference: Marriage Book C Page 50

FARMER, Jesse to Martha Henderson   23 August 1825
    m. 23 August by Geo. Bowman, L. P. of M. E. C.
    Reference: W. P. A.

FARMER, Wm. J. J. to Louisa M. Combs   13 July 1864
    Reference: Marriage Book F Page 5

FARNER, Coonrod to Edy Cearl   9 September 1825
    m. 9 September by Jas. McKamy, J. P.
    Reference: W. P. A.

FARRELL, T. L. to Janettie Borden   4 May 1853
    m. 5 May by S. Sharets, M. G.
    Reference: Marriage Book D Page 66

FARRELL - see also FAIRLL, FERREL, FERRELL

FARRIS, Jasper to Margaret Bunch   13 July 1864
    Reference: Marriage Book F Page 5

FARRIS, Jeremiah to Elizabeth Addison   10 November 1838
    Reference: Marriage Book C Page 10

FARRIS, Pleasant M. to Lucinda Hill   5 April 1838
    Reference: Marriage Book C Page 3

FAUGEWAN, R. J. to Margaret MCRoberts   28 October 1858
    m. 28 October by J. S. Russell, M. G.
    Reference: Marriage Book D Page 149

FAULKNER, D. K. to Miss E. S. Browder   13 October 1869
    m. 14 October by E. L. Miller, M. G.
    Reference: Marriage Book G Page 52

FAULKNER - see also FALKNER

FELTA, G. L. to Miss Angis Brookner   5 November 1868
    m. 5 November by T. Sullins, M. G.
    Reference: Marriage Book G Page 39

FENNY - see also FINNEY

FERGURSON, L. C. to Miss S. H. Fergurson   10 July 1857
    m. 12 July by S. M. Haun, M. G.
    Reference: Marriage Book D Page 127

FERGUSON, John to Susan J. Patty   28 September 1840
    m. 29 September by Robert Gregory, Minister
    of the Baptist Church
    Reference: Marriage Book C Page 32

FERGUSON, John P. to Mary A. Miller   21 October 1847
    m. 21 October by Robert Randolph, E. C. C.
    Reference: Marriage Book C Page 161

FERGUSON - see also FORGUSON, FURGERSON

FIELDS, Dudley to Elizabeth Carroll   7 February 1842
    m. 10 February by Jonathan Thomas, J. P.
    Reference: Marriage Book C Page 53

FIELDS - see also FEILDS

FIFER, John P. to Susan E. Smith   15 March 1859
    m. 18 March by Geo. A. Caldwell, M. G.
    Reference: Marriage Book D Page 159

FILLPOT, James to Margaret J. Letner   22 December 1865
    m. 24 December 1866 /sic/ by Wm. H. Stephenson
    Reference: Marriage Book F Page 33

FILPOT - see also PHILPOT

FILYAW - see also FILIO

FILYEW, John to R. Coxey   12 September 1850
    m. 17 September by A. John, M. G.
    Reference: Marriage Book D Page 32

FINNEY, James to Jane Wells   25 October 1848
    m. 25 October by J. C. Carlock, J. P.
    Reference: Marriage Book D Page 6

FINNEY - see also FENNY

FIRESTONE, Frederick K. to Elizabeth Cobb   5 November 1867
    m. 7 November by G. M. Hutsell, J. P.
    Reference: Marriage Book G Page 23

FIRESTONE, Mathias to Mary Fenny   16 March 1839
    m. 17 March by Jas. C. Carlock, J. P.
    Reference: Marriage Book C Page 15

FIRESTONE, Saml. P. to Mrs. Eglentine Smith   27 September 1865
    m. 1 October by Uriah Payne, M. G.
    Reference: Marriage Book F Page 27

FISHER, Jacob to Francis E. Lowry   1 September 1852
    m. 1 September by W. C. Daily, M. G.
    Reference: Marriage Book D Page 55

FISHER, John A. S. to Mary L. Cogghill   9 June 1849
    Reference: Marriage Book D Page 15

FISHER, Richard M. to Ann M. Gettys   20 April 1843
    m. 20 April by L. R. Morrison, V. D. M.
    Reference: Marriage Book C Page 78

FITCH, George to Nancy B. Jimerson   17 December 1856
    m. 18 December by D. W. Beaver, M. G.
    Reference: Marriage Book D Page 121

FITCH, Jacob to Mary McFarling   10 September 1870
    m. 11 September by G. W. Hendrix, J. P.
    Reference: Marriage Book G Page 65

FITCH, John to Mary McNatt   15 February 1858
    m. 17 February by A. D. Briant, J. P.
    Reference: Marriage Book D Page 136

FITCH, John to Catharin MCollum   4 December 1858
    m. 5 December by M. Paine, M. G.
    Reference: Marriage Book D Page 152

FITCH, Joseph to Rody A. Fitch   28 July 1863
    m. 2 August by D. W. Beaver, M. G.
    Reference: Marriage Book E Page 14

FITCHGEARALD, James T. to Sarah E. Neel   8 September 1851
    m. 8 September by Jas. Douglass
    Reference: Marriage Book D Page 42

FITE, Peter to Mary Barnet   11 March 1829
    m. 15 March by J. W. Norwood
    Reference: W. P. A.

FITZGERALD, Jabez to Caroline Kirkpatrick   8 February 1843
    m. 8 February by Abel Pearson, M. G.
    Reference: Marriage Book C Page 73

FITZGERALD, John K. to Mary J. Jameson   21 August 1844
    m. 22 August by Abel Pearson, M. G.
    Reference: Marriage Book C Page 107

FITZGERALD - see also FITCHGEARALD

FLIMING, Thos. to Jane Giboney   2 September 1858
    m. 2 September by J. N. S. Huffaker, M. G.
    Reference: Marriage Book D Page 146

FLINN, E. M. to Miss R. E. Moore   1 November 1851
    Reference: Marriage Book D Page 45

FLINN, Jessee W. to Nancy M. Smith   26 February 1847
    m. 26 February by W. F. Forrest, M. G.
    Reference: Marriage Book C Page 153

FORD, Micajah M. to Elizabeth C. Myers   21 February 1852
    m. 22 February by William R. Walker
    Reference: Marriage Book D Page 48

FORD, Nimrod to Amandia Anderson   21 February 1846
    m. 5 March by A. Slover, M. G.
    Reference: Marriage Book C Page 134

FORD, Thomas to Lizzie Davis   12 November 1870
    m. 17 November by Jas. Smith, M. G.
    Reference: Marriage Book G Page 68

FORD, William to Elvira Myers   22 February 1843
    m. 28 February by A. Kinser, J. P.
    Reference: Marriage Book C Page 75

FORE, Wm. L. to Nancy Thurman   21 August 1860
    m. 22 August by Stephen Sharitts, M. G.
    Reference: Marriage Book E Page 4

FOREMAN, Bark to Rachel Torbalt   29 March 1821
    Reference: W. P. A.

FOREST, James to Nancy Jane Ellis   23 June 1850
    m. 23 June by J. C. Gaston, M. G.
    Reference: Marriage Book D Page 28

FORESTER - see also FORISTER

FORGEY, John F. to Jane Weaks   4 August 1842
    m. 4 August by Elisha Hays, J. P.
    Reference: Marriage Book C Page 60

FORREST, Albartiy to Miss Malinda Sherman   9 April 1870
    m. 10 April by J. B. Kimbrough, M. G.
    Reference: Marriage Book G Page 60

FORTNER, Henry to Lucinda Harris   20 October 1867
    John J. Helm, Security
    m. 15 November by Calvin Denton, M. G.
    Reference: County Archives: Marriage Book G
    Page 20: Marriage Book G Page 22

FORTNER, William to Anna Huckaby   21 February 1840
    m. 26 February by William Dotson, J. P.
    Reference: Marriage Book C Page 27

FOSTER, Andrew to Elizabeth Goss   12 September 1844
    m. 12 September by G. W. Walis, J. P.
    Reference: Marriage Book C Page 108

FOSTER, Andrew to Sarah Buttram   31 August 1850
    m. 4 September by E. E. Gillenwater, M. G.
    Reference: Marriage Book D Page 31

FOSTER, Chrisley to Miss Degenira Buttram   20 October 1857
    m. 20 October by Hiel Buttram, M. G.
    Reference: Marriage Book D Page 130

FOSTER, Chrisley A. to Mary C. Buttram   17 February 1858
    Reference: Marriage Book D Page 137

FOSTER, Geo. W. to Julia Hope   23 May 1870
    m. 23 May by O. M. Liner, J. P.
    Reference: Marriage Book G Page 61

FOSTER, J. A. to Miss M. M. Barton   10 January 1865
    m. 12 January by W. H. Stephenson, J. P.
    Reference: Marriage Book F Page 13

FOSTER, James to Mary E. Gullidge   29 January 1869
    m. 29 January by E. L. Miller, M. G.
    Reference: Marriage Book G Page 43

FOSTER, John R. to Malissa Buttram   4 March 1850
    m. 7 March by E. E. Gillenwater, M. G.
    Reference: Marriage Book D Page 26

FOSTER, Oliver P. to Malinda C. Gibson   21 December 1841
    m. 23 December by T. B. Love, J. P.
    Reference: Marriage Book C Page 50

FOSTER, Wm. to Elizabeth Jane Bryant   1 August 1848
    m. 2 August by David F. Jamison, J. P.
    Reference: Marriage Book D Page 3

FOSTER, Wm. to Miss M. E. Casey   2 July 1870
    Reference: Marriage Book G Page 62

FOSTER, Wm. S. to Mary P. Handley   14 November 1844
    m. 14 November by J. H. Benton, J. P.
    Reference: Marriage Book C Page 112

FOX, Daniel to Carline Stone   9 January 1846
    m. "A few days after issuing of license"
    by F. McGonigal, M. G.
    Reference: Marriage Book C Page 131

FOX, Daniel to Misouri Rentfro   12 November 1870
    m. 13 November by F. M. Pennington, J. P.
    Reference: Marriage Book G Page 68

FRANCE, Wm. to Martha Shook   24 September 1864
    m. 24 September by Wm. C. Owen, J. P.
    Reference: Marriage Book F Page 7

FRANK, James to Mary Cole   18 January 1866
    m. 18 January by A. D. Briant, J. P.
    Reference: Marriage Book F Page 36

FRANKLIN, Esom to Susan Collier   16 November 1838
    Reference: Marriage Book C Page 10

FRANKLIN, John S. to Permelia Buttram   19 September 1838
    m. 19 September by Henry Price, M. G.
    Reference: Marriage Book C Page 8

FRANKLIN, Jonathan F. to Sarah Collier   5 July 1845
    m. 6 July by J. H. Benton, J. P.
    Reference: Marriage Book C Page 122

FRAZIER, James R. to Eliza Givens   27 July 1864
    m. 27 July by Wm. G. Wilson, M. G.
    Reference: Marriage Book F Page 6

FRAZIER, Lorenzo L. to Hannah Briant   2 July 1839
    m. 9 July by A. Barb, J. P.
    Reference: Marriage Book C Page 20

FRAZIER, Philip to Nancy Wear   24 December 1844
    m. 24 December by W. F. Forrest, M. G.
    Reference: Marriage Book C Page 115

FREEMAN, William H. to Mildred A. Thornton   28 December 1842
    m. 29 December by Wilson Chapman, M. G.
    Reference: Marriage Book C Page 70

FROST, John O. to Emeline C. Trim   18 December 1839
    m. 19 December by J. Courtney, M. G.
    Reference: Marriage Book C Page 24

FRY, David G. to Zeporah Harris   13 September 1844
    m. 13 September by J. W. Barnett, J. P.
    Reference: Marriage Book C Page 108

FRY, G. W. to Elizabeth Ann Newkirk   1 May 1846
    m. 3 May by Rev. Edwin A. Atlee
    Reference: Marriage Book C Page 138

FRY, Harvy to Miss Alpha Ruethurford   29 May 1847
    m. 3 June by G. W. Wallis, J. P.
    Reference: Marriage Book C Page 156

FRY, Harvey to Mary J. Adare   13 November 1856
    m. 13 October /sic7 by C. W. Renfro, M. G.
    Reference: Marriage Book D Page 118

FRY, John to Rebecca E. Adare   20 October 1855
    m. 21 October 1856 /sic7 by H. M. Sloop, M. G.
    Reference: Marriage Book D Page 104

71

FRY, John W. to Jane Garrison   22 May 1855
    m. 23 May by Isah Garrison, J. P.
    Reference: Marriage Book D Page 99

FRY, Joseph M. to Mary Cicill   12 December 1849
    m. 13 December by Leander Wilson, M. G.
    Reference: Marriage Book D Page 23

FRY, Thomas to Sallie Aytes   12 July 1870
    Reference: Marriage Book G Page 62

FUNCHAUSER (FUNKHAUSER), John to Hattie (Hattia)   15 July 1867
    A. McGughey (McGaughey)
    W. M. Cate, Security
    m. 15 July by J. Albert Hyden, M. G.
    Reference: County Archives: Marriage Book G
    Page 18

FUQUA - see alos FAUGEWAN

FURGERSON, J. R. to Marthia Lee   23 December 1868
    m. 24 December by G. M. Bloom, J. P.
    Reference: Marriage Book G Page 41

FYFFE, I. W. to Jennie Townsend   15 December 1870
    m. 15 December by J. D. Lyle, J. P.
    Reference: Marriage Book G Page 71

FYFFE, Isaac W. to Elizabeth Fleming   8 March 1859
    m. 7 April by Joseph A. Dillan, J. P.
    Reference: Marriage Book D Page 158

GADD, A. J. to Elizabeth Ann Wiatt   21 April 1868
    m. 20 /sic7 April by J. S. Russell, M. G.
    Reference: Marriage Book G Page 31

GALAHON, Isaack F. to Mandee Taly   23 September 1869
    m. 23 September by L. W. Crouch, M. G.
    Reference: Marriage Book G Page 51

GALBRAITH, Jas. H. to Jane McElwee   19 December 1865
    m. 19 December by Saml. B. West, M. G.
    Reference: Marriage Book F Page 32

GALLAHAR, Tipton to Matildy Andrews   28 November 1866
    m. 27 December by Hial Buttram. M. G.
    Reference: Marriage Book G Page 5

GALLAHER, Gainey M. to Sarah Lawson   28 August 1849
    m. 28 August by Urial Johnston, J. P.
    Reference: Marriage Book D Page 17

GALLAHER, James M. to Elmira Sparks   2 February 1841
    m. 2 February by Uriel Johnson, Esq.
    Reference: Marriage Book C Page 37

GALLAHER, John to Jane Richards   14 April 1841
    m. by Uriel Johnson, J. P.
    Reference: Marriage Book C Page 40

GALLAHER, Wm. to Sarah Hackler   29 December 1864
    m. 29 December by D. W. Beaver, M. G.
    Reference: Marriage Book F Page 13

GALLAHER - see also GALAHON, GOLLAHON, GOLLARAH

GALLAHON, Crisley P. to Katherine Brooksire   17 November 1847
    Reference: Marriage Book C Page 162

72

GALLANT, Francis to Miss W. R. Ferryman   17 March 1853
    m. 17 March by D. W. Beaver, M. G.
    Reference: Marriage Book D Page 64

GALLANT, John to Sarah Wilson   8 July 1852
    Thoams Gallant, Security
    m. 8 July by David W. Beaver, M. G.
    Reference: Marriage Book D Page 54:
    County Archives

GALLOWAY, Thoams to Miss M. C. Rothwell   7 February 1848
    Reference: Marriage Book C Page 167

GALYON - see GILLIAN

GAMBLE, Patton L. to Nancy Ann Hounshell   18 February 1851
    m. 18 February by Wm. H. Ballew, J. P.
    Reference: Marriage Book D Page 38

GAN, Thos. H. to Rebeckah Crosslin   14 August 1852
    m. 14 August by Wm. H. Ballew, J. P.
    Reference: Marriage Book D Page 54

GARDEN, Jacob to Mary Ann Jones   7 July 1868
    Reference: Marriage Book G Page 33

GARLAND, John R. to Mrs. Sarah A. Chinn   23 December 1840
    m. 23 December by L. R. Morrison, V. D. M.
    Reference: Marriage Book C Page 35

GARNER, J. C. C. to Texanna L. Ballew   29 January 1868
    m. 30 January by C. Long, M. G.
    Reference: Marriage Book G Page 27

GARRETT, R. L. to Mrs. Eliza Bunch   7 April 1870
    Reference: Marriage Book G Page 59;
    McMinn Chancery Case #302

GARRISON, Isaiah to Mahala Arnwine   22 February 1849
    m. 22 February by G. W. Wallace, J. P.
    Reference: Marriage Book D Page 12

GARRISON, Isaiah to Nancy Arnwine   16 August 1852
    m. 17 August by J. R. Fryar, M. G.
    Reference: Marriage Book D Page 55

GARTEN - see GARDEN

GASTON - see also GHASTON

GAUT, George W. to Nancy Dorsey   11 July 1838
    m. 12 July by Robert Frazier, M. G.
    Reference: Marriage Book C Page 4

GAUT, J. Hamilton to Sarah Elizabeth Isbell   4 December 1849
    Milton P. Jarnagin, Security
    Reference: County Archives: Marriage Book
    D Page 22

GAUT, John C. to Sarah A. McReynolds   24 September 1839
    m. 26 September by L. R. Morrison, V. D. M.
    Reference: Marriage Book C Page 23

GEE, John J. to Mary Grubb   17 April 1851
    m. 17 April by Robert Gregory, M. G.
    Reference: Marriage Book D Page 40

GEE, Jonathan to Margaret Grubb   20 July 1853
    John M. Vaughan, Security
    m. 28 July by W. C. Daily, M. G.
    Reference: County Archives: Marriage
    Book D Page 67

GEE, Joseph to Margaret McKinsey   3 September 1870
    m. 4 September by M. Zeigler, J. P.
    Reference: Marriage Book G Page 64

GEE, Milton to Sarah Cooksten   7 September 1869
    m. 8 September by R. T. Hamond, M. G.
    Reference: Marriage Book G Page 50

GEFFEY, Cornelius to Mary J. Combs   7 October 1856
    m. 8 October by R. A. Giddens, M. G.
    Reference: Marriage Book D Page 116

GENOE - see GINOW

GENTERY, Z. T. to Mahaly Jack   29 November 1866
    m. 30 November by Elihu Kelley, J. P.
    Reference: Marriage Book G Page 5

GENTRY, Gilbert to Mrs. Mary Ashley   7 June 1866
    Reference: Marriage Book F Page 42

GENTRY, James P. to Mandy Rew   4 May 1867
    Wm. B. Armstrong, Security
    m. 5 May by Charles Cate, J. P.
    Reference: County Archives: Marriage
    Book G Page 15

GENTRY, John M. - see MC GINTY, John

GENTRY, L. M. to Miss Dicey Wilson   29 December 1869
    m. 5 January 1870 by W. J. Walsh, J. P.
    Reference: Marriage Book G Page 56

GENTRY, Samuel to Charlotte Dougherty   18 August 1842
    m. 22 August by Green L. Reynolds, J. P.
    Reference: Marriage Book C Page 60

GENTRY, William J. to Mary M. Saxton   20 February 1847
    Reference: Marriage Book C Page 153

GEORGE, John C. to Mary Womack   28 August 1850
    Reference: Marriage Book D Page 31

GEORGE, Powell H. to Miss Call Howard   5 June 1867
    J. C. Barbe, Security
    m. 5 June by J. C. Barbe
    Reference: County Archives: Marriage
    Book G Page 16

GERALD, Elijah F. to Nancy McCally   14 December 1840
    m. by A. F. Gerreld, M. G.
    Reference: Marriage Book C Page 35

GERALD - see also JUREL

GERALDS, Wm. J. to Martha E. McCann   3 December 1867
    Hiram Geralds, Security
    m. 8 December by Elihu Kelley, J. P.
    Reference: County Archives: Marriage
    Book G Page 24

74

GETTYS, James R. to Mary Rider   27 September 1865
 m. 28 September by Wallace W. Thorp, M. G.
 Reference: Marriage Book F Page 27

GHASTON, Wesley to Laura Jane Peck   9 May 1848
 m. 11 May by A. F. Shanon, M. G.
 Reference: W. P. A. /Page in Book D missing7

GHORMLY (GHORMAN), J. P. to Miss S. M. Gamble 17 August 1868
 J. C. Barnett, Security
 m. 16 September by Joseph Peeler, M. G.
 Reference: County Archives: Marriage Book
 G Page 34

GIBBONY, Wm. to Miss M. E. Hutsell   25 December 1867
 Sam Hutsell, Security
 m. 26 December by E. L. Miller, M. G.
 Reference: County Archives: Marriage Book
 G Page 25

GIBBS, A. S. to Sophrona Rudd   30 July 1844
 m. 30 July by John Jenkins, J. P.
 Reference: Marriage Book C Page 105

GIBBS, C. B. to Miss S. A. Walker   3 October 1844
 m. 3 October by W. H. Ballew, J. P.
 Reference: Marriage Book C Page 109

GIBBS, Flemming G. to Miz /Mrs.7 Jane Eaton 18 November 1846
 Reference: Marriage Book C Page 147

GIBBS, James to Caroline Patterson   4 August 1855
 m. 6 August 1856 /sic7 by H. M. Sloop, M. G.
 Reference: Marriage Book D Page 101

GIBBS, James J. to Sarah L. Shell   10 October 1866
 m. 11 October by A. D. Bryent, J. P.
 Reference: Marriage Book G Page 2

GIBBS, John M. to Angelina Whetsell, widow of
 Michael Whetsell
 m. 3 January 1833
 Reference: McMinn Chancery Case #244 and
 Number 53

GIBBS, William E. to Melissa McCance   23 November 1852
 m. 25 November by Benj. E. Cass, J. P.
 Reference: Marriage Book D Page 59

GIBBS, William H. to Martha Rudd   13 June 1843
 m. 14 June by Hiram Ingram, M. G.
 Reference: Marriage Book C Page 80

GIBONEY - see also GIBBONY

GIBSON, E. P. to Miss Lue Mayfield   22 November 1866
 m. 22 November 1867 /sic7 by Timothy Sulins, M.G.
 Reference: Marriage Book G Page 5

GIBSON, Elisha S. to Mary Ann Etter   30 November 1853
 M. R. Gibson, Security
 m. 1 December by Moses A. Cass, M. G.
 Reference: County Archives: Marriage Book
 D Page 75

GIBSON, Jas. G. to Mary T. Hurst   9 December 1857
 m. 10 December by Robert Sewell, M. G.
 Reference: Marriage Book D Page 132

GIBSON, John C. to Sarah J. Anderson   21 December 1853
    m. 22 December by Robert Gregory, M. G.
    Reference: Marriage Book D Page 76

GIBSON, John C. to Willametta M. Drake   11 October 1870
    E. P. Gibson, Security
    m. 11 October by S. F. Drake, M. G.
    Reference: County Archives: Marriage
    Book G Page 67

GIBSON, Joseph W. to Sarah Matlock   14 September 1844
    m. 17 September by M. D. Anderson, J. P.
    Reference: Marriage Book C Page 108

GIBSON, Lewis E. to Susan M. Jones   7 November 1865
    m. 12 November by P. W. Long, J. P.
    Reference: Marriage Book F Page 29

GIBSON, M. T. to Miss Salenia C. Griffin   12 January 1865
    Reference: Marriage Book F Page 14

GIBSON, Plesant B. to Nancy Kinchelo   4 December 1848
    m. 7 December by J. M. Spears, J. P.
    Reference: Marriage Book D Page 8

GIBSON, Saml. P. to Nancy Studdard   29 June 1855
    m. 30 June by J. G. Swisher, M. G.
    Reference: Marriage Book D Page 100

GIBSON, T. F. to Miss E. F. Mayfield   17 August 1854
    Reference: Marriage Book D Page 86

GIBSON, T. J. to Elizabeth Braden   19 April 1855
    m. 19 April by Robert Cochran, J. P.
    Reference: Marriage Book D Page 97

GIBSON, William C. to Jane Thompson   12 Mar. or Apr.
    Huson (Hutson) Johnson, Security   1834
    Note: Date on face of Bond is April 12,
    1834 and on back of Bond is "executed
    March 12, 1834"
    Reference: County Archives

GIBSON, William T. to Nancy Dertherow   3 January 1848
    m. 4 January by J. Jenkins, J. P.
    Reference: Marriage Book C Page 165

GIBSON - see also GIPSON

GIFFORD, H. N. to Eugenie E. Rowley   1 January 1866
    m. 1 January by J. F. Spence, M. G.
    Reference: Marraige Book F Page 34

GILBERT, Bernhart to Louisa M. Kelley   23 February 1860
    m. 23 February by E. Rowley, M. G.
    Reference: Marriage Book E Page 2

GILBERT, Edmond to Nancy Swafford   26 April 1856
    m. 27 April by Wm. MCamy, J. P.
    Reference: Marriage Book D Page 109

GILBERT, G. G. to Maggie S. Neal   1 June 1870
    m. 1 June by David M. Wilson, M. G.
    Reference: Marriage Book G Page 61

GILBERT, Marcus to Nancy Maxwell   8 August 1848
    m. 9 August by A. Swafford, J. P.
    Reference: Marriage Book D Page 4

GILBERT, Solomon to Polly Cannon   9 March 1853
    m. by J. Jenkins, J. P.
    Reference: Marriage Book D Page 64

GILBREATH, Joseph to Jemimah Thompson   28 November 1849
    m. 28 November by H. C. Cooke, M. G.
    Reference: Marriage Book D Page 21

GILBREATH, Samuel to Nancy Cobbs   10 September 1851
    m. 19 March 1852 by T. L. Hoyl
    Reference: Marriage Book D Page 43

GILBREATH - see also GALBRAITH

GILES, Houston to Susan A. Carter   18 November 1848
    m. 19 November by James Sewell, Minister
    Reference: Marriage Book D Page 7

GILEZ, Calvin to Elender Carter   19 June 1845
    m. 20 June by James Sewell, Minister
    Reference: Marriage Book C Page 121

GILLESPIE, David E. to Sarah E. Cleage   26 February 1852
    Reference: Marriage Book D Page 48

GILLEY, James to Mary Ann Sivils   10 August 1843
    m. 10 August by M. D. Anderson, J. P.
    Reference: Marriage Book C Page 83

GILLEY, Samuel to Catharine Brock   13 March 1850
    m. 13 March by John Spears, J. P.
    Reference: Marriage Book D Page 26

GILLIAN, Lorenzo Dow to Cealey Ann Dyer   29 February 1840
    Reference: Marriage Book C Page 27

GILLINGWATERS, Elijah to Polly Weavers   10 December 1829
    J____ McMillin, Security
    m. 10 December by Henry Bradford
    Reference: W. P. A.

GILLY, John to Martha Parks   11 December 1854
    m. 11 December by James Baker, J. P.
    Reference: Marriage Book D Page 90

GINOW, James to Emeline Robeson   31 July 1844
    m. 4 August by James A_____, M. G.
    Reference: Marriage Book C Page 105

GINOW, John to Carneth Lawson   3 January 1855
    m. 4 January by Rev. D. Carpenter
    Reference: Marriage Book D Page 93

GIPSON, B. A. to Rebecca Wallin   5 August 1856
    Simion M. Foster, Security
    m. 7 August by H. C. Cook, M. G.
    Reference: County Archives: Marriage Book
    D Page 112

GIPSON, Samuel K. P. to Miss A. C. Edington   12 June 1856
    m. 13 June by J. M. Miller, M. G.
    Reference: Marriage Book D Page 110

GIVINS, Jesse to Mary Firestone   21 March 1848
    Note: Page missing in Book C
    Reference: W. P. A.

GLASE, Henry to Martha Arnwine   20 January 1840
    m. 21 January by Russell Lane
    Reference: Marriage Book C Page 26

GLASE, T. M. to Margret Melton   4 February 1867
    m. 5 February by E. Z. Williams, J. P.
    Reference: Marriage Book G Page 10

GLASS, A. W. to Mandy Melton   18 December 1866
    J. S. Barker, Security
    m. 18 December by Z. Williams, J. P.
    Reference: County Archives: Marriage
    Book G Page 6

GLASS, John to Miss E. Stratton   19 May 1845
    m. 19 May by Wm. McKamy, J. P.
    Reference: Marriage Book C Page 121

GLAZE, B. G. to Lucy J. Reynolds   19 August 1856
    Reference: Marriage Book D Page 112

GLAZE, Jefferson to Mariah Dugan   14 February 1852
    m. 17 February by Wm. C. Lee, M. G.
    Reference: County Archives: Marriage
    Book D Page 48

GLAZE, Jefferson to Martha Jackson   18 November 1865
    m. 23 November by T. R. Bradshaw, M. G.
    Reference: Marriage Book F Page 30

GLAZE, William to Permelia Rudd   4 July 1839
    m. 4 July by D. Cantrell, J. P.
    Reference: Marriage Book C Page 20

GLENN, William to Sally Wilson   13 December 1825
    m. 13 December by Thoams W. Norwood
    Reference: County Archives

GODARD, M. B. to Miss C. V. Hutsell   5 August 1858
    Reference: Marriage Book D Page 144

GOFORTH, Drury to Evaline Pugh   27 December 1854
    m. 28 December by M. R. Ware, J. P.
    Reference: Marriage Book D Page 92

GOFORTH, Henry to Nancy Smart   26 February 1840
    m. 27 February by L. L. Ball, J. P.
    Reference: Marriage Book C Page 27

GOFORTH, John F. to Catharine Childers   17 February 1866
    John B. Smart, Security
    m. 26 February by S. M. Thomas, J. P.
    Reference: County Archives: Marriage
    Book F Page 38

GOFORTH, Miles to Mahala Vernom   29 September 1852
    m. by Nathaniel Barnett, M. G.
    Reference: Marriage Book D Page 57

GOINS, Hugh H. to Narcissa C. Blackwell   23 September 1865
    Reference: Marriage Book F Page 26

GOLD, Martin to Rebecca Fox   23 November 1841
    m. 25 November by M. C. Hawk, M. G. M. E. C.
    Reference: Marriage Book C Page 49

GOLDEN, Abraham to Patsey Branham   1 August 1827
    John Spencer, Security
    Reference: County Archives

                                78

GOLDEN, Caswell to Miss Orinda Harmon   21 November 1840
   m. 22 November 1841 /sic/ by David F. Jamison,
   J. P.
   Reference: Marriage Book C Page 34

GOLLAHON, George W. to Mary Ann Smith   19 May 1841
   m. 20 May by J. Thomas, J. P.
   Reference: Marriage Book C Page 42

GOOD, Richard T. to Martha Dorsey   4 January 1839
   m. 6 January by A. Slover, M. G.
   Reference: Marriage Book C Page 12

GOODNER, John to Nancy Long   16 July 1845
   m. 16 July by Green L. Reynolds, J. P.
   Reference: Marriage Book C Page 122

GOODWIN, John S. to Jane Hannah   25 January 1842
   m. 25 January by John W. Barnett, J. P.
   Reference: Marriage Book C Page 52

GOOLSBY, John to Elizabeth Stansberry   29 September 1857
   m. 30 September by Robert Reynolds, J. P.
   Reference: Marriage Book D Page 130

GORDON, John to Mrs. Jane Shamblin   15 July 1854
   Johnathan Hanks, Security
   m. 16 July by Joel Coupepper, J. P.
   Reference: County Archives: Marriage
   Book D Page 85

GORDON, William to Talitha Harden   17 January 1849
   m. 18 January by John Speares, J. P.
   Reference: Marriage Book D Page 10

GORDON - see also GARDEN

GORE, John T. E. to Rachel A. C. Heck   25 February 1854
   m. 7 March by J. Jack, M. G.
   Reference: Marriage Book D Page 80

GORMAN, David H. to Ruth Long   13 April 1840
   m. 14 April by A. F. Gerald, M. G.
   Reference: Marriage Book C Page 28

GRAHAM, W. J. to Eliza Wilson   23 April 1864
   J. A. Kinser, Security
   m. 5 May by Uriah Payne, M. G.
   Reference: County Archives: Marriage
   Book F Page 2

GRANTHAM, John to Cyntha A. Huffer   25 August /1843/
   Reference: Marriage Book C Page 84

GRAVES, A. J. to Miss Polina Carter   7 January 1857
   m. 8 January by I. S. Garrison, J. P.
   Reference: Marriage Book D Page 122

GRAVES, Andrew F. to Miss Francis T. Carter   8 July 1866
   m. 12 July by A. D. Briant, J. P.
   Reference: County Archives: Marriage Book
   F Page 43

GRAVES, Christifer to Elizabeth Shelton   25 November 1850
   Reference: Marriage Book G Page 34
   Note: See same on Marriage Book G (below)

GRAVES, Christopher to Elizabeth Shelton   5 August 1853
    Isaac Smart, Security
    m. 15 August by William Walker, J. P.
    Reference: County Archives: Marriage
    Book G Page 68

GRAVES, J. H. to Martha M. Carter   11 March 1858
    m. 14 March by A. D. Briant, J. P.
    Reference: Marriage Book D Page 137

GRAVES, William to Margaret A. Hood   11 December 1839
    m. 11 December by L. R. Morrison, V. D. M.
    Reference: Marriage Book C Page 19, Page
    24 and Page 25

GRAW, John to Peggy Moreland   21 October 1821
    Saml. Murphey, Security
    Reference: County Archives

GRAY, W. N. to Miss M. A. Coffee   20 May 1870
    Reference: Marriage Book G Page 61

GREEN, A. P. to Mary Rudd   16 May 1839
    m. 16 May by M. C. Hawk, M. G.
    Reference: Marriage Book C Page 17

GREEN, Alexander to Penelope Cobbs, daughter   30 October 1839
    of A. Cobb, Esq.
    m. 31 October by Floyd McGonegal, M. G.
    Reference: Marriage Book C Page 24:
    "Hiwassee Patriot" 7 November 1839,
    Volume I, #35

GREEN, David to Abigale Sivley   13 March 1847
    Reference: Marriage Book C Page 154

GREEN, Frederick to Jane Romines   9 February 1842
    m. 10 February by M. W. Cunninghan, J. P.
    Reference: Marriage Book C Page 56

GREEN, George M. to Mary Jane West   6 May 1857
    m. 7 May by David W. Beavers, M. G.
    Reference: Marriage Book D Page 126

GREEN, Henry to Josephine Payne   18 July 1868
    m. 19 July by John Jackson, J. P.
    Reference: Marriage Book G Page 29

GREEN, Jacob to Susannah Crisp   26 October 1842
    m. 26 October by J. H. Benton, J. P.
    Reference: Marriage Book C Page 66

GREEN, James to Margaret MCollum   6 September 1857
    m. 6 September by D. W. Beaver, M. G.
    Reference: Marriage Book D Page 130

GREEN, James D. to Sarah Lewis   24 January 1855
    m. 24 January by H. J. Brock, J. P.
    Reference: Marriage Book D Page 94

GREEN, John to Mahala Bledsoe   13 March 1843
    m. 13 March by Tapley Gregory, J. P.
    Reference: Marriage Book C Page 76

GREEN, John A. to Margaret Henry   6 September 1850
    m. 6 September by Moses Sweeny, J. P.
    Reference: Marriage Book D Page 32

GREEN, Philmer W. to Susan R. Cox   24 May 1852
    m. 25 May by Wm. W. Haymes, M. G.
    Reference: Marriage Book D Page 52

GREEN, R. S. to Miss N. E. Trew   1 February 1870
    Reference: Marriage Book G Page 58

GREEN, Rufus to Nancy Cofer   15 April 1840
    m. 15 April by Elijah Hurst, J. P.
    Reference: Marriage Book C Page 28

GREEN, Rufus to Amy Bledsoe   8 February 1843
    m. 8 February by R. A. McAdoo, J. P.
    Reference: Marriage Book C Page 73

GREEN, William to Nancy Curtis   27 February 1868
    J. S. Russell, Security
    m. 28 February by J. S. Russell, M. G.
    Reference: County Archives: Marriage
    Book G Page 28

GREEN, Wm. B. to Haney Owins   21 December 1829
    Russell H. Smith, Security
    Reference: W. P. A.

GREEN, William D. to Louisa A. Fuqua   24 October 1864
    m. 24 October by W. C. Owen, J. P.
    Reference: Marriage Book F Page 9

GREEN, William J. to Lidia Millsaps   31 January 1851
    Reference: Marriage Book D Page 38

GREGG, John to Louisa Mulkey   6 February 1839
    Silvester Blackwell, Security
    m. 10 February by Obadiah Bolding, M. G.
    Reference: County Archives: Marriage
    Book C Page 15

GREGG, Robert W. to Sarah Wilson   24 May 1849
    m. 24 May by R. M. Hickey, M. G.
    Reference: Marriage Book D Page 15

GREGG, Samuel to Jane Dolan   17 February 1857
    m. 18 February by T. L. Hoyl, M. G.
    Reference: Marriage Book D Page 124

GREGG - see also GRIGG

GREGGORY, Stephen E. to Margraet A. Farmer   21 April 1865
    m. 23 April by J. C. Barb, M. G.
    Reference: Marriage Book F Page 17

GREGORY, Benjamin to Mary Wilson   7 January 1858
    m. 7 January by H. M. Roberts, J. P.
    Reference: Marriage Book D Page 134

GREGORY, Benjamin to Eliza Lewis   6 January 1869
    m. 8 January by T. T. Salyer, M. G.
    Reference: Marriage Book G Page 42

GREGORY, James to Elizabeth Bonner   16 March 1846
    m. 19 March by McAtchley, Minister
    Reference: Marriage Book C Page 135

GREGORY, James F. H. to Adareus Fisher   16 November 1858
    m. 16 November by Dan Carpenter, Minister
    M. E. Church South
    Reference: Marriage Book D Page 151

GREGORY, Jathan to Mira Bedford   5 February 1838
    Reference: Marriage Book C Page 2

GREGORY, John to Parilee Atkinson   18 December 1841
    m. 21 December by L. L. Ball, J. P.
    Reference: Marriage Book C Page 50

GREGORY, Tapley to Eleanor Snodgrass   20 December 1843
    m. 21 December by A. Slover, M. G.
    Reference: Marriage Book C Page 94

GREGORY, William E. to Cinthia Ann Lillard   20 February 1851
    m. 23 February by Rev. D. Carpenter, M. G.
    Reference: Marriage Book D Page 39

GREGORY, James L. to Nancy Graves   25 February 1867
    A. P. McClatchy, Security
    Reference: County Archives: Marriage
    Book G Page 12
    Note: This Bond is in County Archives but
    the entry on Record Book G has been marked
    out, as though marriage did not take place.

GREGRY, James L. to Fansina (Fransina) Peak   20 September 1867
    James Gregry, Security
    m. 3 October by L. W. Crouch, M. G.
  · Reference: County Archives: Marriage
    Book G Page 21

GRESHAM, Henry to Emaline Larrimore   4 February 1839
    m. 7 February by Edward Newton, M. G.
    Reference: Marriage Book C Page 15

GRESHAM, James H. to Rebecky Wyett   9 January 1867
    m. 10 January by J. S. Russell, M. G.
    Reference: Marriage Book G Page 8

GRIFFEY, John to Sarah A. Walker   2 November 1863
    Reference: Marriage Book E Page 14

GRIFFIN, John P. to Francis J. Howard   22 January 1857
    m. 22 January by J. W. Gibson, J. P.
    Reference: Marriage Book D Page 123

GRIFFIN, Robert H. to Margaret Chancy   2 August 1856
    m. 3 August by D. W. Beaver, M. G.
    Reference: Marriage Book D Page 112

GRIFFIN, William to Anna L. Davis   20 April 1829
    R. P. Bowman, Security
    Reference: County Archives

GRIFFIT, Ambrose to Jane G. Brookman   1 April 1868
    m. 1 April by S. Sharits, J. P.
    Reference: Marriage Book G Page 30

GRIFFITH, J. T. to Margret Foster   20 November 1869
    m. 26 November by John N. Stamper, M. G.
    Reference: Marriage Book G Page 54

GRIFFITH, John W. to Mariah Might   3 October 1845
    Reference: Marriage Book C Page 127

GRIFFITT, William to Elizabeth Cook   5 November 1845
    m. 6 November by Samuel Wilson, J. P.
    Reference: Marriage Book C Page 129

GRIFFITTS, Delaney to Margaret Griffitts   25 October 1851
    m. 26 October by Saml. Wilson, J. P.
    Reference: Marriage Book D Page 45

GRIFFITTS, Emanuel to Sarah McCluen   8 August 1859
    m. 14 August by Morgan Miller, J. P.
    Reference: Marriage Book E Page 2

GRIFFITTS, Joseph to Sarah Cate   19 July 1866
    m. 22 July by E. B. Cass, J. P.
    Reference: Marriage Book F Page 44

GRIGG, Jesse R. to Jane Prophet   15 August 1850
    m. 15 August by C. R. Hoyl, M. G.
    Reference: Marriage Book D Page 30

GRIGG, M. H. to Eliza A. Triplett   16 August 1870
    m. 18 August by John H. Bruner, M. G.
    Reference: Marriage Book G Page 63

GRIGG, Nelson to Elizabeth Ann Ware   2 August 1847
    Reference: Marriage Book C Page 158

GRIGSBY, J. A. to Mary Jane Jordan   18 August 1870
    m. 18 August by Dan Carpenter, M. G.
    Reference: Marriage Book G Page 64

GRIGSBY, James to Lidy Hedrick   30 June 1824
    Merody Hix, Security
    Reference: County Archives

GRIGSBY, Thomas to Rebecca Davis   11 July 1860
    m. 13 July by J. F. Pugh, J. P.
    Reference: Marriage Book E Page 18

GRILLS, Starke Duprye to Penelope Armstrong   6 April 1854
    J. L. Vaughan, Security
    m. 6 April by M. L. Phillips, J. P.
    Reference: County Archives: Marriage
    Book D Page 82

GRILLS, Thoams J. to Harriet W. Smith   29 May 1825
    of McMinn County
    m. 25 May by Rev. George Atkin
    Reference: Knoxville Enquirer, 2 June 1825

GRISHAM, Elijah to Luvann Browder   20 September 1842
    m. 20 September by J. H. Benton, J. P.
    Reference: Marriage Book C Page 62

GRISHAM, James to Milly Rucker   3 November 1829
    Jesse Grisham, Security
    Reference: County Archives

GRISHAM, James to Polly Newton   2 August 1847
    m. 3 August by Wm. Newton, M. G.
    Reference: Marriage Book C Page 158

GRISHAM, James W. to Mary S. Woods   1 November 1864
    m. 16 November by Wm. C. Owen, J. P.
    Reference: Marriage Book F Page 9

GRISHA, Jesse, Senr. to Mary Jane Erwin   20 September 1849
    Wm. Burns, Security
    m. by Wm. Burns, J. P.
    Reference: County Archives: Marriage Book
    D Page 18

GRISHAM, John to Nancy Bebibin   15 October 1839
    m. 15 October by Jonathan Thomas, J. P.
    Reference: Marriage Book C Page 23

GRISHAM, John to Gemima Kinchlow   10 July 1845
    m. 10 July by Edward Newton, M. G.
    Reference: Marriage Book C Page 122

GRISHAM, John to Elizabeth Wolff   30 August 1847
    m. 30 August by M. R. Gibson, J. P.
    Reference: Marriage Book C Page 159

GRISHAM, John to Nancy McCrary   25 May 1848
    m. 25 May by Wm. H. Ballew, J. P.
    Reference: Marriage Book D Page 2

GRISHAM, Looney to Eliza Peters   7 July 1843
    m. 7 July by W. H. Ballew, J. P.
    Reference: Marriage Book C Page 80

GRISHAM, M. V. to Mary C. Eaton   12 January 1860
    m. 12 January by J. A. Zeigler, J. P.
    Reference: Marriage Book E Page 4

GRISHAM, Marion to Miss Rody Isham   7 October 1839
    m. 7 October by Jonathan Thomas, J. P.
    Reference: Marriage Book C Page 24

GRISHAM - see also GRESHAM

GROGAN, David to Miss N. J. Roddan   14 August 1855
    m. 19 August by H. J. Brock, J. P.
    Reference: Marriage Book D Page 101

GROGAN, David C. to Telitha E. Brumit (Bumit)   1 December 1870
    John Wilkins, Security
    m. 4 December by C. R. Hoyl, M. G.
    Reference: County Archives: Marriage
    Book G Page 70

GRUBB, Alfred to Salena Dodson   13 January 1856
    m. 13 January by R. A. Geddens, M. G.
    Reference: Marriage Book D Page 107

GRUBB, Henry S. to /Bride's name is missing7   29 September 1866
    m. 3 October by J. M. Miller, M. G.
    Reference: Marriage Book G Page 1

GRUBB, John to Nancy A. Robinson   19 October 1847
    m. 19 October by Samuel Wilson, J. P.
    Reference: Marriage Book C Page 161

GRUBB, P. J. to Miss M. F. Pearce   30 April 1867
    C. C. Crow, Security
    Reference: County Archives; Marriage
    Book G Page 14

GRUBB, W. W. to Ellen Crawford   22 November 1866
    m. 22 November by John Bruner, M. G.
    Reference: Marriage Book G Page 5

GUFFEY, Elig /Elijah7 to Miss May Higdon   21 November 1866
    Reference: Marriage Book G Page 5

GUFFEY, George to Rebeckah Shell   19 December 1866
    m. 20 December by A. Barb, J. P.
    Reference: Marriage Book G Page 7

GUFFEY, John to Purmilia Lowry   6 September 1845
    Reference: Marriage Book C Page 126

GUFFEY, Thos. F. to Narcissa Porter   21 September 1858
    m. 22 September by H. M. Roberts, J. P.
    Reference: Marriage Book D Page 147

GUFFEY - see also GEFFEY

GUFFY, James A. to Nancy Creasman   27 April 1867
    m. 27 April by Stephen Hill, J. P.
    Reference: Marriage Book G Page 14

GUFFY, Joseph A. to May C. Robinett   5 January 1860
    m. 5 January by H. M. Roberts, J. P.
    Reference: Marriage Book E Page 6

GUINN, L. B. to Mary Snider   2 September 1869
    m. 2 September by J. Janeway, M. G.
    Reference: Marriage Book G Page 49

GUINN - see also GWINN

GURRIS, John to Elizabeth Butler   3 January 1840
    m. 3 January by Moses A. Cass, J. P.
    Reference: Marriage Book C Page 19

GUTHEY, C. H. to Elizabeth Crisman   19 January 1846
    Reference: Marriage Book C Page 132

GUTHREY, C. W. to Miss M. J. Love   22 December 1866
    m. 23 December by E. L. Miller, M. G.
    Reference: Marriage Book G Page 7

GWINN, Matthew to Margaret Maddux   30 December 1844
    m. 30 December by D. A. Cobbs, M. G.
    Reference: Marriage Book C Page 116

GWINN - see also GUINN

HACKER, F. E. to Virginia Fisher   6 July 1852
    m. 7 July by W. C. Daily, M. G.
    Reference: County Archives: **Marriage**
    Book D Page 53

HACKLER, George to Lousinda Jane Tompson   5 May 1866
    m. 4 /sic/ May by Daniel McPhail, J. P.
    Reference: Marriage Book F Page 41

HACKLER, William to Elizabeth Davis   18 June 1866
    m. 24 June by D. W. Beaver, M. G.
    Reference: Marriage Book F Page 43

HAFELY, William to Jane Seay   17 August 1843
    m. 17 August by J. H. Benton, J. P.
    Reference: Marriage Book C Page 84

HAFLEY - see HEFLY

HAFLY, Frankford W. to Elizabeth Lays   30 November 1843
    m. 30 November by R. A. McAdoo, J. P.
    Reference: Marriage Book C Page 91

HAGGARD, James to Mrs. Isaphena M. McCrosky   6 October 1850
    m. 6 October by Saml. Snoddy, J. P.
    Reference: County Archives: **Marriage Book**
    D Page 33: McMinn Chancery Case #80

HAINES, Thompson to Martha Irvin   9 September 1864
    m. 10 September by James Parkison, J. P.
    Reference: County Archives: Marriage
    Book F Page 7

HAINS, Samuel B. to Martha J. Yerwood   7 July 1851
    Reference: Marriage Book D Page 41

HAIR, Caleb G. to Elja Elizobeth Foster   8 January 1848
    Reference: Marriage Book C Page 165

HAITTY, /HALEY?/ Samuel H. to Julia A. Frisby   24 August 1856
    m. 24 August by Wm. H. Ballew, J. P.
    Reference: Marriage Book D Page 113

HALE, Churchwell to Catharine Roberts   9 December 1841
    m. 9 December by Jonathan Thomas, J. P.
    Reference: Marriage Book C Page 50

HALE, J. H. to Margaret L. Campbell   23 November 1858
    m. 23 December by Geo. A. Caldwell, M. G.
    Reference: Marriage Book D Page 151

HALE, John G. to Nancy Owens   13 January 1853
    Reference: Marriage Book D Page 62

HALE, Jonathan to Polly Shelton   27 July 1825
    m. __th August by Henry Price, J. P.
    Reference: County Archives

HALE, Mark to Jane Long   24 March 1845
    Reference: Marriage Book C Page 119

HALE, S. P. to Mrs. Cordelia V. Yearwood   24 September 1864
    m. 2 October by Jno. Scruggs, M. G.
    Reference: Marriage Book F Page 7

HALE, Tate to Anna Minton   18 April 1839
    m. 18 April by Jonathan Thomas, J. P.
    Reference: Marriage Book C Page 16

HALE, Thomas to Mildred Steed   5 July 1865
    m. 5 July by W. A. Nelson, M. G.
    Reference: Marriage Book F Page 20

HALE, Wm. to Hannah G. Wright   23 September 1847
    m. 23 September by R. A. McAdoo, J. P.
    Reference: Marriage Book C Page 160

HALE - see also HAIL

HALEY, A. S. to Emma C. Ivins   7 June 1865
    m. 7 June by Erastus Rowley, M. G.
    Reference: Marriage Book F Page 19

HALEY, Charles to Margaret Smith   29 September 1846
    Reference: Marriage Book C Page 144

HALEY, John to Mary Thompson   18 September 1841
    m. 19 September by C. Taliaferro, M. G.
    Reference: Marriage Book C Page 46

HALEY - see also HAITTY and HAYLEY

HALL, O. P. to Mrs. Amanda J. Riggs   11 August 1852
    m. 11 August by John Hoyl, M. G.
    Reference: Marriage Book D Page 54

HALL, Samuel to Delila Emmerson   13 July 1847
 William Cate, Security
 m. 14 July by Russell Lane, J. P.
 Reference: County Archives: Marriage
 Book C Page 157

HAMBLETON, James A. to Peggy Booker   17 October 1826
 m. by Thomas Moreland, P. G.
 Reference: County Archives

HAMBRICK, James to Cinthia Malissa Richards 11 May 1848
 m. 11 May by Daniel McPhail, J. P.
 Reference: Marriage Book D Page 1;
 W. P. A.
 Note: Part of page 1 in Book D is missing

HAMBRIGHT, William S. to Sarah B. Moore 23 November 1838
 Reference: Marriage Book C Page 10

HAMES, James P. to Angeline Dodson   4 August 1869
 m. 5 August by S. M. Thomas, J. P.
 Reference: Marriage Book G Page 48

HAMILTON, David J. to Sarah Williams   2 March 1858
 m. 2 March by J. W. Gibson, J. P.
 Reference: Marriage Book D Page 137

HAMILTON, James A. to Mary Ann Lauftus   27 April 1867
 m. 28 April by Morgan Miller, J. P.
 Reference: Marriage Book G Page 14

HAMILTON, John L. to Susan Senter   30 September 1856
 m. 30 September by J. A. Rowles, J. P.
 Reference: Marriage Book D Page 115

HAMILTON, Robert to Mary John   28 November 1867
 m. 28 November by G. W. Colman, M. G.
 Reference: Marriage Book G Page 23

HAMILTON, Robert N. to Mrs. Malindy Therman 13 April 1867
 m. 14 April by J. Albert Hyden, M. G.
 Reference: Marriage Book G Page 13

HAMILTON, Thomas to Ellen Rentfrow   18 September 1869
 m. 19 September by James A. Wallace, M. G.
 Reference: Marriage Book G Page 51

HAMILTON, Wm. R. to Mary Darkes Beck   24 July 1869
 Reference: Marriage Book G Page 48

HAMMOND, William W. to Jane O. Patton   15 August 1850
 m. 16 August by Thomas T. Russell, M. G.
 Reference: Marriage Book D Page 30

HAMMONDS, Jas. P. to Angeline Loughmiller 15 August 1865
 m. 16 August by S. W. Royston, J. P.
 Reference: Marriage Book F Page 24

HAMMONTREE - see also HAMELTREE

HAMPTON, Daniel to Marthy A. McBroom 31 December 1870
 m. 1 January 1871 by Wm. H. Cate, J. P.
 Reference: Marriage Book G Page 72

HAMPTON, Jacob to Margaret E. Varner   12 July 1865
 m. 16 July by Joseph Hamilton, J. P.
 Reference: Marriage Book F Page 21

HAMPTON, R. F. to Mary L. Isbell   5 November 1844
    m. 5 November by A. Slover, M. G.
    Reference: Marriage Book C Page 111

HAMPTON, Wm. to Sarah Wooddy   22 April 1858
    m. 22 April by Johnathan Thomas, J. P.
    Reference: Marriage Book D Page 139

HAMRICK, R. M. to Martha Gregory   6 April 1854
    m. 8 April by E. M. Roberts, J. P.
    Reference: Marriage Book D Page 82

HANCE, Joseph to Sarah Reese   21 October 1846
    Reference: Marriage Book C Page 145

HANCE, Samuel "75 years of age" to   9 August 1849
    Mrs. Martha Brown "same age 75 years"
    Reference: Marriage Book D Page 17

HANDLEY, George W. to Mary Ann Stubblefield   26 January 1852
    m. 27 January by James Douglass, M. G.
    Reference: Marriage Book D Page 47

HANEY, Emanuel to Amanda Irvin   23 February 1849
    m. 1849 by James Douglass, M. G.
    Reference: Marriage Book D Page 12

HANEY, George W. to Margaret Pangle   25 October 1843
    m. 25 October by Samuel Wilson, J. P.
    Reference: Marriage Book C Page 88;
    Marriage Book C Page 89

HANEY, George W. to Caroline Givens   9 February 1866
    m. 9 February by F. M. Avans, M. G.
    Reference: Marriage Book F Page 37

HANEY, Henry to Sarah Givens   31 July 1865
    m. 1 August by D. B. Cunningham, M. G.
    Reference: Marriage Book F Page 22

HANEY, J. L. to Sarah Maloan   18 September 1858
    m. 19 September by Edward Atlee, M. G.
    Reference: Marriage Book D Page 146

HANEY, John to Caroline Gollarah   23 August 1869
    m. 24 August by A. J. Shelton, J. P.
    Reference: Marriage Book G Page 49

HANEY, John J. to Keziah Rowan   12 November 1845
    m. 12 November by J. W. Barnett, J. P.
    Reference: Marriage Book C Page 129

HANEY, Thomas to Nancy Haney   16 September 1846
    Reference: Marriage Book C Page 143

HANEY, Wm. to Mary Jane Lemons   14 January 1868
    m. 17 January by L. W. Crouch, M. G.
    Reference: Marriage Book G Page 26:
    Marriage Book G Page 29

HANEY - see also HAYNIE

HANKINS, Andrew M. to Eliza Waide   14 December 1840
    m. 15 December by C. W. Rice, J. P.
    Reference: Marriage Book C Page 35

HANKINS, Joseph J. to Elizabeth J. Parks   13 January 1853
    m. 13 January by A. Barb, J. P.
    Reference: County Archives: Marriage Bk D p. 62

HANKS, Alfred to Mrs. Sarah Smith   25 December 1840
    m. 25 December by John Jenkins, J. P.
    Reference: Marriage Book C Page 35

HANKS, Jonathan to Mary Kipps   9 July 1839
    m. 11 July by John McCartney, J. P.
    Reference: Marriage Book C Page 20

HANNAH, James to Eliza A. Gilly   13 October 1854
    m. 14 October by Morgan Miller, J. P.
    Reference: Marriage Book D Page 88

HARDEN, William G. to Margret Mins   11 September 1851
    Reference: Marriage Book D Page 43

HARDIN, Amos to Sarah Creasman   28 August 1858
    Reference: Marriage Book D Page 145

HARDIN, Josiah R. to Elizabeth Cox   31 August 1848
    m. 31 August by E. Newton, M. G.
    Reference: Marriage Book D Page 4

HARDY, Samuel, Jr. to Elizabeth Copeland 12 December 1850
    m. 13 December by M. Southard, M. G.
    Reference: Marriage Book D Page 35

HARGIS, David L. to Eliza M. Pike   6 October 1846
    m. 6 October by M. D. Anderson, J. P.
    Reference: Marriage Book C Page 144

HARKRIDER, Reece to Mahala Horton   23 March 1841
    m. 23 March by Richard A. McAdoo, J. P.
    Reference: Marriage Book C Page 39

HARMON, G. W. to Sallie Otter   25 February 1870
    Reference: Marriage Book G Page 59

HARMON, George to Mary C. Ledbetter   25 April 1866
    m. 26 April by Stephen Hill, J. P.
    Reference: Marriage Book F Page 40

HARMON, James to Delily Hames   19 September 1868
    m. 28 September by E. L. Miller, J. P.
    Reference: Marriage Book G Page 36

HARMON, L. J. to Sarah J. Patterson   2 January 1867
    m. 3 January by Martin Sharp, M. G.
    Reference: Marriage Book G Page 8

HARMON, W. R. to Miss C. P. Hale   6 November 1869
    m. 14 November by James T. Smith, M. G.
    Reference: Marriage Book G Page 53

HARREL, Enoch to Elizabeth Miller   25 January 1844
    m. 25 January by J. W. Barnett, J. P.
    Reference: Marriage Book C Page 96

HARREL, Moses to Martha J. Ford   5 January 1854
    Reference: Marriage Book D Page 77

HARRELL, William to Rinda Ford   11 January 1853
    m. 12 January by Samuel Wilson, J. P.
    Reference: County Archives: Marriage
    Book D Page 62

HARRELL, G. A. to Margaret Wyrick   5 September 1864
    m. 7 September by J. H. Magill, J. P.
    Reference: Marriage Book F Page 6

HARRELL - see also HEARALD, HERALD, HERRELL, HERROLD

HARRIS, Andrew to Sarah Crouch   12 September 1840
    m. 17 September by T. B. Love, J. P.
    Reference: Marriage Book C Page 32

HARRIS, Andrew to Margrt A. Dye   8 October 1869
    m. 11 October by C. Cate, J. P.
    Reference: Marriage Book G Page 51

HARRIS, Benjamin to Margaret Grennell   18 November 1865
    m. 18 November by S. W. Royston, J. P.
    Reference: Marriage Book F Page 30

HARRIS, Carter to Nancy Nations   18 September 1847
    m. 21 September by J. Jack, M. G.
    Reference: County Archives: Marriage
    Book C Page 160
    Note: License gives information as copied
    above, but Marriage Book C Page Henry HARRIS

HARRIS, Charles to Isbell Snoddy   5 November 1838
    m. 5 November by Lewis Brewer, M. G.
    Reference: County Archives: Marriage
    Book C Page 10

HARRIS, Henry - see HARRIS, Carter

HARRIS, John to Jane Shelton   31 July 1847
    m. 31 July by M. A. Cass, J. P.
    Reference: County Archives: Marriage
    Book C Page 158

HARRIS, John to Mary Howard   28 January 1852
    m. by G. W. Kirksey
    Reference: Marriage Book D Page 47

HARRIS, Wm. J. to Sarah Jane Forgie   3 February 1869
    m. 4 February by J. A. Womac, M. G.
    Reference: Marriage Book G Page 44

HARRISS, John B. to Sarah Gregg   22 September 1841
    m. 23 September by T. L. Hoyl, J. P.
    Reference: Marriage Book C Page 47

HARROD, Jourdin to Lucianah Coats   12 October 1855
    m. 13 October by T. B. Waller, M. G.
    Reference: Marriage Book D Page 103

HARROD, Wm. M. to Sarah L. Lamar   23 September 1858
    Reference: Marriage Book D Page 147

HARROD - see also HORRID

HART, John to Nancy A. Wammack   3 October 1856
    m. 4 October by T. B. Waller, M. G.
    Reference: Marriage Book D Page 115

HART, Maredeth to Miss Julian Nance   23 April 1844
    Reference: Marriage Book C Page 102

HART, Wm. M. to Rachel Lamare   17 January 1850
    m. 17 January by Wm. Burns, J. P.
    Reference: Marriage Book D Page 24

HARTE, John to Heriet A. Snider   20 December 1866
    m. 20 December by Elder John Davis, M. G.
    Reference: Marriage Book G Page 7

HARWELL, Alexander B. to Catharine L. Greene   7 April 1854
    Reference: Marriage Book D Page 82

HAWK, J. H. to Amanda Crawford   3 May 1845
   m. 29 May by O. F. Cunningham, M. G.
   Reference: Marriage Book C Page 120

HAWK, T. S. M. to Miss R. J. Wilson   3 May 1858
   m. 5 May by J. W. Gibson, J. P.
   Reference: Marriage Book D Page 140

HAWK - see also HAWKS

HAWKS, John to Hetty Shook   29 May 1850
   Reference: Marriage Book D Page 28

HAYDEN, Charles to Mary Ann Sivils   5 March 1852
   Reference: Marriage Book D Page 49

HAYDEN - see also HADEN

HAYES, Absolem C. to Marthy Colwell   28 June 1828
   John S. Heath, Security
   Reference: W. P. A.

HAYES, Absalem C. to Matilda Eaten   21 January 1839
   m. 24 January by A. C. Robison, J. P.
   Reference: Marriage Book C Page 13

HAYES, Isham to Sarah Hayes   4 March 1850
   Reference: Marriage Book D Page 26

HAYES - see also HAYS, HAYSE, HAZE

HAYLEY, Allen to Elizabeth Rice   29 May 1838
   m. 29 May by Benjamin Isbell, J. P.
   Reference: Marriage Book C Page 4

HAYMES, John E. to Lucinda A. Ziegler   13 November 1838
   m. 16 November by A. Slover, G. M.
   Reference: Marriage Book C Page 10

HAYMES, Vincent to Phebe Casada   29 December 1836
   m. 31 December 1837 /sic7 by Henry Price, M.G.
   Reference: County Archives

HAYMES, Vincent to Carline Templeton   2 October 1845
   m. 2 October by M. D. Anderson, J. P.
   Reference: Marriage Book C Page 127

HAYMES, William to Rebeca Zeagler   24 February 1829
   m. 30 /sic7 February by Jacob McDaniel
   Reference: County Archives

HAYMES, William W. to Mary C. Robison   13 July 1839
   m. 18 July by J. M. Kelly, M. G.
   Reference: Marriage Book C Page 20

HAYMES - see also HAMES

HAYNES, James P. to Margaret E. Elliott   11 October 1850
   m. 15 October by J. W. Millirs, M. G.
   Reference: Marriage Book D Page 33

HAYNES - see also HAINES

HAYNIE, G. W. to Sarah J. Newman   20 September 1854
   m. 24 September by Robert Gregory, M. G.
   Reference: Marriage Book D Page 87

HAYNIE, Herrol P. to Mary Davis   10 December 1838
    m. 10 December by L. Brewer, M. G.
    Reference: Marriage Book C Page 11

HAYNIE, James H. to Catharine Walker   21 November 1867
    m. 21 November by L. W. Crouch, M. G.
    Reference: Marriage Book G Page 23

HAYNIE - see also HANEY

HAYS, James to Mrs. Lucinda Russell   2 August 1842
    m. 4 August by Elisha Hays, J. P.
    Reference: Marriage Book C Page 59

HAYS, James to Sarah Cecil   20 August 1846
    m. 20 August by Leander Wilson, M. G.
    Reference: Marriage Book C Page 142

HAYS, James H. to Susan C' McElrath   31 October 1866
    m. 1 November by J. M. Miller, M. G.
    Reference: Marriage Book G Page 3

HAYS, William to Margaret Butler   21 August 1840
    m. 22 August by Ezekiel Ward, M. G.
    Reference: Marriage Book C Page 31

HAYS - see also HAYES

HAYSE, E. T. to Nancy A. Townsend   20 July 1864
    Reference: Marriage Book F Page 5

HAYSE, H. H. to Miss A. A. Gibson   10 September 1864
    Reference: Marriage Book F Page 7

HAYSE, Wm. F. to Sarah Senter   13 September 1864
    m. 18 September by A. T. Brooks, M. G.
    Reference: Marriage Book F Page 7

HAZE, Jas. R. to Louiza C. Parker   11 January 1858
    m. 12 January by Joel Culpepper, J. P.
    Reference: Marriage Book D Page 134

HAZE, Robert R. to Elizabeth J. Woods   31 August 1857
    m. 1 September by S. Philips, M. G.
    Reference: Marriage Book D Page 129

HAZE, Wm. H. to Nancy Collins   7 April 1857
    m. 7 April by J. A. Rowles, J. P.
    Reference: Marriage Book D Page 125

HEARALD, Joseph to Martha A. Hearald   1 June 1867
    m. 4 April /sic/ by A. J. Shelton, J. P.
    Reference: Marriage Book G Page 16
    Note: See HEARD, Joseph

HEARALD - see also HARRELL, HERALD, HERRELL, HERROLD

HEARD, Joseph to Martha A. Hearald   1 June 1867
    m. 2 June by Morgan Miller, J. P.
    Reference: Marriage Book G Page 17
    Note: This issuances and endorsement are
    inserted at bottom of page 17, on which are
    entries for July only. See HEARALD, Joseph
    which is on page 16.

HECKEX /HICKOX/, John E. to Arista Cox   7 October 1851
    m. 9 October by J. W. Miller, Minister
    Reference: Marriage Book D Page 44

HEDDINGTON, Worden C. P. E. to Sarah Ball   25 April 1855
 m. 27 April by W. H. H. Dogan, M. G.
 Reference: Marriage Book D Page 98

HEDDLESTON, Wm. W. to Mary Fairbanks   28 October 1843
 Reference: Marriage Book C Page 89

HEFLY, Winston to Elizabet Blevins   1 June 1868
 m. 4 June by J. C. Barb, M. G.
 Reference: Marriage Book G Page 32
 "Married 4 June 1868 at residence of bride's
 father, by Rev. J. C. Barb, Mr. W. C. Hafley
 of Blount County Tenn. to Miss Elizabeth,
 daughter of Wilson Blevins, Esq. of McMinn County."
 (Notice in the "Athens Republican", 11 June 1868
 Volume 1 Number 47)

HEISKELL, Wm. M. to Virginia W. Netherland   29 December 1852
 m. 30 December by John Scruggs, M. G.
 Reference: Marriage Book D Page 61

HELLON /HELM??7, Ransam to Sarah Carright   10 January 1856
 m. 10 January by Robert Cockran, J. P.
 Reference: Marriage Book D Page 106

HELLUMS, Eli to Elizabeth E. Bryan   17 December 1855
 m. 18 December by O. M. Liner, J. P.
 Reference: Marriage Book D Page 105

HELMS - see also HELEMS, HELUMS

HELTON, James to Sue V. Gregory   1 January 1866
 m. 1 January by T. R. Bradshaw, M. G.
 Reference: Marriage Book F Page 34

HELTON, Peter to Barbary Williams   18 May 1839
 m. 19 May by A. Barb, J. P.
 Reference: Marriage Book C Page 17

HELVEY, Daniel M. to Syphey (Sythuy) Roberts   5 April 1838
 m. 5 April by Henry Price, M. G.
 Reference: County Archives: Marriage
 Book C Page 3

HEMBREE - see EMBREE

HEMPHILL, James T. to Sarah Morrison   30 October 1869
 m. 4 November by Calvin Denton, M. G.
 Reference: Marriage Book G Page 53

HEMPHILL, John w. to Mary J. Roland   3 January 1866
 m. 4 January by E. Z. Williams, J. P.
 Reference: Marriage Book F Page 35

HEMPHILL, Thomas to Lucinda Tinsley   18 February 1828
 John Hemphill, Security
 Reference: County Archives

HEMPHILL, Thomas to Malvina Morris   18 July 1843
 m. 18 July by M. D. Anderson, J. P.
 Reference: Marriage Book C Page 81

HEMPHILL, William P. to Milly Triplett   29 September 1849
 m. 30 September by M. Southard, M. G.
 Reference: County Archives: Marriage
 Book D Page 19

HENDERSON, Alexander to Jane Robison   24 February 1848
 m. 24 February by Wm. H. Ballew, J. P.
 Reference: Marriage Book C Pg. 168; W.P.A.

HENDERSON, Elias to Sarah Boon 22 March 1844
    m. 26 March by John Scruggs, M. G.
    Reference: Marriage Book C Page 99

HENDERSON, J. H. to Miss M. A. Long 4 December 1867
    m. 5 December by C. R. Hoyl, M. G.
    Reference: Marriage Book G Page 24

HENDERSON, James to Eliza Jane Norville 6 June 1855
    m. 7 June by Robert Cochran, J. P.
    Reference: Marriage Book D Page 99

HENDERSON, James P. to Narcissah C. Childers 25 August 1866
    m. 26 August by A. J. Kirksey, J. P.
    Reference: Marriage Book F Page 45

HENDERSON, John R. to Molly C. McMahan 6 December 1869
    m. 12 December by P. M. Long, J. P.
    Reference: Marriage Book G Page 54

HENDERSON, Saml. P. to Miss S. B. Stephenson 1 September 1853
    m. 1 September by John Scruggs, M. G.
    Reference: Marriage Book D Page 69;
    County Archives

HENDERSON, Thomas to Dellily Woodall 3 December 1866
    m. 4 December by Uriah Payne, M. G.
    Reference: Marriage Book G Page 6

HENDERSON, Thos. J. to Margaret C. Mize 11 April 1864
    m. 14 April by W. H. Stephenson, J. P.
    Reference: Marriage Book F Page 1

HENDERSON, W. F. to Miss C. M. Rider 23 November 1870
    m. 24 November by J. B. Lee, M. G.
    Reference: Marriage Book G Page 69

HENDERSON, W. T. to Sallie L. Kimbrough 25 August 1869
    m. 26 August by N. B. Goforth, M. G.
    Reference: Marriage Book G Page 49

HENDERSON, William to Jane Cuningham 23 March 1850
    m. 24 March by Wm. Burns, J. P.
    Reference: Marriage Book D Page 27

HENDRIX, G. W. to Mary E. Shannan 15 September 1866
    Reference: Marriage Book F Page 47

HENEGAR, John H. to Kate Epersom 10 December 1866
    m. 10 December by Charles Cate, J. P.
    Reference: Marriage Book G Page 6

HENLEY, Thomas C. to Maryann F. Swenney 23 July 1846
    m. 23 July by Wm. H. Ballew, J. P.
    Reference: Marriage Book C Page 140

HENLY, W. C. to Mary Owen 7 March 1844
    m. 7 March by M. D. Anderson, J. P.
    Reference: Marriage Book C Page 99

HENRY, John to Jane Cuningham 16 May 1867
    m. 19 May by W. C. Owens, J. P.
    Reference: Marriage Book G Page 15

HENRY, William to Nancy Fulks 25 November 1869
    m. 25 November by E. Z. Williams, J. P.
    Reference: Marriage Book G Page 54

HENSLEY, Benjamin to Catharine Aiken
    both of McMinn County, Tenn.
    m. 1 November 1832 by Rev. C. Putnam
    at Gunters Landing, Alabama
    Reference: "The Knoxville Register"
    Volume 17, Number 859, 9 January 1833

HERALD - see also HARRELL, HEARALD, HERRELL, HERROLD

HERDIN, Joseph to Eliza Christian   26 November 1829
    James Christian, Security
    Reference: W. P. A.

HERON, William H. to Miss J. S. Bridges,
    Daughter of James S. Bridges, Esq.
    m. 23 February 1833
    Reference: "Knoxville Register"
    Volume 17, #867, 6 March 1833

HERST, H. J. to Miss A. Sivels   10 May 1851
    m. 8 June by Wm. Burns, J. P.
    Reference: Marriage Book D Page 41

HESTER, James to Eliza Worden   11 June 1844
    m. 13 June by John Hoyl, M. G.
    Reference: Marriage Book C Page 103

HICKEY, James to Mary W. Paris   15 August 1850
    m. 16 August by John Jenkins, J. P.
    Reference: Marriage Book D Page 30

HICKEY, R. H. to Elizabeth Amurin   22 August 1845
    m. 24 August by Justus Steed, J. P.
    Reference: Marriage Book C Page 125

HICKOX, Richard A. to Mary Jane Willhight   2 April 1851
    Reference: Marriage Book D Page 40

HICKOX - see also HECKEX

HICKS, James to Sarah Ann Stansbury   1 November 1849
    m. 1 November by J. C. Carlock, J. P.
    Reference: Marriage Book D Page 20

HICKS, Jas. M. to Elender J. Sanders   23 October 1847
    m. 24 October by J. W. Barnet, J. P.
    Reference: Marriage Book C Page 161

HICKS, James N. to Miss N. J. Carden   16 April 1864
    m. 17 April by John Scruggs, M. G.
    Reference: Marriage Book F Page 1

HICKS, John to Martha Orick   30 July 1870
    m. 31 July by A. D. Briant, J. P.
    Reference: Marriage Book G Page 63

HICKS, John B. to Jane Surtman   7 October 1851
    m. by P. N. Lee, J. P.
    Reference: Marriage Book D Page 44

HICKS, John H. to Rebecca C. Smith   4 January 1865
    m. 4 January by J. Albert Hyden, Chaplain
    U. S. A.
    Reference: County Archives: Marriage
    Book F Page 13

HICKS, Joseph to Leucy Ann Franklin   25 June 1839
    m. 26 June by Robert Frazier, M. G.
    Reference: Marriage Book C Page 18

HICKS, Thomas to Emely Lewis   28 August 1850
    m. 29 August by C. R. Hoyl, M. G.
    Reference: Marriage Book D Page 31

HICKS, William to Elizabeth Cecil   29 August 1846
    m. 3 September by Leander Wilson, M. G.
    Reference: Marriage Book C Page 142

HICKS, William to Nancy Dorherty   17 May 1849
    m. 17 May by A. L. Dugan, J. P.
    Reference: Marriage Book D Page 15

HICKS, William H. to Martha Bullington   21 January 1858
    m. 21 January by Thos. Russell, M. G.
    Reference: Marriage Book D Page 135

HICKS - see also HIX

HIGDON, John to Mary Ann Rivers   30 September 1847
    m. 1 October by Thoams B. Willes, M. G.
    Reference: Marriage Book C Page 160

HIGDON, Noah to Lydia Ann Rutherford   12 February 1846
    J. N. Cate, Security
    m. 12 February by William C. Lee, M. G.
    Reference: County Archives: Marriage
    Book C Page 133

HIGDON, Robert S. to Sarah M. Sutherland   8 July 1864
    m. 9 July by William H. Cate, M. G.
    Reference: Marriage Book F Page 4

HIGGINS, Thoams to Elizabeth Johnson   25 June 1864
    m. 1 July by G. M. Hutsell, J. P.
    Reference: Marriage Book F Page 4

HILDEBRAN - see HETTERBRAND

HILL, Claiborne to Mary (Polly) Cate
    m. 12 October 1823 in McMinn County, Tenn.
    Reference: Oregon Donation Land Claims,
    Volume 1, #643 and McMinn County Deed Book
    I, page 23

HILL, James to Jane Johnson   3 February 1849
    m. 4 February by Robert Sneed, M. G.
    Reference: Marriage Book D Page 11

HILL, James F. to Elizabeth Mayfield   22 March 1838
    Reference: Marriage Book C Page 3

HILL, Stephen to Mary Stewart   21 February 1849
    m. 22 February by Nathaniel Barnett, M. G.
    Reference: Marriage Book D Page 12

HILL, Sterling to Mary Ann Wallace   24 February 1849
    m. 26 February by Russell Lane, J. P.
    Reference: Marriage Book D Page 12

HINKLE, John to Lydia E. Miller   20 February 1841
    m. 21 February by T. B. Love, J. P.
    Reference: Marriage Book C Page 39

HINKLE - see also HICKEL

HISS, Phillip to Susan Johnson   29 May 1845
    m. 29 May by Justice Steed, J. P.
    Reference: Marriage Book C Page 121

HITCHCOCK, William to Eliza Jurel   15 July 1838
    m. 15 July by Larkin Taylor, J. P.
    Reference: Marriage Book C Page 5

HIX, Abel to Mrs. Mary Sliger   27 January 1853
    m. 27 January by Hiel Buttram, M. G.
    Reference: Marriage Book D Page 63

HIX, Douthet to Marinda Whitten   10 September 1853
    m. 7 May 1854 by Morgan Mill____, J. P.
    Reference: Marriage Book D Page 70

HIX, John to Mary Long   22 February 1845
    m. 23 February by D. A. Cobbs, M. G.
    Reference: Marriage Book C Page 117

HIX, John B. to Mariah Poe   24 October 1853
    m. 24 October by T. T. Russell, M. G.
    Reference: Marriage Book D Page 73

HIX, Lonard to Mary Ann Robison   23 December 1845
    m. 2 February by D. A. Cobbs
    Reference: Marriage Book C Page 130

HOBACK, James A. to Sarah W. Wattenbarger   3 October 1868
    m. 15 October by S. Sharits, M. G.
    Reference: Marriage Book G Page 37

HOGAN, Thomas M. to Juletta Sloop   5 December 1844
    m. 5 December by M. D. Anderson, J. P.
    Reference: Marriage Book C Page 113

HOGUE, W. M. to Ellen Cowin   22 September 1866
    m. 22 September by J. M. Miller, J. P.
    Reference: Marriage Book F Page 47

HOLCOMB, Daniel D. to Glapha Ann Robertson   17 October 1843
    Reference: Marriage Book C Page 88

HOLDER, John to Millie Darlin   25 November 1869
    m. 25 November by C. Cate, J. P.
    Reference: Marriage Book G Page 54

HOLEN, Joseph J. to Marthey E. Fry   23 April 1867
    m. 25 April by H. M. Sloop, M. G.
    Reference: Marriage Book G Page 14

HOLLAN, William to Sarah A. Fry   28 November 1861
    m. 28 November by H. M. Sloop
    Reference: Marriage Book E Page 12

HOLLAND, A. A. to Amanda Spradlin   21 September 1868
    m. 23 September by William Thompson, M. G
    Reference: Marriage Book G Page 36

HOLLAND, John to Martha Hayes   24 December 1838
    Reference: Marriage Book C Page 11

HOLMAN, Brittian to Luvecy Triplet'   19 January 1839
    m. 19 January by A. Slover, M. G.
    Reference: Marriage Book C Page 13

HOLMES, Thos. to Mary E. Cross   21 August 1865
    m. 25 August by S. M. Thomas, J. P.
    Reference: Marriage Book F Page 24

HOLT, Francis A. to Sarah D. Yearwood   26 October 1845
    m. 26 October by A. Slover, M. G.
    Reference: Marriage Book C Page 128

HOLT, Jasper to Sarah H. Wilson   27 November 1865
    m. 28 November by C. Long, M. P.
    Reference: County Archives: Marriage
    Book F Page 31

HOLT, Robert S. of McMinn County to
    Elizabeth Ragan, daughter of Peter Ragan
    of Monroe County
    m. 12 June 1832 by Rev. Abraham Slover
    Reference: "Knoxville Register" Volume 16
    #830, 27 June 1832

HOOD, Hathhorn to Rheny Marshall   11 May 1842
    m. 15 May by R. A. McAdoo, J. P.
    Reference: Marriage Book C Page 57

HOOD, W. G. to Hattie Johnson   12 February 1867
    m. 12 February by George James Norv___M___
    Reference: Marriage Book G Page 11

HOOSER, Jefferson to Margaret Hix   3 April 1843
    m. 3 April by M. A. Cass, J. P.
    Reference: Marriage Book C Page 77

HOOSER, Jefferson to Mary Brown   1 June 1853
    m. 3 June by P. N. Lee, J. P.
    Reference: County Archives: Marriage
    Book D Page 67

HOPGOOD, Lewis W. to Nancy A. Holse   12 January 1865
    m. 15 January by I. R. Chesnutt, M. G.
    Reference: Marriage Book F Page 14

HORNSBY, James H. to Harriet C. Coleman   14 November 1849
    m. 14 November by John J. Robison, M. G.
    Reference: Marriage Book D Page 21

HORRID, William to Amanda Butler   10 February 1840
    m. 10 February by Jonathan Thomas, J. P.
    Reference: Marriage Book C Page 24

HORTON, Elcana D. to Mary C. Rucker   23 August 1849
    m. 23 August 1850 /sic7
    Reference: Marriage Book D Page 17

HORTON, H. C. P. to Nancy M. Bryan   8 September 1853
    m. 8 September by M. A. Cass, M. G.
    Reference: Marriage Book D Page 70

HORTON, H. C. P. to Bettie Steed   30 May 1860
    m. 31 May by T. J. Pope, M. G.
    Reference: Marriage Book E Page 8

HORTON, H. C. P. to Kate Ensminger   30 December 1869
    m. 30 December by T. Sullins, M. G.
    Reference: Marriage Book G Page 56

HORTON, Joseph M. to Margaret J. MCgaughy   24 December 1857
    m. 24 December by G. A. Caldwell, M. G.
    Reference: Marriage Book D Page 133

HORTON, Robert to Anna Simpson   18 May 1839
    m. 18 May by D. Cantrell, J. P.
    Reference: Marriage Book C Page 17

HORTON, William G. to Miss P. C. Steed   12 October 1848
    m. 12 October by M. A. Cass, M. G.
    Reference: Marriage Book D Page 6

HOSKINS, John A. to Mrs. Mary E. Shadden   5 December 1864
    Reference: Marriage Book F Page 11

HOSS, Montgomery to Sarah Bicknell   18 October 1846
    m. 19 October by Hillery Patrick, M. G.
    Reference: Marriage Book C Page 145

HOTCHKISSON, Geo. to Martha Reed   9 March 1849
    m. 9 March by John Jenkins, J. P.
    Reference: Marriage Book D Page 13

HOUSTON, J. B. to Mahala Cate   13 May 1856
    m. 13 May by R. A. Prophet, J. P.
    Reference: Marriage Book D Page 109

HOWARD, C. W. B. to Mariah J. Morris   25 March 1845
    m. 27 March by J. Douglass, M. G.
    Reference: County Archives: Marriage
    Book C Page 119

HOWARD, J. W. to Mary Payn   15 December 1841
    Reference: Marriage Book C Page 50

HOWARD, J. W. to Mary Sowell   9 November 1853
    m. 10 November by Hiel Buttram, M. G.
    Reference: Marriage Book D Page 74

HOWARD, James to Maria Collins   13 November 1865
    m. 14 November by S. M. Thomas, J. P.
    Reference: Marriage Book F Page 30

HOWARD, John R. to Henrietta Rudd   30 November 1865
    Reference: Marriage Book F Page 31

HOWARD, Wlater to Eliza Sallee   4 March 1847
    m. 4 March by A. Slover, M. G.
    Reference: Marriage Book C Page 153

HOWARD, William to Pertina Center   28 January 1840
    m. by H. C. Cook, J. P.
    Reference: Marriage Book C Page 28

HOWARD, William to Elizabeth Henderson   14 June 1843
    Reference: Marriage Book C Page 80

HOWARD, William to Mary Ann Hunt   2 January 1851
    m. 2 January by William H. Ballew, J. P.
    Reference: Marriage Book D Page 36

HOWARD, William H. to Nancy L. Steed   27 September 1842
    m. 27 September by Justus Steed, J. P.
    Reference: Marriage Book C Page 63

HOWELL, Samuel H. to Ruth J. Blevins   9 November 1857
    Reference: Marriage Book D Page 131

HOYL, C. D. to Susan C. Hoyl   15 December 1858
    m. 16 December by Rufus M. Hickey, M. G.
    Reference: Marriage Book D Page 153

HOYL, C. R. to Miss S. M. Cooke   7 July 1841
    m. 8 July by Wilson Chapman, M. G.
    Reference: Marriage Book C Page 43

HOYL, Caleb R. to Atalina Cantrell   29 August /1850/
    m. 29 August 1850 by Jmaes Carson, M. G.
    Reference: Marriage Book D Page 31

HOYL, D. A. to Miss E. E. Dodson   2 November 1868
    m. 4 November by Calvin Denton, M. G.
    Reference: Marriage Book G Page 39

HOYL, John to Mrs. Mary Love, formerly   12 February 1829
    Mary Smith widow of Samuel Love
    Augustine P. Fore, Security
    Reference: W. P. A. and McMinn Chancery
    Case #227

HOYL, Oses to Jane Baker   31 August 1846
    m. 31 August by J. H. Benton, J. P.
    Reference: Marriage Book C Page 142

HOYL, P. W. to Margaret E. Wilson   30 January 1865
    m. 1 February by I. R. Chesnutt, M. G.
    Reference: Marriage Book F Page 15

HUDDLESTON, John to Sarah Newman   2 June 1864
    m. 3 June by Thos. B. Waller, M. G.
    Reference: Marriage Book F Page 3

HUDDLESTON - see also HEDDLESTON

HUDGENS, Eli to Mrs. Elizabeth Hill   12 July 1868
    Reference: Marriage Book C Page 39

HUDGINS, William to Winney Reneau   7 June 1855
    m. 7 June by Robert Cochran, J. P.
    Reference: Marriage Book D Page 99

HUDGINS - see also HUGGINS

HUDSON, Benjamin F. to Ursula Culton   26 April 1842
    m. 26 April by J. H. Benton, J. P.
    Reference: Marriage Book C Page 57

HUDSON, Roland to Mary J. Pearson   17 July 1852
    m. 17 July by David W. Beaver, M. G.
    Reference: County Archives: Marriage
    Book D Page 54

HUDSON, William C. to Mary Ann Lawson   23 September 1846
    m. 24 September by J. H. Benton, J. P.
    Reference: County Archives: Marraige
    Book C Page 144

HUDSON - see also HUTSON

HUFF, William to Mary E. Jones   1 February 1865
    m. 2 February by Stephen Sharits, M. G.
    Reference: Marriage Book F Page 15

HUGHES, George to Ann E. Riggins   30 October 1869
    m. 30 October by G. M. Hutsell, J. P.
    Reference: Marriage Book G Page 53

HUGHES, George W. to Nancy Young   1 October 1848
    m. 2 October by A. L. Dugin, J. P.
    Reference: Marriage Book D Page 5

HUGHES, James to Rebecca Tenney   7 June 1849
    m. 7 June by Hile Buttram, M. G.
    Reference: Marriage Book D Page 15

HUGHES, John to Francis D. Isbell   30 March 1852
    m. 31 March by D. Rose, M. G.
    Reference: Marriage Book D Page 50

HUGHES, Joseph E. to Mrs. Sarah J. Wade
   m. 12 October by Dan Carpenter, M. G.
   Reference: Marriage Book F Page 28
                                  10 October 1865

HUGHES, Joseph Eli to Elizabeth McKeehen
   m. 2 October by Hiram H. Brandon, M. G.
   Reference: Marriage Book D Page 44
                            29 September 1851

HUGHES, Samuel B. to Eliza A. Collins
   m. 18 May by James Baker, J. P.
   Reference: Marriage Book D Page 84
                                      17 May 1854

HUGHES, Samuel B. to Martha A. Stansberry
   m. 22 April by H. P. Wilson, J. P.
   Reference: Marriage Book D Page 139
                                22 April 1858

HUGHES, William to Mahala Rhom
   Henery Rhom. Security
   m. 30 October by William Burns, J. P.
   Reference: County Archives: Marriage
   Book D Page 58
                              30 October 1852

HUGHES - see also HUGES, HUSE

HUGHS, G. W. to Eliza Cate
   m. 17 March by J. H. Benton, J. P.
   Reference: Marriage Book C Page 99
                              13 March 1844

HUGHS, Joseph to Elizabeth Knox
   m. 31 August by J. H. Benton, J. P.
   Reference: Marriage Book C Page 125
                            30 August 1845

HUGHS, Samuel to Easter Roe
   Reference: Marriage Book C Page 98
                          27 February 1844

HUGHS, Williams to Amy A. McKehen
   m. 22 December by Heil Buttram, M. G.
   Reference: Marriage Book D Page 76
                          20 December 1853

HULL, Daniel to Elizabeth E. Smedley
   m. 30 December by John Courtney, M. G.
   Reference: County Archives
                          30 December 1829

HUMPHREY, Norris to Angeline Ellis
   m. 14 February by Jonathan Thomas, J. P.
   Reference: Marriage Book C Page 38
                          13 February 1841

HUNDERWOOD, William to Nancy McKeehan
   m. 3 January by D. Carpenter, M. G.
   Reference: Marriage Book G Page 8
                          2 January 1867

HUNNYCUT, John to Katharine Hackler
   Reference: Marriage Book C Page 1
                          6 January 1838

HUNT, David to Darcus McKenzie
   Reference: Marriage Book D Page 90
                          2 December 1854

HUNT, J. W. to Miss D. E. Zeigler
   J. L. Spradling, Security
   m. 1 November by A. Hawn, M. G.
   Reference: County Archives: Marriage
   Book G Page 68
                          29 October 1870

HUNT, Jessee A. to Salina J. Smith
   m. 25 December by M. R. Wear, J. P.
   Reference: Marriage Book D Page 105
                        22 December 1855

HUNT, John M. to Margaret N. Tunnell   28 December 1843
   m. 28 December by Moses Sweeney, J. P.
   Reference: Marriage Book C Page 95

HURST - see also HERST

HUTSELL, Charles L. to Mollie C. Buttram   10 October 1870
   m. 11 October by Jas. N. Stamper, M. G.
   Reference: Marriage Book G Page 67

HUTSELL, George M. to Mary E. McSpaddin
   m. 3 October 1849 by R. M. Hickey, M. G.
   Reference: Marriage Book D Page 19

HUTSELL, James to Miss S. C. Love   1 May 1866
   m. 1 May by E. L. Miller, M. G.
   Reference: Marriage Book F Page 41

HUTSELL, John E. to Margaret Bonner   3 October 1860
   m. 4 October by L. W. Crouch, M. G.
   Reference: Marriage Book E Page 8

HUTSELL, W. H. to Miss M. M. Rucker   1 January 1870
   m. 2 January by J. N. Moore, M. G.
   Reference: Marriage Book G Page 57

HUTSON, George to Elizia Ray   9 October 1866
   m. 9 October by B. E. Cass, J. P.
   Reference: Marriage Book G Page 1

HUTSON, James F. to Elizabeth Russell   14 February 1867
   m. 14 February by G. M. Bloom, J. P.
   Reference: Marriage Book G Page 11

HUTSON, Peter B. to Jane Walker   20 December 1825
   m. 22 December by Geo. Bowman, L.P.M.E.C.
   Reference: County Archives

HUTTON, Leonard W. to Miss Milner Frances Walker   Not Dated
   Note: This license was issued between those
   of March 5 and March 10, 1851
   Reference: Marriage Book D Page 39

HUTTON, W. C. to Mary Ann Ashley   14 June 1856
   m. 29 June by A. F. Cox, M. G.
   Reference: County Archives: Marriage Book D
   Page 111

HYDEN, Jessee A. to Nancy M. Steed   29 October 1850
   m. 31 October by T. S. Rice, J. P.
   Reference: Marriage Book D Page 34

INGALS, Peter to Narcissa Hambrick   1 January 1845
   m. 2 January by R. A. McAdoo, J. P.
   Reference: Marriage Book C Page 116

INGRAM, C. M. to Miss Bhaney Walker   4 July 1870
   m. 7 July by Wm. Thompson, M. G.
   Reference: Marriage Book G Page 62

INGRAM, Caleb to Julia Riddle   16 April 1867
   m. 21 April by D. W. Beaver, M. G.
   Reference: Marriage Book G Page 13

INGRAM, Caleb M. to Lurena E. Harless   12 June 1850
   m. 13 June by T. S. Rice, J. P.
   Reference: Marriage Book D Page 28

INMAN, John to Sally C. Riddle   7 April 1844
    m. 8 August by Hiel Buttram, M. G.
    Reference: Marriage Book C Page 106

INMAN, Thomas to Louisa E. Cox   7 December 1870
    m. 8 December by W. D. Cox, J. P.
    Reference: Marriage Book G Page 70

INMAN, Willis to Sarah Edgemon   8 October 1870
    m. 9 October by D. W. Beavers, M. G.
    Reference: Marriage Book G Page 67

ISBELL, Thomas N. to Sarah Ann Terry   21 December 1843
    m. 24 December by Tapley Gregory, J. P.
    Reference: Marriage Book C Page 94

ISHAM, Jasper to Adaline Fane   12 October 1867
    P. M. Atchly, Security
    m. 13 October by Levi Fitzgerald, M. G.
    Reference: County Archives: Marriage
    Book G Page 22

IVEY, Edwin S. to Sarah E. Fitzgerald   26 January 1843
    m. 26 January by Robert Snead, M. G.
    Reference: Marriage Book C Page 72

IVINS, G. W. to Mrs. Indanah P. Rice   29 June 1867
    B. Senter, Security
    m. 29 June by _. M. Miller, J. P.
    Reference: County Archives: Marriage
    Book G Page 16

JACK, Francis B. to Sue Kelley   27 August 1862
    m. 28 August by John Jack, J. P.
    Reference: Marriage Book E Page 6

JACK, Francis M. to Miss M. E. McNabb   22 October 1869
    m. 14 November by John Davis, M. G.
    Reference: Marriage Book G Page 52;
    Marriage Book G Page 53

JACK, Jeremiah to Jane Bailey   12 February 1829
    Andrew Jack, Security
    Reference: County Archives

JACK, John to Mary Ditmore   7 April 1829
    Joseph Rabourn, Security
    Reference: County Archives

JACK, Samuel H. to Mary L. White   13 April 1868
    W. A. Davis, Security
    m. 16 April by Jno. Davis, M. G.
    Reference: County Archives: Marriage
    Book G Page 31

JACK, V. H. to Sarah M. Dopherty   14 February 1852
    m. 23 February by Benj. E. Cass, J. P.
    Reference: Marriage Book D Page 48;
    County Archives

JACK, William H. to Jane Cook   16 May 1841
    m. 18 May by M. A. Cass, J. P.
    Reference: Marriage Book C Page 42

JACKSON, James to Rachael Wadkins   17 August 1837
    m. 17 August by D. Cantrell, J. P.
    Reference: County Archives

JACKSON, John to Mary E. Right
    (Other entries for this page are
    dated February 1867)
    Reference: Marriage Book G Page 11   Not Dated

JACKSON, Major Richard C. of Athens to
    Miss Julia A. Brazelton, second daughter
    of General William Brazelton of Newmarket
    m. 26 November 1845 in Newmarket by
    Rev. Gideon S. White
    Reference: "Knoxville Register", Volume 5,
    #259, 3 December 1845

JACKSON, W. D. to Louisa Smith   22 January 1866
    J. C. Lowry, Security
    m. 23 Janaury by T. R. Bradshaw, M. G.
    Reference: County Archives: Marriage
    Book F Page 36

JACKSON, Washington to Lony Bowren   31 December 1838
    Reference: Marriage Book C Page 12

JAMES, Hiram to Nancy Ann Bradly   9 September 1847
    Reference: Marriage Book C Page 159

JAMES, John to Mary Blanshipp   3 November 1836
    Frank K. Reeder, Security
    Reference: County Archives

JAMES, William G. to Annaliza Townsly   4 December 1838
    m. 4 December by William Shamblin, J. P.
    Reference: Marriage Book C Page 11 .

JAMES, William M. to Martha J. Duckworth   6 October 1852
    m. 6 October by Uriel Johnston, J. P.
    Reference: Marriage Book D Page 57

JAMESON, Jacob P. to Mary J. McCammon   7 February 1854
    m. 7 February by John Tate, M. G.
    Reference: Marriage Book D Page 79

JAMISON - see also JAMESON, JEMISON, JIMERSON

JANEWAY, Isaac to Narcissa Moore   1 November 1853
    Looney Janeway, Security
    m. 3 November by A. John, M. G.
    Reference: County Archives: Marriage
    Book D Page 73

JANEWAY, Luna to Nancy Plank   27 November 1848
    m. 30 November by Nathaniel Barnett, M. G.
    Reference: Marriage Book D Page 7

JARNAGAN, William to Margret Rogers   20 April 1868
    m. 21 April by James Parkerson, J. P.
    Reference: Marriage Book G Page 31

JARNAGIN, Hamilton to Nancy Emerson   20 January 1841
    m. 21 January by A. C. Robeson, J. P.
    Reference: Marriage Book C Page 36

JARNAGIN, Hamilton T. to Mrs. Sarah Cook   9 November 1864
    m. 15 November by P. M. Long, J. P.
    Reference: County Archives: Marriage
    Book F Page 9

JARNAGIN, Jas. H. to Mollie J. Johnson   16 July 1870
    Reference: Marriage Book G Page 62

JARNAGIN, Milton P. to Emily L. Murrill   1 December 1852
    J. W. Lillard, Security
    m. 1 December by George A. Caldwell, M. G.
    Reference: Marriage Book D Page 59:
    County Archives

JARNIGAN, Spencer to Mary Ann Kinder
    m. June 20, 1837 by Rev. A. Slover
    Reference: "Knoxville Register" Volume 21
    #1095, 19 July 1837

JARVIS, J. L. to Mary E. Howard   22 September 1866
    m. 23 September by Dan Carpenter, M. G.
    Reference: Marriage Book F Page 47:
    County Archives

JAYS, William A. to Elizabeth Jane Tenney   3 October 1866
    m. 4 October by Carroll Long, M. G.
    Reference: Marriage Book G Page 1

JENKINS, Adison to Elizabeth Dodson   9 January 1846
    m. 15 January by W. Chapman, M. G.
    Reference: Marriage Book C Page 131

JENKINS, Benjamin to C. Haney   20 January 1861
    m. 20 January by J. F. Pugh, J. P.
    Reference: Marriage Book E Page 14

JENKINS, Benjamin to Margaret West   14 September 1865
    Reference: Marriage Book F Page 26

JENKINS, J. B. to Miss Elvy Paris   18 March 1852
    m. 19 March by T. L. Hoyl
    Reference: Marriage Book D Page 49

JENKINS, Richard F. to Arminda Prather   2 July 1855
    m. 4 July by A. P. Early, M. G.
    Reference: Marriage Book D Page 100

JOHN, Benjamin to Mary Baker   27 July 1843
    m. 27 July by Moses Sweeny, Esq.
    Reference: Marriage Book C Page 82

JOHN, Hugh K. to Sarah Ann Prather   16 March 1842
    A. J. Ballew, Security
    m. 16 March by Robert Frazier, M. G.
    Reference: County Archives: Marriage
    Book C Page 55

JOHN, Saml. to Rebeckah Frazier   23 June 1841
    m. 24 June by A. C. Robison, J. P.
    Reference: Marriage Book C Page 43

JOHN (JOHNS), William to Jane Armstrong   31 December 1839
    m. 31 December by D. Cantrell, J. P.
    Reference: Marriage Book C Page 19;
    Marriage Book C Page 26

JOHNS, Ezekiel to Adaline Richard   11 December 1856
    m. 11 December by James Forest, J. P.
    Reference: Marriage Book D Page 121

JOHNS, Jonathan to Ciley (Celia) Browder   6 August 1838
    m. 10 August by A. Slover, M. G.
    Reference: County Archives: Marriage
    Book C Page 5

JOHNS, William to Rebecca Detherage
    m. 21 March by Russell Lane, J. P.
    Reference: Marriage Book C Page 2
21 March 1838

JOHNSON, Berry M. to Phebe L. Pressnell
    m. 17 December by Reuben Faulkner, J. P.
    Reference: County Archives: Marriage
Book D Page 60
16 December 1852

JOHNSON, Elias P. to Mary A. Dixon
    m. 1 March by J. S. Russell, M. G.
    Reference: Marriage Book F Page 16
28 February 1865

JOHNSON, Jackson to Louvicy McDonald
    Reference: Marriage Book C Page 1
26 January 1838

JOHNSON, Jacob to Sarah Moore
    m. 30 October by Elihu H. Randolph
    Reference: County Archives
29 October 1825

JOHNSON, James to Rebecca Ann Kitchen
    m. 12 July by Dan Carpenter, M. G.
    Reference: Marriage Book D Page 41
10 July 1851

JOHNSON, James to Sarah E. Dillon
    m. 11 September by C. J. Wright, M. G.
    Reference: Marriage Book E Page 4
10 September 1860

JOHNSON, Jarrett to Mary McConnell
    J. L. Bridges, Security
    m. 9 March by James Douglass, M. G.
    Reference: County Archives: Marriage
Book C Page 118
1 March 1845

JOHNSON, Jasper to Sallie F. Slack
    m. 24 January by J. S. Russell, M. G.
    Reference: Marriage Book G Page 9
24 January 1867

JOHNSON, John C. to Mary Ann McCallum
    m. 10 October by C. W. Rice, J. P.
    Reference: Marriage Book C Page 24
8 October 1839

JOHNSON, Joseph to Martha A. Green
    m. 20 January by Joseph Neil, J. P.
    Reference: Marriage Book D Page 123
16 January 1857

JOHNSON, Josiah to Eliza Pearman
    m. 16 September by T. S. Rice, J. P.
    Reference: Marriage Book D Page 43
16 September 1851

JOHNSON, Lindley M. to Eliza Jane Burnett
    m. 24 May by G. W. Wallis, J. P.
    Reference: Marriage Book C Page 102;
County Archives
14 May 1844

JOHNSON, Madison to Mrs. Nancy Presly
    m. 13 August by Tandy S. Rice, J. P.
    Reference: Marriage Book C Page 44
13 August 1841

JOHNSON, Marcellis B. to Margaret C. Hiss
    m. 13 March by Justus Steed, J. P.
    Reference: Marriage Book C Page 118
12 March 1845

JOHNSON, Mitchel to Lucinda Presly
    m. 24 April by Justice Steed, J. P.
    Reference: Marriage Book C Page 102
22 April 1844

JOHNSON, Robert to Nancy Carey   4 January 1823
    m. July by Jno. T. Porter, J. P.
    Reference: County Archives

JOHNSON, Robert L. to Nancy Yearwood   12 June 1838
    m. 12 June by James Sevil, M. G.
    Reference: Marriage Book C Page 4

JOHNSON, Ruben to Nancy A. Bryan   8 November 1821
    Andrew Cowan, Security
    Reference: County Archives

JOHNSON, Sycander N. to Mira McDaniel   4 June 1844
    m. 4 June by T. S. Rice, J. P.
    Reference: County Archives: Marriage
    Book C Page 103

JOHNSON, Thomas to Tennessee Johnson   5 March 1866
    George M. Hutsell, Security
    m. 11 March by George M. Hutsell
    Reference: County Archives: Marriage
    Book F Page 39

JOHNSON, W. B. to Sarah A. Teague   5 January 1867
    W. B. Kelley, Security
    m. 6 January by Elihu Kelly, J. P.
    Reference: County Archives: Marriage
    Book G Page 8

JOHNSON, William to Dicy Maples   9 April 1845
    m. 9 April by John Hoyl, M. G.
    Reference: Marriage Book C Page 119

JOHNSON, William to Polly Patterson   13 September 1856
    m. 13 September by Hiel Buttram, M. G.
    Reference: Marriage Book D Page 113

JOHNSON, William to Polly Ann Townsend   6 January 1865
    Reference: Marriage Book F Page 13

JOHNSON, William B. to Mary Ann Dean   5 September 1867
    James S. Burnett, Security
    m. 5 September by A. D. Briant, J. P.
    Reference: County Archives: Marriage
    Book G Page 20

JOHNSTON, Andrew Jackson to Elizabeth West   18 May 1848
    m. 18 May by Russell Lane, J. P.
    Reference: Marriage Book D Page 2

JOHNSTON, Elmadoras R. to Malvina Sloop   21 February 1850
    m. 21 February by Moses Sweny, J. P.
    Reference: Marriage Book D Page 25

JOHNSTON, William B. to Mary Isabilla McCarty   8 June 1848
    m. 16 June by Henry Price, M. G.
    Reference: Marriage Book D Page 2

JOHNSTONE, John W. to Mary E. Edwards   28 April 1866
    m. 28 April by Jno. P. Green, J. P.
    Reference: County Archives: Marriage
    Book F Page 40

JOINES, J. H. to Margaret T. Green   17 February 1865
    m. 23 February by Elder Thomas J. Russell
    Reference: County Archives: Marriage
    Book F Page 16

JONES, George to Delila Morgan   12 February 1851
    m. 14 February by William Walker
    Reference: Marriage Book D Page 38

JONES, Hugh - see JONEZ, Hugh

JONES, J. to Miss M. J. Gipson   29 June 1856
    m. 29 June by H. C. Cook, M. G.
    Reference: Marriage Book D Page 111

JONES, James M. to Matilda Luttrell   22 September 1841
    m. 23 September 1842 /sic7 by
    M. W. Cunningham, J. P.
    Reference: Marriage Book C Page 47

JONES, James M. to Sidney Jane Fry   26 October 1852
    m. 26 October by Rev. H. Brandon, local deacon
    Reference: Marriage Book D Page 58

JONES, John to Margaret Mayabb   29 August 1850
    m. 29 August by William Walker, J. P.
    Reference: Marriage Book D Page 31

JONES, John T. to Susan Eldridge   28 April 1846
    m. 28 April by Samuel Wilson, J. P.
    Reference: Marriage Book C Page 137

JONES, Joshua B. to Evaline T. Jamison   10 August 1842
    m. 10 August by J. Sewell, Minister
    Reference: Marriage Book C Page 60

JONES, Micajah to Sintha Sellers   21 May 1836
    m. by William Jones, M. G.
    Reference: County Archives

JONES, N. C. to Miss S. M. McCaslin   14 June 1860
    m. 14 June by Geo. A. Caldwell, M. G.
    Reference: Marriage Book E Page 4

JONES, Nathaniel to Jane McSpadden   9 October 1854
    m. 9 October by George A. Caldwell, M. G.
    Reference: Marriage Book D Page 88

JONES, Pleasant W. to Sarah E. Morgan   18 August 1845
    m. 25 August by Rev. A. Slover
    Reference: Marriage Book C Page 124;
    "Knoxville Register" Volume 5 #246
    3 September 1845

JONES, R. D. to Martha King   2 January 1840
    Reference: Marriage Book C Page 26

JONES, Samuel to Margret A. Rudd   11 May 1867
    William T. Heningar (Henegar), Security
    m. 12 May by W. H. Stephenson, J. P.
    Reference: County Archives: Marriage
    Book G Page 15

JONES, Silas to Elizabeth Hunt   18 October 1854
    J. V. Walker, Security
    Reference: County Archives: Marriage
    Book D Page 88

JONES, Thos. to Matilda Keeton   12 September 1839
    m. 12 or 13 September by Wm. Jones, M. G.
    Reference: Marriage Book C Page 22;
    Marriage Book C Page 24
    Note: Page 22 has m. 12 and page 24 has
    m. 13

JONES, Thos. A. to Susan N. Mastin   11 November 1856
    Reference: Marriage Book D Page 118

JONES, Thomas H. of Georgia to Susan E. Hoyl   13 May 1845
    m. 14 May by O. F. Cunningham, M. G.
    Reference: Marriage Book C Page 120;
    "Knoxville Register" Volume 5 #232
    28 May 1845

JONES, William M. to Miss M. E. Miller   11 July 1851
    m. 13 July by M. A. Cass, M. G.
    Reference: Marriage Book D Page 41

JONES, William W. W. to Harriet M. Crews   13 August 1855
    m. 14 August by J. Cunningham, M. G.
    Reference: Marriage Book D Page 101

JONEZ, Hugh to Margaret Keeling   6 December 1848
    m. 8 December by Russell Lane, J. P.
    Reference: Marriage Book D Page 8

JORDAN, Columbus A. W. to Mary Jane Youry (Ury)   18 May 1848
    Reference: Marriage Book D Page 2
    "Knoxville Register" Volume 8 #388,
    31 May 1846

JORDAN, John V. to Julie Ann Wallis   26 April 1867
    m. 12 May by Hamilton Pearsce, J. P.
    Reference: Marriage Book G Page 14

JORDON, Thomas W. to Elizabeth Mansell   12 February 1840
    Reference: Marriage Book C Page 25

JULIAN, Robert P. to Rosanna Bond   21 December 1839
    m. 24 December by A. Barb, J. P.
    Reference: Marriage Book C Page 19

JULIAN, Samuel to Mary B. Smith   7 October 1839
    m. 7 October by A. Barb, J. P.
    Reference: Marriage Book C Page 23

KALBACK, Daniel to Mary Sharets   22 July 1856
    m. 22 July by Geo. A. Caldwell, M. G.
    Reference: Marriage Book D Page 112

KALBACK - see also COLBOCK

KAYLOR, Geo. W. to Julia A. Hamilton   15 March 1869
    m. 16 March by James Parkerson, J. P.
    Reference: Marriage Book G Page 45

KAYLOR, James M. to Mattie Rose   22 January 1869
    m. 24 January by A. Marshman, J. P.
    Reference: Marriage Book G Page 43

KEELIN, William to Malinda Green   9 September 1829
    William McDonald, Security
    Reference: W. P. A.

KEELON, W. J. to Margaret Hope   12 September 1870
    m. 12 September by Stephen Hill, J. P.
    Reference: Marriage Book G Page 65

KEETON, Allen to Elizabeth Love   6 May 1840
    Reference: Marriage Book C Page 29

KEETON, Jacob to Rebecca Ann Newman   5 March 1866
    G. C. Williams, Security
    m. 13 March by Hiel Buttram, M. G.
    Reference: County Archives: Marriage
    Book F Page 39

KEGGLE, John to Manday J. Gigg   16 July 1867
    m. 16 July by E. Z. Williams, J. P.
    Reference: Marriage Book G Page 18

KEGLEY, Absalem D. to Elizabeth Tunnel   3 November 1840
    Reference: Marriage Book C Page 33

KEITH, Alexander H. to Sarah Fore   20 May 1841
    m. 20 May by R. W. Patty, M. M. E. C.
    Reference: Marriage Book C Page 42

KEITH, N. J. to Hannah E. Laughmiller   4 July 1867
    m. 4 July by Joseph Peeler, M. G.
    Reference: Marriage Book G Page 17

KEITH, William to Martha J. Shumate
    m. 3 March 1835 by Rev. Jared R. Avery
    at home of J. W. M. Breazeale, Esq. in
    the town of Athens.
    Reference: "Tennessee Journal", Athens,
    Volume II, Number 29, 4 March 1835

KELLEY, A. C. to Emeline Kizer   9 March 1866
    m. 11 March by Morgan Miller, J. P.
    Reference: Marriage Book F Page 39

KELLEY, Elihu to Mrs. Eliza Brock   18 July 1868
    m. 19 July by C. Cate, J. P.
    Reference: Marriage Book G Page 29;
    McMinn Chancery Case Number 233

KELLEY, F. P. to Martha A. Cate   4 May 1865
    m. 11 May by W. A. Nelson, M. G.
    Reference: County Archives: Marriage
    Book F Page 18

KELLEY, Jas. to Martha E. Landers   17 November 1863
    m. 19 November by C. R. Hoyl, M. G.
    Reference: Marriage Book E Page 18

KELLEY, James to Dianner Bonner   29 October 1867
    m. 31 October by Stephen Hill, J. P.
    Reference: Marriage Book G Page 22

KELLEY, James M. to Nancy H. Long   21 December 1865
    m. 21 December by W. A. Nelson, M. G.
    Reference: Marriage Book F Page 33

KELLEY, Leeroy to Letty Elliott   9 February 1852
    m. 9 February by J. Jack, M. G.
    Reference: County Archives: Marriage
    Book D Page 48

KELLEY, Nathan to Mary Triplet   28 August 1838
    m. 30 August by L. R. Morrison, V. D. M.
    Reference: County Archives: Marriage
    Book C Page 6

KELLEY, Nathan to Miss V. K. Thompson   15 September 1870
    m. 15 September by C. R. Hoyl, M. G.
    Reference: Marriage Book G Page 65

KELLEY, W. W. to Miss L. A. McKnight   13 May 1856
    m. 14 May by J. M. Miller, J. P.
    Reference: Marriage Book D Page 109

KELLEY, William G. to Mary S. Small   28 February 1865
    m. 1 March by A. D. Briant, J. P.
    Reference: County Archives: **Marriage**
    Book F Page 16

KELLY, Eli to Elizabeth Worly   10 November 1866
    m. 17 November by Elihu Kelly, J. P.
    Reference: County Archives: Marriage
    Book G Page 4

KELLY, James to Lois A. Bridges   26 April 1843
    m. 26 April by L. R. Morrison, V. D. M.
    Reference: Marriage Book C Page 78

KELLY, James H. to Sarah J. Cade   12 October 1864
    Reference: Marriage Book F Page 8

KELLY, Richard to Mary Jackson   2 December 1829
    William Kelly, Security
    m. 3 December by E. Cantrell, J. P.
    Reference: County Archives: W. P. A.

KELLY, Terry to Delily Emmerson   4 January 1839
    m. 4 January by Jas. Barnett, J. P.
    Reference: Marriage Book C Page 12

KELSEY, Stanton to Catharine Parker   14 June 1864
    m. 15 June by J. M. Miller, M. G.
    Reference: County Archives; **Marriage**
    Book F Page 4

KENNEDY, James Sr. of Knoxville to
    Mrs. Nancy Heard of McMinn County
    m. 15 Janaury 1824 by Rev. David Wear
    Reference: "Knoxville Register",
    Volume VIII, #389, 23 January 1824

KENNEDY, James B. to Rebecca J. Newman   15 October 1857
    m. 15 October by Daniel McPhail, J. P.
    Reference: Marriage Book D Page 130

KENNEDY - see also CANNADY

KERBY, George to Mrs. Lorenah Green   14 August 1867
    m. 14 August by Elihu Kelley, J. P.
    Reference: Marriage Book G Page 19

KEY, John to Martha J. Wattenbarger   18 October 1859
    m. 20 October by Rev. D. Carpenter
    Reference: Marriage Book E Page 16

KEY, Thomas to Lizzie Camel   28 July 1868
    m. 28 July by Dan Carpenter, M. G.
    Reference: Marriage Book G Page 33

KEYES, Alexander D. of Athens to Mary Adaline Love,
    daughter of Major John Love of Knox County
    m. 10 January 1832 by Rev. J. F. Montgomery
    (In Knox County)
    Reference: "Knoxville Register" Volume 16,
    #807, 18 January 1832

KEYKENDALL, J. H. to Miss Kizzie Hopkings   5 April 1870
    m. 7 April by Joseph Neil, J. P.
    Reference: County Archives: Marriage
    Book G Page 59

KEYLON - see KEELIN, KEELING, KEELON

KEYTON, Benton to Artemesy Bales   28 September 1850
    m. 28 September by Hiel Buttram, M. G.
    Reference: Marriage Book D Page 33

KEYTON - see also KEATON, KEETEN, KEETON

KIBBLE, Daniel to Martha Onley   29 January 1851
    m. 29 January by William Walker
    Reference: Marriage Book D Page 37

KIBBLE, Elias to Martha C. Jones   9 July 1845
    Reference: Marriage Book C Page 122

KIBBLE, James to Mary Reed   1 January 1850
    m. 2 January by William Walker, J. P.
    Reference: Marriage Book D Page 24

KIKER, Andrew J. to Louisa J. Kennedy   16 November 1852
    m. 16 November by Hiel Buttram, M. G.
    Reference: County Archives: Marriage
    Book D Page 59

KIKER, Benjamin E. to Mahaly Beever   23 December 1867
    m. 24 December by George W. Morton, J. P.
    Reference: Marriage Book G Page 24

KIKER, William F. to Emily C. Newman   10 November 1858
    Reference: Marriage Book D Page 150

KIKER - see also KEIKER, KYKER

KILE, Hugh to Mrs. Mary Dixon   11 April 1840
    m. 11 April by M. W. Cunningham; J. P.
    Reference: Marriage Book C Page 28

KILLINGSWORTH, William to Jane Ellison   18 December 1838
    m. 20 December by William Shamblin, J. P.
    Reference: Marriage Book C Page 11

KIMBROUGH, Duke H. to Mary E. Cook   10 November 1857
    m. 11 November by C. R. Hoyl, M. G.
    Reference: Marriage Book D Page 131

KIMBROUGH, Duke W. to Mrs. Julia Ann Parkinson   1 July 1854
    m. 6 July by H. C. Cooke, M. G.
    Reference: Marriage Book D Page 84

KIMBROUGH, Elisha to Miss Lemira Jane Hickox   15 March 1849
    Reference: Marriage Book D Page 13

KIMBROUGH, I. B. to Miss M. A. E. Thompson   1 July 1854
    m. 4 July by H. C. Cooke, M. G.
    Reference: Marriage Book D Page 84

KIMBROUGH, John to Melissa Jane Cate   25 June 1855
    Reference: Marriage Book D Page 99

KINCHLOW - see also KINZALOW

KINDRICK, Tempe to Miss Thena Hambrick   22 September 1860
    m. 22 September by John McGaughey, J. P.
    Reference: Marriage Book E Page 6

KING, E. F. to Mary J. Sugart   18 October 1858
    m. 19 October by C. Long, M. G.
    Reference: Marriage Book D Page 148

KING, E. W. to Miss Vilenia W. Atkinson   19 December 1854
   m. 20 December by W. H. H. Duggan, M. G.
   Reference: County Archives: Marriage
   Book D Page 91

KING, George to Rebecca Slaughter   2 July 1829
   John D. Slaughter, Security
   Reference: County Archives

KING, Henry to Elizabeth J. Haymes   23 July 1839
   m. July by C. W. Rice, J. P.
   Reference: Marriage Book C Page 21

KING, James C. to Orlenia Lattimore   29 March 1859
   m. 30 March by Uriah Payne, J. P.
   Reference: Marriage Book D Page 159

KING, James H. to Lousian Center   4 July 1825
   m. 5 July by Irby Holt, P. G.
   Reference: County Archives

KING, John to Athens to Elizabeth I Fain,
   daughter of John Fain, Esq. of Dandridge
   m. at Dandridge 6 June 1849 by Rev. John
   McCampbell
   Reference: "Knoxville Register", Volume 33,
   #1675, Wednesday 13 June 1849

KING, Robert to Elizabeth Guthrie   18 December 1846
   m. 20 December by John Tate, M. G.
   Reference: Marriage Book C Page 149

KING, Robert to Malinda Loudermilk   26 January 1865
   m. 26 January by Rev. William Thompson
   Reference: County Archives: Marriage
   Book F Page 15

KING, William to Caliona Odom   19 September 1864
   m. 20 September by S. M. Thomas, J. P.
   Reference: Marriage Book F Page 7

KINGEN, David to Eliza J. Williams   20 July 1864
   Reference: Marriage Book F Page 5

KINMAN, James F. E. to Elizabeth A. Killingsworth   12 June 1841
   m. 27 June by C. W. Rice, J. P.
   Reference: Marriage Book C Page 43

KINNER, Elias H. to Elizabeth Grisham   18 August 1838
   m. 19 August by Charles W. Rice, J. P.
   Reference: Marriage Book C Page 5

KINSER, Andrew to Phereby A. (Feribe Ann) Kinchelo   26 October 1842
   m. 2 November by L. L. Ball, J. P.
   Reference: Marriage Book C Page 66

KINSER, F. J. to Miss N. J. Cloninger   17 November 1870
   m. 17 November by J. C. Barb, M. G.
   Reference: Marriage Book G Page 69

KINSER, James L. to Judith Hunt   30 January 1849
   m. 30 January by Nathaniel Barnett, M. G.
   Reference: Marriage Book D Page 11

KINSER, John to Rachel Barb   27 December 1843
   m. by J. Cunningham, M. G.
   Reference: Marriage Book C Page 95

KINZALOW - see also KINCHELOW

KIRBY, Calvin to Elizabeth Sanders   9 October 1845
    m. 9 October by Moses A. Cass, J. P.
    Reference: Marriage Book C Page 128

KIRBY, George to Sarah Manrey   17 February 1850
    m. 18 February by A. L. Dugan, J. P.
    Reference: Marriage Book D Page 25

KIRBY, John to Marthey McCrary   7 January 1855
    m. 7 January by James Baker, J. P.
    Reference: County Archives: Marriage
    Book D Page 93

KIRBY - see also KERBY

KIRK, Daniel to Eliza Edwards   6 July 1839
    Reference: Marriage Book C Page 20

KIRK, Matthew S. to Louisa Philips   2 February 1841
    m. 2 February by R. A. McAdoo, J. P.
    Reference: Marriage Book C Page 37

KIRKLIN, George to Mary Rollins   1 /July/ 1858
    m. 1 July by Joseph Zigler, J. P.
    Reference: Marriage Book D Page 143

KIRKSEY, A. J. to Mary A. Brock   24 December 1855
    m. 25 December by C. R. Hoyl, M. G.
    Reference: Marriage Book D Page 106

KIRKSEY, George W. to Talitha Boling   2 December 1839
    m. 2 January 1840 by C. Sanders, M. G.
    Reference: Marriage Book C Page 26

KIRKSEY, J. W. to Elizabeth Duckett   21 November 1866
    m. 22 November by John P. Green, J. P.
    Reference: County Archives: Marriage
    Book G Page 4

KISER, John to Elvira Casteel   10 May 1851
    m. 11 May by William C. Lee, M. G.
    Reference: Marriage Book D Page 41

KISER - see also KIZER

KITCHEN, Harrison to Martha Ball   14 March 1860
    m. 15 March by D. Carpenter, M. G.
    Reference: Marriage Book E Page 8

KITCHEN, William to Letty Urserry   22 October 1829
    m. 23 October by J. Evans, J. P.
    Reference: County Archives

KIZER - see also KISER

KLINE, John L. to Serena J. Holt   30 January 1839
    Reference: Marriage Book C Page 14

KNIGHT, Isaac P. to Jane Triplett   10 May 1864
    m. 12 May by W. A. Nelson, M. G.
    Reference: County Archives: Marriage
    Book F Page 3

KNOX, Benjamin to Celia Bingham   23 December 1844
    m. 24 December by R. A. McAdoo, J. P.
    Reference: Marriage Book C Page 114

KNOX, Elijah to Jennett Nance   22 October 1845
    m. 23 October by R. A. McAdoo, J. P.
    Reference: Marriage Book C Page 128

KNOX, Henry H. to Nancy J. Vaughn   29 December 1863
    m. 30 December by C. Long, M. G.
    Reference: Marriage Book E Page 12

KNOX, Jeremiah to Martha McAdoo   7 February 1849
    m. 8 February by A. Barb, J. P.
    Reference: Marriage Book D Page 11

KNOX, John W. to Miss E. C. G. Stanton   1 November 1844
    m. 2 November by J. H. Benton, J. P.
    Reference: Marriage Book C Page 111

KNOX, Nathaniel to Julian Smith   25 November 1845
    m. 27 November by J. H. Benton, J. P.
    Reference: Marriage Book C Page 129

KNOX, Samuel M. to Mary E. Grills   11 January 1846
    m. 15 January by W. F. Forrest, M. G.
    Reference: Marriage Book C Page 131

KNOX, W. G. to Mary E. E. Hamilton   25 August 1864
    m. 25 August by Chas. Cate, J. P.
    Reference: Marriage Book F Page 6

KNOX, William to Mrs. Martha Underwood   30 June 1849
    m. 2 /sic7 June by Thos. B. Waller, M. G.
    Reference: Marriage Book D Page 16

KNOX, William to Tennessee Smith   11 March 1861
    m. 14 March by J. M. Miller, M. G.
    Reference: Marriage Book E Page 4

KYKER, Thomas J. to Loduska Bryant   5 August 1869
    m. 5 August by George W. Morton, J. P.
    Reference: Marriage Book G Page 48

KYKER - see also KEIKER, KIKER

LADD, James to Mary A. Studdard   22 November 1864
    m. 24 November by Charles Cate, J. P.
    Reference: County Archives: Marriage
    Book F Page 11

LADD, Thomas to Catharine J. Wilson   8 September 1865
    m. 14 September by E. N. Sawtell, Clerg.
    Reference: County Archives: Marriage
    Book F Page 25

LAEMONS, Munrow to Mrs. Elizabeth Wilson   25 May 1866
    Reference: Marriage Book F Page 42

LAMAR, Aman to Martha Cooley   26 June 1858
    m. 26 June by William H. Ballew, J. P.
    Reference: Marriage Book D Page 141

LAMAR - see also LEAMAR

LAMBERT, Z. T. to Martha Hardin   24 February 1859
    m. 24 February by Joseph Gibson, J. P.
    Reference: Marriage Book D Page 157

LANCYFORD, E. F. to Miss T. J. Partin   14 August 1866
    m. 10 September by Jacob Womack, M. G.
    Reference: Marriage Book F Page 45

LAND, James to Fanny Ailey   4 July 1859
    m. 4 July by Robert Cochran, J. P.
    Reference: Marriage Book E Page 4

LAND, James J. to Susan M. Dawny   20 April 1869
    m. 22 April by Jacob Brillhart, M. G.
    Reference: Marriage Book G Page 46

LANDERS, James to Rachel Maynor   30 March 1846
    m. 30 March by C. Sanders, M. G.
    Reference: Marriage Book C Page 136

LANDERS, James to Partheny Smallwood   23 September 1869
    m. 26 September by W. H. Cooper, J. P.
    Reference: Marriage Book G Page 51

LANDERS, Luk to Mary C. Marr   8 September 1855
    m. 8 September by B. A. Prophet, J. P.
    Reference: Marriage Book D Page 102

LANE, Daneil to Emily E. Dickard   10 April 1840
    Reference: Marriage Book C Page 28

LANE, Daniel to Mrs. Mina Monroe   24 September 1864
    F. S. Ray, Security
    Reference: County Archives: Marriage
    Book F Page 7

LANE, Eldred to Miss Armenia Miller   9 August 1843
    m. 9 August by W. H. Ballew, J. P.
    Reference: Marriage Book C Page 83

LANE, James T. to Quintina Moss
    m. 21 March 1837
    Reference: Newspaper clipping in scrapbook
    of Miss Cora Boyd in possession of Mrs. F. O.
    Mahery, Athens, Tenn. Copy in files of
    compliler. Family Bible in possession of
    Miss Virginia Lane Brown, Chattanooga, Tenn.

LANE, John to Melinda Tinnell   15 April 1829
    Sherwood W. Pearson, Security
    Reference: County Archives

LANE, John F. to Parallee C. Miller   7 October 1844
    m. 7 October by W. H. Ballew, J. P.
    Reference: Marriage Book C Page 110

LANE, John F. to Caroline Walker   21 March 1860
    m. 22 March by L. W. Crouch, M. G.
    Reference: Marriage Book E Page 10

LANE, John J. to Catharine L. Atley   27 September 1866
    m. 27 September by R. D. Black, M. G.
    Reference: Marriage Book G Page 1

LANE, Patton to Susan Haynie   19 November 1838
    m. 19 November by Wilson Chapman, M. G.
    Reference: Marriage Book C Page 10

LANE, Samuel to Maxey E. Wear   16 April 1851
    m. 16 April by Robert Gregory, M. G.
    Reference: Marriage Book D Page 40

LANG, Mikel P. to Mrs. Nancy J. Wilson   21 February 1867
    m. 21 February by G. M. Bloom, J. P.
    Reference: County Archives: Marriage
    Book G Page 12

LANGDON, Garrett F. to McMinn County to Mary
    Beard, daughter of Welcome Beard, Esq. of
    Monroe County
    m. 7 November 1848 /Place of marriage not
    stated7
    Reference: "Knoxville Register", Volume
    8, #414, 29 November 1848

LANGFORD, Gibson to Sarah Wray   27 June 1843
    Reference: Marriage Book C Page 80

LANGFORD, John W. to Eliza E. Sharp   17 June 1843
    m. 17 June by B. E. Blain, J. P.
    Reference: Marriage Book C Page 80

LANGFORD, Robert to Mary Hughs   20 July 1843
    m. 26 July by J. H. Benton, J. P.
    Reference: Marriage Book C Page 81

LANGFORD, William to Lucy Hughes   16 December 1850
    m. 17 December by William Burns, J. P.
    Reference: Marriage Book D Page 35

LANGSTON, G. W. to Mrs. Eliza J. Igou   29 May 1865
    m. 29 May by Jas. Baker, J. P.
    Reference: Marriage Book F Page 19;
    County Archives

LANKFORD (LANGFORD), Licil /sic7 to Sarah Randolph   21 March 1829
    George Weathers, Security
    Reference: County Archives

LARASON - see LORISON

LARGE, George to Nancy Faulkner   25 January 1853
    m. 26 January by Daniel McPhail, J. P.
    Reference: Marriage Book D Page 62

LARGE, Henry M. to Martha C. Hughes   25 October 1865
    Lewis Stanton, Security
    m. 25 October by Henry Baldwin, J. P.
    Reference: County Archives: Marriage
    Book F Page 28

LARGE, Isaac to Miss N. R. Miller   9 August 1865
    William M. Stanton, Security
    m. 10 August by Daniel McPhail, J. P.
    Reference: County Archives: Marriage
    Book F Page 23

LARGE, James to Lizer (Louisa) Monroe   11 January 1851
    m. 16 January by Daniel McPhail, J. P.
    Reference: Marriage Book D Page 36

LARGE, John W. to Melvina Cooke   1 January 1859
    Reference: Marriage Book D Page 154

LARGEN, J. J. to Julia A. Kinchelow   12 November 1849
    m. 14 November by William R. Walker, J. P.
    Reference: Marriage Book D Page 21

LARGENT, McCamy to Eliza Lafforty   3 September 1845
    m. 4 September by M. C. Hawk, M. G.
    Reference:' Marriage Book C Page 126

LASATER, Wiley to Elizabeth Ross   31 December 1845
    m. 1 January 1846 by John Key, M. G.
    Reference: Marriage Book C Page 131

LATHAM, Silas G. to Miss Elmy Green   9 August 1855
    m. 9 August by D. McPhail, J. P.
    Reference: Marriage Book D Page 101

LATIMORE, Joseph to Clementine Ware   5 March 1870
    m. 6 March by A. J. Kirksey, J. P.
    Reference: Marriage Book G Page 59

LATIMORE, Samuel to Nancy Starr   29 December 1829
    William S. Cowan, Security
    m. 29 December by John Belding, M. G.
    Reference: County Archives: W. P. A.

LATTIMORE, Thomas to Elizabeth Queener   1 January 1840
    m. 2 January by J. C. Carlock, J. P.
    Reference: Marriage Book C Page 25

LAUGHMILLER, Hiram to Evaline Carroll   22 December 1840
    Reference: Marriage Book C Page 35

LAW, James D. to Elizabeth J. Wilkins   8 April 1867
    James H. Pickel, Security
    m. 23 April by A. G. Small, M. G.
    Reference: County Archives: Marriage
    Book G Page 13

LAWSON, David to Jane Williams   21 March 1854
  · Dan Carpenter, Security
    m. 21 March by Rev. D. Carpenter
    Reference: County Archives: Marriage
    Book D Page 82

LAWSON, Elias to Martha J. Williams   13 June 1854
    m. 18 June by D. Carpenter, M. G.
    Reference: Marriage Book D Page 84

LAWSON, Huster to Nancy Falkner   14 January 1845
    m. 16 January by G. W. Wallis, J. P.
    Reference: Marriage Book C Page 116

LAWSON, James H. to Elizabeth Glass   1 January 1857
    m. 2 January by Joel Culpepper, J. P.
    Reference: County Archives: Marriage
    Book D Page 122

LAWSON, Jeremiah to Miss Dicy Ellis   26 October 1840
    Reference: Marriage Book C Page 33

LAWSON, Nathan to Delelea Green   13 October 1838
    m. 13 October by Johnathan Thomas, J. P.
    Reference: Marriage Book C Page 9

LAWSON, Nathaniel to Mary L. Lillard   23 December 1853
    m. 25 December by Rev. D. Carpenter
    Reference: Marriage Book D Page 76

LAWSON, Nathanil to Jane Cate   5 February 1859
    m. 6 February by Johnathan Thomas, J. P.
    Reference: Marriage Book D Page 156

LAWSON, Nelson to Joanna Martin   13 November 1846
    Reference: Marriage Book C Page 147

LAWSON, William L. to M. Caroline Snider   4 September 1854
  · Calaway Blankinship, Security
    m. 7 September by E. L. Miller, J. P.
    Reference: County Archives: Marriage
    Book D Page 86

LEA, James to Lucinda Cantrell   14 August 1843
     Reference: Marriage Book C Page 83

LEA, Magor to Miss Roady Ireland   27 July 1829
     m. 26 /sic/ July by D. Cantrell, Esq.
     Reference: County Archives

LEA, Prior (Pryor) of Knoxville to Minerva Ann   4 May 1829
     Heard
     William B. A. Ramsey, Security
     m. 5 May by Rev. William Wood
     Reference: County Archives: "Knoxville
     Register", Volume XIII, #664, 13 May 1829

LEADBETTER, Lewis to Sarah Whaley   15 February 1858
     Reference: Marriage Book D Page 136

LEAMON, Robert to Peggy Conner   20 September 1838
     m. 4 October by WM. Shamblin, J. P.
     Reference: Marriage Book C Page 8

LEAMON - see also LAEMONS, LEEMAN, LEMMONS,
     LEMON, LEMONS

LEAPER, Drew to Miss /name is missing/   25 October 1839
     Reference: Marriage Book C Page 24

LEATHERWOOD, Aquilla to Jane Cox   4 December 1834
     Joseph Wilson, Security
     Reference: County Archives

LEATHERWOOD, John M. to Elizabeth C. Garland   11 August 1858
     Reference: Marriage Book D Page 144

LEDBETTER, Joseph to Nancy Right   24 November 1868
     m. 25 November by James H. Hamilton, J. P.
     Reference: Marriage Book G Page 40

LEDBETTER - see also LEADBETTER

LEDFORD, Amos M. to Tempy A. Pane   6 October 1870
     Luke Landers, Security
     m. 7 November by W. C. Barnett, J. P.
     Reference: County Archives; Marriage
     Book G Page 66

LEDFORD, Jahugh to Sarah Ann Hampton   18 May 1867
     S. W. Wade, Security
     m. 7 /sic/ May by M. D. Carpenter
     Reference: County Archives: Marriage
     Book G Page 15

LEE, Edward to Esther S. Fitzgerald   14 August 1850
     m. 15 August by E. A. Smith, V. D. M.
     Reference: Marriage Book D Page 30

LEE, John Sevier to Emaline Henderson   14 January 1839
     m. 17 January by Robert Gregory, M. G.
     Reference: Marriage Book C Page 13

LEE, Pleasant N. to Susan Lee   14 September 1842
     m. 15 September by Robert Gregory,
     Minister of Baptist Church
     Reference: Marriage Book C Page 62

LEE, William to Emaline Reynolds   11 September 1839
     m. 12 September by Robert Gregory, M. G.
     Reference: Marriage Book C Page 22

LEE - see also LEA

LEEMAN, Thomas to Mary A. Allaway   11 July 1867
   m. 11 July by P. M. Long, J. P.
   Reference: Marriage Book G Page 17

LEMING, Chandler to Mary A. Higgins   6 April 1841
   m. by Uriel Johnson, J. P.
   Reference: Marriage Book C Page 40

LEMMONS, Houston to Mary Blackwell   13 August 1854
   m. 14 August by Jas. Douglass, M. G.
   Reference: Marriage Book D Page 86

LEMMONS, James to Anna Blackwell   25 December 1847
   m. 26 December by John Scarbrough, J. P.
   Reference: Marriage Book C Page 164

LEMMONS, Levi to Miss Ursley Hicks   4 May 1829
   Samuel Edmissons, Security
   m. 6 May by James Senter, J. P.
   Reference: County Archives

LEMMONS, Reuben to Matilda Woodall   12 November 1844
   m. 12 November by John Jenkins, J. P.
   Reference: Marriage Book C Page 111

LEMON, G. W. to Jane Price   15 September 1838
   m. 23 September by William Shamblin, J. P.
   Reference: Marriage Book C Page 7

LEMONS, F. J. to Elizabeth M. Lusk   21 January 1858
   m. 21 January by H. C. Cook, M. G.
   Reference: Marriage Book D Page 135

LEMONS - see also LAEMONS, LEAMON, LEEMAN, LEMMONS,
LEMON, LEMONS

LENOIR, W. F. to Elizabeth C. Goddard   16 November 1841
   m. 20 November by James Sewell, Minister
   Reference: Marriage Book C Page 49

LESLEY, John to Marthey Jane Cass   25 October 1866
   m. 28 October by Thomas J. Russell, M. G.
   Reference: County Archives: Marriage
   Book G Page 3

LETNER, Caswell to Catharine Watson   1 November 1865
   m. 2 November by D. W. Beaver, M. G.
   Reference: County Archives: Marriage
   Book F Page 29

LEUPER - see LOOPER

LEUTY, John R. to Elizabeth Matlock   3 January 1850
   m. 3 January by Crocket Gorlley, Traveling
   Elder in the M. E. Church South Holston
   Conference
   Reference: Marriage Book D Page 24

LEWIS, Ansel to Mrs. Jane Gibson   13 July 1865
   m. 13 July /no signature/
   Reference: County Archives: Marriage
   Book F Page 21

LEWIS, Burton to Elizabeth Logan   24 March 1842
   m. 24 March by E. P. Bloom, J. P.
   Reference: County Archives: Marriage
   Book C Page 55

LEWIS, David to Margaret Cline   6 October 1856
    m. 18 October by Robert Cochran, J. P.
    Reference: Marriage Book D Page 115

LEWIS, Isaac to Miram Buckner   25 December 1852
    Reference: Marriage Book D Page 60

LEWIS, J. F. J. to Laura A. Mitchell   8 July 1858
    Will B. Heron, Security
    Reference: County Archives: Marriage
    Book D Page 143

LEWIS, James to Mary Kile   10 August 1846
    m. 12 August by Green L. Reynolds, J. P.
    Reference: Marriage Book C Page 141

LEWIS, James to Elizabeth Emery   11 October 1849
    m. 11 October by J. C. Carlock, J. P.
    Reference: Marriage Book D Page 20

LEWIS, James to L. A. Dennis   20 March 1868
    m. 29 March by L. W. Crouch, M. G.
    Reference: Marriage Book G Page 30

LEWIS, John to Elizabeth Patterson   14 December 1848
    m. 14 December by J. C. Carlock, J. P.
    Reference: Marriage Book D Page 8

LEWIS, John to Nancy Gore   7 February 1851
    Reference: Marriage Book D Page 38

LEWIS, John to Jane Dennis   7 February 1867
    m. 17 February by L. W. Crouch, M. G.
    Reference: Marriage Book G Page 10

LEWIS, John C. to Patsy Bullard   25 December 1829
    Jacob Bullard, Security
    Reference: County Archives

LEWIS, Larkin to Miss E. M. Mize   30 January 1849
    W. H. Maples, Security
    m. by T. L. Hoyl, Local Preacher
    Reference: County Archives: Marriage
    Book D Page 11

LEWIS, Marshal to Sarah B. Bonner   25 January 1868
    m. 30 January by L. W. Crouch, M. G.
    Reference: Marriage Book G Page 27

LEWIS, Oliver to Sarah Emeline Rodden   5 January 1852
    Reference: Marriage Book D Page 47

LEWIS, Thomas to Catharine C. Lyle   30 June 1850
    m. 30 June by Reuben Faulkner, J. P.
    Reference: Marriage Book D Page 28

LILE - see also LYLE

LILES, John to Darcus E. Strutten   25 January 1858
    m. 28 January by H. M. Roberts, J. P.
    Reference: County Archives: Marriage
    Book D Page 136

LILES, Stephen to Malinda Powers   5 March 1859
    m. 6 March by W. B. Mansell, M. G.
    Reference: Marriage Book D Page 158

LILES, William to Emaline Hambrick   19 March 1857
    m. 20 March by I. S. Garrison, J. P.
    Reference: Marriage Book D Page 125

LILES, William to Martha Whales   13 December 1870
    Reference: Marriage Book G Page 70

LILLARD, Austin to Margret Cobb   14 October 1869
    Reference: Marriage Book G Page 52

LILLARD, J. W. to Miss M. E. Matlock   12 August 1869
    m. 12 August by J. B. Kimbrough, M. G.
    Reference: Marriage Book G Page 49

LINER, Carroll C. to Elizabeth D. Smith   10 August 1846
    m. 20 August by William Newton, M. G.
    Reference: Marriage Book C Page 141

LINER, F. M. to Lizzie Lide
    m. 3 September 1862 by Rev. J. M. Miller
    at home of Bride's Mother in Calhoun
    Reference: "The Athens Post", Volume XV,
    #733, 10 October 1862

LINER, James B. to Sarah A. Clark   7 February 1866
    J. M. Bishop, Security
    m. 9 February by J. M. Miller, M. G.
    Reference: County Archives: Marriage
    Book F Page 37

LINER, James S. to Lucinda V. Ahl   7 February 1843
    m. 8 February by Joel Culpepper, J. P.
    Reference: Marriage Book C Page 72

LINER, John W. to Jane Hampton   7 February 1849
    m. 7 February by A. Swafford, J. P.
    Reference: Marriage Book D Page 11

LINER, O. M. to Malinda Ellen DeWitt   26 November 1870
    W. B. Carr, Security
    m. 27 November by J. D. Lyle, J. P.
    Reference: County Archives: Marriage
    Book G Page 70

LINER - see also LINOR

LINGERFELT, Jacob to Martha Gregory   8 October 1870
    C. C. Witt, Security
    m. 9 October by C. C. Witt, J. P.
    Reference: County Archives: Marriage
    Book G Page 67

LINN, Absolom N. to Mary A. Hicks   17 June 1865
    m. 22 June by D. W. Beaver, M. G.
    Reference: Marriage Book F Page 19

LLOYD, David P. to Eliza Pitner   12 February 1829
    Jeptha Civils, Security
    Reference: County Archives

LLOYD - see also LOYD

LOCHMILLER, Jedson to Miss S. R. Stanton   3 January 1859
    m. 4 January by Johnathan Thomas, J. P.
    Reference: Marriage Book D Page 154

LOCKMILLER - see also LAUGHMILLER, LOCHMILLER,
    LOUGHMER, LOUGHMILLER

LOFTIS - see LAUFTUS

LOGAN, Bloomfield to Mary Ann Cantrell   30 April 1840
 m. 30 April by C. Sanders, M. G.
 Reference: Marriage Book C Page 29

LOGAN, John A. to Margaret L. Smith   15 September 1866
 m. 16 September by C. Cate, J. P.
 Reference: Marriage Book F Page 47

LOGAN, W. C. to Miss Judy E. Weatherly 22 January 1859
 m. 22 January by H. J. Brock, J. P.
 Reference: Marriage Book D Page 155

LOGAN, William to Malinda Cantrell   19 February 1838
 m. 20 February by James C. Carlock, J. P.
 Reference: Marriage Book C Page 1

LONG, Albert D. to Martha R. Davis   22 December 1852
 m. 23 December by H. M. Dodson, M. G.
 Reference: Marriage Book D Page 60

LONG, Alexander to Narcissa Talent   6 September 1866
 m. 9 September by L. W. Crouch, M. G.
 Reference: Marriage Book F Page 46

LONG, Isaac to Rebecca Purkins   26 March 1839
 m. 26 February /sic/ by Reece Jones, M. G.
 Reference: Marriage Book C Page 15

LONG, Isaac to Dianah Wells   25 July 1853
 William T. Long, Security
 m. 25 July by Robert Gregory, M. G.
 Reference: County Archives: Marriage
 Book D Page 67

LONG, J. B. to Miss M. A. McKinsey   13 October 1869
 m. 24 October by Jno W. Moore, M. G.
 Reference: Marriage Book G Page 52

LONG, J. D. to Phebe Cassidy   29 August 1868
 m. 30 August by G. W. Coleman, M. G.
 Reference: Marriage Book G Page 35

LONG, Jacob B. to Rebeca E. Newton 25 September 1852
 Jesse A. Ware, Security
 m. 26 September by William Newton, M. G.
 Reference: County Archives: Marriage
 Book D Page 56

LONG, James to Margret Henderson   12 April 1847
 m. 12 April by Robert Gregory, Minister
 Baptist Church
 Reference: Marriage Book C Page 155

LONG, James to Mary Jane Marton   19 December 1851
 m. 21 December by William McKamy, J. P.
 Reference: Marriage Book D Page 47

LONG, John to Leah Smelser   3 November 1843
 Reference: Marriage Book C Page 90

LONG, John A. to Mahala Jane Newman 18 September 1844
 m. 19 September by R. W. Patty, Minister
 of M. E. Church
 Reference: County Archives: Marriage
 Book C Page 109

LONG, John H. to Mrs. Milly Gray   1 April 1843
    m. 2 April by M. A. Cass, J. P.
    Reference: Marriage Book C Page 77

LONG, John L. to Eliza Cox   17 July 1838
    m. 17 July by John Courtney, M. G.
    Reference: Marriage Book C Page 5

LONG, Joshua to Mary Emmerroson   2 September 1857
    m. 3 September by H. C. Cooke, M. G.
    Reference: Marriage Book D Page 129

LONG, Levi to Mary Wilson   13 February 1843
    Reference: Marriage Book C Page 74

LONG, Moses to Miss Currinda Mitchell   10 January 1859
    Reference: Marriage Book D Page 155

LONG, P. M. to Louiza Jane Crittenden   30 July 1857
    Thomas Long, Security
    m. 30 July by H. C. Cooke, M. G.
    Reference: Marriage Book D Page 128;
    County Archives

LONG, Pleasant M. to Elizabeth Long   26 October 1843
    m. 26 October by William F. Forest, M. G.
    Reference: Marriage Book C Page 88

LONG, Riley R. to Catharine Ziegler   7 March 1855
    m. 7 March by C. P. Vandyke, M. G.
    Reference: Marriage Book D Page 96

LONG, Robert to Sarah Leamon   5 June 1863
    m. 7 June by J. M. Miller, M. G.
    Reference: Marriage Book E Page 2

LONG, William to Nancy E. Liner   6 September 1852
    m. 12 September by O. M. Liner, J. P.
    Reference: Marriage Book D Page 56

LONG, William to Isabella McNelly   21 June 1855
    m. 24 June by Joel Culpeper, J. P.
    Reference: Marriage Book D Page 99

LONG, Rev. William R. of Holston Conference   4 November 1847
    to Sarah Elizabeth Atlee
    m. 4 November by J. Atkins, M. G.
    Reference: County Archives: Marriage
    Book C Page 162: "Knoxville Register",
    Volume 7, #362, 24 November 1847

LONG, William T. to Mary B. Becket   14 July 1855
    Reference: Marriage Book D Page 100

LONGFORTH, Henry to Miss S. A. Morrison   26 August 1848
    m. 27 August by Reuben Falkner, J. P.
    Reference: Marriage Book D Page 4

LOOPER (LEUPER), Calvin to Nancy Shumaker   24 August 1853
    George W. More (Moore) Security
    m. 25 August by Reuben Faulkner, J. P.
    Reference: Marriage Book D Page 69:
    County Archives

LORISON (LARASON), William to Emelia Billingsley 11 August 1829
    Joseph Billingsley, Security
    Reference: County Archives

LOUDER, George to Judah McCall   2 April 1845
    Reference: Marriage Book C Page 119

LOUDER, John to Catharine McCall   4 August 1845
    Reference: Marriage Book C Page 123

LOUGHMER, William H. to Telitha Logan   2 March 1864
    m. 3 March by C. R. Hoyl, M. G.
    Reference: Marriage Book E Page 14

LOUGHMILLER, Alfred to Eveline Wetherly   6 March 1854
    Reference: Marriage Book D Page 81

LOUGHMILLER, Geo. W. to Fanny E. Rutherford   30 September 1850
    m. by T. L. Hoyl, M. G.
    Reference: Marriage Book D Page 33

LOUGHMILLER, George W. to Nancy A. C. Hester   24 November 1853
    J. W. Cox, Security
    m. 24 November by J. W. Cox, J. P.
    Reference: County Archives: Marriage
    Book D Page 75

LOUGHMILLER, H. J. to Jane Bolin   4 February 1854
    m. 9 February by G. W. Kirksey, J. P.
    Reference: Marriage Book D Page 79

LOUGHMILLER, John to Frances L. Curry   23 January 1866
    m. 25 January by A. J. Kirksey, J. P.
    Reference: Marriage Book F Page 36

LOVE, J. B. to Miss N. E. Hutsell   23 July 1870
    m. 24 July by J. W. Gilbert, J. P.
    Reference: Marriage Book G Page 63

LOVE, James R. to Julia Reagan   17 November 1868
    m. 18 November by J. K. Stringfield, M. G.
    Reference: Marriage Book G Page 40

LOVE, John P. to Elizabeth N. Barker   2 January 1855
    m. 2 January by J. B. Cobb, J. P.
    Reference: County Archives: Marriage
    Book D Page 92

LOVE, William to C. A. Luttrell   20 November 1866
    m. 20 November by E. L. Miller, M. G.
    Reference: County Archives: Marriage
    Book G Page 5

LOVE, William M. to Sarah J. Pickens   26 July 1867
    A. Casey, Security
    m. 30 July by G. W. Coleman, M. G.
    Reference: County Archives: Marriage
    Book G Page 18

LOVEL, David to Katherine Lowers   20 February 1840
    Reference: Marriage Book C Page 27

LOVEL, John to Polly Stephens   24 July 1840
    m. 30 July by Moses A. Cass, J. P.
    Reference: Marriage Book C Page 30

LOW, Isaac to Elizabeth H. Long   13 June 1839
    m. 13 June by D. Cantrell, J. P.
    Reference: Marriage Book C Page 18

LOW, Jacob to Sarah Akin   15 June 1839
    m. 16 June by John McGaughy, J. P.
    Reference: Marriage Book C Page 18

LOW, Joshua to Mary Jane Lowry   23 December 1847
    m. by J. Cunningham, M. G.
    Reference: Marriage Book C Page 164

LOWE, Nathan to Sarah M. Burnett   9 November 1844
    m. 24 April 1845 by Thos. H. Small,
    M. G. C. T. C.
    Reference: County Archives: Marriage
    Book C Page 111

LOWE, Nathan to Gazilda Pearson   30 June 1853
    Mathew J. Pearson, Security
    m. 30 June by Reuben Faulkner, J. P.
    Reference: County Archives: Marriage
    Book D Page 67

LOWE, William J. to Martha Benton   27 December 1865
    m. 27 December by A. J. Kirksey, J. P.
    Reference: Marriage Book F Page 34

LOWER, George W. to Adeline Manery   18 November 1852
    m. 18 November by J. Jack, M. G.
    Reference: County Archives: Marriage
    Book D Page 59

LOWER, Michael M. to Amanda Hoozier   22 December 1847
    m. 23 December by J. Jack, M. G.
    Reference: Marriage Book C Page 164

LOWERY, Daniel C. to Mattie W. Ross   28 July 1868
    Reference: Marriage Book G Page 33

LOWERY, John M. to Louisa E. C. Anderson   22 December 1856
    m. 6 January by Geo. A. Caldwell, M. G.
    Reference: Marriage Book D Page 121

LOWERY, P. C. to Miss Rhue H. Dillean   3 July 1858
    m. 4 July by Joel Culpepper, J. P.
    Reference: Marriage Book D Page 142

LOWERY, R. A. to Lydia C. Wassan   16 September 1856
    m. 16 September by George A. Caldwell, M. G.
    Reference: Marriage Book D Page 114

LOWERY, T. J. to Clarrissa Jackson   18 June 1860
    m. 21 June by Geo. A. Caldwell, M. G.
    Reference: Marriage Book E Page 8

LOWERY, Willie to Miss Artie E. Power   20 April 1858
    m. 21 April by Geo. A. Caldwell, M. G.
    Reference: Marriage Book D Page 139

LOWREY, John D. to Elizabeth Small   26 November 1867
    T. J. Lowry, Security
    m. 28 November by J. S. Russell, M. G.
    Reference: County Archives: Marriage
    Book G Page 5; Marriage Book G Page 23

LOWRY, A. A. to Clarissa E. Guffey   15 December 1854
    Reference: Marriage Book D Page 91

LOWRY, A. M. to Emeline Smith   16 November 1847
    William Lowry, Jr., Security
    m. 16 November by A. Slover, G. M.
    Reference: County Archives: Marriage
    Book C Page 162

LOWRY, Daniel A. to Lucinda Stead   6 December 1843
    m. 7 December by M. D. Anderson, J. P.
    Reference: Marriage Book C Page 92

LOWRY, James H. to Margaret Emaline Kirkpatrick   19 December 1838
    m. 20 December by Abel Pearson, J. P.
    Reference: Marriage Book C Page 11

LOWRY, James R. to Elizabeth M. McClatchy   10 January 1854
    R. C. Rowan, Security
    m. 11 January by W. C. Daily, M. G.
    Reference: County Archives: Marriage
    Book D Page 77

LOWRY, John D. Jr. to Sarah C. Forest   7 January 1856
    m. 8 January by John Scruggs, M. G.
    Reference: Marriage Book D Page 106

LOWRY, Thomas J. to Nancy B. Smith   9 October 1843
    m. 11 October by J. Cunningham, M. G.
    Reference: Marriage Book C Page 87

LUMPKIN, John H. to Mary Jane Crutchfield   5 May 1840
    m. 5 May by L. R. Morrison, V. D. M.
    "Col. Lumpkin of Rome, Georgia to Mary
    Jane Crutchfield, daughter of Thomas
    Crutchfield"
    Reference: Marriage Book C Page 29:
    "Knoxville Register", Volume I, # 24,
    3 June 1840

LUNSFORD, Calven to Sarah Jane Bennett   8 January 1850
    Reference: Marriage Book D Page 24

LUNSFORD - see also LANCYFORD

LUNTSFORD, Andrew to Martha C. Ferrell   18 June 1846
    m. 18 June by A. Slover, M. G.
    Reference: Marriage Book C Page 139

LUSK, Hugh to Joannah Matheys   11 February 1835
    John D. Lowrey, Security
    Reference: County Archives

LUSK, Samuel to Elizabeth Dixon   9 October 1826
    m. 12 October by Benj. Isbell, J. P.
    Reference: County Archives

LUTTRELL, Erastis R. to Sarah F. Coffee   14 January 1867
    m. 15 January by J. C. Barb, M. G.
    Reference: County Archives: Marriage
    Book G Page 8

LUTTRELL, John H. to Susan Brock   25 November 1843
    m. 26 November by M. D. Anderson, J. P.
    Reference: Marriage Book C Page 91

LYLE - see also LILE

LYNCH, Isaac P. to Elizabeth Jane Blankinship   20 July 1848
    m. 20 July by James J. Troth, M. G.
    Reference: Marriage Book D Page 3

LYNN - see LINN

MC ADOO, Elijah to Clarinda Wilson   19 October 1864
   Reference: Marriage Book F Page 8

MC ADOO, Samuel to Isabelah Sligar   20 May 1867
   W. H. Stephenson, Security
   m. 22 May by William Newman, M. G.
   Reference: County Archives: Marriage
   Book G Page 16

MC AFEE, J. F. to Miss N. J. Collier   25 August 1858
   m. 26 August by Thos. Rogers, J. P.
   Reference: Marriage Book D Page 144

MC AFFREY, James W. to Nancy McGuire   5 December 1849
   Edward Leed, Security
   Reference: County Archives: Marriage
   Book D Page 22

MC AFFREY - see also MC CAFERY

MCALISTER (MC CALLISTER), J. M. to Fanny A. Talent   24 January 1866
   J. M. Bishop, Security
   m. 25 January by J. M. Miller, M. G.
   Reference: County Archives: Marriage
   Book F Page 36

MC ALISTER - see also MC CALISTER, MC LESTER

MCALLESTER, P. G. to Henrietta Coffey   15 February 1866
   Thos. Hale, Security
   Reference: County Archives: Marriage
   Book F Page 38

MCAMIS, Samuel to Elizabeth Underwood   24 December 1858
   m. 24 December by A. D. Briant, J. P.
   Reference: Marriage Book D Page 154

MC AMIS - see also MC CAMIS

MC ANALLY, W. T. to Miss N. E. Jones   7 January 1865
   m. 8 January by E. S. Miller, J. P.
   Reference: Marriage Book F Page 13

MC ANNELLY, William to Isabella Millsaps   4 April 1859
   m. 6 April by Jas. H. Melton, J. P.
   Reference: Marriage Book D Page 159

MC BRAYER, J. H. to Nancy A. Thompson   11 August 1865
   J. F. Wallis, Security
   m. 13 August by J. Janeway, M. G.
   Reference: County Archives: Marriage
   Book F Page 23

MC BRIEN, John to Margaret Barns   25 September 1844
   m. 26 September by J. Scarborough, J. P.
   Reference: Marriage Book C Page 109

MC BROOM, James A. to Sarah M. Patty   8 September 1853
   Taylor Russell, Security
   Reference: County Archives: Marriage
   Book D Page 70

MC BROON, A. J. to Miss Liddy A. Sneede   24 March 1868
   m. 25 March by G. M. Hutsell, J. P.
   Reference: Marriage Book G Page 30

MC CAIN, Carrick H. to Margaret McCall   21 November 1864
William Ward, Security
m. 23 November by D. Beaver, M. G.
Reference: County Archives: Marriage
Book F Page 10

MC CALL, James to Rebecca E. Jemison   16 September 1847
m. 16 September by B. E. Blain, J. P.
Reference: Marriage Book C Page 160

MC CALLIE, William T. to Mrs. Mary Forgey 16 September 1842
m. 18 September by Joel Culpepper, J. P.
Reference: Marriage Book C Page 62

MC CALLIE - see also MC CALLY, MC CAULLEY, MC COLLIE

MC CALLESTER, Eliga to Ann Jones   6 June 1868
Reference: Marriage Book G Page 32

MC CALLISTER, Elijah to Ruth Bishop   19 December 1842
m. 19 December by Thomas Camp, J. P.
Reference: Marriage Book C Page 69

MC CALLISTER - see also MC ALISTER, MC LESTER

MC CALLUM - see also MCOLLUM, MC COLLUM, MC CULLEM

MC CAMIS, James to Miss E. J. Cooper   22 October 1840
m. 22 October by L. R. Morrison, V. D. M.
Reference: Marriage Book C Page 33

MC CAMIS - see also MC AMIS

MC CANCE, J. E. to Martha J. Prophet   13 August 1868
m. 23 August by B. E. Cass, J. P.
Reference: Marriage Book G Page 34

MC CARTNEY, Alexander A., Editor of the
Alabama Gazette, to Miss Jane Beaty,
both formerly of Huntingdon, Pa.
m. in Athens by Rev. D. P. Bester on
Tuesday, 7 October 1823
Reference: "Knoxville Register", Volume
VIII, # 376, October 17, 1823

MC CARTNEY, James B. to Elizabeth L. Michail 14 July 1838
m. 19 July by J. Wimpy, M. G.
Reference: Marriage Book C Page 5

MC CARTY, Benj. to Mary A. Weir   18 July 1864
m. 3 August by J. M. Miller, M. G.
Reference: Marriage Book F Page 5

MC CARTY, James C. to Elizabeth W. Hanks   1 October 1851
m. 2 October by J. M. Miller, M. G.
Reference: Marriage Book D Page 44

MC CARTY, John T. to M. A. H. Ball   20 November 1854
m. 21 November by W. C. Reynolds, M. G.
Reference: Marriage Book D Page 89

MC CASKEY, James S. to Eliza Flinn   20 December 1845
m. 21 December by W. F. Forrest, M. G.
Reference: Marriage Book C Page 130

MC CASLAND, Jeremiah to Mary Ann Pierce
    Daughter of David Pierce
    m. 19 September 1837
    Reference: Newspaper clipping in old
    scrap book of Miss Cora Boyd, in possession
    of Mrs. F. O. Mahery, Athens, Tenn. Copy
    in files of compiler.

MC CASLIN, Matthew L. to Ellin H. Deaton   6 October 1853
    Joab H. Terry, Security
    m. 6 October by James L. Russell, M. G.
    Reference: County Archives: Marriage
    Book D Page 72

MC CAULLEY, J. H. to Martha Long   2 May 1868
    m. 2 May by J. M. Miller, M. G.
    Reference: Marriage Book G Page 31

MC CLARY, B. F. to Mattie F. Wilson   20 December 1867
    Lon Blizard, Security
    m. 24 December
    Reference: County Archives: Marriage
    Book G Page 24

MC CLATCHY, Adolphus P. to Malissa A. Gregory   20 September 1864
    m. 4 October by J. M. Miller, M. G.
    Reference: Marriage Book F Page 7

MC CLATCHY, W. J. to Miss M. L. Rowles   11 May 1842
    m. 12 May by Henry Price, M. G.
    Reference: Marriage Book C Page 57

MC CLENEN, A. to Mr. /Mrs.7 Catharine Stephenson 31 August 1867
    m. 5 September by Jas. Parkerson, J. P.
    Reference: Marriage Book G Page 20

MC CLEWER, Markes _ to Mary M. Ervin   15 September 1866
    m. 16 September by J. C. Barb, M. G.
    Reference: Marriage Book F Page 47

MC CLOUD, W. W. to Jane D. McCarty   17 February 1851
    m. 2 /sic7 February by James Scarbrough, M. G.
    Reference: Marriage Book D Page 38

MC CLURE, W. H. H. to Melissa Benton   13 December 1864
    Reference: Marriage Book F Page 12

MC CLURE - see also MC CLEWER

MC CLUSKEY, Madison W. of Columbus County, Ga.
    to Mary Eleanor Campbell, formerly of
    Knoxville
    m. 10 August 1840 in Athens by A. Slover, M.G.
    Reference: Marriage Book C Page 31:
    "Knoxville Register", Volume I, # 36,
    26 August 1840

MC COLLIE, William T. to Elizabeth Perryman   16 October 1838
    m. 25 October by William McKamy, J. P.
    Reference: Marriage Book C Page 9

MC COLLUM - see also MC CALLUM, MCOLLUM, MC CULLEM

MC COMBS - see MCOMBS

MC CONNELL, Joseph S. to M. M. McClatchey   28 February 1833
    Hamilton L. Alexander, Security
    Reference: County Archives

MC COY, James to Emeline Southard 6 November 1843
    m. 7 November by Rev. Edwin A. Allen
    Reference: Marriage Book C Page 90

MC CRARY, Robert to Elizabeth Grisham 2 September 1852
    m. 2 September by William Burns, J. P.
    Reference: Marriage Book D Page 55

MC CRARY, Robert C. to Becky E. Crocket 26 May 186
    m. 27 May by Morgan Miller, J. P. /1866/
    Reference: Marriage Book F Page 48

MC CROSKEY, David P. to Sarah Ann Detherrow 20 April 1853
    James S. McCroskey, Security
    m. by J. Jenkins, J. P.
    Reference: County Archives: Marriage
    Book D Page 65

MC CUISTION (MC CUISTON), Andrew J. to Sarah 8 September 1853
    Jane Turk
    Robert McCuistion, Security
    m. 8 September by S. Sharits, M. G.
    Reference: County Archives: Marriage
    Book D Page 70

MC CUISTION - see also MCUISTIAN, MC QUESTEAN

MC CULLEM, Thos. to Elizabeth Jane Marnoe 28 January 1846
    m. 28 January by Hiel Buttrem, M. G.
    Reference: Marriage Book C Page 132

MC CULLEY, Adam to Anna Jane Fry 3 April 1846
    m. 3 April by Russel Lane, J. P.
    Reference: Marriage Book C Page 136

MC CULLEY, Geo. M. to Ann A. Porter 19 August 1846
    m. 20 August by Archibald A. Mathis, M. G.
    Reference: Marriage Book C Page 142

MC CULLY, Granvill H. to Sarah E. Beene 23 January 1867
    W. H. Hollan,. Security
    m. 23 January by H. M. Sloop, M. G.
    Reference: County Archives: Marriage
    Book G Page 9

MC CULLY - see also MCULLEY

MC DANIEL, Daniel to Emeline Redfearn 5 August 1840
    m. 6 August by Richard A. McAdoo, J. P.
    Reference: Marriage Book C Page 30

MC DANIEL, R. C. to Miss M. A. Manis 30 December 1869
    m. 30 December by A. D. Briant, J. P.
    Reference: Marriage Book G Page 56

MCDANIEL, W. J. to Sarah C. MCDaniel 22 October 1857
    m. 22 October by A. D. Briant, J. P.
    Reference: Marriage Book D Page 130

MC DANIEL, William to Jemima Liles 26 October 1851
    m. 28 October by William C. Lee, M. G.
    Reference: Marriage Book D Page 45

M. C. DANIL /sic/, T. J. to Sarah J. Turner 11 September 1856
    m. 11 September by I. S. Garrison, J. P.
    Reference: Marriage Book D Page 113

MC DONAL, Thomas M. to Lucindy March   20 March 1852
Reference: Marriage Book D Page 49

MC DONALD, **Alex to Omey** Ayres   20 January 1867
m. 20 January by Robert Mancell, M. G.
Reference: Marriage Book G Page 9

MC DONALD, Daniel to Charlotte R. Campbell   2 January 1839
m. 3 January by Robert Gregory, M. G. of
Baptist Church
Reference: Marriage Book C Page 13

MC ELHANY - see also MCULHANY

MC ELHAMY, Thomas N. to Sarah J. Frank   22 February 1854
m. 22 February by Hugh P. Wilson, J. P.
Reference: Marriage Book D Page 80

MC ENTURFF, Thomas to Mrs. Nancy Pugh   5 December 1849
Martin Burnet, Security
m. 9 December by James Bonner, J. P.
Reference: County Archives: Marriage
Book D Page 22

MC EWEN, Robert N. to Sarah C. Balfour   11 December 1851
m. 11 December by J. W. Miller, M. G.
Reference: Marriage Book D Page 46

MC GAUGHEY - see also MC GUGHEY

MC GEHEE, Alfred to Mary E. Coates   9 November 1864
m. 10 November by Z. Rose, M. G.
Reference: Marriage Book F Page 9

MC GEHEN, George W. to Nancy Jane Large   16 February 1853
m. 17 February by Hiel Buttram, M. G.
Reference: Marriage Book D Page 63

MC GENDEY, Joseph to Nancy Brown   20 March 1821
Reference: W. P. A.

MC GHEE - see MEGHEE

MC GILL, Walter M. to Isabella Anderson   16 August 1838
m. 16 August by Abel Pearson, M. G.
Reference: Marriage Book C Page 5

MC GINLEY, John to Mary Ann Matthews   18 August 1842
Reference: Marriage Book C Page 60

MC GINTY, Elbert to Emaline Baker   18 October 1852
m. 18 October by Samuel Wilson, J. P.
Reference: Marriage Book D Page 58

MC GINTY, John (GENTRY, John M.) to Nancy **Gentry** 9 November 1842
m. 9 November by C. Sanders, M. G.
Reference: Marriage Book C Page 67
(Note: This license issued to John McGinty
but endorsed in return as John M. McGinty.
McMinn County Deed Book J 464 states that
Nancy Shelton, daughter of John Shelton is wife
or John McGinty)

MC GINTY, John to Polly Whitten   11 January 1854
Peter K. Whetsel, Security
m. 13 January by G. W. Cox, J. P.
Reference: County Archives: Marriage
Book D Page 78

MC GINTY, Madison to Martha Brock   5 March 1851
    m. 6 March by W. McKamy, J. P.
    Reference: Marriage Book D Page 39

MC GONEGAL, Floyd to Nancy Dorsey   23 April 1849
    Joseph Robinson, Security
    Reference: County Archives: Marriage
    Book D Page 14

MC GONEGAL, J. M. to Mary Ann Shults   12 September 1850
    m. 12 September by Joseph Robertson, M. G.
    Reference: Marriage Book D Page 32

MC GRAW - see GRAW

MC GRWE, John H. to Josephine Crittenden   26 January 1858
    m. 26 January by Neddy Newton, M. G.
    Reference: Marriage Book D Page 136

MC GREW, William T. to Mrs. Elizabeth A. Johnston   23 November 1864
    m. 23 November by P. M. Long, J. P.
    Reference: Marriage Book F Page 11

MC GUIR, Michael to Sarah O. Deatin   18 December 1844
    m. 18 December by W. H. Ballew, J. P.
    Reference: Marriage Book C Page 114

MC GUIRE, Jackson to Milly Craige   31 August 1847
    Reference: Marriage Book C Page 159

MC GUIRE, Robert to Mrs. Letitia M. McGuire   13 December 1865
    m. 14 December by J. S. Russell, M. G.
    Reference: Marriage Book F Page 32;
    McMinn Chancery Case # 179

MC GUIRE - see also MAGEER

MCINTURF, John to Nancy Graves   4 December 1857
    J. M. Patton, Security
    Reference: County Archives: Marriage
    Book D Page 132

MC INTURF - see also MC ENTURFF

MC KAMEY, Jasper N. to Mattie E. Cate   18 January 1868
    Reference: Marriage Book G Page 26

MC KEEHAN - see also MC GEHEN, MCGHEHAN

MC KEEHEN, Elbert S. to Sarah M. Canron   29 September 1852
    m. 30 September by H. Brandon, local Deacon
    Decatur Circuit
    Reference: Marriage Book D Page 57

MC KEEHEN, George H. to Malinda Cuningham   22 April 1851
    m. 22 April by William Burns, J. P.
    Reference: Marriage Book D Page 40

MC KEEHEN, James to Elisa B. Munrow   31 January 1867
    m. 31 January by J. January /Janeway?7, M. G.
    Reference: Marriage Book G Page 10

MC KEHAN, James to Mary Ann Cunningham   22 March 1853
    William Lasater, Security
    m. 22 March by James W. Shelton, M. G.
    Reference: County Archives: Marriage
    Book D Page 64

MC KELDIN, Andrew, merchant of Athens, to
   Miss Emily Brazelton, daughter of Gen.
   William Brazelton of New Market
   m. in New Market, 5 September 1839
   by Rev. John McCampbell, D. D.
   Reference: "Hiwassee Patriot"
   19 September 1839, Volume I, #28

MC KELDIN, W. B. to Mary Seahorn   22 March 1866
   m. 22 March by E. Rowley, M. G.
   Reference: Marriage Book F Page 41

MC KENY, Thos. to Susan Melton   6 September 1867
   William Sibsts, Security
   m. 5 September by E. Z. Williams, J. P.
   Reference: County Archives: Marriage
   Book G Page 20
   /Note: Date of issue on bond is Sept.
   6 and on Record Book as September 5/

MC KENZIE, Charles to Stacia Murry   21 February 1853
   F. M. Lusk, Security
   m. by J. Jenkins, J. P.
   Reference: County Archives: Marriage
   Book D Page 64

MC KENZIE - see also MC KINSEY

MC KEOWN, William M. to Clarissa Wilson   6 October 1852
   m. 6 October by Rev. D. Carpenter
   Reference: Marriage Book D Page 57

MC KINNEY, Frances E. to Miss Lucinda Melton   2 November 1865
   m. 2 November by E. Z. Williams, J. P.
   Reference: Marriage Book F Page 29

MC KINNEY, John to Mary Long   15 November 1838
   Reference: Marriage Book C Page 10

MC KINNEY, John to Martha Bookout   14 September 1865
   m. 14 September by E. Z. Williams, J. P.
   Reference: Marriage Book F Page 26

MC KINNEY - see also MC KENY

MC KINSEY, David A. to Sarah Mitchael   25 February 1870
   m. 27 February by G. H. Cate, M. G.
   Reference: Marriage Book G Page 59

MC KINSEY, Frank to Nannie Shell   15 October 1870
   m. 16 October by S. H. Cate, M. G.
   Reference: Marriage Book G Page 67

MC KINSEY, J. M. to Martha A. Fisher   10 January 1866
   m. 11 January by John N. Moore, M. G.
   Reference: Marriage Book F Page 35

MC KINSY, H. M. to Mrs. Elisey Warde   28 August 1867
   Jas. M. King, Security
   m. 28 August by John Davis, M. G.
   Reference: County Archives: Marriage
   Book G Page 20

MCKINZEY, Henry to Arvizena Wells   15 October 1856
   m. 15 October by James Parkerson, J. P.
   Reference: Marriage Book D Page 116

MC KNABE, Alcany to Rebecca Hunt   26 September 1850
    m. 26 September by A. John, M. G.
    Reference: Marriage Book D Page 32

MC LESTER, William W. to Amelia Metcalfe   31 August 1842
    m. 1 September by Robert Snead, M. G.
    Reference: Marriage Book C Page 61

MC LIN, William C. to Nancy A. Lasiter   19 June 1839
    m. 20 June by A. Barb, J. P.
    Reference: Marriage Book C Page 18

MC MAHAN, J. C. to Sarah C. Jackson   4 May 1864
    N. A. Cardwell, Security
    m. 5 May by C. J. Wright, M. G.
    Reference: County Archives: Marriage
    Book F Page 2

MC MILLAN, John to Pharibe Wassom   6 December 1854
    m. 6 December by I. S. Garrison, J. P.
    Reference: Marriage Book D Page 90

MC MILLAN, R. A. to Miss M. A. Isbell   3 September 1844
    m. 3 September by A. Slover, M. G.
    Reference: Marriage Book C Page 107

MC MILLEN, Madison to Luisa Eaton   30 August 1869
    m. 31 August by A. J. Shelton, J. P.
    Reference: Marriage Book G Page 49

MC MILLIAN, John to Susan Reneau   17 December 1843
    m. 17 December by Daniel McPhail, Esq.
    Reference: Marriage Book C Page 93;
    W. P. A.

MC MILLIAN, Joseph W. to Mrs. Sarah A. Ingram   23 January 1851
    m. 23 January by Henry Price, M. G.
    Reference: Marriage Book D Page 37

MC MILLIN, D. C. to Mary L. Campbell   24 May 1843
    m. 24 May by L. R. Morrison, V. D. M.
    Reference: Marriage Book C Page 79

MC MILLION, R. A. to Miss J. M. Isbell   9 July 1855
    m. 9 July by S. M. Haun, M. G.
    Reference: Marriage Book D Page 100

MC MINN, James to Matilda Brock   18 October 1842
    m. 20 October by M. C. Hawk, Minister of
    M. E. Church
    Reference: Marriage Book C Page 65

MC MINN, James M. to Sarah Haymes   29 August 1870
    m. 23 October by L. W. Crouch, M. G.
    Reference: Marriage Book G Page 64

MC MINN, Joseph to Syvilla Weir   17 November 1864
    m. 28 November by J. M. Miller, M. G.
    Reference: Marriage Book F Page 10

MC NABB, Henry Cay to Sinthy Morris Cline   20 December 1869
    m. 23 December by John Davis, M. G.
    Reference: Marriage Book G Page 55

MC NABB, Isaac H. to Jane M. Wear   11 September 1841
    m. 16 September by R. A. McAdoo, J. P.
    Reference: Marriage Book C Page 46

MC NABB, James to Levesta Mynatt   15 November 1853
    C. W. Mynatt, Security
    m. 15 November by James C. Bryan, J. P.
    Reference: County Archives: Marriage
    Book D Page 74

MC NABB, Matthew G. to Sarah Hunt   1 October 1846
    m. 1 October by William Rucker, J. P.
    Reference: Marriage Book C Page 144

MC NABB, Nathaniel to Serena Caroline McInturff   5 November 1839
    m. 12 November by A. Kinser, J. P.
    Reference: Marriage Book C Page 9;
    Marriage Book C Page 24

MC NELLY, Robert to Ann T. Fisher   26 October 1843
    m. 27 October by Justus Steed, J. P.
    Reference: Marriage Book C Page 89

MC NUTT, John A. to Sarah Stone   27 October 1841
    m. 28 October by R. W. Patty, M. G. E. C.
    Reference: Marriage Book C Page 48

M. C. OMBS, James to Sarah Shell   12 October 1855
    Reference: Marriage Book D Page 103

MC PHAIL, Birde to Mary Ann Cannady   25 July 1866
    m. 29 July by E. L. Minten, M. G.
    Reference: Marriage Book F Page 44

MCPHAIL, John P. to Mary J. Sharits   3 July 1858
    m. 4 July by D. Carpenter, M. G.
    Reference: Marriage Book D Page 142

MCPHAIL, William D. to Margaret A. Wattenbarger   24 September 1857
    m. 24 September by Hiel Buttram, M. G.
    Reference: Marriage Book D Page 130

MC PHAL, William D. to Mrs. Sarah J. Hughs   5 September 1867
    m. 5 September by G. W. Morton, J. P.
    Reference: Marriage Book G Page 20;
    McMinn Chancery Case Number 614

MC QUESTEAN, J. L. to Margraet Monroe   19 July 1865
    m. 20 July by E. L. Miller, J. P.
    Reference: Marriage Book F Page 21

MC REYNOLDS, D. L. (M) to Larorah (Laura) L. Rice   10 September 1867
    G. Shults, Security
    m. 25 September by Robert Snead, M. G.
    Reference: County Archives: Marriage
    Book G Page 20

MC ROBERTS, H. to Miss M. F. Smith   18 September 1868
    O. R. Dixon, Security
    m. 20 September by J. K. Stringfield, M. G.
    Reference: County Archives: Marriage
    Book G Page 36

MC ROY, John to Sarah Arnel (Arnell)   24 March 1829
    Curtus McRoy, Security
    Reference: County Archives

MC SPADDEN, Saml. of Monroe County to Charity   22 February 1844
    Cunningham
    m. 29 February
    Reference: Marriage Book C Page 98:
    "Knoxville Register" New Series # 174,
    Volume IV, 17 April 1844

MC SPADDEN, W. L. to Miss M. J. Porter　　　　　　　20 December 1866
　　m. 20 December by T. W. Bradshaw, M. G.
　　Reference: Marriage Book G Page 7

MCUISTIAN, Miles H. to Elizabeth Turk　　　　　　　25 November 1857
　　m. 25 December by E. L. Miller, J. P.
　　Reference: Marriage Book D Page 131

MCUISTIAN, Miles H. to Harriet A. Delia Smith　　　12 August 1858
　　m. 12 August by Johnathan Thomas, J. P.
　　Reference: Marriage Book D Page 144

MCUISTION, Holoway T. to Sarah Rabourn　　　　　　　19 August 1857
　　m. 19 August by Stephen Sharets, M. G.
　　Reference: Marriage Book D Page 128

MCULLEY, George M. to Jane M. Godard　　　　　　　　27 October 1858
　　m. 27 October by J. M. Miller, M. G.
　　Reference: Marriage Book D Page 149

MC VAY, Joseph to Nancy Edwards　　　　　　　　　　　11 May 1828
　　Abraham Gonce, Security
　　Reference: W. P. A.

MACACY, John to Nancy Chapman　　　　　　　　　　　　20 December 1842
　　m. 20 December by Wilson Chapman, M. G.
　　Reference: Marriage Book C Page 69

MADDEN, John H. to Lois Roberts　　　　　　　　　　　15 January 1856
　　m. 16 January by M. R. Wear, J. P.
　　Reference: Marriage Book D Page 107

MADDOX, Joseph to Leticia Green　　　　　　　　　　　21 October 1840
　　m. 22 October by Floyd McGonegal
　　Reference: Marriage Book C Page 33

MADDOX - see also MADOX, MADUX, MATTOCKS

MADISON - see also MATTERSON

MADURIUS, Hiram to Elizabeth Boon　　　　　　　　　　30 May 1839
　　m. 30 May by D. Cantrell, J. P.
　　Reference: Marriage Book C Page 17

MAGILL, James to Miss A. E. Lowery　　　　　　　　　14 October 1858
　　m. 14 October by Geo. A. Caldwell, M. G.
　　Reference: Marriage Book D Page 148

MAGILL - see also MC GILL

MAHAN, Robert L. to Miss Joriah Pierce　　　　　　　15 November 1841
　　m. 18 November by Edward Newton, M. G.
　　Reference: Marriage Book C Page 48

MAINER, Jobe to Delily E. Dennis　　　　　　　　　　28 September 1866
　　m. 30 September by S. W. Royston, J. P.
　　Reference: County Archives: Marriage
　　Book G Page 1

MAINOR, John F. to Nancy Dauny　　　　　　　　　　　25 December 1867
　　m. 26 December by L. H. Cate, M. G.
　　Reference: Marriage Book G Page 25

MAINOR, Joseph to Perlina Johnson　　　　　　　　　21 July 1868
　　m. 22 July by William Thompson, M. G.
　　Reference: Marriage Book G Page 33

MAIROT, Archibald to Sarah Lawson   10 August 1850
    m. 15 August by Rev. Dan Carpenter
    Reference: Marriage Book D Page 30

MAISAY, Renne to Rebeckah Lacy   1 June 1840
    m. 2 June by Jesse Locke, M. G.
    Reference: Marriage Book C Page 29

MALLER (MARLER), Allen to Elizabeth Snodgrass   11 April 1839
    Reference: Marriage Book C Page 16;
    Deed Book H Page 310

MALONE, Finley M. to Martha Jane Ward   4 February 1852
    m. 5 February by Nathaniel Barnett, M. G.
    Reference: Marriage Book D Page 47

MALONE, James to Eliza Mandagriff   24 January 1868
    m. 24 January by W. C. Owens, J. P.
    Reference: Marriage Book G Page 27

MALONE, John W. to Sarah Casteel   17 September 1839
    Reference: Marriage Book C Page 23

MALONE, Joseph to Mary Miller   16 December 1842
    m. 16 December by Samuel Wilson, J. P.
    Reference: Marriage Book C Page 69

MALONE, Joseph to Margret Casteel   7 January 1867
    m. 7 January by W. C. Owen, J. P.
    Reference: County Archives: Marriage
    Book G Page 11

MALONE, Michael to Jincy Meredith   15 September 1855
    m. 16 September by William H. Ballew, J. P.
    Reference: Marriage Book D Page 102

MALONE, Samuel to Malinda Cavet   22 August 1838
    m. 22 August by A. Barb, J. P.
    Reference: Marriage Book C Page 6

MALONE, William to Matilda Woods   20 November 1838
    Reference: Marriage Book C Page8

MALONE, William to Elizabeth Casteel   18 January 1841
    m. 19 January by John W. Barnett, J. P.
    Reference: Marriage Book C Page 36

MALONE, William to Hannah Hicks   7 January 1858
    m. 7 January by James Baker, J. P.
    Reference: Marriage Book D Page 134

MANARY, William to Zany Lower   17 November 1842
    m. 17 November by M. A. Cass, J. P.
    Reference: Marriage Book C Page 68

MANERY, John to Lucy Ann Floyd   29 October 1845
    m. 30 October by J. Jack, M. G.
    Reference: Marriage Book C Page 128

MANERY - see also MANNERY, MANRY

MANIS, Asberry to Matilda J. Manis   6 September 1852
    m. 9 September by G. W. Wallis, J. P.
    Reference: Marriage Book D Page 55

MANIS, James H. to Sarah E. Randolph   15 February 1866
    m. 15 February by Zachariah Rose, M. G.
    Reference: Marriage Book F Page 38

MANIS - see also MANUS

MANRY, Richard to Mary Jane Rue   28 May 1853
   George W. Lower, Security
   m. 29 May by J. Jack, M. G.
   Reference: Marriage Book D Page 66;
   County Archives

MANSEL, Walter B. to Mary Roberts   14 April 1841
   m. 15 April by William Stewart, M. G.
   Reference: Marriage Book C Page 40

MANSELL, John B. to Mary S. Newmon   14 February 1839
   Reference: Marriage Book C Page 14

MANTOOTH, Robert to Martha J. Burnett   25 September 1844
   Reference: Marriage Book C Page 109

MANUS, James to Sarah Vaughn   1 October 1864
   m. 2 October by E. Z. Williams, J. P.
   Reference: Marriage Book F Page 8

MANZE, John to Lydia Herrell   7 February 1858
   Reference: Marriage Book D Page 156

MAPLE, Perry to Elizabeth Webb   25 April 1839
   m. 25 April by John McGaughy, J. P.
   Reference: Marriage Book C Page 16

MAPLES, Absolem to Sarah Maples   4 April 1844
   m. 4 April by John Hoyl, M. G.
   Reference: Marriage Book C Page 100

MAPLES, Noah to Sarahann Greenway   18 March 1846
   m. 18 March by W. F. Forrest
   Reference: Marriage Book C Page 135

MAPLES, Peter to Elizabeth Henson   16 December 1846
   m. 16 December by Robert Gregory,
   Minister of Baptist Church
   Reference: Marriage Book C Page 149

MARCUM, Ransom A. to Jane Matthews   30 December 1843
   m. 31 December by M. D. Anderson, J. P.
   Reference: Marriage Book C Page 95

MARIOTT - see MAIROT, MAYRIOD

MARLER, Alfred T. to Mary S. Coats   31 January 1854
   Matthew Campbell, Security
   m. 2 February by A. John, M. G.
   Reference: County Archives: Marriage
   Book D Page 79

MARLER, Allen - see MALLER, Allen

MARLER, George W. to Sarah Moore   26 April 1853
   Henry P. Ward, Security
   m. 28 April by A. John, M. G.
   Reference: County Archives: Marriage
   Book D Page 65

MARLER, Jas. to Malinda Fields   25 March 1857
   m. 6 /sic7 March by H. Roberts, J. P.
   Reference: Marriage Book D Page 125

MARLER, Simpson to Olivia Hamrick   3 September 1853
    Henry P. Ward, Security
    m. 4 September by William R. Elder, M. G.
    Reference: County Archives: Marriage
    Book D Page 70

MARLEY (MARLER), James to Elizabeth Moore   26 January 1853
    Duke Ward, Security
    m. 27 January by Nathaniel Barnett, M. G.
    Reference: County Archives: Marriage
    Book D Page 63

MARNEY, Francis E. to Miss C. C. Brock   3 July 1858
    m. 4 July by John Jack, M. G.
    Reference: Marriage Book D Page 142

MARNEY, William to Sarah Ann F_____r   9 September 1869
    m. 9 September by A. Marshman, J. P.
    Reference: Marriage Book G Page 50

MARSHALL, David to Elizabeth Jane Hickman   18 January 1848
    m. 18 January by James Coffee, J. P.
    Reference: Marriage Book C Page 166

MARSHALL, Henry S. to Mary Elizabeth Smith   10 December 1849
    John N. Griffith, Security
    m. 13 December by J. Cuningham, M. G.
    Reference: County Archives: Marriage
    Book D Page 22

MARSHALL, John to Jane Branham   15 August 1838
    Reference: Marriage Book C Page 5

MARSHALL, John W. to Nancy Smith   18 October 1841
    m. 22 October by James Sewell, Minister
    Reference: Marriage Book C Page 48

MARSHALL, William C. to P. M. M. Hickman   6 August 1845
    Reference: Marriage Book C Page 124

MARTAIN, M. P. to Ellen M. McElhaney   25 September 1851
    m. 25 September by Wiliam H. Ballew, J. P.
    Reference: Marriage Book D Page 43

MARTIN, Benjamin M. to Manervy Jane Foster   9 July 1849
    Thos. R. White, Security
    m. 12 July by A. Barb, J. P.
    Reference: County Archives: Marriage
    Book D Page 16

MARTIN, Charles to Malinda Shelton   18 July 1839
    Reference: Marriage Book C Page 21

MARTIN, F. W. to Miss S. G. Lide   10 November 1858
    m. 11 November by J. A. Hyders, M. G.
    Reference: Marriage Book D Page 150

MARTIN, George W. to Mary Ann Brummut   7 December 1854
    Reference: Marriage Book D Page 90

MARTIN, James to Patsey Herald   12 November 1838
    m. 13 November by David F. Jamerson, J. P.
    Reference: Marriage Book C Page 10

MARTIN, Jas. P. to Nancy A. T. Cline   24 Ocotber 1868
    H. M. Kirby, Security
    m. 25 October 1869 /sic7 by Elihu Kelly, J.P.
    Reference: County Archives: Marriage
    Book G Page 39

MARTIN, Jerome N. to Emma J. Shults   21 June 1869
    m. 22 June by J. B. Kimbrough, M. G.
    Reference: Marriage Book G Page 47

MARTIN, John to Harriet E. Greenway   24 June 1847
    m. 24 June by W. F. Forrest, M. G.
    Reference: Marriage Book C Page 156

MARTIN, John S. to Lucy Greenwood   17 March 1838
    m. 18 April by Jas. Barnett, J. P.
    Reference: Marriage Book C Page 3

MARTIN, Robert E. to Eliza Blackburn   1 January 1866
    B. F. Green, Security
    m. 2 January 1866 by John N. Moore, M. G.
    Reference: County Archives: Marriage
    Book F Page 34
    /Note: Record Book has dates as given
    above but Bond has date as January 1, 1865,
    evidently in error7

MARTIN, Thomas to Polly A. Lawson   17 February 1844
    m. 18 February by E. P. Bloom, J. P.
    Reference: Marriage Book C Page 97

MARTIN, Thos. to Prussia Firestone   10 February 1859
    m. 15 February by Robert Cochran, J. P.
    Reference: Marriage Book D Page 156

MARTIN, Valentine to Miss Vashti Boon   31 October 1846
    m. 1 November by E. P. Bloom, J. P.
    Reference: Marriage Book C Page 146

MARTIN, William to Caroline Cline   5 March 1866
    John F. Slover, Security
    m. 6 March by Elihu Kelly, J. P.
    Reference: County Archives: Marriage
    Book F Page 38

MARTIN, William E. to Nancy W. Dodson   18 April 1843
    m. 20 April by Wilson Chapman, M. G.
    Reference: Marriage Book C Page 78

MARTIN, William G. to E. C. Liner
    m. 3 September by J. H. Scarbrough
    Reference: Marriage Book D Page 31

MASEY, Reuben to Sarah Wheeler   27 February 1850
    m. 27 February by J. D. Henley, J. P.
    Reference: Marriage Book D Page 26

MASINGALE, H. L. to Sarah E. Melton   21 October 1868
    m. 22 October by William H. Cate, M. G.
    Reference: Marriage Book G Page 38

MASON, Jesse to Nancy Norman   11 March 1843
    Reference: Marriage Book C Page 76

MASON, John J. to Amanda Pierce   9 February 1857
    m. 12 February by M. R. Ware, J. P.
    Reference: Marriage Book D Page 124

MASSENGALE, James C. to Elizabeth Morris   30 March 1844
    m. 31 March by E. P. Bloom, J. P.
    Reference: Marriage Book C Page 100

MASSEY - see also MAISAY, MASEY, MASSY

141

MASSINGALE, Husten T. to Martha Blankinship   5 June 1869
    m. 6 June by E. Z. Williams, J. P.
    Reference: Marriage Book G Page 47

MASSINGALE, James to Jane Watson   5 November 1853
    John Rudd, Security
    m. 6 November by J. W. Cox, J. P.
    Reference: County Archives: Marriage
    Book D Page 74

MASSINGALE, James H. to Elizabeth Blankenship   7 July 1864
    m. 7 July by A. R. Wilson, M. G.
    Reference: Marriage Book F Page 4

MASSY, John to Emily Hayes   11 January 1839
    m. 17 January by John Farmer, M. G.
    Reference: Marriage Book C Page 12

MATE, William P. to May Jane Parmly   25 May 1867
    m. 30 May by J. M. Backley, M. G.
    Reference: Marriage Book G Page 16

MATHENY, Samuel to Ester Lacy   10 August 1839
    Reference: Marriage Book C Page 21

MATHEWS, Aaron to Margaret Edgmon   27 February 1856
    m. 27 February by James Baker, J. P.
    Reference: Marriage Book D Page 108

MATHEWS, J. L. to Margret Thomas   27 April 1870
    m. 28 April by Stephen Hill, J. P.
    Reference: Marriage Book G Page 60

MATHEWS, William to Joysey Beavers   18 May 1839
    Reference: Marriage Book C Page 17

MATLOCK, C. L. to Ellen Hutsell   15 December 1870
    H. M. Rice, Security
    m. 19 December by J. S. Petty, M. G.
    Reference: County Archives: Marriage
    Book G Page 71

MATLOCK, Charles L. to Nancy L. Howard   9 November 1852
    L. Dodson, Security
    m. 9 November by W. C. Daily, M. G.
    Reference: Marriage Book D Page 58;
    County Archives

MATLOCK, Henry H. to L. E. Calloway   14 November 1870
    m. 14 November by J. B. Kimbrough, M. G.
    Reference: Marriage Book G Page 69

MATLOCK, Thos. B. to Miram Dixon   18 March 1857
    m. 24 March by John Scruggs, M. G.
    Reference: Marriage Book D Page 125

MATTERSON, William to Martha Stalions   18 December 1848
    m. 19 December by Joseph Cobbs, J. P.
    Reference: Marriage Book D Page 9

MAULDIN, James K. to Elizabeth Owens   27 September 1838
    m. 28 September by Thos. L. Hoyl, J. P.
    Reference: Marriage Book C Page 8

MAXWELL, Alexander to Martha J. Norvell   16 October 1850
    m. 18 October
    Reference: Marriage Book D Page 33;
    McMinn Chancery Case 45

MAXWELL, George W. to Sarah J. Ferguson   2 December 1865
    m. 3 December by Joseph Hamilton, J. P.
    Reference: Marriage Book F Page 32

MAXWELL, Robert N. to Eliza Jane Haney   16 August 1845
    m. 19 August by Samuel Wilson, J. P.
    Reference: Marriage Book C Page 124

MAXWELL, William to Josephine Elmore   7 November 1867
    m. 7 November by Jas. Hamilton, J. P.
    Reference: Marriage Book G Page 22

MAYES, Henry of Sweetwater to Mrs. Adaline   26 April 1860
    Treadway of Rome, Georgia
    m. 26 April 1860 at residence of
    William Burns by Rev. G. A. Caldwell
    Reference: Athens Post Volume XII, #606,
    4 May 1860

MAYFIELD, Ezekiel H. to Susan C. Lattimore   5 February 1866
    John Harrell, Security
    m. 8 February by Jacob Brillhart, M. G.
    Reference: County Archives: Marriage
    Book F Page 37

MAYFIELD, Jno. to Jane Poe   1 August 1844
    m. 1 August by William Walsh, J. P.
    Reference: Marriage Book C Page 106

MAYFIELD, John G. to Mary Elizabeth Cobbs   17 January 1855
    m. 18 December /sic/ 1855 by T. L. Hoyl, M.G.
    Reference: Marriage Book D Page 93

MAYFIELD, L. H. to Martha Rice   30 November 1857
    m. 3 December by J. Atkens, M. G.
    Reference: Marriage Book D Page 132

MAYFIELD, Thomas B. to Sarah Jane Rudd   12 September 1847
    Reference: Marriage Book C Page 160

MAYFIELD, Williams to Narcissa Hoyl   17 December 1850
    Reference: Marriage Book D Page 35

MAYFIELD - see also MOFIELD

MAYNOR, Fournis F. to Nancy M. Cantrell   20 July 1841
    m. 27 July by Rev. Joseph Peeler
    Reference: Marriage Book C Page 43

MAYNOR - see also MAINER

MEADOWS, James L. to Susan Carter   21 August 1849
    G. W. Wallis, Security
    m. 23 August by David F. Jamison, J. P.
    Reference: County Archives: Marriage
    Book D Page 17

MEHANEY, William P. to Elizabeth Hicks   10 December 1855
    m. 10 December by Morgan Miller, J. P.
    Reference: Marriage Book D Page 105

MELTON, Alfred to Jane Barker   25 October 1856
    m. 2 November by J. M. Melton, J. P.
    Reference: Marriage Book D Page 117

MELTON, Calloway to Eliza Tucker   30 November 1844
    m. 20 December by William Rucker, J. P.
    Reference: Marriage Book C Page 113

MELTON, Elisha to Rebecca M. Cate
   m. 5 August by Jas. Douglass, M. G.
   Reference: Marriage Book C Page 158
                5 August 1847

MELTON, Elisha to Anis Crabtree
   m. 30 August by Samuel Snoddy, J. P.
   Reference: Marriage Book D Page 4
                29 August 1848

MELTON, George W. to Eliza J. P. Rogers
   Micajah M. Ford, Security
   m. 14 December by A. Swafford, J. P.
   Reference: County Archives: Marriage
   Book D Page 75
                2 December 1853

MELTON, James to Adaline Bunch
   m. 13 February by S. M. Thomas, J. P.
   Reference: Marriage Book G Page 10
                6 February 1867

MELTON, James A. to Thursa A. Barker
   m. 9 December by E. Z. Williams, J. P.
   Reference: Marriage Book G Page 55
                8 December 1869

MELTON, Jesse to Nancy Erskin
   m. 17 September by Hiram Ingram, M. G.
   Reference: Marriage Book C Page 46
           16 September 1841

MELTON, Jessy to May E. Ham____
   m. 11 February by C. Cate, J. P.
   Reference: Marriage Book G Page 11
              11 February 1867

MELTON, John to Nancy C. Kelley
   m. 22 December by Morgan Miller, J. P.
   Reference: Marriage Book F Page 12
             21 December 1864

MELTON, John to Sarah Atchley
   m. 19 August by J. W. L. Fore, M. G.
   Reference: Marriage Book G Page 49
             13 August 1869

MELTON, Nathan to Susannah Melton
   m. 4 June by John Hays, M. G.
   Reference: Marriage Book C Page 139
                4 June 1846

MELTON, Peter to Nancy E. McKinney
   m. 24 December by E. Z. Williams, J. P.
   Reference: Marriage Book F Page 33
           23 December 1865

MELTON, Reuben to Elizabeth Jane Smith
   m. 22 October by Samuel Snoddy, J. P.
   Reference: Marriage Book C Page 161
           21 October 1847

MELTON, Robert to Elisabeth Eliott
   Reference: Marriage Book C Page 163
           24 November 1847

MELTON, Stephen J. to Adaline Walker
   James H. Melton, Security
   Reference: County Archives: Marriage
   Book D Page 69
              11 August 1853

MELTON, Taylor to Lucinda Glaze
   m. 20 October by E. Z. Williams, J. P.
   Reference: Marriage Book G Page 38
           20 October 1868

MELTON, Thomas to Mrs. Margret Gradey
   m. 27 April by J. D. Henly, J. P.
   Reference: Marriage Book D Page 27
              27 April 1850

MELTON, William to Rebecca Hampton   14 March 1849
    J. W. Liner, Security
    m. 14 March by A. Swafford, J. P.
    Reference: County Archives: Marriage
    Book D Page 13

MELTON, William to Elizia Owens   21 October 1869
    m. 21 October by G. M. Bloom, J. P.
    Reference: Marriage Book G Page 52

MELTON, Wright to Nancy Crittenden   24 January 1854
    m. 24 January by James C. Bryan
    Reference: Marriage Book D Page 78

MESERMAN or MESSIMON, Thomas to Miss A. E.   4 February 1846
    Torbert or Miss E. S. Torbett
    m. 5 February by Robert Gregory,
    Minister of Baptist Church
    Reference: Marriage Book C Page 131;
    Marriage Book C Page 133
    /Note: Page 131 has Thos. Meserman to
    Miss A. E. Torbert and page 133 has
    Thomas Messimon to Miss E. S. Torbett
    and m. as given above7

METCALF, Thomas to Martha Smith   15 September 1838
    Reference: Marriage Book C Page 7

MICHAEL, Alexander to Martha J. Strain   14 December 1854
    m. 17 December by J. N. Blackburn, M. G.
    Reference: Marriage Book D Page 91

MICHAEL, Frederick to Charlotte R. Courtney   14 December 1846
    m. 16 December by J. M. Courtney, M. G.
    Reference: Marriage Book C Page 148

MICHAELS, John to Martha Wolff   26 September 1849
    m. 27 September /sic7 1850 by Wm. McKamy, J.P.
    Reference: Marriage Book D Page 19

MIDDLE /MIDDLETON7, John G. to Martha Wilson   20 December 1839
    m. 24 December by A. Barb, J. P.
    Reference: Marriage Book C Page 19

MIDDLETON, H. L. to Mary Wilson   23 September 1839
    m. 26 September by A. Barb, J. P.
    Reference: Marriage Book C Page 23

MIERS, F. J. to Elizabeth Newton   9 March 1868
    m. 10 March by F. A. Dixon, J. P.
    Reference: Marriage Book G Page 28

MILLER, Alexander A. to Elizabeth J. Maples   7 November 1865
    m. 9 November by George M. Hutsell, J. P.
    Reference: Marriage Book F Page 30

MILLER, Elisha to Elizabeth McCully   4 December 1839
    Reference: Marriage Book C Page 19

MILLER, Enoch to Sophrona Adaline Wilson   10 August 1848
    Reference: Marriage Book D Page 4

MILLER, J. B. to Mary Smith   27 November 1845
    m. 27 November by Green L. Reynolds, J. P.
    Reference: Marriage Book C Page 129

MILLER, Jackson to Manada Ellis   3 January 1849
    m. 9 January by A. A. Mathies, M. G.
    Reference: Marriage Book D Page 10;
    "Knoxville Register" Volume 9, #420,
    17 January 1849

MILLER, Jacob L. to Edny Fair   2 October 1843
    m. 5 October by T. S. Rice, J. P.
    Reference: Marriage Book C Page 86

MILLER, James to Mrs. Mary Allen   4 April 1866
    m. 5 April by F. A. Dixon, J. P.
    Reference: Marriage Book F Page 40

MILLER, James A. to Elmira A. Shearer   10 November 1866
    m. 11 November by G. M. Eloom, J. P.
    Reference: County Archives: Marriage
    Book G Page 4

MILLER, James A. to Susan Jackson   25 January 1868
    Joseph Miller, Security
    m. 26 January by G. M. Hutsell, J. P.
    Reference: County Archives: Marriage
    Book G Page 27

MILLER, John to Eliza Carter   8 January 1840
    Reference: Marriage Book C Page 20

MILLER, John to Manila Dobbs   1 December 1841
    m. 2 December by Joseph Minzes, J. P.
    Reference: Marriage Book C Page 49

MILLER, John to Lydia Morgan   19 October 1855
    Reference: Marriage Book D Page 104

MILLER, John to Mandy Green   13 November 1867
    Joshua Willson, Security
    m. 13 November by G. M. Hutsell, J. P.
    Reference: County Archives: Marriage
    Book G Page 22

MILLER, John F. to Mary A. Miller   26 September 1857
    Joshua Wilson, Security
    m. 27 September by H. M. Roberts, J. P.
    Reference: County Archives: Marriage
    Book D Page 130

MILLER, John W. to Nancy McDaniel   2 February 1848
    m. 8 February by T. S. Rice, J. P.
    Reference: Marriage Book C Page 167

MILLER, Luke L. to Jane C. Vinson   3 September 1846
    m. 3 September by G. C. Metcalf, Evt.
    Reference: Marriage Book C Page 143

MILLER, N. B. to Harriate Duff   23 January 1869
    m. 24 January by Charles Cate, J. P.
    Reference: Marriage Book G Page 43

MILLER, Robert to Letty McGuire   21 May 1842
    m. 22 May by R. A. McAdoo, J. P.
    Reference: Marriage Book C Page 58

MILLER, Russell to Jane Wilson   15 January 1850
    Reference: Marriage Book D Page 24

MILLER, William to Mary Lanb   23 May 1839
    Reference: Marriage Book C Page 17

MILLER, William to Nancy Vincent   30 November 1865
   A. J. Mathis, Security
   m. 30 November by S. W. Royston, J. P.
   Reference: County Archives: Marriage
   Book F Page 31

MILLER, William W. to Elizabeth Belcher   24 October 1849
   Henry M. Davis, Security
   m. 24 October by R. A. McAdoo, J. P.
   Reference: County Archives: Marriage
   Book D Page 20

MILLION, A. J. to Martha Lawson   18 April 1864
   m. 19 April by Dan Carpenter, M. G.
   Reference: Marriage Book F Page 1

MILLION, Frances N. to Elizabeth Hart   24 January 1855
   m. 25 January by J. B. Waller, M. G.
   Reference: Marriage Book D Page 93

MILLION, George W. to Nancy Robison   13 February 1841
   m. 14 February by Jonathan Thomas, J. P.
   Reference: Marriage Book C Page 38

MILLS, Charles H. to Sarah C. Brown   6 September 1849
   Thos. W. Barter and William W. Barter, Sec.
   m. 6 September by Thos. H. Small, M. G.
   Reference: County Archives: Marriage
   Book D Page 18

MINSEY, John M. to Mary McElhaney   21 October 1851
   m. 21 October by William H. Ballew, J. P.
   Reference: Marriage Book D Page 45

MINZES, Ewin S. to Sophrona Buttram   3 January 1843
   m. 8 January by Heil Buttram, P. of Gospel
   Reference: Marriage Book C Page 70

MINZES - see also MINS, MINSEY, MANZE

MISEMER, William B. to Mary Ann Torbett   5 November 1850
   m. 6 November by J. Cunningham, M. G.
   Reference: Marriage Book D Page 34

MIZE, Daniel W. to Sarah J. Bean   28 July 1856
   m. 5 August by Joseph Peeler, M. G.
   Reference: Marriage Book D Page 112

MIZE, Hearvy Jackson to Elizabeth Jane Cartright   19 December 1849
   m. 19 December by J. Jack, M. G.
   Reference: Marriage Book D Page 23

MIZE, Henery D. to Mary Elizabeth Stansbury   2 November 1848
   Isaac N. Ryan, Security
   m. 2 November by M. A. Cass, M. G.
   Reference: County Archives: Marriage
   Book D Page 7

MIZELL, James to Barzilla Peters   29 August 1844
   Reference: Marriage Book C Page 107

MIZELL, Samuel to Synthia Stephenson   3 January 1850
   m. 3 January by Samuel Snoddy, J. P.
   Reference: Marriage Book D Page 24

MIZELL, Samuel to Lamira Ann Barker   26 March 1854
   P. W. Brewer, Security
   Reference: Marriage Book D Page 82;
   County Archives

MIZER, Isaac to Nancy Cunningham   30 January 1838
    Reference: Marriage Book C Page 2

MIZER, John to Mrs. Susannah Lewis   5 November 1840
    m. 5 October /sic/ by C. W. Rice, J. P.
    Reference: Marriage Book C Page 33

MONGER, John E. to Elizabeth Bond   28 July 1842
    m. 28 July by Samuel Wilson, J. P.
    Reference: Marriage Book C Page 59

MONGER, Joseph to Jackabena Southard   14 September 1843
    m. 14 September by Justus Steed, J. P.
    Reference: Marriage Book C Page 85

MONROE, B. to Elizabeth Smith   23 December 1870
    m. 25 December by Joseph Neil, J. P.
    Reference: Marriage Book G Page 71

MONROE, George to Eliza Pearson   25 April 1840
    m. 25 April by David F. Jameson, J. P.
    Reference: Marriage Book C Page 29

MONROE, George to Margart Simpson   2 July 1855
    m. 15 July by Robert Gregory, M. G.
    Reference: Marriage Book D Page 100

MONROE, James to Miss C. M. Hughes   1 August 1851
    m. 3 August by G. W. Wallis, J. P.
    Reference: Marriage Book D Page 41

MONROE, James to Miss Willer M. Dixon   29 April 1858
    m. 29 April by J. W. Gibson, J. P.
    Reference: Marriage Book D Page 140

MONROE, Robert to Mary Fields   12 May 1828
    Robert Dugan, Security
    Reference: County Archives

MONROE - see also MUNROW

MOON, John to Eliza L. Hoback   25 May 1865
    m. 25 May by Jas. Baker, J. P.
    Reference: Marriage Book F Page 18

MOORE, Alexander to Elizabeth Armstrong   28 December 1864
    m. 29 December by E. N. Sawtell, M. G.
    Reference: Marriage Book F Page 13

MOORE, Allen to Miss Leantine Dugan   5 November 1857
    m. 5 November by Joseph Neil, J. P.
    Reference: Marriage Book D Page 131;
    County Archives

MOORE, Allen to Jane Small   27 December 1870
    G. S. Manis, Security
    m. 29 December by D. McReynolds, M. G.
    Reference: County Archives: Marriage
    Book G Page 71

MOORE, Archabald R. to Martha Cowden   8 March 1854
    J. N. McCoy, Security
    m. 8 March by William H. Ballew, J. P.
    Reference: Marriage Book D Page 81;
    County Archives

MOORE, Cham to Mary Cantrell   (4) 6 June 1839
   m. 6 June by John Walker, M. G.
   Reference: Marriage Book C Page 18;
   Marriage Book C Page 27

MOORE, G. W. to Mary J. Wamack   26 October 1859
   m. 27 October by A. J. Mathis, M. G.
   Reference: County Archives
   Note: There is no entry on the
   Marriage Books for this license.

MOORE, George W. to Mary Goss   1 December 1842
   m. 1 December by G. W. Wallace
   Reference: Marriage Book C Page 68

MOORE, George W. to Rebeckah Jane Feilds   30 August 1852
   m. 31 August by Hiel Buttram, M. G.
   Reference: Marriage Book D Page 55

MOORE, H. L. to Miss N. C. Hamilton   21 December 1865
   m. 21 December by J. C. Barb, M. G.
   Reference: Marriage Book F Page 33

MOORE, Henry to Ann Fyke   15 January 1840
   Reference: Marriage Book C Page 27

MOORE, Henry to Mary Haze   14 March 1857
   m. 17 March by J. A. Rolls, J. P.
   Reference: Marriage Book D Page 124

MOORE, Jacob to Arrena Newton   10 July 1844
   Reference: Marriage Book C Page 104

MOORE, James to Julia A. Mitchell   27 January 1857
   m. 27 January by Jas. Baker, J. P.
   Reference: Marriage Book D Page 123

MOORE, Martin B. to Mrs. Martha C. Keith   23 April 1864
   Jno. R. Tuell, Security
   m. 24 April by J. R. Fryar, M. G.
   Reference: Marriage Book F Page 2;
   County Archives

MOORE, Nimrod to Cassa Davis   26 August 1826
   Joseph Dunn, Security
   Reference: W. P. A.

MOORE, Thomas P. to Margaret T. Lipscomb   21 October 1840
   m. 21 October by L. R. Morrison, V. D. M.
   Reference: Marriage Book C Page 32;
   Marriage Book C Page 33

MOORE, William to Katharine Armstrong   5 January 1854
   m. 5 January by Robt. Gregory, M. G.
   Reference: Marriage Book D Page 77

MORE, G. W. to Mary E. Duff   16 March 1867
   m. 17 March by J. S. Russell, M. G.
   Reference: Marriage Book G Page 12

MORE, Jamez to Catharine Hall   8 August 1846
   m. 8 August by R. A. McAdoo, J. P.
   Reference: Marriage Book C Page 141

MORE (MOORE), William Sen. to Margaret Elizabeth   15 January 1857
    Eadens (Eaton)
    P. H. George, Security
    Reference: County Archives: Marriage Book
    D Page 123: McMinn Chancery Case Number 267
    Note: There was no marriage

MORELAND, James A. to Margaret Romack   19 October 1848
    m. 19 October by T. S. Rice, J. P.
    Reference: Marriage Book D Page 6

MORELOCK, Alexander to Mrs. Giminey Lewis   18 September 1866
    m. 19 September 1867 /sic7 by L. W. Crouch,M.G.
    Reference: Marriage Book F Page 47

MORGAN, David to Marthy Jane Nickelson   28 July 1866
    James Morgan, Security
    m. 28 July by L. W. Crouch, M. G.
    Reference: Marriage Book F Page 45;
    County Archives

MORGAN, George W. to Martha K. Mayo   26 October 1848
    m. 26 October by Hillery Patrick, M. G.
    Reference: Marriage Book D Page 6

MORGAN, Harvey to Polly Kinchelo   18 August 1845
    James Morgan, Security
    m. 25 August by Rev. A. Slover
    Reference: County Archives: Marriage
    Book C Page 124: "Knoxville Register"
    Volume 5, Number 246, 3 September 1845

MORGAN, Henry to Caroline Brock   10 September 1849
    T. J. Pleasant, Security
    m. 11 September by William R. Walker, J. P.
    Reference: County Archives: Marriage
    Book D Page 18

MORGAN, James to Jane Liner   7 December 1866
    Reference: Marriage Book G Page 6

MORGAN, John to Polly Abbot   28 April 1849
    James Walker, Security
    m. 29 April by W. R. Walker, J. P.
    Reference: Marriage Book D Page 14;
    County Archives

MORGAN, John to Sarah Potter   26 August 1865
    m. 27 August by L. W. Crouch, M. G.
    Reference: Marriage Book F Page 24

MORGAN, John R. to Polly Stainer   23 July 1849
    S. S. Morgan, Security
    m. by William R. Walker, J. P.
    Reference: Marriage Book D Page 16;
    County Archives

MORGAN, Mordick (Mordecai) H. to Susannah   16 November 1853
    (Susan) H. Elder
    Henry P. Ward, Security
    m. 17 November by J. Whiteside, M. G.
    Reference: Marriage Book D Page 74;
    County Archives

MORGAN, Rufus to Laura Britt   25 June 1870
    m. 25 June by C. C. Witt, J. P.
    Reference: Marriage Book G Page 61

MORGAN, Samuel to Margaret Vinzant   26 December 1829
   Ezekiel Vansant, Security
   Reference: County Archives

MORGAN, Samuel to Marthia L. Harmon   21 December 1868
   Reference: Marriage Book G Page 41

MORGAN, Silas to Christen Moore   23 December 1843
   Reference: W. P. A.
   /Note: Page 94 in Book C is torn_7

MORGAN, Silas to Mahaly Givins   26 November 1867
   H. Haney, Security
   Reference: County Archives: Marriage
   Book G Page 23

MORGAN, Silas M. to Mary Walker   7 July 1865
   m. 9 July by L. W. Crouch, M. G.
   Reference: Marriage Book F Page 20

MORGAN, Thomas to Adeline Potter   10 February 1866
   Jesse Walker, Security
   m. 11 February by S. M. Thomas
   Reference: County Archives: Marriage
   Book F Page 37

MORGAN, Timothy to Harriate Pressely   11 September 1868
   Samuel K. Morgan, Security
   m. 13 September by Levi Fitzgerald, M. G.
   Reference: County Archives: Marriage
   Book G Page 36

MORGAN, W. L. to Miss Lurana Sivils   22 October 1870
   m. 30 October by Stephen Hill, J. P.
   Reference: Marriage Book G Page 68

MORGAN, William M. to Mary Ann Shuemake 16 September 1853
   George W. Marler, Security
   m. 17 September by J. Whiteside, M. G.
   Reference: County Archives: Marriage
   Book D Page 71

MORGAN, William R. to Carline Boring   8 May 1846
   m. 10 May by Thomas J. Russel,
   Minister of United Baptist Church
   Reference: Marriage Book C Page 138

MORGAN, William S. to Mary J. Jones   5 September 1856
   m. 7 September 1857 /sic_7 by M. R. Wear,J.P.
   Reference: Marriage Book D Page 113

MORLEY, William G. to Mary E. Jones   6 July 1865
   m. 6 July by L. W. Crouch, M. G.
   Reference: Marriage Book F Page 20

MORRIS, Alfred W. to Narcissa Trim   28 November 1850
   m. 28 November by G. W. Wallis, J. P.
   Reference: Marriage Book D Page 34

MORRIS, Geo. W. to Mary C. Fitzgerald   6 January 1851
   m. 7 January by Robert _____, M. G.
   Reference: Marriage Book D Page 36

MORRIS, Isaac to Susan Peters   20 October 1846
   m. 20 October by John Hoyl, M. G.
   Reference: Marriage Book C Page 145

MORRIS, J. C. to Mary Cate   14 September 1867
    H. L. Massingale, Security
    m. 16 September by W. H. Cate, M. G.
    Reference: County Archives: Marriage
    Book G Page 20

MORRIS, James C. to Elin F. McElrath   1 October 1867
    O. S. Morgan, Security
    Reference: County Archives: Marriage
    Book G Page 21

MORRIS, Jesse K. to Rebecca Wells   6 September 1864
    N. G. Peters, Security
    m. 7 September by Uriah Payne, M. G.
    Reference: Marriage Book F Page 6:
    County Archives

MORRIS, R. H. to Amy A. Hughes   24 December 1864
    m. 25 December by Stephen Sharits, M. G.
    Reference: Marriage Book F Page 12

MORRIS, Thomas to Julia Amanda Wells   4 December 1848
    m. 5 December by J. C. Carlock, J. P.
    Reference: Marriage Book D Page 8

MORROW, H. J. to Lydiann Forister   3 November 1858
    m. 3 November by H. M. Roberts, J. P.
    Reference: Marriage Book D Page 150

MORROW, Robert M. to Martha E. Myers   2 August 1865
    m. 3 August
    Reference: Marriage Book F Page 22

MORTON, Joseph to Elizabeth Long   4 April 1828
    James Lonley, Security
    Reference: W. P. A.

MORTON - see also MARTON, MOTEN

MOSES, John H. to Katharine Huse   3 December 1840
    Reference: Marriage Book C Page 34

MOSS, Bartly H. to Eliza G. Martin   1 October 1853
    Lawrence Brock, Security
    m. 2 October by J. Jack, M. G.
    Reference: County Archives: Marriage
    Book D Page 71

MOSS, Hardy to Adaline Reatherford   9 May 1857
    m. 10 May by H. J. Brock, J. P.
    Reference: Marriage Book D Page 126

MOSS, John R. to Nancy E. Forgey   29 January 1860
    m. 29 January by O. M. Liner, J. P.
    Reference: Marriage Book E Page 16

MOSS, Warren to Patsy Cloud   14 March 1844
    m. 14 March by C. Sanders, M. G.
    Reference: Marriage Book C Page 99

MOSS, Warren D. to Elizabeth Cloud   5 November 1850
    m. 8 November
    Reference: Marriage Book D Page 34

MOSS, William to Elizabeth Lower   20 January 1848
    m. 20 January by J. Jack, M. G.
    Reference: Marriage Book C Page 166

MOTEN, George to Martha Haynes
    m. 10 December by B. Floyd Nuckles, M. G.
    Reference: Marriage Book G Page 55
              10 December 1869

MULVANY, Mark to Eliza Ann Davis
    m. 6 February by Jonathan Thomas, J. P.
    Reference: Marriage Book C Page 20
              3 February 1840

MUNROW, S. M. to Matildey McKichin
    m. 18 September by S. Sharits, M. G.
    Reference: Marriage Book F Page 47
           18 September 1866

MURPHEY, John N. to Clarinda A. White
    m. 10 July by J. Davis, M. G.
    Reference: Marriage Book G Page 47
                9 July 1869

MURPHY, Jefferson D. to Susan Orten
    Reference: Marriage Book C Page 87
             13 October 1843

MURPHY, John to Mary Mahan
    m. by A. Fitzgerald, M. G.
    Reference: Marriage Book D Page 78
            25 January 1854

MURPHY, Robert to Rebecca Jane Shields
    Edmund Ramsey, Security
    Reference: County Archives
            7 December 1829

MURRAY, John H. to Rebecca Grigsby
    m. 8 December 1855 /sic7 by Hugh P. Holland,M.G.
    Reference: Marriage Book D Page 90
            8 December 1854

MURRAY, Samuel R. to Mary R. Foster
    9 November by Robert Snead, M. G.
    Reference: Marriage Book F Page 29
           2 November 1865

MURRELL, Major George M. to Athens to
    Minerva Ross, daughter of Lewis Ross
    of Cherokee Agency
    m. 7 July 1834
    Reference: "Knoxville Register" Volume 19,
    Number 938, 16 July 1834

MURRELL, Onslow G. to Mrs. Parthena Hickel
    m. by J. W. Miller, M. G.
    Reference: Marriage Book D Page 28
                /May 1850
                not dated7

MURRY, C. C. to Miss M. E. Stallcup
    Reference: Marriage Book G Page 19
           28 August 1867

MYERS, John to Mary J. Snoddy
    m. 6 October by John Rogers, J. P.
    Reference: Marriage Book C Page 47
            5 October 1841

MYERS, M. L. to Nancy L. C. Bowerman
    m. 7 January by John Jenkins, J. P.
    Reference: Marriage Book C Page 116
           7 January 1845

MYERS - see also MIERS, MIRES, MYRES

MYRES, Franklin to Malinda Davis
    Thos. J. Ford, Security
    Reference: County Archives: Marriage
    Book G Page 70
          13 December 1870

MYRES, James to Sarah C. Snoddy
    m. 15 January by J. Jenkins, J. P.
    Reference: Marriage Book C Page 165
           14 January 1848

NANCE, Payton T. to Polly Ann Womack   2 May 1848
    m. 3 May by Thos. B. Weller, M. G.
    Reference: W. P. A.
    Note: Page missing in Marriage Book

NAPIER, Thomas N. to Mary Shelton   14 January 1835
    Robert K. Hamilton, Security
    Reference: W. P. A.

NATION - see also NACION

NATIONS, William to Nancy Higdon   16 December 1846
    m. 17 December by C. Sanders, M. G.
    Reference: Marriage Book C Page 149

NEAL, Abraham B. to Rebecca Pickins   11 February 1829
    Reece Pickins, Security
    Reference: W. P. A.

NEAL, Joseph O. to Sarah Teague   20 August 1868
    Reference: Marriage Book G Page 34

NEAL - see also NAILE, NEEL, NEIL, NEILL, NIEL

NEATHERLAND, J. P. to Miss Francis Midelton   9 October 1869
    m. 9 October by J. B. Kimbrough, M. G.
    Reference: Marriage Book G Page 52

NEELY, Dr. William H. to Elizabeth McPherson   4 September 1851
    Reference: Marriage Book D Page 42

NEET, Philip to Eliza J. Marcum   13 April 1858
    m. 13 April by George A. Caldwell, M. G.
    Reference: Marriage Book D Page 138

NEIL, John to Harriet Cate   22 February 1856
    m. 22 February by William R. Elder, M. G.
    Reference: Marriage Book D Page 108

NEIL, John R. to Eleanor J. Wallis   16 March 1848
    Reference: W. P. A.
    Note: Page missing in Marriage Book

NEIL, Joseph to Elizabeth Glaize   15 August 1849
    m. 16 August by William C. Lee, M. G.
    Reference: Marriage Book D Page 17

NEIL - see also NAILE, NEAL, NEEL, NEILL, NIEL

NEILL, C. E. to Miss M. M. Suthard   28 December 1844
    m. 29 December by M. D. Anderson, J. P.
    Reference: Marriage Book C Page 115

NEILL, Hamilton to Nancy Ann Burnet   11 December 1854
    m. 11 December by William R. Elder, M. G.
    Reference: Marriage Book D Page 90

NEILL, James, Senr. to Elizabeth J. Johnston   26 July 1842
    m. 26 July by Nathan Harrison, Minister M. E.
    Church
    Reference: Marriage Book C Page 59

NEILL, William to Katharine Dodson   25 February 1839
    m. 26 February by L. R. Morrison, V. D. M.
    Reference: Marriage Book C Page 15

NELSON, Arthur to Synthy Robison   14 December 1838
    m. 15 December by Thos. L. Hoyl, J. P.
    Reference: Marriage Book C Page 11

NELSON, Henry to Jane Bailey   17 September 1840
    m. 17 September by T. L. Hoyl, J. P.
    Reference: Marriage Book C Page 32

NELSON, M. to Rebecca A. McGaughey   25 April 1855
    m. 25 April by George A. Caldwell, M. G.
    Reference: Marriage Book D Page 97

NETHERLAND - see also NEATHERLAND

NEWMAN, Arthur to Louisa Reneau   27 January 1844
    m. 28 January by B. E. Blain, J. P.
    Reference: Marriage Book C Page 96

NEWMAN, Clinton B. to Clementine Cantrell   9 December 1846
    m. 9 December by W. Chapman, M. G.
    Reference: Marriage Book C Page 148

NEWMAN, Jacob P. to L. M. Fetzl   26 September 1851
    m. 26 September by Nathaniel Barnet, M. G.
    Reference: Marriage Book D Page 43

NEWMAN, John to Martha A. Keiker   3 January 1856
    m. 3 January by Daniel McPhail, J. P.
    Reference: Marriage Book D Page 106

NEWMAN, John C. to Sydney Ann Myers   5 October 1854
    Reference: Marriage Book D Page 88

NEWMAN, John D. to Sarah Holland   5 January 1870
    m. 6 January by William Thompson, M. G.
    Reference: Marriage Book G Page 57

NEWMAN, John L. to Catharine St. John   28 December 1841
    m. 30 December by Robert Gregory,
    Minister of Baptist Church
    Reference: Marriage Book C Page 51

NEWMAN, Robert to Ellen Scarbrough   10 December 1868
    Reference: Marriage Book G Page 40

NEWMAN, Robert M. to Sarah E. Jones   15 October 1844
    m. 16 October by Green L. Reynolds, J. P.
    Reference: Marriage Book C Page 110

NEWMAN, Samuel to Malinda Baine   25 February 1859
    m. 27 February by William Newman, J. P.
    Reference: Marriage Book D Page 157

NEWMAN, Tayler M. to Miss Frances E. Blevins   15 October 1868
    m. 15 October by D. W. Beaver, M. G.
    Reference: Marriage Book G Page 38

NEWMAN, Thomas J. to Mary J. Day   22 January 1867
    m. 22 January by N. B. Goforth, M. G.
    Reference: Marriage Book G Page 9;
    County Archives

NEWTON, E. M. to Rebecca M. Allison   6 May 1845
    m. 11 May by William Newton, M. G.
    Reference: Marriage Book C Page 120

NEWTON, Edward to Mary D. Rogers   10 October 1863
    m. 15 October by Calvin Denton, M. G.
    Reference: Marriage Book E Page 2

NEWTON, G. W. to Mary L. Wilson   2 February 1848
   m. 3 February by Ed Newton, M. G.
   Reference: Marriage Book C Page 167

NEWTON, James A. to Scynthia C. Allison   23 January 1842
   m. 27 January by William F. Forest, M. G.
   Reference: Marriage Book C Page 52

NEWTON, Jasper to Percilia Crabtree   17 September 1851
   Reference: Marriage Book D Page 43

NEWTON, Thomas to Eliza Morris   30 August 1838
   m. 6 September by John Walker, M. G.
   Reference: Marriage Book C Page 6

NEWTON, William to Jane L. Smith   27 March 1841
   m. 27 March by Henry M. Dodson, M. G.
   Reference: Marriage Book C Page 40

NEWTON, William to Elizabeth H. Roberts   2 November 1846
   m. 3 November by William Rucker, J. P.
   Reference: Marriage Book C Page 146;
   County Archives

NICE, William G. to Elizabeth R. Balfour   9 December 1852
   m. 9 December by Geo. A. Caldwell, M. G.
   Reference: Marriage Book D Page 60

NICHOLS, Thos. to Lucy Cofman   8 February 1848
   m. 10 February by William Rucker, J. P.
   Reference: Marriage Book C Page 167

NICHOLSON, Henry of McMinn County to Nancy
   Jane McSpadden, daughter of Rev. J. McSpadden
   of Bradley County
   m. 2 November 1848 (place not stated)
   Reference: "Knoxville Register", Volume 8,
   #414, 29 November 1848

NIEL, David to Elizabeth A. Shults   29 March 1843
   Reference: Marriage Book C Page 77

NIEL, William R. to Elizabeth Burnet   25 October 1843
   m. 26 October by G. W. Wallis, J. P.
   Reference: Marriage Book C Page 88

NORMAN, Flemming S. to Susan Miller   19 October 1846
   m. 22 October by R. A. McAdoo, J. P.
   Reference: County Archives: Marriage
   Book C Page 145

NORTH, Squire to Eliza Kird   25 /March7 1844
   m. 28 March 1844 by Samuel Wilson, J. P.
   Reference: Marriage Book C Page 100

NORVELL, Greenberry to Sarah Dobbins   24 November 1847
   m. 25 November by John Jenkins, J. P.
   Reference: Marriage Book C Page 162

NORVILL, C. L. to Mary M. Smith   30 November 1858
   m. 2 December by John H. Brewer, M. G.
   Reference: Marriage Book D Page 152

NOVEL, William to Marinda Hartly   5 August 1841
   m. 5 August by James Sewell, Minister
   Reference: Marriage Book C Page 44

NUNN, P. B. to Talitha Breedin   26 July 1853
 m. 26 July by William Burns, J. P.
 Reference: Marriage Book D Page 68;
 County Archives

O'DANIEL, William H. to Mary Ann Burns   28 December 1853
 m. 28 December by J. W. Cox, J. P.
 Reference: Marriage Book D Page 76

OLIVER, Jas. M. to Emeline (Caroline) Keeton 10 November 1851
 m. 10 November by Daniel McPhail, J. P.
 Reference: Marriage Book D Page 46

O NAIL, James to Nancy Parsons   2 March 1840
 m. 2 March by A. Kinser, J. P.
 Reference: Marriage Book C Page 28

ONEAL, Andrew to Anna Caroline Delday   24 January 1838
 Reference: Marriage Book C Page 1

O'NEAL, Larsens to Hayney Owens   2 January 1839
 Reference: Marriage Book C Page 12

ONLY, Levi to Marinda Bolen   10 January 1866
 m. 12 January by A. Marshman, M. G.
 Reference: Marriage Book F Page 35

ORICK, Felix to Eliza Newcum   7 June 1858
 m. 8 July by C. L. Owen, J. P.
 Reference: Marriage Book D Page 141

ORICK - see also ARIC, ORRICH, ORRICK

ORLEMAN, William to Avalene Southerling   26 June 1865
 m. 26 June by W. A. Nelson, M. G.
 Reference: Marriage Book F Page 20

ORR, David G. to Susan Johnson   20 February 1840
 Reference: Marriage Book C Page 27

ORR, William to Elizabeth Ann Copeland   26 November 1849
 m. 26 November by Uriel Johnson, Esq.
 Reference: Marriage Book D Page 21

ORRICH, Martin to Eva Dobbs   7 October 1843
 m. 8 October by G. W. Wallis, J. P.
 Reference: Marriage Book C Page 86

ORRICK, Felix to Dorcas Ann Decker   19 August 1852
 m. 19 August by G. W. Wallis, J. P.
 Reference: Marriage Book D Page 55

ORTEN, Charles to Milly _____   22 August 1845
 m. 26 August by R. A. McAdoo, J. P.
 Reference: Marriage Book C Page 125

ORTEN, James W. to May L. White   8 July 1867
 m. 11 July by B. E. Cass, J. P.
 Reference: Marriage Book G Page 17

ORTEN, John to Elizabeth McNabb   30 January 1855
 m. 31 January by M. R. Ware, J. P.
 Reference: Marriage Book D Page 94

ORTON, Chas. V. to Clarinda A. Erickson   22 January 1866
 m. 23 January by John Davis, M. G.
 Reference: Marriage Book F Page 36

ORTON, John to Marthy C. Wear   4 April 1867
    Reference: Marriage Book G Page 13

OSBORN - see AUSBORN

OSHIELDS, James M. to Miss Ruth Lands   16 September 1862
    m. 16 September 1862 by E. W. Carlock Esq.
    All of McMinn County
    Reference: Athens Post Volume XV, #730,
    19 September 1862

OVERHOLSER, Jacob to Malinda Whaley   11 June 1842
    Reference: Marriage Book C Page 58

OWEN, A. J. to Susan Chambers   24 December 1857
    m. 15 October 1858 by S. Sharets, M. G.
    Reference: Marriage Book D Page 133

OWEN, C. L. to Mary A. Patton   23 February 1853
    m. 24 February by Thos. Brown, V. D. M.
    Reference: Marriage Book D Page 64

OWEN, James R. to Catharine Hunt   20 October 1853
    m. 20 October by Dan Carpenter, M. G.
    Reference: Marriage Book D Page 73

OWEN, James W. to Amelia Kirkpatrick   3 October 1842
    m. 4 October by L. R. Morrison, V. D. M.
    Reference: Marriage Book C Page 63

OWEN, Marshal C. to Caroline Thomas   19 October 1854
    m. 19 October by L. B. Waller, M. G.
    Reference: Marriage Book D Page 89

OWENS, Andrew to Elizabeth J. Kennedy   6 September 1865
    m. 7 September by E. L. Miller, M. G.
    Reference: Marriage Book F Page 25

OWENS, C. O. to Miss Texas Dunn   14 March 1868
    Reference: Marriage Book G Page 30;
    Marriage Book G Page 31

OWENS, J. A. to Elizabeth A. Buckner   11 September 1865
    m. 12 September by W. A. Nelson, M. G.
    Reference: Marriage Book F Page 25

OWENS, John to Elizabeth A. Rutherford   5 June 1838
    m. 5 June by David Cantrell, J. P.
    Reference: Marriage Book C Page 4

OWENS, Philip to Susan Bedford   27 September 1838
    m. 4 February by Larkin Taylor, J. P.
    Reference: Marriage Book C Page 8

OWENS, Thomas A. to Nancy P. Rice   17 July 1848
    m. by W. F. Forrest, M. G.
    Reference: Marriage Book D Page 16

OWENS, W. C. to Jane Reid   31 December 1844
    m. 31 December by M. D. Anderson, J. P.
    Reference: Marriage Book C Page 116

OWNBY, R. J. to Anney E. Swisher   13 July 1868
    m. 14 July by L. W. Crouch, M. G.
    Reference: Marriage Book G Page 33

PACK, Timothy to Lidia Burger   5 May 1838
    m. 6 May by Jas. C. Carlock, J. P.
    Reference: **Marriage Book C Page** 3

PAIN, James to Reminda Mulkey   22 August 1839
    m. 23 August by T. Hoyl, J. P.
    Reference: Marriage Book C **Page** 22

PAIN, Martin to Manervia Haney   19 February 1847
    Reference: Marriage Book C Page 153

PALMER, Wellington to Caroline Rogers   19 July 1865
    m. 24 July by Morgan Miller, J. P.
    Reference: Marriage Book F Page 22

PANGLE, Eli S. to Miss H. J. Wiate   6 October 1844
    m. 6 October by Wilson Chapman, M. G.
    Reference: Marriage Book C Page 109

PANGLE, James to Lydia McKehan   13 August 1842
    Reference: Marriage Book C Page 60

PARIS, John W. to Margaret Wheeler   15 August 1854
    m. 17 August by J. C. Carlock, J. P.
    Reference: Marriage Book D Page 86

PARIS, Robert H. to Mary Jane Jenkins   /November 1849_7
    m. 22 November 1849 by J. C. Pendergrass, M.G.
    Reference: Marriage Book D Page 21

PARIS, William to Patsy Weathery   15 April 1857
    m. 19 September by T. L. Hoyl, M. G.
    Reference: Marriage Book D Page 125

PARKER, G. P. to Sarah M. Wooden   10 August 1865
    m. 11 August by S. M. Thomas, J. P.
    Reference: Marriage Book F Page 23

PARKER, John J. to Chresada McMinn   21 January 1845
    m. 21 January by E. P. Bloom, J. P.
    Reference: Marriage Book C Page 117

PARKER, Samuel H. to Emily Templeton   27 October 1845
    m. 28 October by James Blair, M. G.
    Reference: Marriage Book C Page 128

PARKERSON, James A. to Miss M. E. Emmerson   30 October 1869
    Reference: Marriage Book G Page 53

PARKERSON, L. K. to Miss S. C. Newton   9 August 1869
    m. 10 August by James Parkison, J. P.
    Reference: Marriage Book G Page 48

PARKISON, Daniel to Rebecca K. Dodson   14 September 1842
    m. 16 September by W. F. Forrest, M. G.
    Reference: Marriage Book C Page 62

PARKISON, James to Mary Ann Clemenson   7 July 1840
    m. 7 July by John Tate, M. G.
    Reference: Marriage Book C Page 30

PARKISON, Manuel to Julian Dougherty   6 January 1842
    m. 6 January by John Jenkins, J. P.
    Reference: County Archives: Marriage
    Book C Page 51

PARRETT, Thomas to Sarah Ann Grayson   19 August 1845
    m. 20 August by Green L. Reynolds, J. P.
    Reference: Marriage Book C Page 125;
    County Archives

PARRIS, Benjamin to Elizabeth Dodson   2 December 1867
    m. 3 December by E. Z. Williams, J. P.
    Reference: Marriage Book G Page 23

PARRIS, Stephen to Mrs. Hudah Ball   10 January 1842
    Reference: Marriage Book C Page 51

PARRIS, William to Milla Ann Porter   3 April 1846
    m. 10 April by Robert Mansell, M. G.
    Reference: Marriage Book C Paeg 136

PARRIS - see also PARIS

PARSHALL, J. G. to Miss M. M. Rowan   27 November 1856
    m. 2 /sic7 November by Geo. A. Caldwell, M.G.
    Reference: Marriage Book D Page 120

PARSON, George to Mary Ann Gilbert   31 October 1844
    m. 31 October by J. M. Kelley, M. G.
    Reference: Marriage Book C Page 111;
    County Archives

PARSONS, George to Jane Moss   17 January 1868
    m. 19 January by C. R. Hoyl, M. G.
    Reference: Marriage Book G Page 26

PARSONS, Thomas to Nancy Waters   1 October 1839
    m. 2 October by C. W. Rice, J. P.
    Reference: Marriage Book C Page 23

PARTIN - see also PARDON

PATRICK, John to Margaret Mires   5 October 1838
    Reference: Marriage Book C Page 8

PATTERSON, Andrew to Sarah Turnmiles   3 July 1865
    m. 5 July by G. W. Millard, J. P.
    Reference: Marriage Book F Page 20

PATTERSON, Frederick W. to Mary E. Williams   30 August 1855
    m. 30 August by R. A. Prophet, J. P.
    Reference: Marriage Book D Page 102

PATTERSON, James E. to Caroline Sloop   29 November 1848
    m. 30 November by J. C. Carlock, J. P.
    Reference: Marriage Book D Page 8

PATTERSON, Samuel to Mrs. Malvina Johnson   5 January 1856
    m. 6 January by H. M. Sloop, M. G.
    Reference: Marriage Book D Page 106;
    McMinn Chancery Case #156

PATTERSON, Washington to Mary Ann Collier   13 September 1838
    m. 13 September by A. Barb, J. P.
    Reference: Marriage Book C Page 7

PATTERSON, William H. to Lea____ E. South   28 April 1866
    m. 28 April by Uriah Payne, M. G.
    Reference: Marriage Book F Page 41

PATTLY, James M. to Mary Jane McCafery   9 October 1851
    m. 9 October by T. T. Russell, M. G.
    Reference: Marriage Book D Page 44

PATTON, John P. to Mary O. Barnett   20 August 1844
    m. 20 August by B. T. Smith, V. D. M.
    Reference: Marriage Book C Page 107

PATTON, Robert to Mary L. Ward   5 March 1861
    m. 5 March by Geo. A. Caldwell, M. G.
    Reference: Marriage Book E Page 12

PATTY, George O. to Laura S. Newman   29 March 1842
    m. 29 March by Robert Greogry, Minister
    of Baptist Church
    Reference: Marriage Book C Page 56

PATTY, I. R. to Miss Leah Smith   2 December 1850
    Reference: Marriage Book D Page 35

PATTY, Josiah to Elizabeth Ann Black   18 September 1848
    m. 5 October by David F. Jamison, J. P.
    Reference: Marriage Book D Page 5

PATTY, Obed C. to Eliza S. Millard   14 October 1840
    m. 15 October by Robert Gregory, Minister
    of Baptist Church
    Reference: Marriage Book C Page 32

PATTY, Owen West to Nancy Eveline Reynolds   8 September 1848
    m. 4 October by Wilson Chapman, M. G.
    Reference: Marriage Book D Page 4

PATTY, R. J. to Miss Pelina Reynolds   11 November 1844
    m. 12 November by Reobert Gregory, Minister
    of Baptist Church
    Reference: Marriage Book C Page 111

PATTY, William H. to Ede Ferguson   29 November 1843
    m. 30 November by Robert Gregory, Minister
    of Baptist Church
    Reference: Marriage Book C Page 91;
    County Archives

PAUL, G. W. to Marthy Logan   3 November 1866
    m. 4 November by G. M. Bloom. J. P.
    Reference: Marriage Book G Page 4;
    County Archives

PAUL, Marida to Miss Orpha Wassom   2 July 1852
    m. 4 July by William R. Elder, M. G.
    Reference: Marriage Book D Page 53;
    County Archives

PAUL, Thomas T. to Mary Washam   4 July 1847
    m. 4 July by G. W. Kirksey, J. P.
    Reference: Marriage Book C Page 157

PAYNE, F. J. to Miss C. A. Lathan   22 January 1867
    m. 22 January by J. January, M. G.
    Reference: Marriage Book G Page 9

PAYNE, J. P. to Margret J. Cole   28 July 1869
    m. 1 August by J. W. Wiggins, M. G.
    Reference: Marriage Book G Page 48

PAYNE, John J. to Lucinda Parris   11 October 1842
    m. 12 October by Hiram Ingram, M. G.
    Reference: Marriage Book C Page 64

PAYNE, Madison to Margaret Tally   2 January 1839
    m. 3 January by Andrew Crawford
    Reference: Marriage Book C Page 12

PAYNE, Thomas J. to Mary O. Greene   3 November 1866
     m. 4 November by Carroll Long, F. E. (M.G.)
     Reference: County Archives; Marriage
     Book G Page 3

PAYNE, U. M. to Miss Victory McLane   11 November 1865
     m. 15 November by C. Long, M. G.
     Reference: Marriage Book F Page 30;
     County Archives

PAYNE, Uriah to Nancy Atkinson   16 July 1844
     m. 17 July by C. R. Hoyl, J. P.
     Reference: Marriage Book C Page 105

PAYNE - see also PAIN, PANE

PEAK (PEAKE), Blewford (Bluford) to Malinda Brock   11 December 1841
     m. 17 December by L. L. Ball, J. P.
     Reference: County Archives: Marriage
     Book C Page 50

PEAK, T. to Miss H. Prigmore   23 January 1840
     Reference: Marriage Book C Page 26

PEAK, William C. to Nancy P. Matlock   1 January 1855
     m. 4 January by Geo. A. Caldwell, M. G.
     Reference: Marriage Book D Page 92;
     County Archives

PEARCE, Daniel to Barbara Barnett   14 April 1842
     m. 14 April by John Scruggs, M. G.
     Reference: Marriage Book C Page 56

PEARCE, David to Mary Triplett   7 January 1843
     m. 8 January by W. F. Forest, M. G.
     Reference: Marriage Book C Page 71

PEARCE, David to Lucinda Evans   11 February 1850
     m. 12 February by J. N. Scarbrough
     Reference: Marriage Book D Page 25

PEARCE, David to Mary Ensminger   21 September 1865
     m. 23 September by A. J. Mathis, M. G.
     Reference: Marriage Book F Page 26;
     County Archives

PEARCE, David Jr. to Sarah Jane Hutson   4 July 1850
     m. 4 July by A. Barb, J. P.
     Reference: Marriage Book D Page 29

PEARCE, Frances M. to Amanda J. Armstrong   13 September 1849
     m. 13 September by Moses Sweny, J. P.
     Reference: Marriage Book D Page 18

PEARCE, James to Elizabeth Galion (Gallion)   28 June 1845
     m. 30 June by C. Sanders, M. G.
     Reference: Marriage Book C Page 122

PEARCE, James H. to Elizabeth Gollahon   22 July 1865
     m. 23 July by N. H. Haggard, M. G.
     Reference: Marriage Book F Page 22

PEARCE, John L. to Lucy Harrod   23 March 1859
     m. 23 March by Johnathan Thomas, J. P.
     Reference: Marriage Book D Page 159

PEARMAN, Henry to Martha L. Standifer   25 January 1855
     Reference: Marriage Book D Page 94

PEARMAN, Mike to Louisa C. Renoe   21 April 1858
     C. M. Presswood, Security
     m. 21 April by L. R. Hust, J. P.
     Reference: Marriage Book D Page 139;
     County Archives

PEARMAN - see also PERMAN

PECK, W. W. to Miss Dialtha R. Wilson   21 February 1854
     m. 21 February by W. Witcher, M. G.
     Reference: Marriage Book D Page 80

PECK, William F. to Sarah E. Workman   22 January 1844
     m. 23 January by L. Wetten, M. G.
     Reference: Marriage Book C Page 96

PECK, William T. to Nancy Cooper   8 September 1857
     m. 15 September by C. R. Hoyl, M. G.
     Reference: Marriage Book D Page 129

PEEL, James to Permelia Firestone   27 May 1865
     m. 28 May by A. R. Wilson, M. G.
     Reference: Marriage Book F Page 18

PENCE, James to Narcissa McFalls   5 April 1865
     m. 6 April by N. H. Haggard, M. G.
     Reference: Marriage Book F Page 17

PENCE, Triplet to Catharine Elssly   11 September 1869
     m. 11 September by E. Z. Williams, J. P.
     Reference: Marriage Book G Page 50

PENDERGRASS, Robert to Matilda Bell   24 December 1844
     Reference: Marriage Book C Page 115

PENNINGTON, David to Matilda Bigham   16 August 1839
     Reference: Marriage Book C Page 22

PENNINGTON, F. M. to Virginia M. Lowery   30 November 1859
     m. 1 December by Geo. A. Caldwell, M. G.
     Reference: Marriage Book E Page 8

PENNINGTON, J. C. to Esther C. Bryant   17 March 1855
     m. 20 March by Robert Sewell, M. G.
     Reference: Marriage Book D Page 96

PENNINGTON, James to Jane Vincent   8 November 1842
     m. 8 November by John Jenkins, J. P.
     Reference: Marriage Book C Page 67

PENNINGTON, Nelson to Nancy Ann Lunna Bigham   19 September 1845
     m. 20 September by William McKamy, J. P.
     Reference: Marriage Book C Page 127;
     County Archives

PEOPLES, James to Louvina Stratton   24 September 1870
     m. 25 September by E. L. Miller, M. G.
     Reference: Marriage Book G Page 65

PERCELL, William M. to Martha Matlock   2 November 1848
     Reference: Marriage Book D Page 6

PERKINS, James D. to Elzira Hughs   15 August 1852
     m. by John Jenkins, J. P.
     Reference: Marriage Book D Page 54

PERKINS, Robert to Mrs. Malinda Gossett   28 April 1866
     m. 29 April by P. M. Long
     Reference: Marriage Book F Page 40

PERKINS - see also PURKINS

PERMAN (PEARMAN), James to Sarah Jane Reathford   21 October 1870
   m. 22 October by Joseph Neil, J. P.
   Reference: Marriage Book G Page 68;
   County Archives

PERRINE, Nathan E. to Jane E. Bunch   24 June 1865
   m. 24 June by N. H. Haggard, M. G.
   Reference: Marriage Book F Page 20

PERRY, James to Polly Harte   /27-29 August 1838/
   Reference: Marriage Book C Page 6
   (Noate: Date of issuance is not given
   and there is no return)

PERRY, John to Susan Norris   14 August 1865
   m. 8 March 1866 by S. M. Thomas, J. P.
   Reference: Marriage Book F Page 23

PERRY, Thomas to Mrs. Sarah Ritchey   2 November 1864
   m. 3 November by E. Z. Williams, J. P.
   Reference: Marriage Book F Page 9;
   County Archives

PETERS, Christian to Nancy Pearce   28 November 1829
   Thomas G. Willett, Security
   m. by Robert Cowan, J. P.
   Reference: County Archives: W. P. A.

PETERS, Christian to Olevia Benton   12 September 1839
   m. 12 September by John McGaughy, J. P.
   Reference: Marriage Book C Page 22

PETERS, Christian to Ellen Grisham   9 January 1844
   m. 9 January by William H. Ballew, J. P.
   Reference: Marriage Book C Page 95

PETERS, J. P. to Miss K. H. Basinger   18 January 1864
   m. 19 January by W. H. Stephenson, J. P.
   Reference: Marriage Book E Page 14

PETERS, Landon C. to Mrs. Margaret Smith   9 June 1841
   m. 10 June by T. B. Love, J. P.
   Reference: Marriage Book C Page 43

PETERS, N. J. to Permelia Frazier   18 December 1844
   Reference: Marriage Book C Page 114

PETERS, Robert G. to Elizabeth Bond   22 January 1840
   m. 23 January by John McGaughy, J. P.
   Reference: Marriage Book C Page 25

PETERS, Samuel A. to Phebe S. Peters   13 June 1839
   Reference: Marriage Book C Page 18

PETITT, Elijah to Malinda Deaton   6 August 1859
   m. 7 August by Thomas Rogers, J. P.
   Reference: Marriage Book E Page 8

PETTITT, Francis A. to Sarah E. Carson   21 January 1865
   m. 23 January by W. A. Nelson, M. G.
   Reference: Marriage Book F Page 14;
   County Archives

PETTITT, James to Matilda Senter   17 March 1838
   Reference: Marriage Book C Page 2

PHILIPS, Edwad to Nancy Haney   17 January 1859
    m. 20 Januar by I. B. Haney, J. P.
    Reference: Marriage Book D Page 155

PHILIPS, Thomas to Elizabeth Standifer   10 June 1853
    m. 11 June by M. D. Anderson, J. P.
    Reference: Marriage Book D Page 67;
    County Archives

PHILIPS, William to Katharine Miller   21 April 1845
    m. 21 April by Wilson Chapman, M. G.
    Reference: Marriage Book C Page 120

PHILLIPS, Horace to Miss Mat A. Sehorn   18 February 1867
    m. 19 February by R. D. Black, M. G.
    Reference: Marriage Book G Page 11

PHILLIPS, John C. to Hily Reggins   16 January 1845
    m. 16 January by T. Gregory, J. P.
    Reference: Marriage Book C Page 116

PHILLIPS, John P. to Matilda Durham   1 May 1864
    m. 2 May by Jas. Atkins, M. G.
    Reference: Marriage Book F Page 2;
    County Archives

PHILLIPS, Thomas P. to Sarah Elizabeth Dyer   7 June 1848
    m. 7 June by Thomas Sewell, Minister
    Reference: Marriage Book D Page 2

PHILPOT, William to Rachel Nations   9 March 1844
    m. 10 March 1846 by C. Sanders, M. G.
    Reference: Marriage Book C Page 135

PHILPOT - see also FILLPOT, FILLPOTS, FILPOT

PHILPOTS. John to Polly Little   6 June 1850
    m. 6 June by J. Jack, M. G.
    Reference: Marriage Book D Page 28

PHILPOTT, William B. to Nancy J. Elliott   28 April 1860
    m. 29 April by William H. C. Thompson, J. P.
    Reference: County Archives
    (Note: This license is not entered on the
    Marriage Book)

PICKENS, Robert to Mary Smith
    m. 7 March 1826 by Geo. Bowman, L. P. of M. E. C.
    Reference: County Archives

PICKINS, Charles A. to Malinda Smith   19 August 1840
    m. 19 August by T. B. Love, J. P.
    Reference: Marriage Book C Page 31

PICKLE, Lewis M. to Nancy L. Lowry   5 April 1855
    m. 5 April by John Tate, M. G.
    Reference: Marriage Book D Page 97

PIERCE, Ephraim to Lucinda Hambrick   27 July 1826
    Robert Ritchardson & William H. Newman, Security
    Reference: W. P. A.

PIERCE, John to Sarah M. Lawson   1 March 1845
    m. 2 March by Moses A. Cass, J. P.
    Reference: Marriage Book C Page 118;
    County Archives

PIERCE, Samuel to Anna Niceley   17 July 1868
    m. 17 July by J. W. Gilbert, J. P.
    Reference: Marriage Book G Page 29;
    County Archives

PIERCE - see also PEARCE

PIKE, Carter to Nancy Hawk   10 September 1866
    m. 10 September by W. H. Spherson, J. P.
    Reference: Marriage Book F Page 46

PIEK, James to Polly Ann Seivils   7 March 1859
    m. 7 March by Jas. M. Henderson, J. P.
    Reference: Marriage Book D Page 158

PINION, John to Hiley Riggins   25 April 1866
    m. 26 April by S. W. Royston, J. P.
    Reference: Marriage Book F Page 40

PINNION, McKamy to Nancy Frazier   26 September 1839
    m. 26 September by John McGaughy, J. P.
    Reference: Marriage Book C Page 23

PIPER, George M., Editor of "The Hiwassee   11 February 1845
    Republican", to Clarrissa Jane Lyle
    m. 11 February by L. R. Morrison, V. D. M.
    Reference: Marriage Book C Page 117;
    "Knoxville Register", Volume 5, #218,
    19 February 1845

PLANK, James W. to Mary Ann Hays   11 October 1843
    m. 12 October by Hiel Buttram, M. G.
    Reference: Marriage Book C Page 87

PLANK, John to Sarah J. Hill   13 September 1865
    Reference: Marriage Book F Page 25

PLEASANT, Thomas J. to Rebecca Walker   4 February 1839
    m. 4 February by John Courtney, M. G.
    Reference: Marriage Book C Page 14

PLUMLY, Daniel to Amanda Cuningham   23 January 1845
    m. 23 January by Thomas Russell, M. G.
    Reference: Marriage Book C Page 117

POE, Asael to Anna Hellums   10 October 1838
    m. 18 October by A. B. Niel, J. P.
    Reference: Marriage Book C Page 9

POE, John L. to Nancy Kible   21 August 1851
    m. 22 August by James Bonner, J. P.
    Reference: Marriage Book D Page 42

POE, Stephenson to Hannah Bishop   9 March 1842
    m. 10 March by John Jenkins, J. P.
    Reference: Marriage Book C Page 54

POE, William to Jane Hilliard   25 July 1843
    Reference: Marriage Book C Page 82

POE, William to Susanah Largent   15 February 1850
    m. 1850 by William Walker, J. P.   or
    Reference: Marriage Book D Page 25;   23 September 1850
    Marriage Book D Page 32
    (Note: Page 25 has issued 15 Feb. 1850
    with no return. Page 32 has issued
    23 Sept. 1850 and married 1850 by
    William Walker, J. P.)

POES, F. M. to Sarah Ann Stapp   19 August 1868
   m. 21 August by J. S. Russell, M. G.
   Reference: Marriage Book G Page 34

POINDEXTER, Robert L. to Mary E. Dillbeck   26 Juen 1865
   m. 27 June by M. A. Cass, M. G.
   Reference: Marriage Book F Page 20

POLLER, Uriah E. to Delila E. Jones   20 September 1856
   Reference: Marriage Book D Page 114

POPE, Fielding to Theresa C. Meigs   24 March 1829
   Solomon Bogart, Security
   m. 24 March by R. McAlpin
   Reference: County Archives: W. P. A.

PORTER, William S. S. to Martha Dodson   14 December 1843
   m. 17 December by William McKamy, J. P.
   Reference: Marriage Book C Page 93

POTER, Robert W. to Menada Cates   29 July 1827
   Henery Amarine, Security
   Reference: County Archives

POWER, G. H. to Martha J. Hamilton   12 January 1858
   m. 14 January by E. L. Miller, J. P.
   Reference: Marriage Book D Page 135

POWER, William to Elizabeth White   29 November 1858
   m. 3 December by W. B. Manell, M. G.
   Reference: Marriage Book D Page 152

POWERS, David to Tabitha Hously   14 August 1841
   m. 15 August by Russell Lane, J. P.
   Reference: Marriage Book C Page 44

POWERS, Forest M. to Sarah S. Powers   5 May 1864
   m. 5 May by William G. Wilson, M. G.
   Reference: County Archives: Marriage
   Book F Page 2

POWERS, James to Nancy M. Hope   26 May 1864
   m. 29 May by Rev. D. Carpenter
   Reference: Marriage Book F Page 3;
   County Archives

POWERS, John T. to Mary M. Rose   26 December 1865
   m. 26 December by William Thompson, M. G.
   Reference: Marriage Book F Page 34

POWERS, Robert to Mary Light   1 January 1848
   m. 5 January by David F. Jamison, J. P.
   Reference: Marriage Book C Page 165

POWERS, Robert S. to Malinda McDowel   9 February 1839
   John B. Smart, Security
   Reference: Marriage Book C Page 14;
   County Archives

POWERS, Samuel to Margaret Ann Smith   9 June 1855
   m. 10 June by I. S. Garrison, J. P.
   Reference: County Archives: Marriage
   Book D Page 99
   Note: By License married 10 June and
   by Record Book married 9 November

POWERS, William to Ann Housely   31 August 1840
   Reference: Marriage Book C Page 30

PRATHER, C. H. to Sarah T. Steed   21 January 1865
    m. 22 January by C. Long, M. G.
    Reference: Marriage Book F Page 15;
    County Archives

PRATHER, John A. to Matilda Steed   29 November 1855
    m. 29 November by William C. Daily, M. G.
    Reference: Marriage Book D Page 105

PRATHER, William M. to Roselvirn Kemp   20 December 1854
    m. 20 December by Geo. A. Caldwell, M. G.
    Reference: Marriage Book D Page 91

PRESLEY, G. W. to Simanthia Owen   21 January 1869
    m. 21 January by J. W. Gilbert, J. P.
    Reference: Marriage Book G Page 43

PRESSWOOD, David to Sarah Jane Eliot   5 February 1867
    m. 10 February by Elihu Kelley, J. P.
    Reference: Marriage Book G Page 10

PRESSWOOD, James A. to Sallie A. Cuningham   9 May 1867
    m. 9 May by J. S. Russell
    Reference: Marriage Book G Page 15

PRICE, A. J. to Julia A. Teague   21 May 1869
    m. 23 May by E. L. Miller, M. G.
    Reference: Marriage Book G Page 46

PRICE, Dossy to Mrs. Nancy Coats   22 August 1867
    John L. Pearce, Security
    Reference: Marriage Book G Page 19;
    County Archives

PRICE, Edward to Elza Jemison   7 December 1846
    m. 10 December by B. E. Blain, J. P.
    Reference: Marriage Book C Page 148

PRICE, Henry B. to Mary A. Smith   7 July 1870
    m. 7 July by J. A. Womac, M. G.
    Reference: Marriage Book G Page 62;
    County Archives

PRICE, John to Catharine Baker   18 January 1855
    m. 18 January by Jonathan Thomas, J. P.
    Reference: Marriage Book D Page 93

PRICE, William to Lecy Johnson   6 June 1870
    m. 6 June by James Thomas, J. P.
    Reference: Marriage Book G Page 61

PRICHARD - see also PRITCHARD

PRIESTWOOD, John to Maryann J. F. Johnson   13 February 1845
    m. 13 February by Justus Steed, J. P.
    Reference: Marriage Book C Page 117;
    County Archives

PRINCE, Jackson to Mahala Cross   25 December 1839
    Reference: Marriage Book C Page 25

PRINCE, James to L. L. Hayes   21 November 1844
    m. 21 November by Matthew R. Gibson, J. P.
    Reference: Marriage Book C Page 113

PRINCE, Sandford to Joana Thomas   18 December 1838
    m. 27 December by A. C. Robison, J. P.
    Reference: Marriage Book C Page 11

PRIOR, John to Easter Manus   29 August 1864
    m. 1 September by William Thompson, M. G.
    Reference: Marriage Book F Page 6;
    County Archives

PRITCHARD, Jas. to Nancy A. Wilson   16 December 1857
    m. 18 December by M. L. Philips, J. P.
    Reference: Marriage Book D Page 132

PROCTOR, Chas. A. to Sarah A. Mastin   18 December 1854
    Reference: Marriage Book D Page 91

PROFPHET, B. A. to Eunice Grigg   5 March 1849
    m. 5 March by J. C. Carlock, J. P.
    Reference: Marriage Book D Page 12

PROPHET, John W. to Margaret S. Newman   7 October 1852
    m. 7 October by J. W. Cox, J. P.
    Reference: Marriage Book D Page 57;
    County Archives

PUGH, James J. to Sarah Jane Willes   23 January 1867
    m. 23 January by S. M. Thomas, J. P.
    Reference: Marriage Book G Page 9

PUGH, Jonathan F. to Elizabeth Reed   18 June 1844
    m. 4 July by L. L. Ball, J. P.
    Reference: Marriage Book C Page 103;
    County Archives

PUGH, Josiah to Martha Morris   3 April 1848
    Reference: W. P. A.
    (Note: Page 1 in Marriage Book is
    missing)

PUGH - see also PEW

PURDY, J. G. to Sarah A. Firestone   7 September 1859
    m. 8 September by Robert Cochran, J. P,
    Reference: Marriage Book E Page 2

PURSER, Pleasant M. to Miss Reuhamy Fisher   21 January 1843
    m. 22 January by John Jenkins, J. P.
    Reference: Marriage Book C Page 71

PURVINE, M. G. to Mary A. E. Neil   2 January 1868
    m. 2 January by J. C. Barbe, M. G.
    Reference: Marriage Book G Page 25

PU__RY, William J. to Mary E. Webb   2 May 1867
    m. 5 May by S. M. Thomas, J. P.
    Reference: Marriage Book G Page 14

QUEENER, George W. to Rachel Lattimore   1 January 1839
    m. 3 January by J. C. Carlock, J. P.
    Reference: Marriage Book C Page 13

QUEENER, Jacob to Susan E. Queener   9 August 1865
    m. 10 August by Uriah Payne, M. G.
    Reference: Marriage Book F Page 23

QUEENER, James C. to Eliza Trew   3 February 1841
    m. 11 February by T. B. Love, J. P.
    Reference: Marriage Book C Page 37

QUEENER, John to Elizabeth Butler   3 December 1839
    Reference: Marriage Book C Page 26

QUEENER, John to Mabel Gregg   12 December 1843
    m. 14 December by Hiram Ingram, M. G.
    Reference: Marriage Book C Page 93;
    W. P. A.

QUENER, Thomas Y. to Arminda Wells   19 May 1868
    m. 21 May by Uriah Payne, M. G.
    Reference: Marriage Book G Page 32

QUINN, Morris O. to Nancy Malinda Secrest   15 May 1850
    Reference: Marriage Book D Page 27

RABURN, Charles to Mary E. Brock   9 October 1869
    m. 10 October by Elihu Kelley, J. P.
    Reference: Marriage Book G Page 52

RABURN, J. J. to Mary Perry   17 May 1865
    m. 17 May by I. R. Chesnutt, M. G.
    Reference: Marriage Book F Page 18;
    County Archives

RABURN, William to Miss Zilpha Breden   18 February 1855
    m. 19 February by Robert Cochran, J. P.
    Reference: Marriage Book D Page 95

RABURN - see also RAYBURN

RABY, William S. to Elizabeth Sharp   10 November 1864
    m. 13 November by D. W. Beaver, M. G.
    Reference: Marriage Book F Page 10;
    County Archives

RACKLY, A. M. to Miss Derendy Cooke   1 October 1867
    E. F. Kirksey, Security
    m. 6 October by C. R. Hoyl, M. G.
    Reference: Marriage Book F Page 21;
    County Archives

RAGAN, William S. to Sarah J. Helums   21 January 1853
    m. 23 January by O. M. Liner, J. P.
    Reference: Marriage Book D Page 62;
    County Archives

RAGGSDALE, Wilie to Susana Elliston   3 March 1821
    John McClorg (McCog), Security
    Reference: County Archives

RAGSDALE, Benjamin to Mary Ann Rudd   5 June 1828
    m. 5 June by Fielding Pope
    Reference: County Archives

RAMAY, Claiborn W. to Lucinda Foster   27 February 1850
    Reference: Marriage Book D Page 26

RAMSEY, Lewis to Mrs. Susannah Newman   23 August 1842
    m. 23 August by R. A. McAdoo, J. P.
    Reference: Marriage Book C Page 61

RAMY, Thos. to Hassie Lock Miller   8 October 1870
    James Peoples, Security
    m. 9 October by William G. Horton, J. P.
    Reference: Marriage Book G Page 67;
    County Archives

RANDOLPH, G. C. to Miss H. M. Mashburn   24 April 1858
    m. 29 April by G. Randolph, M. G.
    Reference: Marriage Book D Page 140

170

RANDOLPH, Gilbert to Marinda Miers   15 September 1838
    m. 16 September by Robert Randolph, M. G.
    Reference: Marriage Book C Page 7

RANDOLPH, Gilmore to Mary Brookshire   24 March 1840
    m. 26 March by Reece Jones, M. G.
    Reference: Marriage Book C Page 28

RANDOLPH, Hezekiah to Eliza Ditmore   21 September 1839
    m. 22 September by R. J. Moore, J. P.
    Reference: Marriage Book C Page 23

RANDOLPH, Lankister to Nancy Rice   5 November 1825
    m. 6 November by Elihu H. Randolph
    Reference: County Archives

RANDOLPH, Peyton to Rody (Rhoda) Mirers (Miers)   10 November 1837
    (Mires)
    m. 12 November by Robert Randolph, M. G.
    Reference: County Archives

RANDOLPH, Robert to Mrs. Jemima Miller   2 December 1843
    m. 3 December by William McKamy, J. P.
    Reference: Marriage Book C Page 91;
    Deed Book I, Page 234

RANDOLPH, Robert to Salina J. Coatney   23 October 1865
    m. 25 October by Gilmore Randolph, M. G.
    Reference: Marriage Book F Page 28;
    County Archives

RANDOLPH, Robert to M. Bolan   2 October 1868
    m. 3 October by A. Marshman, J. P.
    Reference: Marriage Book G Page 37

RANDOLPH, William to Mary Murray   8 May 1860
    m. 8 May by John Scarbrough, J. P.
    Reference: Marriage Book E Page 12

RANDOLPH, William to Mrs. Mary Fleming   3 November 1870
    Gilbert Murry, Security
    m. 13 November by Gilmore Randolph, M. G.
    Reference: Marriage Book G Page 68;
    County Archives

RANINS, John to Miss E. E. Rogers   6 May 1842
    Reference: Marriage Book C Page 57

RAPER, John S. to Mary Ann Robison   27 September 1843
    m. 28 September by John Scruggs, M. G.
    Reference: Marriage Book C Page 86;
    County Archives

RAPER, William to Elizabeth Maxwell   19 November 1864
    m. 20 November by John Scruggs, Minister
    Reference: Marriage Book F Page 10;
    County Archives

RATLEDGE, George L. to Nancy E. Dooley   17 January 1857
    m. 18 January by Jas. Parkerson, J. P.
    Reference: Marriage Book D Page 123;
    County Archives

RATLEDGE, James to Malinda Barlow   7 February 1856
    m. 7 February by Robert Reynolds, J. P.
    Reference: Marriage Book D Page 107

RATLEDGE, Jas. to Elizabeth A. Goins   1 September 1858
    Reference: Marriage Book D Page 145

RATLIFF, A. J. to Nancy Hambright   13 March 1867
    m. 27 March by G. W. Colman, M. G.
    Reference: Marriage Book G Page 12

RAWLINGS, Elijah to Catharine Vincen   24 May 1846
    m. 24 May by John Scarbrough, J. P.
    Reference: Marriage Book C Page 138

RAY, F. S. to Eliza T. C. Ware   30 December 1854
    m. 31 December by M. A. Cass, M. G.
    Reference: Marriage Book D Page 92

RAY, William to Polly Zenny Dobbs   25 October 1838
    m. 25 October by Johnathan Thomas, J. P.
    Reference: Marriage Book C Page 9

RAY - see also RHA, RHEA, WRAY

RAYBURN, Henry to Martha Manery   18 May 1850
    m. 20 May by J. Jack, M. G.
    Reference: Marriage Book D Page 28

RAYBORN, J.J. to Miss M. L. Bigham   4 October 1870
    J. W. Epperson, Security
    m. 6 October by P. M. Long, J. P.
    Reference: Marriage Book G Page 66;
    County Archives

RAYBORN, John to Rebeca Ann Rue   9 February 1859
    m. 9 February by Robert Cochran, J. P.
    Reference: Marriage Book D Page 156

RAYBURN, James J. to Catharine Saunders   31 March 1849
    James T. Fitzgerald, Security
    m. 1 April by A. L. Dugan, J. P.
    Reference: Marriage Book D Page 14;
    County Archives

RAYBURN - see also RABOURN, RABURN

READ, John H. to Eliza Pugh   29 December 1841
    Reference: Marriage Book C Page 51

READ - see also REED, REID

REAGAN - see also RAGAN, REGAN, REGGINS

REAVELY, Frances to Miss Mariah J. Culpepper   9 January 1858
    m. 12 January by William R. Long, M. G.
    Reference: Marriage Book D Page 134

RECTOR, Elijah to Martha Liles   4 August 1845
    m. 4 August by J. H. Benton, J. P.
    Reference: Marriage Book C Page 123

RECTOR, Maxamillan to Mary Elizabeth Dethroe   4 September 1845
    m. 4 September by J. H. Benton, J. P.
    Reference: Marriage Book C Page 126

RECTOR, William to Elizabeth (Isabella M.)   24 March 1841
    McPherson (MCpherson)
    m. 25 March by Jos. Minzes, J. P.
    Reference: Marriage Book C Page 41
    Note: License issued to Elizabeth McPherson
    and endorsed Isabella M. MCpherson.

REDING (REEDING), Joseph to Eliza Newman   30 July 1845
    m. 31 July by Daniel McPhail, J. P.
    Reference: Marriage Book C Page 123

REED, Baxter to Nancy Fry   22 April 1865
    m. 29 April by E. Z. Williams, J. P.
    Reference: Marriage Book F Page 17;
    County Archives

REED, Fleming to Mary Wear   21 September 1865
    m. 21 September by S. M. Thomas, J. P.
    Reference: Marriage Book F Page 26;
    County Archives

REED, James to Margaret Young   22 May 1847
    m. 23 May by R. A. McAdoo, J. P.
    Reference: Marriage Book C Page 156

REED (REID), John to Sarah Burnett   18 February 1845
    Hezekiah Pruet, Security
    Reference: Marriage Book C Page 117;
    County Archives

REED, Joseph to Margaret P. Dodson   1 February 1854
    Reference: Marriage Book D Page 79

REED, S. W. to Catharine Guthery   7 December 1858
    m. 7 December by M. Love, M. G.
    Reference: Marriage Book D Page 152

REED, Simeon to Elizabeth Guthrey   17 December 1851
    Reference: Marriage Book D Page 47

REED - see also READ, REID

REEDER, S. K. to Mary M. Bridges   7 April 1841
    m. 9 April by L. R. Morrison, V. D. M.
    Reference: Marriage B-ok C Page 41

REID (REED), John S. to Larinda Dearin   6 March 1847
    m. 7 March by J. H. Benton, J. P.
    Reference: Marriage Book C Page 154;
    County Archives

REID - see also READ, REED

REINHARDT, Ephraim to Juliet Duke   8 May 1829
    m. 14 May by D. Cantrell, Esq.
    Reference: County Archives

REINHART, Thomas to Frances N. Carr   25 December 1866
    Reference: Marriage Book G Page 7

REIZNER (REISNER), John to Sarah A. (E.) McCartney   24 August 1840
    m. 24 August by Ralph E. Tedford, M. G.
    Reference: Marriage Book C Page 31

RENEAU - see also RENO

RENFROW - see also RENTFREL, RENTFRO

RENO, William to Matilda Haney   5 March 1847
    m. 10 March by Thoams Witte, G. M.
    Reference: Marriage Book C Page 154

RENOW, Samuel to Martha T. Sellers   28 February 1865
    m. 2 March by D. W. Beaver, M. G.
    Reference: Marriage Book F Page 16;
    County Archives

RENOW - see also RENEAU

RENTREL, Langden C. to Nancy Parkison   1 October 1846
    m. 1 October by William F. Forrest, M. G.
    Reference: Marriage Book C Page 144

RENTFRO, Robert to Catharine Goodwin   3 February 1829
    m. 3 February by William Lowry, J. P.
    Reference: County Archives

RENTFRO, William to Melvina Ray   27 March 1856
    m. 27 March by James Baker, J. P.
    Reference: Marriage Book D Page 109

RENTFROW, Thoams to Katharine Wyrick   30 June 1848
    Reference: Marriage Book D Page 3

RENTFROW - see also RENFRO

REYNOLDS, Charles L. to Francis E. Regan   30 May 1854
    m. 1 June by O. M. Liner, J. P.
    Reference: Marriage Book D Page 84

REYNOLDS, H. C. to Elizabeth Lee   4 December 1844
    m. 5 December by Robert Gregory, Minister
    of Baptist Church
    Reference: Marriage Book C Page 113

REYNOLDS, Henry of McMinn County to Mary Gault,
    daughter of William Gault, Esq. of Blount Co.
    m. Tuesday, August 12, 1823 in Blount Co. by
    Rev. Isaac Anderson
    Reference: "The Knoxville Register", Vol. 8,
    #369, 22 August 1823

REYNOLDS, I. W. to Emily Copeland   30 April 1846
    m. 30 April by Green L. Reynolds, J. P.
    Reference: Marriage Book C Page 138

REYNOLDS, James M. to Mary B. Haney   15 November 1855
    m. 15 November by T. T. Russell, M. G.
    Reference: Marriage Book D Page 104

REYNOLDS, James T. to Lou D. Dodson   15 October 1868
    m. 15 October by J. S. Russell, M. G.
    Reference: Marriage Book G Page 38

REYNOLDS, John to Mary M. M. Smith   21 December 1854
    Reference: Marriage Book D Page 91

REYNOLDS, John M. to Martha L. Russell   7 December 1864
    T. J. Reynolds, Security
    m. 8 December by John Scruggs, M. G.
    Reference: Marriage Book F Page 12;
    County Archives

REYNOLDS, Joseph C. to Rebecca Reynolds   24 February 1852
    m. 29 February by William McKamy, J. P.
    Reference: Marriage Book D Page 48

REYNOLDS, M. C. to Mary C. Hoyl   14 December 1848
    m. 15 December by Wilson Chapman, M. G.
    Reference: Marriage Book D Page 9

REYNOLDS, Montraville to Rachel Bond   1 September 1845
    m. 2 September by L. R. Morrison, V. D. M.
    Reference: Marriage Book C Page 126

174

REYNOLDS, Perry to Mariah Philips   14 June 1866
    m. 14 June by J. C. Barb, M. G.
    Reference: County Archives
    (Noate: This license was not
    entered on the Marriage Books)

REYNOLDS, Pleasant M. to Elizabeth A. Oliver   20 November 1843
    Reference: Marriage Book C Page 91

REYNOLDS, Robert to Mary Jane Dodson   22 July 1846
    m. 23 July by Wilson Chapman, M. G.
    Reference: Marriage Book C Page 140

REYNOLDS, T. J. to Eliza J. C. Dixon   7 December 1864
    m. 8 December by John Scruggs, M. G.
    Reference: Marriage Book F Page 12;
    County Archives

REYNOLDS, William to Eliza Ann Simmonds   9 February 1867
    m. 10 February by Timothy Sullins, M. G.
    Reference: Marriage Book G Page 10;
    County Archives

REYNOLDS, William H. to Mary E. Derrick   12 December 1868
    m. 13 December by C. Cate, J. P.
    Reference: Marriage Book G Page 41

REYNOLDS - see also RUNNELZ, RUNOLDS, RYNOLDS

RHA, James M. to Lucinda Cash   25 May 1841
    m. 26 May by John Jenkins, J. P.
    Reference: Marriage Book C Page 42;
    County Archives

RHODES, William A. to Sarah Douglas   26 April 1848
    m. 27 April by John Jenkins, J. P.
    Reference: W. P. A.
    (Note: Page 1 in Marriage Book D,
    is missing now)

RHODES - see also ROADS, RODES

RHOHDES, S. S. to Margart E. Kantz   5 January 1856
    m. 7 January by R. A. Gidens, M. G.
    Reference: Marriage Book D Page 106

RICE, A. H. to Miss P. T. Terry   4 October 1866
    m. 4 October by Calvin Denton, M. G.
    Reference: Marriage Book G Page 4;
    County Archives

RICE, C. W. to Miss Juliet C. Cobbs   1 April 1844
    m. 2 April by Hiram Ingram, M. G.
    Reference: Marriage Book C Page 100

RICE, Henry of McMinn County to Elizabeth K.
    Senter, daughter of Stephen W. Senter of
    Grainger County
    m. 16 July 1833 by Rev. Charles McAnnally
    (Probably not a McMinn County marriage)
    Reference: "Knoxville Register", Vol. 17,
    #889, 7 August 1833

RICE, Henry to Mary E. Hawks   15 June 1854
    H. H. Burke, Security
    m. 15 June by Robert Gregory, M. G.
    Reference: Marriage Book D Page 84;
    County Archives

RICE, Jesse C. to Martha Benson   7 December 1862
    m. 7 December by Geo. A. Caldwell, M. G.
    Reference: Marriage Book E Page 4

RICE, Orville to Miss Molley Reynolds   13 September 1858
    m. 14 September by John Scruggs, M. G.
    Reference: Marriage Book D Page 146

RICE, W. L. to Jenira Wattenbarger   10 September 1861
    m. 11 September by D. Carpenter, M. G.
    Reference: Marriage Book E Page 16

RICE, W. L. to Mrs. F. J. Huges /Hughes7   16 July 1867
    m. 16 July by Thoams Russell, M. G.
    Reference: Marriage Book G Page 18

RICE, William J. to Martha Lusk   13 October 1842
    m. 13 October by W. H. Ballew, J. P.
    Reference: Marriage Book C Page 64

RICE, William L. to Elizabeth A. Rayburn   3 May 1843
    m. 3 May by W. F. Forest, M. G.
    Reference: Marriage Book C Page 78

RICHARDS, J. S. to Lydia H. Johns,   23 May 1861
    all of McMinn County
    m. 23 May 1861 by James Forrest, Esq.
    Reference: Athens Post, Volume XIII,
    #663, 7 June 1861

RICHARDSON, Samuel H. to Sarah E. Buttram   8 October 1866
    m. 1 November by Hiel Buttram, M. G.
    Reference: Marriage Book G Page 1;
    County Archives

RICHARDSON, Thomas L. to Francis Cate   7 December 1829
    Wesley Kinman, Security
    Reference: County Archives

RICHEY, S. A. to Elizabeth J. Rudd   11 February 1870
    m. 13 February by James M. Watson, M. G.
    Reference: Marriage Book G Page 58

RICHEY, Silas H. to Polly Cry   11 July 1850
    m. 11 July by J. D. Henley, J. P.
    Reference: Marriage Book D Page 29

RICHEY, William to Margret S. Cry   7 November 1850
    m. 7 November by J. D. Henly, J. P.
    Reference: Marriage Book D Page 34

RICHEY, William to Emeline Tallent   18 September 1870
    m. 18 September by J. D. Gaston, J. P.
    Reference: Marriage Book G Page 65

RICHEY, William W. to Elizabeth Cauldwell   30 October 1851
    m. 30 October by Robert Gregory, M. G.
    Reference: Marriage Book D Page 45

RICHEY - see also RITCHEY

RICK, Isaack G. to Milvena Casteel   8 May 1867
    James Gresham, Security
    Reference: Marriage Book G Page 15;
    County Archives

RICKS, C. C. to Rebecky P. Casteel   14 February 1867
    m. 14 February by S. W. R_____, J. P.
    Reference: Marriage Book G Page 11

RIDDLE, Benj. to Elizabeth J. Fairll   3 December 1846
    m. 3 December by R. A. McAdoo, J. P.
    Reference: Marriage Book C Page 148

RIDDLE, James to Mary Read   27 June 1846
    m. 28 June by J. H. Benton, J. P.
    Reference: Marriage Book C Page 139

RIDDLE, John M. to Nancy M. Kennedy   6 February 1857
    m. 8 February by Daniel McPhail, J. P.
    Reference: Marriage Book D Page 124

RIDDLE, Miles H. to Mary A. Bishop   2 March 1858
    m. 4 March by Dan McPhail, J. P.
    Reference: Marriage Book D Page 137

RIDDLE, Pleasant to Nancy A. Bishop   25 January 1865
    m. 26 January by Henry Baldwin, J. P.
    Reference: Marriage Book F Page 15;
    County Archives

RIDDLE, Plesant to Miss Keziah Ervin   8 April 1852
    m. 11 April by Daniel McPhail, J. P.
    Reference: Marriage Book D Page 51

RIDDLE, Samuel L. to Sarah C. Dake   17 August 1841
    Reference: Marriage Book C Page 45

RIDEN, J. T. to Martha J. Eaden (Eaton)   1 August 1867
    Lewis Hampton, Security
    m. 1 August by H. M. Sloop
    Reference: Marriage Book G Page 18;
    County Archives

RIDINGS, John R. to Mrs. Sarah E. Emmerson   8 July 1867
    m. 8 July by E. Z. Williams, J. P.
    Reference: Marriage Book G Page 17

RIGGINS, Thomas to Mathursa Pugh   18 September 1841
    m. 18 September by J. H. Benton, J. P.
    Reference: Marriage Book C Page 46

RIGGS, A. A. to Mary Prestwood   7 August 1868
    m. 9 August by Elihu Kelly, J. P.
    Reference: Marriage Book G Page 34

RIGGS, B. A. to Mary Daugherty   29 September 1858
    m. 3 October by M. A. Cass, M. G.
    Reference: Marriage Book D Page 148

RIGGS, Martin to Elizabeth A. Elliott   4 December 1857
    m. 6 December by H. J. Brock, J. P.
    Reference: Marriage Book D Page 132

RIGGS, S. P. to Nancy Elliott   19 March 1846
    m. 19 March by M. A. Cass, J. P.
    Reference: Marriage Book C Page 136

RISDEN, James to Tempy Keaton   11 July 1865
    m. 12 July by Daniel McPhail, J. P.
    Reference: Marriage Book F Page 21;
    County Archives

RITCHEY, Alexander to Mary L. Bogart   1 November 1865
    m. 2 November by W. W. Thorpe, M. G.
    Reference: Marriage Book F Page 29;
    County Archives

RITCHEY, Alexander to Cathirin Talent   11 April 1869
    m. 11 April by H. Pearce, J. P.
    Reference: Marriage Book G Page 46

RITCHEY, Robert to Sarah Cry   15 November 1856
    m. 16 November by Robert Gregory, M. G.
    Reference: Marriage Book D Page 119

RITCHEY - see also RICHEY

RITCHIE, John J. to Frances Henley   24 March 1847
    William J. Ware, Security
    m. 25 March by William H. Ballew, J. P.
    Reference: Marriage Book C Page 154;
    County Archives

ROBBINETT, John F. to Rhoda T. McNabb   3 December 1851
    m. 3 December by A. John, M. G.
    Reference: Marriage Book D Page 46

ROBERSON, Benjamin to Catharine Coats   18 October 1866
    m. 21 October by E. L. Miller, M. G.
    Reference: Marriage Book G Page 5;
    County Archives

ROBERSON, Nacy to Margaret Coats   30 November 1866
    m. 4 December by Rev. D. Carpenter
    Reference: Marriage Book G Page 5;
    County Archives

ROBERTS, Benjamin to Ann Helvy   5 December 1842
    m. 11 December by Tapley Gregory, J. P.
    Reference: Marriage Book C Page 68

ROBERTS, David F. to Elizabeth Maddin   4 October 1854
    m. 5 October by H. M. Roberts, J. P.
    Reference: Marriage Book D Page 88;
    County Archives

ROBERTS, E. A. to Jane Benton   1 March 1866
    John Lockmiller, Security
    m. by J. J. Kirksey, J. P.
    Reference: Marriage Book F Page 38;
    County Archives

ROBERTS, E. W. to Mrs. Mary Womack   4 December 1854
    m. 5 December by W. H. H. Duggan, M. G.
    Reference: Marriage Book D Page 90

ROBERTS, Edmund to Elizabeth C. Pettitt   2 November 1848
    m. 2 November by Robert Gregory, M. G.
    Reference: Marriage Book D Page 7

ROBERTS, Edmund D. to Susanah Mansell   6 September 1838
    m. 7 September by Robert Randolph, M. G.
    Reference: Marriage Book C Page 6;
    County Archives

ROBERTS, Henry M. to Elizabeth A. Horton   23 April 1839
    m. 23 April by John Moyers, M. G.
    Reference: Marriage Book C Page 16

ROBERTS, Hugh to Jane Green   24 May 1852
    m. 24 May by Daniel McPhail, J. P.
    Reference: Marriage Book D Page 52;
    County Archives

ROBERTS, James to Mrs. J. Romines   6 June 1870
    m. 7 June by W. G. Horton, J. P.
    Reference: Marriage Book G Page 61

ROBERTS, James F. to Esther C. Tunnell   15 August 1855
    m. 16 September by J. Swishir, M. G.
    Reference: Marriage Book D Page 101

ROBERTS, Joel to Mary Spearman   16 February 1848
    m. 17 February by William McKamy, J. P.
    Reference: Marriage Book C Page 168;
    W. P. A.

ROBERTS, Joseph to Lucy Mofield   7 November 1846
    m. 8 November by Hiel Buttram, M. G.
    Reference: Marriage Book C Page 146

ROBERTS, Mathew to Margaret A. Witt   27 January 1860
    m. 29 January by Rev. D. Carpenter
    Reference: Marriage Book E Page 8

ROBERTS, Peter to Cloe Guffey   14 October 1843
    m. 15 October by Hiel Buttram, M. G.
    Reference: Marriage Book C Page 87

ROBERTS, Thomas C. to Nancy Miller   24 July 1844
    m. 25 July by C. A. Smith, M. G.
    Reference: Marriage Book C Page 105

ROBERTS, Thos. M. to Permelia E. Cate   1 October 1868
    m. 1 October by W. Ereckson, M. G.
    Reference: Marriage Book G Page 37

ROBERTS, William to Harriet Owens   1 June 1844
    m. 2 June by J. H. Benton, J. P.
    Reference: Marriage Book C Page 103

ROBERTS, William E. to Elizabeth J. Carter   18 May 1853
    Jon F. Brumit, Security
    Reference: Marriage Book D Page 66;
    County Archives

ROBERTS, William S. to Katherine Walker   2 November 1842
    m. 3 November by L. L. Ball, J. P.
    Reference: Marriage Book C Page 66

ROBERTS - see also ROBBERTS

ROBERTSON, Hugh to Mrs. Sarah E. Snider   25 April 1864
    Elijah Benton, Security
    m. 27 April by A. J. Mathis, M. G.
    Reference: Marriage Book F Page 2;
    County Archives

ROBERTSON, Joseph to Elizabeth Ann Dodson 14 November 1850
    Reference: Marriage Book D Page 34

ROBERTSON (ROBESON), Milton (William) to   20 September 1849
    Mary Hardy
    Byrum Allen, Security
    m. 21 September by M. Southard, M. G.
    Reference: Marriage Book D Page 19;
    County Archives
    Note: Bond signed Milton Robertson and
    Marriage Book endorsed William Robeson.

ROBERTSON - see also ROBERSON

ROBESON, Edward M. to Catharine Campbell   13 December 1843
     m. 17 December by James Carter
     Reference: Marriage Book C Page 92

ROBESON (ROBISON), Elihu to Mary E. Moore   15 November 1832
     m. 15 November by Robert Randolph, C. C. C.
     Reference: County Archives

ROBESON, Hiram to Sally Keeton   4 July 1844
     m. 4 July by Daniel McPhail, J. P.
     Reference: Marriage Book C Page 104

ROBESON, Hunt to Jane Cannon   18 December 1868
     m. 18 December by W. C. Owens, J. P.
     Reference: Marriage Book G Page 41

ROBINETT, Hugh to Celia Murphy   25 October 1856
     m. 25 October 1857 /sic/ by M. R. Wear, J.P.
     Reference: Marriage Book D Page 117
     Note: Celia Murphy is bride in two
     consecutive entries. See Vinsant, Henry.

ROBINETT - see also ROBBINET

ROBINSON, Daniel to Sarah Johnson   29 August 1870
     Reference: Marriage Book G Page 64

ROBINSON, James M. to Elizabeth Million   12 January 1870
     m. 12 January by A. Haun, M. G.
     Reference: Marriage Book G Page 57;
     County Archives

ROBISON, Dempsey to Mary Lewis   20 September 1848
     m. 20 September by Daniel McPhail, J. P.
     Reference: Marriage Book D Page 5

ROBISON, James to Caroline Anderson   12 January 1866
     Thomas Akins, Security
     m. 13 January by W. C. Owens, J. P.
     Reference: Marriage Book F Page 35;
     County Archives

ROBISON, Joseph to Mrs. Nancy C. Mayfield   6 August 1842
     m. 7 August by Robert Frazier, M. G.
     Reference: Marriage Book C Page 60

ROBISON, William S. to Sarah E. Smith   16 March 1856
     m. 16 March by T. J. Russell, M. G.
     Reference: Marriage Book D Page 108

ROCKHOLT, Thomas to Caroline Kinser   22 August 1865
     Paul Bunch, Security
     m. 24 August by S. M. Thomas, J. P.
     Reference: Marriage Book F Page 24;
     County Archives

RODDEN, James M. to Cathrin Lambert   27 March 1858
     m. 1 April by H. P. Wilson, J. P.
     Reference: Marriage Book D Page 138

RODERICK, William to Susan Guffy   5 February 1868
     m. 5 February by L. H. Cate, M. G.
     Reference: Marriage Book G Page 28

RODES, John to Tabitha Ann Richardson   16 October 1848
     m. 16 October by Uriah Johnston, J. P.
     Reference: Marriage Book D Page 6

RODGERS, Hiram W. to Elizabeth Campbell   3 February 1824
    John W. Overton, Security
    Reference: County Archives

ROGERS, A. F. to Mrs. Savilla McMinn   28 September 1870
    W. T. Hayes, Security
    m. 29 September by L. W. Crouch, M. G.
    Reference: Marriage Book G Page 66;
    County Archives; McMinn Chancery Case
    Number 437

ROGERS, Andrew L. to C. (Cherokee) A. Morgan   20 December 1849
    G. W. Morgan, Security
    m. 20 December by A. A. Mathews, M. G.
    Reference: Marriage Book D Page 23;
    County Archives

ROGERS, Henry to C. S. Thompson   26 July 1863
    m. 27 July by W. H. C. Thompson, J. P.
    Reference: Marriage Book E Page 2

ROGERS, Hugh to Elizabeth Amos   17 December 1844
    m. 17 December by William Newton, M. G.
    Reference: Marriage Book C Page 114

ROGERS, J. M. to Sallie Davis   14 February 1866
    Henry Hyman, Security
    m. 15 February by J. M. Miller, M. G.
    Reference: Marriage Book F Page 37;
    County Archives

ROGERS, James W. to Elizabeth Barksdale   1 September 1841
    Reference: Marriage Book C Page 46

ROGERS, Lawson W. to Marenda L. Jordon   16 June 1829
    William Hogan, Security
    Reference: County Archives

ROGERS, M. E. to Sarah J. Thompson   30 December 1856
    m. 6 January 1857 by C. R. Hoyl, M. G.
    Reference: Marriage Book D Page 122

ROGERS, Samuel to Mrs. Sureptha Freeman   9 December 1867
    m. 13 December (no signature)
    Reference: Marriage Book G Page 23

ROGERS, Thos. to Letticia Wallin   7 January 1846
    m. 8 January by M. C. Hawk
    Reference: Marriage Book C Page 131

ROGERS, William to Morning E. Womack   16 February 1867
    Thomas J. Rogers, Jr., Security
    m. 20 February by L. W. Crouch, M. G.
    Reference: Marriage Book G Page 11;
    County Archives

ROGES, William S. to Rachel Thompson   26 September 1849
    Joseph M. Roges, Security
    m. 27 September by John Jenkins, J. P.
    Reference: Marriage Book D Page 19;
    County Archives

ROGGERS, Isaac to Charlotty Cannon   12 July 1866
    m. 12 July by Elder F. M. Avans
    Reference: Marriage Book F Page 44

ROLAND, Abraham to Nancy Clark   1 March 1838
    m. 4 March by John Camp, J. P.
    Reference: Marriage Book C Page 2

ROLIN, Isaac to Rebecca Helms   14 February 1847
    Reference: Marriage Book C Page 152

ROLLING, Andrew to Rachel Martin   8 October 1849
    Elijah Rolling, Security
    m. 8 October by Samuel Snoddy, J. P.
    Reference: Marriage Book D Page 20;
    County Archives

ROLLINS, A. K. to Miss P. C. Johnson   10 December 1868
    m. 13 December by J. S. Russell, M. G.
    Reference: Marriage Book G Page 41

ROMACK, James to Polly McDonell   14 May 1829
    Robert John, Security
    m. 14· May by Benj. Isbell, J. P.
    Reference: County Archives

ROMINES, Johnathan to Lucinda Goode   20 August 1838
    m. 21 August by Elijah Hurst, J. P.
    Reference: Marriage Book C Page 5

ROPKA, Onne H. to Mary A. Malone   2 June 1864
    m. 2 June by W. C. Owen, J. P.
    Reference: Marriage Book F Page 3

ROSS, David to Sarah Ann Newland   Pg. 38:18 February 1841
    Page 38: No return   Pg. 41:27 February 1841
    Page 41: m. 28 Feb. by John W. Barnett,
    J. P.
    Reference: Marriage Book C Page 38;
    Marriage Book C Page 41

ROSE, John B. to Nancy M. Ensminger   7 December 1865
    Reference: Marriage Book F Page 32

ROSE, Samuel to Nancy Elliott   31 October 1856
    m. 2 November by William Newman, J. P.
    Reference: Marriage Book D Page 117

ROSE, William to Mary Ann Wilson   13 April 1854
    G. W. Standefer, Security
    m. 20 April by J. C. Carlock, J. P.
    Reference: Marriage Book D Page 83;
    County Archives

ROTHWELL, J. M. to Susan E. Baldwin   2 November 1865
    m. 2 November by Rev. Dan Carpenter
    Reference: Marriage Book F Page 29;
    County Archives

ROTHWELL, W. H. to Miss Vinila Arnwine   4 December 1841
    m. 9 December by Jonathan Thomas, J. P.
    Reference: Marriage Book C Page 49

ROTHWELL, Walter to Charlotte Lawson   21 December 1842
    m. 21 December (No signature)
    Reference: Marriage Book C Page 69

ROWAN, F. M. to Sarah E. Dixon   14 January 1865
    m. 17 January by J. S. Russell, M. G.
    Reference: Marriage Book F Page 14;
    County Archives

ROWAN, Francis M. to Miss Sidney Ann Lane   26 September 1848
    m. 28 September by W. C. Lee, M. G.
    Reference: Marriage Book D Page 5

ROWAN, R. C. to Alice E. Cantrell   11 October 1865
    m. 11 October by Calvin Denton, M. G.
    Reference: Marriage Book F Page 28;
    County Archives

ROWLAND, Isaac to Eliza Shook   26 November 1856
    m. 26 November by O. M. Liner, J. P.
    Reference: Marriage Book D Page 119

ROWLAND, J. T. to Louisa J. Keith   27 May 1852
    m. 27 May by John Scruggs, M. G.
    Reference: Marriage Book D Page 53

ROWLAND, Philip to Sarah A. McCroskey   23 July 1857
    m. 23 July by W. W. Haymes, M. G.
    Reference: Marriage Book D Page 127

ROWLAND - see also ROLAND

ROWLY, John A. to Rebecca Elizabeth McCallia   15 April 1848
    m. 16 April by M. C. Hawk, M. G.
    Reference: W. P. A.
    (Note: Page 1 in Book D is missing)

ROYSTON, Samuel W., Attorney of Greene Co.,   5 December 1848
    to Elizabeth Parshall, daughter of late
    Dr. J. Parshall of Athens, Surgeon U. S.
    Army,
    m. 5 December by A. A. Mathis, M. G.
    Reference: Marriage Book D Page 8;
    "Knoxville Register", Volume 8, #417,
    20 December 1848

RUCKER, James to Elizabeth Gregory   26 February 1838
    m. 27 February by Larkin Taylor, J. P.
    Reference: Marriage Book C Page 2

RUCKER, James C. to Virginia McDonald   8 September 1849
    m. 9 September by Jas. C. Bryan, J. P.
    Reference: Marriage Book D Page 18

RUCKER, James H. to E. C. Douglass   23 April 1858
    Reference: Marriage Book D Page 140

RUCKER, Jas. M. to ____ Wasson (Name missing)   4 October 1854
    m. 4 October by A. John, M. G.
    Reference: Marriage Book D Page 88

RUCKER, Jesse to Mivinda Gregory   26 Ocotber 1844
    m. 26 October by R. A. McAdoo, J. P.
    Reference: Marriage Book C Page 110

RUCKER, Joseph to Erthula Hutsell   15 November 1869
    m. 15 November by Jno. N. Moore, M. G.
    Reference: Marriage Book G Page 54

RUCKER, Samuel B. to Eliza Jane Ivans   17 March 1856
    m. 20 March by O. M. Liner, J. P.
    Reference: Marriage Book D Page 108

RUCKER, Silas N. to Martha Zeigler   23 May 1861
    m. 23 May by D. L. Miler, M. G.
    Reference: Marriage Book E Page 4

RUCKER, Wilford to Margaret Young Bates
    m. 17 June 1830 by Rev. John Walker
    Reference: "Knoxville Register", Vol. 14,
    #726, 7 July 1830

RUCKER, William to Mary A. Burk   10 July 1856
    m. 10 July by Jas. Ziglar, J. P.
    Reference: Marriage Book D Page 111

RUDD, Elijah to Eliza Garland   25 May 1841
    Reference: Marriage Book C Page 42

RUDD, Herrod to Margaritt Reatherford   16 February 1842
    (Rutherford)
    James Bales, Security
    Reference: Marriage Book C Page 53;
    County Archives

RUDD, Isaiah to Martha Owen   27 August 1839
    m. "on Tuesday last" by Rev. A. Slover
    Reference: Marriage Book C Page 22;
    "Hiwassee Patriot" 29 August 1839,
    Volume I, #25

RUDD, Jas. B. to Mary A. Brown   6 January 1858
    m. 6 January by S. Philips, M. G.
    Reference: Marriage Book D Page 134

RUDD, John to Mrs. Jane Stansberry   28 April 1852
    m. 29 April by A. Swafford, J. P.
    Reference: Marriage Book D Page 52;
    County Archives

RUDD, John to Judith A. Guthery   20 December 1855
    m. 20 December by E. C. Miller, M. G.
    Reference: Marriage Book D Page 105

RUDD, Parker to Malissa Jane Hughes   31 July 1845
    m. 31 July by William H. Ballew, J. P.
    Reference: Marriage Book C Page 123

RUDD, William H. to Miss C. M. Zeigler   27 September 1854
    m. 27 September by M. A. Cass, M. G.
    Reference: Marriage Book D Page 87

RUE, John to Silday M. Reatherford   27 February 1859
    m. 27 February by James Baker, J. P.
    Reference: Marriage Book D Page 157

RUE - see also REW

RUNOLDS (RENOLDS), H. T. to Matildy Elizabeth Dugan   6 June 1866
    m. 10 June by C. R. Hoyl, M. G.
    Reference: Marriage Book F Page 42;
    County Archives

RUSSELL, G. T. to Emma Mayfield   22 September 1869
    m. 23 September by Jno. H. Brunner, M. G.
    Reference: Marriage Book G Page 51

RUSSELL, Isaac to Mary D. Slack   15 November 1866
    m. 15 November by J. S. Russell, M. G.
    Reference: Marriage Book G Page 4;
    County Archives

RUSSELL, James B. to Mary J. Stepp   12 September 1865
    m. 13 September by John Scruggs, M. G.
    Reference: Marriage Book F Page 25;
    County Archives

RUSSELL, James S. to Maldonethy Cate   10 October 1842
    m. 20 October by Wilson Chapman, M. G.
    Reference: Marriage Book C Page 64

RUSSELL, John to Sarah Weatherly   1 June 1858
   William S. Gouldy, Security
   m. 10 June by R. Reynolds, J. P.
   Reference: Marriage Book D Page 141;
   County Archives

RUSSELL, W. N. to Jennie Bonner   11 February 1870
   m. 13 February by L. W. Crouch, M. G.
   Reference: Marriage Book G Page 58

RUTERHFORD, A. H. to Lucinda Harris   17 September 1844
   m. 19 September by Samuel Snoddy, J. P.
   Reference: Marriage Book C Page 108

RUTHERFORD, Calvin M. to Kezia Carter   30 July 1850
   m. 1 August by Geo. W. Wallis, J. P.
   Reference: Marriage Book D Page 29

RUTHERFORD, J. L. to Hariet R. Rodden   8 January 1866
   F. M. Cantrell, Security
   m. 9 January by A. J. Kirksey, J. P.
   Reference: Marriage Book F Page 35;
   County Archives

RUTHERFORD, James to Rebecca A. Gamble   11 November 1843
   m. 12 November by James Sewell, M. G.
   Reference: Marriage Book C Page 90

RUTHERFORD, James H. to Polly Ann Dickson   11 November 1837
   Reference: W. P. A.

RUTHERFORD, James M. to Nancy Cantrell   12 July 1843
   m. 15 July by A. Carlock, J. P.
   Reference: Marriage Book C Page 81

RUTHERFORD, John to Diletha Grogan   24 August 1868
   m. 1 September by Uriah Payne, M. G.
   Reference: Marriage Book G Page 35;
   County Archives

RUTHERFORD, Joseph R. to Louisa E. Pearce   17 April 1850
   m. 18 April by Thomas T. Russell, M. G.
   Reference: Marriage Book D Page 27

RUTHERFORD, Larkin B. to Julian Wetherly   2 January 1854
   Reference: Marriage Book D Page 76

RUTHERFORD, Randle to Artimelia Dy   9 February 1850
   Reference: Marriage Book D Page 25

RUTHERFORD, Robert A. to Mary Jane Loughmiller   3 May 1855
   m. 3 May by J. C. Carlock, J. P.
   Reference: Marriage Book D Page 98

RUTHERFORD, Rufus T. to Mary E. Crockett   5 May 1866
   m. 6 May by A. J. Kirksey
   Reference: Marriage Book F Page 41

RUTHERFORD, William to Elizabeth Stainer   6 January 1840
   Reference: Marriage Book C Page 26

RUTHERFORD, William to Frances Atkinson   25 February 1846
   m. 26 February by C. R. Hoyle, J. P.
   Reference: Marriage Book C Page 134;
   County Archives

RUTHERFORD, William J. to Mira Humpheys   1 October 1845
   m. 1 October by Samuel H. Jordon, J. P.
   Reference: Marriage Book C Page 127

RUTHERFORD, William P. to Elizabeth A. Loughmiller   4 March 1850
    m. 5 March by J. C. Carlock, J. P.
    Reference: Marriage Book D Page 26

RUTHERFORD - see also FEATHERFORD, RUETHURFORD

RUTLEDGE, Thomas to M. E. Patterson   19 March 1869
    m. 21 March by George W. Maston, J. P.
    Reference: Marriage Book G Page 45

RYAN, Samuel D. to Mary L. McMaCauts
    m. 11 September 1849 at 35 minutes after 9 o'clock
    in the morning by H. C. Cooke, M. G.
    Reference: Marriage Book D Page 17

RYERSON, William to Sally Murray   24 October 1864
    m. 24 October by E. Rowley, M. G.
    Reference: Marriage Book F Page 9;
    County Archives

RYNOLDS (REYNOLDS), John M. to Maggie A. Dixon   9 March 1869
    T. J. Reynolds, Security
    m. 10 March by Calvin Denton, M. G.
    Reference: Marriage Book G Page 44;
    County Archives

SAMPLE, John to Jemima Divine   30 September 1848
    m. 1 October by J. C. Carlock, J. P.
    Reference: Marriage Book D Page 5

SAMPLE, T. B. to Miss C. R. Campbell   4 November 1856
    m. 4 November by Geo. A. Caldwell, M. G.
    Reference: Marriage Book D Page 118

SAMPLES, Jesse of Rhea County to Debora Browder
    of McMinn County
    m. 25 December 1832 by Rev. A. Slover
    Reference: "Knoxville Register", Volume 17,
    #859, 9 January 1833

SAMPLEY, William B. to Caroline Rider   11 October 1856
    m. 12 October by A. John, M. G.
    Reference: Marriage Book D Page 116

SAMPSON, Josiah to Hannah E. Smith   22 July 1859
    m. 24 July by A. D. Brient, J. P.
    Reference: Marriage Book E Page 12

SANDERS, Arden to Elisabeth Lile   22 December 1845
    Reference: Marriage Book C Page 130

SANDERS, Clemmons to Caroline Peoples   23 September 1845
    Reference: Marriage Book C Page 127

SANDERS, James to Rody Beck   28 September 1855
    m. 29 September by Jacob Whitsides, M. G.
    Reference: Marriage Book D Page 103

SANDERS, Thompson to Nancy Fox   5 April 1830
    m. 8 April by Jas. M. Cartney, J. P.
    Reference: W. P. A.

SANDERS - see also SAUNDERS

SARLIN, John to Mary O'Daniel   8 April 1843
    m. 9 April by A. Carlock, J. P.
    Reference: Marriage Book C Page 77

SCARBEROUGH, John to Ellen Cass   7 July 1870
    m. 7 July by P. M. Long, J. P.
    Reference: Marriage Book G Page 62

SCARBOROUGH, John H. to Sarah A. Wallen   19 August 1858
    m. 26 August by Joel Culpepper, J. P.
    Reference: Marriage Book D Page 144

SCARBOROUGH, William to Denize Hambright   9 December 1843
    Reference: Marriage Book C Page 92

SCARBROUGH, William to Elizabeth Rogers   28 June 1855
    m. 28 June by William McAmy, M. G.
    Reference: Marriage Book D Page 100

SCHICK, L. /S ?/ Finley to Huldah H. Haden   19 June 1852
    William E. Pride, Security
    m. 28 June by T. L. Hoyl, M. G.
    Reference: Marriage Book D Page 53;
    County Archives

SCOGGIN, Burgess to Rebecca Gold   25 February 1839
    m. 26 February by J. Edmonson, M. G.
    Reference: Marriage Book C Page 15

SCOGGINS. D. F. to Margaret Buttram   5 March 1846
    m. 12 March by James Sewell, Minister
    Reference: Marriage Book C Page 135

SCOTT, George W. to Mary Fox   5 November 1849
    John Reynolds, Security
    m. 6 November by George W. Kirksey, J. P.
    Reference: Marriage Book D Page 20;
    County Archives

SCOTT, John A. to Narcissa Walker   2 April 1866
    m. 10 April by A. Marshman, M. G.
    Reference: Marriage Book F Page 40

SCOTT, Joseph to Sarah Ann Sams   8 August 1839
    m. 8 August by L. R. Morrison, V. D. M.
    Reference: Marriage Book C Page 21

SCOTT, Thomas C. to Emaline Burns   23 September 1852
    m. 24 September by J. W. Cox, J. P.
    Reference: Marriage Book D Page 56

SCOTT, William to Manurvy Buster   5 April 1869
    m. 7 April by W. J. Walsh, J. P.
    Reference: Marriage Book G Page 45

SCROGGINS, Jackson to Julia Buttram   20 December 1848
    Elihu E. Buttram, Security
    Reference: Marriage Book D Page 9;
    County Archives

SCROGINS, Mathew to Nancy Carroll   14 November 1867
    m. 15 November by Levi Fitzgerald, M. G.
    Reference: Marriage Book G Page 22

SCRUGGS, Thomas to M. J. Hale   13 October 1848
    m. 1848 by Nathaniel Barnett, M. G.
    Reference: Marriage Book D Page 6

SCYBERT, Henry to Elizabeth Melton   30 October 1865
    m. 31 October by P. M. Long, J. P.
    Reference: Marriage Book F Page 29

SEAY, Woodson to Keziah Larrew   20 August 1828
    A. H. Bradock, Security
    .m. 20 August by John S. Wilson, J. P.
    Reference: County Archives; W. P. A.

SEBERT - see SCYBERT, SEYBERT

SECREST, T. M. to Miss D. A. Thompson   9 June 1868
    m. 11 June by B. E. Cass, J. P.
    Reference: Marriage Book G Page 32

SEHORN, William to Ann E. Coleman   17 March 1842
    Reference: Marriage Book C Page 55

SEHORN - see also SEAHORN

SELF - see SELPH

SELLERS, Isaiah to Mary Gallant   19 October 1840
    m. 22 October by George Monroe, M. G.
    Reference: Marriage Book C Page 32

SELLERS, J. W. to Nancy Wassom   7 January 1847
    m. 7 January by G. W. Wallis, J. P.
    Reference: Marriage Book C Page 150

SELLERS, James M. to Martha Wasson   18 January 1847
    m. 21 January by G. W. Wallis, J. P.
    Reference: Marriage Book C Page 151

SELLERS, Joseph H. to Margaret Turnmire   12 December 1858
    m. 13 December by Joel Culpepper, J. P.
    Reference: Marriage Book D Page 153

SELPH, John A. to Mary Ann Mcinturff   Not Dated
    m. 6 September 1849 by Andrew John, M. G.
    Reference: Marriage Book D Page 17

SENTER, Calvin H. to Sarah Gage   15 December 1848
    Reference: Marriage Book D Page 9

SENTER, James P. to Jane (Nancy Jane) Matlock   21 April 1858
    James H. Rice, Security
    m. 21 April by Henry Rice, M. G.
    Reference: Marriage Book D Page 139;
    County Archives

SENTER - see also CENTER

SEWELL, George S. to Margaret E. Wilson   8 December 1856
    m. 11 December 1857 /sic/ by Stephen Sharets, M.G.
    Reference: Marriage Book D Page 120

SEWELL, Marcus E. L. to Miss Vina Parr   2 September 1846
    m. 2 September by M. C. Atchley, Minister
    Reference: Marriage Book C Page 142

SEWELL - see also SOWELL

SEXTON, James K. to Sarah E. Landers   21 July 1866
    Z. F. Gentery, Security
    m. 22 July by Elihu Kelley, J. P.
    Reference: Marriage Book F Page 44;
    County Archives

SEXTON, James R. to Betsey Batson   7 August 1826
    Joel Broch, Security
    Reference: W. P. A.

SEYBERT, John to Martha Stephenson   6 March 1837
    m. 11 March by A. B. Neal, J. P.
    Reference: W. P. A.

SHAMBLIN, John H. to Martha Helms   16 January 1866
    William M. Shamblin, Security
    m. 21 January by F. A. Dixon, J. P.
    Reference: Marriage Book F Page 36;
    County Archives

SHAMBLIN, William M. to Mary S. Johnston   12 (19) October 1864
    D. H. Brock, Security
    m. 24 November by William S. McKnight, J. P.
    Reference: Marriage Book F Page 8;
    County Archives

SHANNON, Saml. to Martha Weston   22 November 1870
    m. 22 November by T. Sullins, M. G.
    Reference: Marriage Book G Page 69

SHAPMAN, Jacob to Marthee Burk   12 Ocotber 1826
    m. 12 Ocotber by John Miller, J. P.
    Reference: W. P. A.

SHARP, Addison to Mary D. Porter   25 Ocotber 1849
    William W. Porter, Security
    m. 25 October by A. A. Mathews, M. G.
    Reference: Marriage Book D Page 20;
    County Archives

SHARP, Jacob to Vilana Graves   21 August 1847
    Reference: Marriage Book C Page 159

SHARP, James to Malinda Robison   23 June 1865
    m. 24 June by Henry Baldwin, J. P.
    Reference: Marriage Book F Page 20

SHARP, Joseph to Eliza Richards   14 January 1851
    m. 16 January by William McKamy, J. P.
    Reference: Marriage Book D Page 37

SHARP, Robert to Nancy Ann Brown   28 February 1839
    Reference: Marriage Book C Page 14

SHARP, Robert P. to Calista Cassada   19 January 1841
    Reference: Marriage Book C Page 36

SHARP, Samuel T. to Mary Rhea   14 April 1847
    m. 13 /sic/ April by Wilson Chapman, M. G.
    Reference: Marriage Book C Page 155

SHARP, Turner to Winney Bicknell   7 August 1845
    m. 9 August by B. E. Blain, J. P.
    Reference: Marriage Book C Page 124

SHARPE, Hiram of McMinn County to Catharine Herring
    m. 26 June 1833 in Anderson County by
    Isaac Miller, Esq.
    Reference: "Knoxville Republican", Volume 2,
    Number 93, 10 July 1833

SHEARER, John H. to Paralee Bonner   22 November 1865
    Reference: Marriage Book F Page 31

SHEARER, John M. to Nancy E. Bradley   4 December 1867
    James A. Miller, Security
    m. 5 December by Charles Cate, J. P.
    Reference: Marriage Book G Page 24;
    County Archives

SHEETS, William to Lotty Townsend   19 March 1845
    m. 20 March by William Newton, M. G.
    Reference: Marriage Book C Page 118

SHELL, Benjamin to Malissa Moore   25 August 1847
    m. 2 September by Tapley Gregory, J. P.
    Reference: Marriage Book C Page 159

SHELL, Charles to Manerva Ellis   11 November 1857
    m. 12 November 1858 /sic/ by William H.
    Newman, M. G.
    Reference: Marriage Book D Page 131

SHELL, E. Mc. to Miss C. E. Carroll   29 March 1849
    D. B. Carlisle, Security
    m. 1 April by R. A. McAdoo, J. P.
    Reference: Marriage Book D Page 13;
    County Archives

SHELL, James to Lucinda White   27 July 1841
    m. 27 July by J. H. Benton, J. P.
    Reference: Marriage Book C Page 44

SHELL, James to Laura Ann Turk   4 March 1854
    m. 5 March by S. Sharritts
    Reference: Marriage Book D Page 81

SHELL, McKamry to Mary Howard   4 March 1851
    m. 4 March by L. D. Billingsly, M. G.
    Reference: Marriage Book D Page 39

SHELL - see also SHILL

SHELTON, David F. to Mary Terry   7 October 1843
    m. 8 October by Robert Gregory, Minister
    of Baptist Church
    Reference: Marriage Book C Page 87

SHELTON, Elisha to Miss Tenness Cate   5 September 1866
    m. 6 September by C. R. Hoyl, M. G.
    Reference: Marriage Book F Page 46

SHELTON, George to Sela Burks   10 April 1834
    John Roberts, Security
    Reference: County Archives

SHELTON, J. D. to Elizabeth A. Brown   16 March 1840
    Reference: Marriage Book C Page 28

SHELTON, Jackson to Rachel Cassaday   16 January 1841
    m. 17 January by David F. Jamison, J. P.
    Reference: Marriage Book C Page 36

SHELTON, James W. to Sarahann Lane   21 August 1844
    m. 22 August by Russell Lane, J. P.
    Reference: Marriage Book C Page 107

SHELTON, John E. to Lucinda Perrin   8 August 1853
    M. D. Anderson, Security
    m. 12 August by William Walker
    Reference: Marriage Book D Page 68;
    County Archives

SHELTON, Larkin to Martha A. Meltan   15 May 1856
    Elisha Gee, Security
    m. 15 May by A. F. Cox, M. G.
    Reference: Marriage Book D Page 110;
    County Archives

SHELTON, Samuel to Mary Wessengton   12 December 1836
    m. 15 December by Jonathan Thomas, J. P.
    Reference: W. P. A.

SHELTON, Sterling to Charlotte A. Cregory   13 November 1841
    m. 14 November by Jonathan Thomas, J. P.
    Reference: Marriage Book C Page 48

SHELTON, Thomas to Elizabeth Wright   28 December 1841
    m. 6 January 1842 by R. A. McAdoo, J. P.
    Reference: Marriage Book C Page 51

SHELTON, William to Miss Becket /first name missing7   2 August 1854
    m. 3 August by Robert Gregory, M. G.
    Reference: Marriage Book D Page 85

SHEPARD, John to Nancy Jane Hameltree   11 March 1868
    m. 11 March by E. Z. Williams, J. P.
    Reference: Marriage Book G Page 30

SHEREL, Ezekiel to Miss Luzany F. Staples   23 September 1858
    m. 23 September by William H. Ballew, J. P.
    Reference: Marriage Book D Page 147

SHERMAN, Thomas J. to Sarah E. Cate   8 January 1853
    m. 11 January by J. H. Reagan, J. P.
    Reference: Marriage Book D Page 61

SHERRILL, Benjamin C. to Lucinda Lawson   17 June 1840
    m. 18 June by Jonathan Thomas, J. P.
    Reference: Marriage Book C Page 30

SHERRILL, Ezekiel to Mrs. Margart Burk   2 August 1854
    m. 2 August by Robert Gregory, M. G.
    Reference: Marriage Book D Page 85

SHERRILL, Isaac to Jane Cate   26 October 1843
    m. 26 Ocotber by John Gaston, M. G.
    Reference: Marriage Book C Page 88

SHERRILL, James to Sarah Matilda Childers   31 August 1848
    m. 1 September by A. F. Shannon, M. G.
    Reference: Marriage Book D Page 4

SHERRILL, John B. to Mary Shook   8 April 1846
    m. 9 April by M. D. Anderson, J. P.
    Reference: Marriage Book C Page 137

SHERRILL - see also SHEREL

SHIELD, William to Elizabeth Lee   27 February 1840
    m. 27 February by Hamilton Bradford, J. P.
    Reference: Marriage Book C Page 27

SHIELDS, Banner to Nancy Bailey   29 November 1823
    Elijah Dodson, Security
    Reference: W. P. A.

SHIELDS, John to Ann Shook   19 September 1847
    m. 21 September by S. H. Jordan, J. P.
    Reference: Marriage Book C Page 160

SHIPLEIGH, Adam to Louisa Cash   1 February 1840
    m. 3 February by Madison C. Hawk,
    M. G. in M. E. Church
    Reference: Marriage Book C Page 20;
    Marriage Book C Page 25

SHIPLEY, Alexander to Naomy Gibson
    m. 5 September by M. C. Hawk, M. G.
    Reference: Marriage Book C Page 107
                                              3 September 1844

SHIPLEY, David F. to Elizabeth Sharp
    m. 6 January by Hiel Buttram, M. G.
    Reference: Marriage Book D Page 24
                                              2 January 1850

SHIPLEY, E. S. to Mary E. Love
    m. 8 November by Joseph Neil, J. P.
    Reference: Marriage Book D Page 150
                                            8 November 1858

SHIPLEY, John to Theby Fitch
    m. 2 October /sic7 by D. W. Beaver, M. G.
    Reference: Marriage Book D Page 117
                                          31 October 1856

SHIPLEY, Martin J. to Eveline Dyer
    m. 11 September by Daniel McPhail, J. P.
    Reference: Marriage Book C Page 108
                                      11 September 1844

SHIPLEY, Martin J. to Barbary Goodwin
    m. 6 January by A. D. Bryant, J. P.
    Reference: Marriage Book D Page 106
                                          5 January 1856

SHIPLEY, Martin V. to Polly Sivils
    m. 23 December by M. C. Hawk, M. G.
    Reference: Marriage Book C Page 149
                                      16 December 1846

SHIPLEY, Nehemiah to Mary E. Fitch
    m. 26 November by William Thompson, M. G.
    Reference: Marriage Book G Page 61
                                            20 May 1870

SHIPLEY, R. W. to Catharine Shelton
    m. 17 September by James Bonner, J. P.
    Reference: Marriage Book D Page 129
                                      8 September 1857

SHIPLEY, Sterling to Lurana Buttram
    m. 1 September by Rev. D. Carpenter
    Reference: Marriage Book D Page 31
                                      27 August 1850

SHIPLEY, Thomas to Nancy Jane Wattenbarger
    m. 6 April by Thos. Witten, G. M.
    Reference: Marriage Book C Page 155
                                        6 April 1847

SHIPLEY, William to Ann E. Brandon
    m. 18 February by James Sewell, M. G.
    Reference: Marriage Book C Page 97
                                    17 February 1844

SHIPLEY, William to Mrs. (Miss) Sarah Ball
    Russell Lane, Security
    m. 11 March by A. D. Morison, M. G.
    Reference: Marriage Book F Page 39;
    County Archives
                                      10 March 1866

SHIPLY, Robert Q. to Ann R. Gore
    m. 22 July by D. A. Cobbs, M. G.
    Reference: Marriage Book C Page 157
                                        22 July 1847

SHOAP, Rily to Martha Hudelsten
    m. 12 July by Stephen Hill, J. P.
    Reference: Marriage Book G Page 33
                                           9 July 1868

SHOEMAKER, A. J. to Hariet E. Davis
    m. 12 September by Jno. N. Stamper, M. G.
    Reference: Marriage Book G Page 50
                                  11 September 1869

SHOEMAKER, Calvin to Lucinda N. Brewer
    John C. Stephenson, Security
    Reference: Marriage Book D Page 65; County Archives
                                  21 April 1853

SHOEMAKER, Evan to Minerva C. Harless   22 July 1865
    J. L. Green, Security
    m. 6 August by A. D. Briant, J. P.
    Reference: Marriage Book F Page 22;
    County Archives

SHOEMAKER, Evin to Miss S. J. Crews   1 February 1868
    Thos. P. Pearson, Security
    Reference: Marriage Book G Page 27;
    County Archives

SHOEMAKER, John W. to Sarah Bowerman   12 August 1857
    m. 12 August by Jas. Parkerson, J. P.
    Reference: Marriage Book D Page 128

SHOEMAKER, Noah to Melvina Forester   3 September 1856
    m. 4 September by E. L. Miller, M. G.
    Reference: Marriage Book D Page 113

SHOEMAKER, William to Mary J. Morrow   3 March 1859
    m. 3 March by Jas. Parkerson, J. P.
    Reference: Marriage Book D Page 158;
    Marriage Book E Page 16

SHOEMAKER, William M. A. to Elizabeth Cannon   24 February 1850
    m. 25 February by John Jenkins, J. P.
    Reference: Marriage Book D Page 26

SHOEMAKER - see also SHUEMAKE, SHUMAKER

SHOOK, M. V. to Mrs. Jane Carden   13 January 1866
    B. L. Ward, Security
    m. 14 January by A. J. Kirksey, J. P.
    Reference: Marriage Book F Page 35;
    County Archives

SHOOK, Peter to Elizabeth B_____   6 April 1844
    m. 7 April by J. H. Benton, J. P.
    Reference: Marriage Book C Page 101

SHOOK, William, Jr. to Margaret Robeson   9 March 1848
    Reference: W. P. A.
    Note: Page 169 in Marriage Book C is
    missing

SHOPE - see SHOAP

SHUGART, E. B. C. to Mrs. Jane Fleming   26 March 1868
    m. 26 March by C. Long, M. G.
    Reference: Marriage Book G Page 31

SHUGART, John C. to Margaret S. E. Peeler   22 Ocotber 1864
    m. 27 October by C. Long, M. G.
    Reference: Marriage Book F Page 8

SHUGART - see also SUGART

SHULTZ, Humphrey to Isabella Terry   20 December 1849
    Granville Shultz, Security
    m. 20 December by Thos. W. Cuningham, J. P.
    Reference: Marriage Book D Page 23;
    County Archives

SHUTZ, Henry to Theressa Toomy   9 January 1849
    m. 11 January by J. P. Cobbs, J. P.
    Reference: Marriage Book D Page 10

SIMPSON, Elisha H. to Mary J. Rodgers   11 August 1865
    m. 13 August by Calvin Denton, M. G.
    Reference: Marriage Book F Page 23

SIMPSON, Henry M. to Eliza Ann Woody   14 August 1845
    m. 14 August by L. R. Morrison, V. D. M.
    Reference: Marriage Book C Page 124

SIMPSON, Henry M. to Hiley Carter   10 August 1853
    James H. Reagan, Security
    m. 11 August by J. H. Reagan, J. P.
    Reference: Marriage Book D Page 69;
    County Archives

SIMPSON, James M. to Martha T. Studdard   19 December 1867
    Thos. J. Cate, Security
    m. 19 December by G. W. Coleman, M. G.
    Reference: Marriage Book G Page 25;
    County Archives

SIMPSON, Samuel to Nancy Rudd
    m. 29 August 1838 by John McGaughey, J. P.
    Reference: Marriage Book C Page 6

SIMPSON, William H. to Angeline Triplett   11 January 1855
    m. 14 January by J. Douglass, M. G.
    Reference: Marriage Book D Page 93

SIMPSON, William M. to E. A. Metcalfe   20 December 1858
    m. 20 December by G. A. Caldwell, M. G.
    Reference: Marriage Book D Page 153

SIMS. G. W. to Miss Caldena Lawson   15 July 1844
    m. 17 July by J. R. Fryor, M. G.
    Reference: Marriage Book C Page 104

SIMS, John W. to Mary E. Moore   23 May 1854
    m. 22 /sic7 May by T. J. Russell, M. G.
    Reference: Marriage Book D Page 84

SISK, James to Mary King   13 September 1843
    m. 17 September by Tapley Gregory, J. P.
    Reference: Marriage Book C Page 85

SIVILS, Clinton to Emmie Allen   13 November 1870
    John Kimbrough, Security
    m. 13 November by W. Gettys, J. P.
    Reference: Marriage Book G Page 69;
    County Archives

SIVILS - see also SEIVILS

SLACK, A. E. to Nancy J. Filpot   6 September 1866
    m. 6 September by T. K. Bradshaw, M. G.
    Reference: Marriage Book F Page 46

SLACK, Abraham to Caroline Trew   26 November 1851
    Reference: Marriage Book D Page 46

SLAGER, Christopher to Jane Buttram   19 September 1838
    m. 19 September by William Jones, M. G.
    Reference: Marriage Book C Page 7

SLAPE, J. R. to Urlinia Bunch   23 January 1868
    m. 26 January by Stephen Hill, J. P.
    Reference: Marriage Book G Page 27

SLATER, Heny to Sarah A. Parke   12 July 1846
    m. 13 July by John Jenkins, J. P.
    Reference: Marriage Book C Page 139

SLAUGHTER, Jacob W. to Elizabeth King   24 June 1829
    Benj. Hambright, Security
    Reference: County Archives

SLAWTER, Gilbert to Mary Bell   2 March 1867
    m. 2 March by Gilmore Randolph, M. G.
    Reference: Marriage Book G Page 12

SLIGAR, A. J. to Sarah Cole   2 March 1864
    m. 9 March by William G. Wilson, M. G.
    Reference: Marriage Book E Page 14

SLIGAR, Jacob E. to Mary C. Hix   15 February 1868
    m. 19 February by D. Carpenter, M. G.
    Reference: Marriage Book G Page 28

SLIGER, A. J. to Miss E. J. Green   5 May 1864
    m. 8 May by A. D. Briant, J. P.
    Reference: Marriage Book F Page 3

SLIGER, Adam to M. E. Bales   24 July 1849
    m. 26 July by Hile Buttram, M. G.
    Reference: Marriage Book D Page 16

SLIGER, Asa to Matilda N. Frank   25 Ocotber 1856
    m. 6 November by A. D. Briant, J. P.
    Reference: Marriage Book D Page 117

SLIGER, Christopher to Mary Ann Gibson   3 April 1855
    m. 3 April by Robert Gregory, M. G.
    Reference: Marriage Book D Page 97

SLIGER, Francis M. to Hester E. Brock   20 August 1855
    m. 21 August by James Parkerson, J. P.
    Reference: Marriage Book D Page 102

SLIGER, J. L. to Sarah Brock   17 December 1866
    m. 17 December by L. W. Crouch, M. G.
    Reference: Marriage Book G Page 6

SLIGER, James E. to Amanda Spradling   27 February 1843
    m. 28 February Heil Buttram, M. G.
    Reference: Marriage Book C Page 75

SLIGER, Joseph to Nancy Butram   28 December 1844
    m. 29 December by Hiel Buttram, M. G.
    Reference: Marriage Book C Page 115

SLIGER, Joseph to Phebe E. Stanton   30 April 1864
    m. 5 May by Dan Carpenter, M. G.
    Reference: Marriage Book F Page 2

SLIGER, William to Pheby E. Knox   4 Ocotber 1866
    m. 7 Ocotber by Rev. Dan Carpenter
    Reference: Marriage Book G Page 1

SLIGER, Wyatt to Miss Nearva Hampton   25 October 1856
    m. 28 October by James Parkerson, J. P.
    Reference: Marriage Book D Page 116

SLIGER - see also SLAGER

SLOAN, Archibald to Jane Baker   21 February 1827
    m. 22 February by Robert W. McClary, J. P.
    Reference: County Archives

SLOOP, Henry to Magga Gilbert   3 April 1867
    P. F. Coffey, Security
    m. 3 April by E. Z. Williams, J. P.
    Reference: Marriage Book G Page 13;
    County Archives

SLOVER, John F. to Mary C. King   12 May 1847
    m. 13 May by W. G. E. Cunningham, M. G.
    Reference: Marriage Book C Page 155

SLOVER, William H. to Sarah J. Jarnigan   7 February 1842
    O. H. Lide, Security
    m. 8 February by M. C. Haw, Minister
    M. E. Church
    Reference: Marriage Book C Page 54;
    County Archives

SMALL, Albert G. to Mary P. Burnett   26 September 1848
    m. 26 September by Thos. H. Small, M. G.
    Reference: Marriage Book D Page 5

SMALL, James A. to Martha J. Rollings   1 June 1841
    m. 3 June by Thomas H. Small, M. G. C. P. C.
    Reference: Marriage Book C Page 43

SMALL, Wilson to Hannah Lamar   9 August 1843
    m. 10 August by D. Morris, M. G.
    Reference: Marriage Book C Page 83

SMALL, Wilson to Mary Owen   24 January 1853
    m. 25 January by David W. Beaver, M. G.
    Reference: Marriage Book D Page 62

SMALLEN, Solomon M. to Mrs. Sarah Pugh   17 August 1840
    m. 1 September by A. C. Robson, J. P.
    Reference: Marriage Book C Page 31;
    Will Book D Page 424

SMALLWOOD, James to Isabell Racket   30 Ocotber 1866
    m. 4 November by C. R. Hoyl, M. G.
    Reference: Marriage Book G Page 3

SMALLWOOD, Thomas N. to Sarah Ann Cantrell   11 September 1869
    m. 16 September by W. H. Cooper, J. P.
    Reference: Marriage Book G Page 50

SMART, A. J. to Miss Tobitha Benson   8 March 1845
    m. 9 March by M. C. Atchley, Minister
    Reference: Marriage Book C Page 118

SMART, Archibald F. to Isbell Farris   31 August 1843
    Reference: Marriage Book C Page 85

SMART, Isaac to Elizabeth Graves   26 February 1851
    m. 27 February by William Walker, J. P.
    Reference: Marriage Book D Page 39

SMART, Isaac L. to Sarah A. Guffey   17 February 1866
    m. 20 February by S. M. Thomas, J. P.
    Reference: Marriage Book F Page 38

SMART, William to Lucinda Graves   26 November 1840
    m. 3 December
    Reference: Marriage Book C Page 34

SMEDLEY, Henry K. to Eliza Dearmon   24 March 1834
    Abner B. Smedley, Security
    Reference: County Archives

SMEDLEY, John L. to Mary E. Trout   22 September 1863
    m. 27 September by C. R. Hoyl, M. G.
    Reference: Marriage Book E Page 18

SMITH, A. C. to Miss E. A. McKinsey   13 December 1865
    H. C. Fisher, Security
    m. 13 December by John N. Moore, M. G.
    Reference: Marriage Book F Page 32;
    County Archives

SMITH, Adam to Louisa Hampton   29 December 1868
    James H. Hornsby, Security
    m. 7 February 1869 by A. J. Shelton, J. P.
    Reference: Marriage Book G Page 41;
    County Archives

SMITH, Asa to Rhoda Dodson   4 February 1829
    m. 5 February by Jesse Dodson
    Reference: W. P. A.

SMITH, B. W. to Miss L. G. Prigmore   20 February 1844
    Reference: Marriage Book C Page 98

SMITH, Blueford to Eliza Jane Lemmon   2 May 1846
    m. 3 May by John Jenkins, J. P.
    Reference: Marriage Book C Page 138

SMITH, Boling to Mildred Rogers   25 April 1829
    Humphrey Reynolds, Security
    Reference: County Archives

SMITH, Eli to Elizabeth Vale   1 June 1840
    m. 1 June by John Tate, M. G.
    Reference: Marriage Book C Page 29

SMITH, Elijah to Eliza Coleir   20 February 1840
    m. 25 February 1839 /sic7 by D. Cantrell, J.P.
    Reference: Marriage Book C Page 27

SMITH, Elijah S. to Martha J. Morris   12 March 1854
    Raleigh Chesnutt, Security
    m. 12 March by Samuel Snoddy, J. P.
    Reference: Marriage Book D Page 81;
    County Archives

SMITH, F. M. to Miss S. E. Cullpeper   17 October 1868
    Reference: Marriage Book G Page 38

SMITH, George P. to Mary Ann Ball   14 September 1870
    m. 15 September by D. W. Beaver, M. G.
    Reference: Marriage Book G Page 65

SMITH, Hesekiah to Lucinda Swaford   29 December 1851
    m. by J. Jenkins, J. P.
    Reference: Marriage Book D Page 47

SMITH, Hugh, Merchant of Philadelphia, Monroe   13 December 1829
    County, to Elizabeth Jane Fyffe
    m. 13 December "on Tuesday evening last"
    by Robert Tate, M. G.
    Reference: W. P. A. and "Knoxville Register",
    Volume 14, #698, Wednesday 30 December 1829

SMITH, Irby H. to Keziah L. Barker   30 September 1841
    m. 7 October by T. B. Love, J. P.
    Reference: Marriage Book C Page 47

```
SMITH, Israel C. to Elizabeth A. Pesterfield               11 January 1853
    m. 11 January by J. Cunningham, M. G.
    Reference:  Marriage Book D Page 61

SMITH, J. N. to Nancy Snoddy                            29 September 1854
    m. 29 September by J. B. Cobb, J. P.
    Reference:  Marriage Book D Page 88

SMITH, James to Nancy Field                               30 August 1828
    Hiram Cooper, Security
    Reference:  County Archives

SMITH, Jas. to Miss Eglinetin Logan                     13 December 1851
    m. 13 December by Geo. W. Kirksey, J. P.
    Reference:  Marriage Book D Page 46

SMITH, James to Sarah J. Thompson                          10 June 1870
    m. 13 June
    Reference:  Marriage Book G Page 61

SMITH, James A. to Malinda J. Armstrong                    4 October 1856
    m. 5 October by Rober Cochran, J. P.
    Reference:  Marriage Book D Page 115

SMITH, James A. to Marthey E. Cox                       8 September 1866
    m. 9 September by William L. Burns, J. P.
    Reference:  Marriage Book F Page 46

SMITH, Jas. D. to Nancy A. Winters                         29 July 1857
    m. 29 July by I. S. Garrison, J. P.
    Reference:  Marriage Book D Page 128

SMITH, Jas. T. to Nancy Wilson                          28 December 1844
    m. 29 December by James Sewell, Minister
    Reference:  Marriage Book C Page 115

SMITH, Jas. T. to Nancy Wallen                             20 July 1858
    Reference:  Marriage Book D Page 143

SMITH, Jesse W. to Dorothy Clark                        22 February 1854
    Reference:  Marriage Book D Page 80

SMITH, John to Elizabeth Heck                              6 October 1841
    Reference:  Marriage Book C Page 47

SMITH, John B. to Sarah Thompson                           17 July 1850
    m. 25 July by Wilson Chapman, M. G.
    Reference:  Marriage Book D Page 29

SMITH, John C. to Manerva J. Smith                       14 August 1867
    m. 14 August by W. L. Burn, J. P.
    Reference:  Marriage Book G Page 19

SMITH, John W. to Nancy M. Naile                        12 December 1839
    m. 12 December by Rev. A. Slover
    Reference:  Marriage Book C Page 19;
    "Hiwassee Patriot", 19 December 1839,
    Volume I, Number 41

SMITH, Johnathan D. to Margaret Esmon                  13 September 1838
    m. 13 September by David F. Jamerson, J. P.
    Reference:  Marriage Book C Page 7

SMITH, Johnson to Savanah Lawson                        16 February 1846
    m. 16 February by Jas. Douglass, M. G.
    Reference:  Marriage Book C Page 133
```

SMITH, Jonathan T. to Elizabeth Shipley   10 March 1846
    m. 10 March by Russell Lane, J. P.
    Reference: Marriage Book C Page 135

SMITH, Joseph to Elizabeth Roberts   21 August 1828
    James Roberts, Security
    Reference: County Archives
    Note: In body of bond "James Williams"
    is bondsman, but bond is signed "James
    Roberts".

SMITH, Joseph to Delila Orr   10 February 1841
    m. 11 February by James Smith, Minister
    Reference: Marriage Book C Page 38

SMITH, Joseph to Visa Askins   23 May 1844
    m. 23 May by W. C. Atchley, Ord. Minister
    Reference: Marriage Book C Page 102

SMITH, Joseph to Mrs. Elizabeth Bookout   18 May 1867
    m. 19 May by W. C. Owens, J. P.
    Reference: Marriage Book G Page 15

SMITH, Joseph H. to Elizabeth C. Dixon   24 June 1852
    John J. Dixon, Security
    m. 24 June by Samuel Wilson, J. P.
    Reference: Marriage Book D Page 53

SMITH, Marshal to Nancy Dyer   16 December 1854
    m. 17 December by David W. Beaver, M. G.
    Reference: Marriage Book D Page 91

SMITH, Dr. Milo, of Smith's Cross Roads to
    Caroline L. Lipscomb, daughter of the late
    Spotswood Lipscomb of Bean's Station
    m. 25 July 1833 by Rev. Benj. Wallace
    at Athens
    Reference: "Knoxville Register", Volume 17,
    #889, 7 August 1833

SMITH, Morris M. to Amanda M. Jarnagin   14 December 1843
    m. 14 December by William H. Ballew, J. P.
    Reference: Marriage Book C Page 93

SMITH, Nat. D. to Eliza Goode   29 January 1839
    Reference: Marriage Book C Page 14

SMITH, Nemire to Sally Woody   24 May 1865
    m. 28 May by Z. Rose, M. G.
    Reference: Marriage Book F Page 18

SMITH, Newton to Eliza Smith   27 December 1847
    m. 27 December by W. F. Forrest, M. G.
    Reference: Marriage Book C Page 164

SMITH, Samuel A. to Martha E. McCarty   1 April 1846
    m. 2 April by M. C. Hawk, M. G.
    Reference: Marriage Book C Page 136

SMITH, Thos. to Sarah E. Wells   27 May 1857
    m. 30 May by R. Reynolds, J. P.
    Reference: Marriage Book D Page 126

SMITH, Thoams H. to Jemima Wammak   3 December 1855
    m. 6 December by H. M. Roberts, J. P.
    Reference: Marriage Book D Page 105

SMITH, William to Ann Robeson   8 February 1839
    Reference: Marriage Book C Page 15

SMITH, William to Malinda McGhehee   7 March 1848
    m. 9 March by George Monroe, M. G.
    Reference: Marriage Book C Page 168;
    W. P. A.

SMITH, William to Rebecca Morgan   29 March 1851
    m. 1 April by William Walker
    Reference: Marriage Book D Page 39

SMITH, William A. to Phebe J. Liner   17 August 1847
    m. 19 August by William Newton, M. G.
    Reference: Marriage Book C Page 158

SMITH, William D. to Jane H. Lowry   27 January 1848
    m. 27 January by A. Slover, M. G.
    Reference: Marriage Book C Page 166

SMITH, William H. to Lydia N. Cates   12 November 1864
    m. 13 November by Jas. Baker, J. P.
    Reference: Marriage Book F Page 10

SMITH, William P. to Eliza J. Huggins   25 December 1857
    m. 27 December by William Newman, J. P.
    Reference: Marriage Book D Page 133

SMITH, William R. to Francis Jane Wilson   7 June 1848
    m. 7 June by John Key, M. G.
    Reference: Marriage Book D Page 2

SMITH, Willis to Polly Tabor   28 September 1825
    m. 1 October by W. Porter, J. P.
    Reference: W. P. A.

SMYTHE, Augustus to Catharine Taylor   6 September 1865
    m. 6 September by Jno. F. Spence, M. G.
    Reference: Marriage Book F Page 25

SNEED, J. T. to Mandy Lane   14 July 1866
    m. 15 July by E. L. Miller, M. G.
    Reference: Marriage Book F Page 44

SNEED, William H. to Marthy L. Avens   19 November 1866
    m. 20 November by Hile Buttram, M. G.
    Reference: Marriage Book G Page 4

SNIDER, Andrew J. to Mary T. Conner   5 May 1855
    m. 6 May by E. W. King, M. G.
    Reference: Marriage Book D Page 98

SNIDER, Andrew R. to Mahaly Leamar (Lemare) 20 October 1847
    Thomas B. Wright, Security
    m. 22 October by G. C. Metcalfe, Esq.
    Reference: County Archives: Marriage
    Book C Page 161

SNIDER, L. B. to Miss S. H. Hale   5 November 1867
    m. 5 November
    Reference: Marriage Book G Page 22

SNIDER, Peter to Sarah E. Ensminger   3 (5) November 1853
    Moses Snider, Security
    m. 3 November by E. L. Miller, J. P.
    Reference: Marriage Book D Page 74;
    County Archives

SNIDER, Robert M. to Martha Guthry   16 March 1854
    John Thurman, Security
    m. 16 March by E. L. Miller, J. P.
    Reference: Marriage Book D Page 81; County Archives

SNIDER, W. G. to Miss S. E. Denton   22 October 1867
    B. F. Hudson, Security
    Reference: Marriage Book G Page 22;
    County Archives

SNIDER - see also SNYDER

SNODDY, George to Sarah A. Armstrong   18 September 1854
    George W. Standley, Security
    m. 13 September by J. W. Cox, J. P.
    Reference: Marriage Book D Page 87;
    County Archives

SNODDY, William to Eveline Mizell   21 November 1844
    m. 21 November by John Jenkins, J. P.
    Reference: Marriage Book C Page 112

SNODGRASS, Thomas to Caroline Moore   3 January 1839
    Reference: Marriage Book C Page 12

SNYDER, James H. Z. to Dora A. Freeman   18 September 1869
    m. 19 September by G. W. Morton, J. P.
    Reference: Marriage Book G Page 51

SNYDER, R. G. to Miss S. A. Freeman   26 June 1869
    m. 27 June by George W. Morton, J. P.
    Reference: Marriage Book G Page 47

SNYDER - see also SNIDER

SOUTHARD, Aaron to Lydia John   2 March 1843
    m. 2 March by Justus Steed, J. P.
    Reference: Marriage Book C Page 75

SOUTHARD, James M. to Rachel A. Doan   23 December 1852
    Waitslell Duckworth, Security
    m. 23 December by M. Southard, M. G.
    Reference: Marriage Book D Page 60;
    County Archives

SOUTHARD, John to Elizabeth Southard   7 March 1842
    m. 8 March by T. S. Rice, J. P.
    Reference: Marriage Book C Page 54

SOUTHARD, William to Katharine Trout   7 December 1839
    m. 12 December by Russell Lane, J. P.
    Reference: Marriage Book C Page 19

SOUTHARD, William to Rebecca R. N. John   12 October 1842
    m. 13 October by Justus Steed, J. P.
    Reference: Marriage Book C Page 64

SOUTHARD - see also SUTHARD

SOWELL, Osten to Nancy E. Runnion   3 February 1858
    m. 4 February by E. L. Miller, J. P.
    Reference: Marriage Book D Page 136

SOWELLS, Sipe (Sipy) T. to Catherine Crow   18 June 1829
    Thomas Guthrey, Security
    Reference: County Archives

SPARKS, John to Mary Ann Gallaher   26 September 1843
    m. 26 September by Green L. Reynolds, J. P.
    Reference: Marriage Book C Page 86

SPARKS, John to Zelpha Helms   12 September 1857
    m. 17 September by O. M. Liner, J. P.
    Reference: Marriage Book D Page 129

SPARKS, Lee to Elizabeth Shook   12 March 1849
   G. M. Gallahar, Security
   m. 12 March by A. L. Dugan, J. P.
   Reference: Marriage Book D Page 13;
   County Archives

SPEARS, John to Eliza C. Maxfield   9 March 1841
   m. 9 March by John Tate, M. G.
   Reference: Marriage Book C Page 39

SPENCER, John to McMinn County to Martha A.
   Lilins of Monroe County
   m. 10 April 1835 by Rev. John G. Likins
   Reference: "Tennessee Journal", Athens,
   Volume II, #36, April 22, 1835
   /Place of marriage not stated7

SPERLIN, Joseph J. to Sarah S. Sharites   2 (27) November 1867
   James M. Dodd, Security
   m. 28 November by J. A. Hyden, M. G.
   Reference: Marriage Book G Page 23;
   County Archives

SPRADLIN, J. L. to Elsy Triplett   30 January 1867
   m. 30 January by W. H. Newman, M. G.
   Reference: Marriage Book G Page 9

SPRADLIN, Mortimer to Louvicy Lawson   29 Ocotber 1838
   m. 29 October by Johnathan Thomas, J. P.
   Reference: Marriage Book C Page 9

SPRADLIN, R. J. to G. S. Holland   24 March 1868
   J. L. Spradlin, Security
   m. 25 March by Rev. D. Carpenter, M. G.
   Reference: Marriage Book G Page 30;
   County Archives

SPRADLING, Richard, Sen. to Mrs. Hannah West   24 November 1843
   m. 28 November by Hiel Buttram, M. G.
   Reference: Marriage Book C Page 91

SPRIGGS, Ezekiel to Mrs. Marye Ann Houston   12 September 1850
   m. 12 September by Young L. McLemore, M. G.
   Reference: Marriage Book D Page 32

STALLION, Matthew to Nancy Ann Goins   17 November 1844
   m. 17 November by Samuel Snoddy, J. P.
   Reference: Marriage Book C Page 112

STANDEFER, Jackson to Mary Sweeney Ahl   16 December 1850
   m. 17 December by L. B. Dodson, J. P.
   Reference: Marriage Book D Page 35

STANDIFER, Benjamin to M. L. Wilson   19 February 1870
   m. 20 February by P. M. Long, J. P.
   Reference: Marriage Book G Page 58

STANDIFER, W. H. to Sarah F. Myres   6 August 1866
   m. 9 August by F. A. Dixon, J. P.
   Reference: Marriage Book F Page 45

STANER, Peter to Almira Coxey   25 December 1848
   m. 25 December by William Walker, J. P.
   Reference: Marriage Book D Page 9

STANFIELD, Thomas to Malinda Rush   6 April 1832
   Syrus Rush, Security
   Reference: County Archives

STANFIELD - see also STANSFIELD

STANPHILE, James to Carolene (Caroline) Roberts   21 February 1842
     McConnell Chambers, Security
     m. 24 February by M. C. Hawk, Minister M. E.
     Church
     Reference: Marriage Book C Page 53;
     County Archives

STANSBERRY, I. N. to Miss E. R. Everton   28 August 1855
     m. 30 August by J. Jack, M. G.
     Reference: Marriage Book D Page 102

STANSBERRY, L. L. to Margarit A. Hance   23 December 1858
     m. 23 December by Jas. Baker, J. P.
     Reference: Marriage Book D Page 153

STANSFIELD, Isreal to Susanah Pearman   25 December 1855
     Reference: Marriage Book D Page 106

STANTON, J. K. to Miss M. E. Fry   3 December 1870
     Lewis Stanton, Security
     m. 4 December 1871 /sic/ by Dan Carpenter, M.G.
     Reference: Marriage Book G Page 70;
     County Archives

STANTON, Kelsey - see KELSEY, Stanton

STANTON, William M. to Surmintha P. Monroe   13 March 1865
     m. 15 March by E. L. Miller, M. G.
     Reference: Marriage Book F Page 17

STAPLES, W. H. to Martha S. Franklin   6 Ocotber 1855
     m. 10 Ocotber by M. A. Cass, M. G.
     Reference: Marriage Book D Page 103

STAPP - see also STEP, STEPP

STARMER, Jefferson to Miss Francis Dodson   16 November 1844
     Reference: Marriage Book C Page 112

STARNES, Jacob K. to A. N. Cofman   20 Ocotber 1845
     m. 23 Ocotber by William Rucker, J. P.
     Reference: Marriage Book C Page 128

STEAD, John to Sarrah Harkrider   29 December 1829
     Elias Presnell, Security
     Reference: County Archives

STEED, Henry to Tilitha Noel of Anderson County   30 Ocotber 1839
     m. 30 Ocotber by Rev. A. Slover
     Reference: Marriage Book C Page 24
     "Hiwassee Patriot", 7 November 1839;
     Volume I, Number 35

STEED, Henry to Elizabeth Vanderporl   8 Ocotber 1850
     m. 8 Ocotber by William Burns, J. P.
     Reference: Marriage Book D Page 33

STEED, Justus C. to Sarah Jane Laseter   20 November 1843
     m. 21 November by Wilson Chapman, M. G.
     Reference: Marriage Book C Page 90

STEP, William A. to Miss Francis Herald   9 July 1870
     m. 14 July by T. J. Russell, M. G.
     Reference: Marriage Book G Page 62

STEP - see also STAPP, STEPP

STEPERSON, T. M. to Sarah C. Melton   2 December 1858
  m. 2 December by M. L. Philips, J. P.
  Reference: Marriage Book D Page 152

STEPHENS, Allen to Elizabeth Rodden   1847
  m. 14 Ocotber 1847 by G. W. Kirksey, J. P.
  Reference: Marriage Book C Page 161

STEPHENS, David to Sarah Clemmons   25 December 1828
  Aby Coats, Security
  Reference: County Archives

STEPHENS, G. W. to Sarah J. Kimbrough   29 July 1857
  m. 30 August by John Jack, M. G.
  Reference: Marriage Book D Page 128

STEPHENS, George to Mrs. Mary Cate   16 November 1853
  Thomas Stephens, Security
  m. 17 November by William C. Lee, M. G.
  Reference: Marriage Book D Page 74;
  County Archives

STEPHENS, H. G. to Addie Lambert   27 September 1870
  W. A. Corbet, Security
  m. 28 September by B. F. Nuckles, M. G.
  Reference: Marriage Book G Page 66;
  County Archives

STEPHENS, J. N. to Miss M. W. Rice   15 January 1856
  m. 17 January by T. J. Russell, M. G.
  Reference: Marriage Book D Page 107

STEPHENS, J. T. to Miss Elinera Harmon   17 February 1859
  Reference: Marriage Book D Page 157

STEPHENS, Joseph to Polly Conner   4 April 1832
  William Shook, Security
  Reference: County Archives

STEPHENS, N. B. to Elizabeth Joines   13 June 1855
  m. 14 June by John Scruggs, M. G.
  Reference: Marriage Book D Page 99

STEPHENS, Sampson to Elizabeth Foster   19 April 1838
  "Returned to the office without any
  endorsement."
  Reference: Marriage Book C Page 3

STEPHENS, William A. to Sarah S. Jourdin   4 December 1856
  m. 4 December by Thos. J. Russell, M. G.
  Reference: Marriage Book D Page 120

STEPHENSON, Andrew to Elmira Kinzalow   18 November 1856
  Reference: Marriage Book D Page 119

STEPHENSON, Daniel D. to Mary Ann Anderson   1 March 1852
  m. 2 March by W. C. Daily, M. G.
  Reference: Marriage Book D Page 49;
  Oregon Donation Land Claim Number 4851

STEPHENSON, Edward to Martha Torbet   16 September 1837
  m. 18 September by R. Gregory
  Reference: W. P. A.

STEPHENSON, J. C. to Nannie E. Brown   14 April 1870
  m. 20 April by Calvin Denton, M. G.
  Reference: Marriage Book G Page 60

STEPHENSON, J. M. to Martha Hanks   20 Ocotber 1866
    Reference: Marriage Book G Page 2

STEPHENSON, James A. to Mary E. Jarnagin   16 December 1868
    Reference: Marriage Book G Page 41

STEPHENSON, James M. to Martha J. Wilson   28 April 1852
    m. 29 April by William R. Walker
    Reference: Marriage Book D Page 52

STEPHENSON, John J. to Cynthia E. Ritchey   31 May 1864
    m. 31 May by E. Z. Williams, J. P.
    Reference: Marriage Book F Page 3

STEPHENSON, Robert A. to Matilda C. Smith   8 September 1853
    Calvin Shoemaker, Security
    m. by William W. Hay, M. G.
    Reference: County Archives; Marriage
    Book D Page 70

STEPHENSON, W. A. to Sarah Jane Ellis   3 May 1867
    Reference: Marriage Book G Page 14

STEPHENSON, William to Nancy Elder   23 December 1847
    m. December 1847 by Robert Gregory, Minister
    Baptist Church
    Reference: Marriage Book C Page 163

STEPHENSON - see also STEPERSON, STEVENSON

STEPP - see also STAPP, STEP

STEVENSON, J. M. to Mary J. Crittendon   10 November 1869
    m. 10 November by Williamson Ereckson, Elder
    Reference: Marriage Book G Page 53

STEWARD, Richard to Salley J. Rothwell   14 January 1868
    Reference: Marriage Book G Page 26

STEWART, Saml. to Mary Hammontree   14 March 1841
    m. 14 March by John Rogers, J. P.
    Reference: Marriage Book C Page 39

STEWART - see also STUART

STILES - see also STYLES

STONE, William to Elizabeth Cofer   26 January 1843
    m. 26 January by M. D. Anderson, J. P.
    Reference: Marriage Book C Page 72

STONE, William G. to Miss P. Errickson   7 August 1850
    Reference: Marriage Book D Page 29

STOUT, Abrahan to Ann Brookshire   5 July 1826
    m. 6 July by Thos. W. Norwood, M. G.
    Reference: W. P. A.

STOUT, Alfred P. to Anna Brock   3 September 1846
    m. 3 September by William Rucker, J. P.
    Reference: Marriage Book C Page 143

STOUT, Robert L. to Mariam Wassom   6 December 1849
    m. 6 December by William McKamy, J. P.
    Reference: Marriage Book D Page 22

STOVER, Solomon L., Jr. to Mary Ann Godard   16 January 1846
    m. 20 January by James Sewell, Minister
    Reference: Marriage Book C Page 132

STRANGE, J. W. to Mrs. E. A. Grigg   3 Ocotber 1865
    m. 5 Ocotber by Uriah Payne, M. G.
    Reference: Marriage Book F Page 27

STROUD, Merrit B. to Rebecca Proffit   24 December 1840
    m. 24 December by F. McGonigal, M. G.
    Reference: Marriage Book C Page 35

STRUTTEN, Riley to Leathy Jones   4 June 1857
    m. 5 June by M. A. Cass, M. G.
    Reference: Marriage Book D Page 126

STUART, Richard to Elizabeth Nickels   16 January 1851
    m. 16 January by Tapley Gregory, J. P.
    Reference: Marriage Book D Page 37

STUART - see also STEWART

STUBBLEFIELD, William to Mahale Griffin   16 August 1827
    James Miller, Security
    Reference: County Archives

STUBBLEFIELD, William H. to Elizabeth Studdard   25 November 1854
    m. 26 November by J. W. Cox, J. P.
    Reference: Marriage Book D Page 89

STUBBLEFIELD - see also STUBLEFLIED

STUBBS, James M. to Rachel Smith   15 February 1840
    Reference: Marriage Book C Page 25

STUBLEFLIED, P. C. to Catharine Martin   17 Ocotber 1851
    m. 19 October by Uriel Johnson, J. P.
    Reference: Marriage Book D Page 45

STUDDARD, Hugh to Ailcy Melton   13 July 1840
    m. 28 July 1841 /sic/ by Uriel Johnson, J. P.
    Reference: Marriage Book C Page 30

STUDDARD, Thomas to Arme Jane Melton   6 November 1850
    m. 7 November by John Jenkins, J. P.
    Reference: Marriage Book D Page 34

STUDDARD, William to Lemyra Wilson   12 January 1848
    m. 12 January by William H. Ballerd, J. P.
    Reference: Marriage Book C Page 165

STYLES, Charles to Mrs. Jincy Malone   23 April 1864
    m. 24 April by E. Rowley, M. G.
    Reference: Marriage Book F Page 2

STYLES - see also STILES

SUMMER, Nehemiah to Mrs. Eveline Jones   8 July 1865
    m. 8 July by Jas. Baker, J. P.
    Reference: Marriage Book F Page 21

SUTTEN, M. G. to Miss M. E. Pilgrim   5 September 1868
    Reference: Marriage Book G Page 35

SUTTON, G. D. to Louisy Jack   29 July 1869
    m. 31 August by Elihu Kelley, J. P.
    Reference: Marriage Book G Page 48

SUTTON, John to Nancy McCall   2 March 1829
    Benjamin S. Crow, Security
    Reference: W. P. A.

SUTTON, John O. to Martha C. Prichard
    m. 8 September by G. M. Hicks, M. G.
    Reference: Marriage Book G Page 65
8 September 1870

SUTTON, O. P. to Miss J. E. Herrold
    m. 3 February by J. Janeway, M. G.
    Reference: Marriage Book G Page 58
1 February 1870

SWAFFOR, John W. to Margret Gibson
    m. 20 January by F. A. Dixon, J. P.
    Reference: Marriage Book G Page 8
18 January 1867

SWAFFORD, Alfred to Mary A. Carver
    Edmon Gilbert, Security
    Reference: Marriage Book F Page 28;
    County Archives
12 October 1865

SWAFFORD, Daniel to Catherin Swafford
    Reference: Marriage Book G Page 42
4 January 1869

SWAFFORD, J. A. to Miss M. T. Green
    Thos. L. Swafford, Security
    m. 27 December by Jno. N. Stamper, M. G.
    Reference: Marriage Book G Page 71;
    County Archives
26 December 1870

SWAFFORD, John to Elizabeth Hampton
    m. 26 November by William McCamy, J. P.
    Reference: Marriage Book D Page 131
21 November 1857

SWAFFORD, John to Sarah Swafford
    m. 5 April by F. A. Dixon, J. P.
    Reference: Marriage Book F Page 40
5 April 1866

SWAFFORD, L. to Martha C. Wilson
    Reference: Marriage Book C Page 98
21 February 1844

SWAFFORD, Larkin F. to Miss Effee N. Wilson
    m. 15 June by Joel Culpepper, J. P.
    Reference: Marriage Book D Page 110
14 June 1856

SWAFFORD, William to Mary E. Avans
    m. 18 August by O. M. Liner, J. P.
    Reference: Marriage Book G Page 64
17 August 1870

SWAGERITY, Jackson to Sally Henry
    m. 31 Ocotber by D. W. Beaver, M. G.
    Reference: Marriage Book D Page 149
29 Ocotber 1858

SWAN, Joseph L. to Huldah Mayfield
    m. 19 November by John Tate, M. G.
    Reference: Marriage Book C Page 34
19 November 1840

SWAN, Robert, Esq. of McMinn County to Miss
    Ann Amelia Ramsey, daughter of the late
    Rev. S. G. Ramsey of Knox County.
    m. in Knox County 16 December 1824 by Rev.
    Thomas H. Nelson
    Reference: "Knoxville Register", Volume
    9, # 437, 24 December 1824; "Knoxville
    Enquirer", Volume I, #23, 22 December 1824

SWANER, David to Sarah Teague
    Robert A. Richardson, Security
    m. 8 Juneby E. L. Miller, M. G.
    Reference: Marriage Book G Page 47;
    County Archives
8 June 1869

SWANSON, James to Nancy Pinion   26 October 1869
    m. 26 October by J. A. Hyden, M. G.
    Reference: Marriage Book G Page 52

SWEENEY, Joseph to Martha Murry   9 June 1866
    m. 10 June by E. Z. Williams, J. P.
    Reference: Marriage Book F Page 42

SWEENY, John D. to Jane M. Underdown   18 April 1844
    m. 18 April by John Hoyl, M. G.
    Reference: Marriage Book C Page 101

SWEENY, Jonathan H. to Sarah Cate   12 December 1847
    m. 12 December by Saml. L. Yearout, J. P.
    Reference: Marriage Book C Page 163

SWEENY, Martin M. to Mary Moore   4 March 1855
    m. 4 March by James Baker, J. P.
    Reference: Marriage Book D Page 95

SWEENY - see also SWINNY

SWINFORD, Elijah to Caroline (Selia Emley) Glass   8 August 1850
    m. 8 August by M. G. Scarbrough
    Reference: Marriage Book D Page 30

SWINFORD, Isaac to Kiziah Woods   12 June 1844
    m. 13 June by L. L. Ball, J. P.
    Reference: Marriage Book C Page 103

SWINFORD, James to Jane Randell   1 January 1839
    m. 1 January by George W. Mayo, J. P.
    Reference: Marriage Book C Page 12

SWINFORD, James to Safira Davis   23 August 1851
    Reference: Marriage Book D Page 42

SWINFORD, James to Mary M. Runyans   30 December 1869
    Reference: Marriage Book G Page 42   /1868/
    Note: This license is dated 1869 in
    Marriage Book but is on page for 1868

SWINFORD, Levi to Nancy E. Rucker   19 January 1850
    m. 19 January by J. C. Bryan, J. P.
    Reference: Marriage Book D Page 25

SWINFORD, Zacchariah to Jucilla Davis   1 March 1841
    m. 1 March by John Rogers, J. P.
    Reference: Marriage Book C Page 38

TAFF, Frances A. to Miss Manerva Gaut   17 June 1857
    m. 17 June by S. Philips, M. G.
    Reference: Marriage Book D Page 127

TAGUE, J. M. to Miss Hetty McCarroll   8 July 1845
    m. 10 July by M. A. Cass, J. P.
    Reference: Marriage Book C Page 122

TALENT, Leroy J. to Elizabeth Richey   29 March 1865
    m. 2 April by D. B. Cunningham, M. G.
    Reference: Marriage Book F Page 17

TALLENT, E. N. to Miss B. A. Watson   20 December 1869
    Reference: Marriage Book G Page 55

TALLENT, Jonathan to Rutilda Brown   26 November 1869
    Reference: Marriage Book G Page 54

TALLEY, J. W. to Miss Tempy L. Reed   9 November 1864
    m. 10 November by M. Paine, M. G.
    Reference: Marriage Book F Page 9;
    County Archives

TATE, Rev. John of Monroe County to Eliza Jane   30 July 1829
    Wear (Weir), daughter of George Weir
    m. 30 July by S. W. Aston, M. G.
    Reference: County Archives; "Knoxville
    Register", Volume XIV, # 681, 2 Sept. 1829

TAWENSEL, James C. to Serena McGrew   25 February 1868
    m. 25 February by E. Z. Williams, J. P.
    Reference: Marriage Book G Page 28

TAYLER, George D. to Susan A. Robison   30 January 1866
    m. 4 February by Morgan Miller, J. P.
    Reference: Marriage Book F Page 37

TAYLOR, James B. to Rebecca Moss   30 April 1845
    m. 30 April by T. K. Munsey
    Reference: Marriage Book C Page 120

TAYLOR, Rufus to Edna Saxten   24 October 1866
    m. 14 /sic/ October
    Reference: Marriage Book G Page 2

TAYLOR, Stephen to Serenah Hail   8 February 1849
    m. 18 February by Nathaniel Barnett, M. G.
    Reference: Marriage Book D Page 11

TEAFFATALER, Jefferson to Elizia Dover   17 August 1867
    m. 18 August by W. G. Horton, J. P.
    Reference: Marriage Book G Page 19

TEAGUE, David to Emelin Orton   15 /August/ 1850
    Reference: Marriage Book C Page 30

TEAGUE, Franklin C. to Malinda L. Newton   10 August 1850
    m. 11 August by J. M. Scarborough, M. G.
    Reference: Marriage Book D Page 30

TEAGUE, John W. to Sarah A. Brock   2 January 1861
    m. 2 January by J. Jack, M. G.
    Reference: Marriage Book E Page 10

TEAGUE, Joseph to Malinda Kelly   31 January 1847
    m. 31 January by J. Jack, M. G.
    Reference: Marriage Book C Page 151

TEAGUE - see also TAGUE

TEMPLETON, George to Eve Massongale   5 April 1852
    m. 5 April by James Douglass, M. G.
    Reference: Marriage Book D Page 50

TEMPLETON, William B. to Elizabeth Ramy   9 September 1852
    m. 9 September by Stephen Sharrets, M. G.
    Reference: Marriage Book D Page 56

TENNILL, George W. to Rachel Orr   27 July 1839
    Reference: Marriage Book C Page 21

TENNY, Isaac to Angeline Blackwell   3 May 1841
    m. 4 May by T. B. Love, J. P.
    Reference: Marriage Book C Page 42

TERY, James to Myran Mageer
    m. 28 November by J. S. Russell, M. G.
    Reference: Marriage Book G Page 23
                           28 November 1867

TEWELL, J. A. to Lucy Shook
    m. 4 August by S. Philips, M. G.
    Reference: Marriage Book D Page 128
                           4 August 1857

THERMAN, William H. to Emily Jane Williams
    m. 24 June 1866 by S. M. Thomas, J. P.
    Reference: Marriage Book F Page 42
                       15 June 1856
                         /ͪ866͇/

THERMAN - see also THURMAN

THOMAS, Bazzel to Susan S. Dixon
    m. 4 November by Morgan Miller, J. P.
    Reference: Marriage Book G Page 3;
    County Archives
                       3 November 1866

THOMAS, G. W. to Miss Celie Keggal
    Reference: Marriage Book F Page 43
                           7 July 1866

THOMAS, John L. to Maryan Wattenbarger
    m. 1 February by Thos. B. Wallen, M. G.
    Reference: Marriage Book D Page 11
                     31 January 1849

THOMAS, Samuel M. to Abigail A. Pearce
    Reference: Marriage Book C Page 113
                     5 December 1844

THOMAS, Samuel W. to Mary C. Davis
    m. 9 May by M. C. Hawk, M. G.
    Reference: Marriage Book C Page 102
                          9 May 1844

THOMASSON, John to Louize Casst
    Daniel McCoy, Security
    Reference; W. P. A.
                         14 July 1828

THOMPSON, Bryant to Margarett Miller
    m. 23 December by Tapley Gregory, J. P.
    Reference: Marriage Book C Page 164
                   23 December 1847

THOMPSON, Charles to Lucinda Shelton
    m. 26 October by Richard A. McAdoo, J. P.
    Reference: Marriage Book C Page 48
                   26 October 1841

THOMPSON, G. W. to Miss A. J. Qualls
    m. 2 September by G. W. Morton, J. P.
    Reference: Marriage Book G Page 50
                 1 September 1869

THOMPSON, George W. to Hetta S. Newman
    m. 22 July by Elihu Kelly, J. P.
    Reference: Marriage Book F Page 44
                     21 July 1866

THOMPSON, H. M. to Malinda Melton
    m. 30 June by J. C. Masingale, J. P.
    Reference: Marriage Book E Page 8
                     20 June 1859

THOMPSON, Isaac R. to Amanda Crayn
    m. 31 August by William F. Forest, M. G.
    Reference: Marriage Book C Page 84
                   30 August 1843

THOMPSON, J. M. to Nancy J. Carlock
    m. 15 August by C. R. Hoyl, M. G.
    Reference: Marriage Book E Page 8
                   15 August 1860

THOMPSON, James to Nancy Reed
    m. 4 May by Henry Bradford, J. P.
    Reference: W. P. A.
                         4 May 1824

THOMPSON, James to Elvira Branum   1 November 1858
   m. 3 November by R. Reynolds, J. P.
   Reference: Marriage Book D Page 149

THOMPSON, James to Nancy Ann Wyett   23 December 1867
   m. 26 December by J. B. McCallon, M. G.
   Reference: Marriage Book G Page 24

THOMPSON, James B. to Nancy L. Yonce   /March/ 1867
   m. 26 March 1868 /sic/ by Elihu Kelly, J. P.
   Reference: Marriage Book G Page 12

THOMPSON, James B. to Sarah J. Crockett   12 November 1868
   m. 19 November by B. E. Cass, J. P.
   Reference: Marriage Book G Page 39

THOMPSON, John to Elizabeth Campbell   24 June 1848
   m. 29 June by Thomas L. Russell, M. G.
   Reference: Marriage Book D Page 3

THOMPSON, John to Martha Jones   30 November 1850
   m. 1 November /sic/ by Moses Sweeny, J. P.
   Reference: Marriage Book D Page 35

THOMPSON, John A. to Joana Pierce   5 September 1829
   James B. Thompson, Security
   Reference: W. P. A.

THOMPSON, John A. to Manervy J. Burk   18 August 1855
   m. 19 August by M. A. Cass, M. G.
   Reference: Marriage Book D Page 101

THOMPSON, Mathew to Serbriney Vandary Welch   3 January 1852
   m. 4 January by William McKamy, J. P.
   Reference: Marriage Book D Page 47

THOMPSON, Mathew to A. R. Walsh   2 July 1855
   m. 2 July by William McAmy, J. P.
   Reference: Marriage Book D Page 100

THOMPSON, R. R. to Miss M. A. Gandd   7 April 1856
   m. 8 April by H. J. Brock, J. P.
   Reference: Marriage Book D Page 109
   Note: Tombstone inscription at Conasauga
   Baptist Church Cem.: Mary Ann Duggan, wife of
   R. R. Thompson

THOMPSON, S. R. to Mary J. Wallis   16 May 1865
   m. 21 May by Joseph Janeway, M. G.
   Reference: Marriage Book F Page 18

THOMPSON, Samuel H. to L. Brock   Not Dated
   m. 7 March 1852 by J. Jack, M. G.
   Reference: Marriage Book D Page 27
   Note: Although the return is dated 1852,
   the license entry is between 23 March 1850
   and 17 April 1850

THOMPSON, Samuel H. to Marha E. McCann   10 February 1869
   Reference: Marriage Book G Page 44

THOMPSON, Thos. J. to Mary A. Knight   30 June 1855
   m. 1 July by William McAmy, M. G.
   Reference: Marriage Book D Page 100

THOMPSON, Uriah to Susan Largent   27 May 1844
   "Returned by Thompson not executed"
   Reference: Marriage Book C Page 102

THOMPSON, William to Mary J. S. Hunter   24 October 1844
    m. 24 October by L. R. Morrison, V. D. M.
    Reference: Marriage Book C Page 110

THOMPSON, William to Matilda Gregory   25 April 1847
    m. 25 April by M. A. Cass, J. P.
    Reference: Marriage Book C Page 155

THOMPSON, William J. to Margaret Holmes   23 October 1840
    m. 23 October by R. A. McAdoo, J. P.
    Reference: Marriage Book C Page 33

THOMPSON, William P. to Nancy A. Newman   5 Ocotber 1868
    m. 8 October by George W. Morton, J. P.
    Reference: Marriage Book G Page 37

THOMPSON - see also TOMPSON, TOMSON

THOMSON, Joseph to Martha L. Thompson   3 November 1870
    m. 3 November by Geo. W. Hendrix, J. P.
    Reference: Marriage Book G Page 68

THORP, Harris D., merchant of Athens to Miss
    Solina Ayres, daughter of David B. Ayres, dec'd.
    formerly of Knoxville
    m. 31 May 1827 /Place not stated7
    Reference: Quoted from "Athens Hiwassean" by
    the "Knoxville Register", Volume XI, # 564,
    13 June 1827

THURMAN, Peter to Eliza Shipley   6 September 1854
    Reference: Marriage Book D Page 87

THURMAN - see also THERMAN

TINNEY, Isaac to Mary Moore   26 December 1846
    Reference: Marriage Book C Page 150

TIPPEN, W. H. to Miss Elizia Owens   19 September 1867
    m. 19 September by J. W. Mo____, M. G.
    Reference: Marriage Book G Page 21

TIPTON, William B. to Phebe Hunt   19 June 1851
    m. 19 June by S. Sharets, M. G.
    Reference: Marriage Book D Page 41

TOOMEY, T. L. to Miss Juliann Tira   26 June 1858
    m. 26 June by J. J. Eliot, J. P.
    Reference: Marriage Book D Page 142

TORBET, John O. to Eviline C. Trim   18 December 1839
    Reference: Marriage Book C Page 19

TOWNSEN, William to Sarah Parsons   24 December 1866
    m. 25 December by E. Z. Williams, J. P.
    Reference: Marriage Book G Page 7;
    County Archives

TOWNSEND, Thomas to Marjara Hays   9 March 1846
    m. 9 March by John Scarbrough, J. P.
    Reference: Marriage Book C Page 135

TOWNSEND, William C. to Katharine Roland   13 October 1838
    m. 18 October by J. Wimpy
    Reference: Marriage Book C Page 9;
    County Archives

TOWNSEND - see also TAWENSEL

TREW, J. J. to Eliza E. Cook   8 December 1868
    m. 8 December by Calvin Denton, M. G.
    Reference: Marriage Book G Page 40

TREW, John M. to Mary Ann Trew   6 February 1843
    m. 8 February by Samuel Snoddy, J. P.
    Reference: Marriage Book C Page 72

TREW, Perry to Jane Wallace   2 May 1864
    m. 2 May by James A. Womac, M. G.
    Reference: Marriage Book F Page 2;
    County Archives

TREW, Warren to Martha Pickens   23 October 1839
    m. 26 October by M. C. Hawk, M. G.
    Reference: Marriage Book C Page 24

TREW - see also TRUE

TRIBBUE (TRIBBUR), Jacob (Jessee) to Mahala Duff   21 September 1848
    m. 25 September by A. L. Dugan, J. P.
    Reference: Marriage Book D Page 5

TRIM, Lafayett to Lurany S. Giles   8 September 1849
    John Giles, Security
    Reference: Marriage Book D Page 18;
    County Archives

TRIPLET, Elzcy to Maiden Chapmon   24 January 1838
    m. 24 January by Wilson Chapmon, M. G.
    Reference: Marraige Book C Page 2

TRIPLET, James C. to Mahala Melton   22 July 1846
    m. 22 July by James Douglass, M. G.
    Reference: Marriage Book C Page 140

TRIPLET, William A. to Hopy Duckworth   9 November 1848
    m. 9 November by Urial Johnston, J. P.
    Reference: Marriage Book D Page 7

TRIPLETT, Franklin to Martha Lawson   9 October 1849
    m. 9 October by Urial Johnston, J. P.
    Reference: Marriage Book D Page 20

TRIPLETT, Iverson to Miss Rhoda Varnel   16 November 1840
    m. 19 November by T. B. Love, J. P.
    Reference: Marriage Book C Page 33

TRIPLETT, Pery to Elizabeth Hunt   15 September 1847
    m. 16 September by W. F. Forrest, M. G.
    Reference: Marriage Book C Page 160;
    County Archives

TROTTER, George to Nancy Howard   26 January 1841
    m. 26 January by T. B. Love, J. P.
    Reference: Marriage Book C Page 37

TROTTER, Green C. to Sinthey C. Triplett   1 August 1843
    m. 1 August by William Newton, M. G.
    Reference: Marriage Book C Page 83

TROTTER, T. R. to Mrs. Lillith Lock Miller   8 October 1868
    m. 11 Ocotber by J. A. Cass, J. P.
    Reference: Marriage Book G Page 38

TRUE, George W. to Polly T. Walton   22 February 1850
    Reference: Marriage Book D Page 26

TUCK, Joseph to Louisa Goodwin   14 May 1855
    Reference: Marriage Book D Page 98

TUCK, Moses to Nancy A. Rabay   3 December 1856
    m. 3 December by David W. Beaver, M. G.
    Reference: Marriage Book D Page 120

TUCK, Taltore B. to Mary A. Pierce   26 November 1856
    m. 27 November by David W. Beaver, M. G.
    Reference: Marriage Book D Page 119

TUCKER, Benjamin to Eliza Erskin   21 May 1842
    m. 23 May by Tapley Gregory, J. P.
    Reference: Marriage Book C Page 58

TUCKER, Joseph to Mary Fox   5 April 1839
    m. 5 April by John McGaughy, J. P.
    Reference: Marriage Book C Page 16

TUCKER, Leroy to Caroline Newton   16 August 1854
    m. 17 August by Jas. Parkison, J. P.
    Reference: Marriage Book D Page 86

TUCKER, Leroy to Catharine Reynolds   9 September 1870
    m. 9 September by B. Floyd Nuckles, M. G.
    Reference: Marriage Book G Page 65

TUNLEY, James A. to Miss Mary Bates
    both of McMinn County
    m. 3 March 1825 by Rev. Mr. Bailey
    Reference: "Knoxville Register",
    Volume IX, Number 448, 11 March 1825

TUNNEL, Jesse to Rebecca Davis   18 August 1838
    m. 19 August by A. Slover, M. G.
    Reference: Marriage Book C Page 6

TUNNELL, John W. to Martha Briant   26 May 1838
    m. 28 May by Jacob McDaniel, M. G.
    Reference: Marriage Book C Page 3

TURK, William P. to Nancy G. McMinn   6 March 1839
    Reference: Marriage Book C Page 14

TURNER, Andrew to Susan Hounsell   2 October 1849
    James Turner, Security
    m. 3 October by R. M. Hickey, M. G.
    Reference: Marriage Book D Page 19;
    County Archives

TURNER, James to Harriet Porter   4 November 1849
    m. 4 November by John J. Robinson, M. G.
    Reference: Marriage Book D Page 22

TURNLEY, Mathew J. to Nancy M. Isbell   27 May 1839
    m. 27 May by William C. C. C. George, M. G.
    Reference: Marriage Book C Page 17

TURNLEY - see also TUNLEY

TWOMEY, Hugh to Lettice W. Smith, daughter of
    Caleb Smith, Esq.
    m. 7 February by T. B. Love, J. P.
    Reference: Marriage Book C Page 38;
    "Hiwassee Patriot", 16 February 1841,
    Volume II, Number 49

UBANKS, George to Eliza Burch   28 November 1829
    John Morris, Security
    Reference: W. P. A.

UNDERDOWN, John to Mrs. Margaret Burk   16 March 1865
    m. 16 March by E. Z. Williams, J. P.
    Reference: Marriage Book F Page 17;
    County Archives

UNDERDOWN, Thos. A. to Catharine A. Barker   26 August 1846
    m. 27 August by William H. Ballew, J. P.
    Reference: Marriage Book C Page 142

UNDERWOOD, A. J. to Miss Hiley Pinion   30 December 1870
    m. 30 December by S. H. Cate, M. G.
    Reference: Marriage Book G Page 72

UNDERWOOD, James to Mary West   18 April 1840
    Reference: Marriage Book C Page 29

UNDERWOOD, James to Polly West   23 August 1841
    m. 27 August by T. S. Rice, J. P.
    Reference: Marriage Book C Page 45

UNDERWOOD, John to Harriett L. Sellars   20 March 1860
    m. 21 March by Joel Culpepper, J. P.
    Reference: Marriage Book E Page 2;
    Marriage Book E Page 6

UNDERWOOD, R. to Miss E. A. Coats   7 October 1867
    m. 10 October by George W. Morton, J. P.
    Reference: Marriage Book G Page 21

UNDERWOOD, T. M. to Miss Surrepta C. Childers   8 December 1870
    m. 8 December by S. H. Cate, M. G.
    Reference: Marriage Book G Page 70

UNDERWOOD, W. J. to Eliza Ball   25 June 1870
    Reference: Marriage Book G Page 61

UNDERWOOD, William to Peggy Salina Mires   17 January 1839
    Reference: Marriage Book C Page 13

UNDERWOOD - see also HUNDERWOOD

VAN ALDEHOFF - see ALDEHOFF

VANCE, Huston to Jane McDaniel   4 January 1870
    m. 5 January by J. Janeway, M. G.
    Reference: Marriage Book G Page 57

VANCE, John to Nancy Crews   9 March 1843
    m. 9 March by J. H. Benton, J. P.
    Reference: Marriage Book C Page 75

VANDEGRIFF, Andrew to Scyntha Orrick   16 January 1865
    m. 16 January by William Thompson, M. G.
    Reference: Marriage Book F Page 14

VANDERGRIFF, Gilber to Eve Templton   22 April 1858
    m. 22 April by William R. Long, M. G.
    Reference: Marriage Book D Page 140

VANDERGRIFF - see also MANDAGRIFF

VAN DYKE, Cornelius to Louisa Jane Yount   23 January 1851
    m. 23 January by Stephens Sharetts, M. G.
    Reference: Marriage Book D Page 37
                              215

VANDYLE, Cornelius P. to Rachel Thompson   25 August 1841
    Reference: Marriage Book C Page 45

VAN DYKE, Thos. Nixon, 3rd son of Thos. J.
    Van Dyke and Penelope Smith Campbell to
    Eliza Ann Deaderick, 2nd daughter of
    William H. Deaderick and Penelope Smith
    (Hamilton) Deaderick
    m. 23 May 1833
    Reference: Bible in possession of Mrs.
    Penelope J. Allen, Chattanooga, Tenn.

VANZANT, J. A. to Mary E. Browder   2 January 1867
    m. 2 January by John H. Brown, M. G.
    Reference: Marriage Book G Page 8

VANZANT, John to Sarah Paris   11 January 1849
    m. 11 January by J. C. Carlock, J. P.
    Reference: Marriage Book D Page 10

VANZANT, John to Nancy Hill   10 October 1853
    James R. Buckner, Security
    m. 12 October by William R. Walker, J. P.
    Reference: Marriage Book D Page 72;
    County Archives

VARNELL, D. N. to Mary F. Porter   30 November 1865
    m. 30 November by L. W. Crouch, M. G.
    Reference: Marriage Book F Page 31

VARNELL, David N. to Mary L. Lowery   8 May 1849
    John King, Security
    m. 8 May by James Atkinson, M. G.
    Reference: Marriage Book D Page 15;
    County Archives

VARNELL, William C. to Mary M. C. K. Yount   16 August 1855
    m. 16 August by C. P. Vandike, M. G.
    Reference: Marriage Book D Page 101

VARNELL, William J. to Mary E. Roberts   11 October 1855
    Reference: Marriage Book D Page 103

VAUGHAN, Robert Y. to Martha A. Triplett   15 November 1854
    m. 15 November by George A. Caldwell, M. G.
    Reference: Marriage Book D Page 89

VAUGHAN, William C. to Mary Ann Chesnut   12 January 1847
    m. 12 January by W. F. Forrest, M. G.
    Reference: Marriage Book C Page 150

VAUGHAN, Wilson to Katharine McDougald   3 January 1838
    Reference: Marriage Book C Page 1

VAUGHN, David C. to Josephine A. Crockett   20 October 1866
    m. 21 October by C. Cate, J. P.
    Reference: Marriage Book G Page 2

VAUGHN, J. H. to Miss Syrrefita Wyatt   26 January 1865
    m. 26 January by J. S. Russell, M. G.
    Reference: Marriage Book F Page 15

VAUGHN, L. R. (B.) to Caroline Emerson   24 January 1852
    m. 28 January by William G. Lee, M. G.
    Reference: Marriage Book D Page 47

VENABLE, William R. to Sarah Cornelia Hoyt   10 March 1851
    m. 12 March by Rev. John Lyons, M. G.
    Reference: Marriage Book D Page 39

VICARS, John R. to Martha A. Crawford   6 July 1858
    m. 14 July by J. A. Ziglar, J. P.
    Reference: Marriage Book D Page 142

VICKERS, Jacob to Martha Wolffe   24 January 1855
    m. 25 January by William McKamy, J. P.
    Reference: Marriage Book D Page 94

VINCEN, Samuel to Lucindy Martin   4 November 1848
    Reference: Marriage Book D Page 7

VINCENT, Charles to Nancy Colbock   13 December 1865
    Marion Marler, Security
    Reference: Marriage Book F Page 32;
    County Archives

VINCENT - see also VANZANT

VINSANT, Henry to Celia Murphy   25 October 1856
    Reference: Marriage Book D Page 117
    /Note: Celia Murphy is bride in two
    consecutive entries - there is no return
    to this entry - see Robinett, Hugh._7

VINSANT, James to Elisabeth Hill   21 February 1846
    m. 21 February by John Walker
    Reference: Marriage Book C Page 134

VINSON, Caleb to Margaret Vinson   25 January 1842
    m. 29 January by Jonathan Thomas, J. P.
    Reference: Marriage Book C Page 52

WADE, George to Ann Reid   19 November 1829
    m. 19 November by J. Ivans, J. P.
    Reference: W. P. A.

WADE, Selas to Adaline MCghehan   15 December 1856
    m. 18 December by Daniel Carpenter, M. G.
    Reference: Marriage Book D Page 121

WADE - see also WAIDE

WADKINS, Harris J. to Martha J. Bodwell   9 September 1865
    m. 10 September by James Parkison, J. P.
    Reference: Marriage Book F Page 25

WAGNER, W. N. J. to Nellie I. King   13 September 1869
    m. 14 September by Joseph H. Martin, M. G.
    Reference: Marriage Book G Page 50

WAIDE, James M. of Texas to Martha W. H. Bridges   31 May 1849
    m. 31 May by J. Atkinson, Min. Meth. Ch. South
    Reference: Marriage Book D Page 15; "Knoxville
    Register", Volume 33, #1674, Wed. 6 June 1849

WAIDE, William D. to Louisa Wattenbarger   4 October 1853
    m. 6 October by Dan Carpenter, M. G.
    Reference: Marriage Book D Page 71

WAKEFIELD, Alexander to Nancy Orr   11 April 1827
    m. 12 April by Thos. W. Norwood
    Reference: W. P. A.

WALKER, Abraham to Mahala Kinchelow   17 November 1841
    m. 17 November by L. L. Ball, J. P.
    Reference: Marriage Book C Page 49

WALKER, Abraham to Martha Jones   12 April 1854
    m. 24 May by J. A. Wilson, Esq.
    Reference: Marriage Book D Page 83

WALKER, Daniel to Mary Jane McKenzie   30 July 1850
    m. 4 August by William Walker, J. P.
    Reference: Marriage Book D Page 29

WALKER, E. S. to Sallie L. Cass   3 April 1869
    m. 4 April by W. W. Neal, M. G.
    Reference: Marriage Book G Page 45

WALKER, George I. to Martha E. Mabs   30 May 1856
    m. 1 June by M. R. Wear, J. P.
    Reference: Marriage Book D Page 110

WALKER, Gustavus A. to Ellen S. Cate   21 August 1869
    m. 22 August by J. Janeway, M. G.
    Reference: Marriage Book G Page 49

WALKER, Henry P. to Mary T. Smith   21 September 1855
    m. 2 October by Joseph McSpaden, M. G.
    Reference: Marriage Book D Page 102

WALKER, J. H. to Lucy F. Franklin   29 December 1852
    m. 29 December by William C. Daily, M. G.
    Reference: Marriage Book D Page 60

WALKER, James to Charlotte Craven Dean   12 October 1824
    Robert W. McClary, Security
    m. 12 October by Robert McClary, J. P.
    Reference: W. P. A.

WALKER, James R. to Evanna Turnmeir   24 February 1848
    Reference: Marriage Book C Page 168

WALKER, James V. to Susan Hunk   8 January 1855
    m. 16 January by M. R. Ware, J. P.
    Reference: Marriage Book D Page 93

WALKER, James V. to Keziah A. Morgan   4 September 1865
    m. 7 September by L. W. Crouch, M. G.
    Reference: Marriage Book F Page 25

WALKER, John H. to Sarah E. Shipley   21 August 1866
    m. 21 August by Bery H. B. Bralan
    Reference: Marriage Book F Page 45

WALKER, Joseph to Anna Stephenson   2 September 1838
    Reference: Marriage Book C Page 6

WALKER, Joseph to Sarah Bonner   20 December 1848
    m. by A. F. Shanno, M. G.
    Reference: Marriage Book D Page 9

WALKER, Prior H. to Mary Ann Cate   12 January 1843
    m. 12 January by A. Slover, M. G.
    Reference: Marriage Book C Page 71

WALKER, Robert to Juliann Philips   10 February 1843
    m. 12 February by D. L. Godsey, M. G.
    Reference: Marriage Book C Page 73

WALKER, Samuel to Eliza White Cotton   13 March 1839
    m. 13 March by Jos. Billings, J. P.
    Reference: Marriage Book C Page 14

WALKER, Silas M. to Eliza Morgan   4 October 1852
   m. 7 October by William R. Walker, J. P.
   Reference: Marriage Book D Page 57

WALKER, Thomas to Texana Wells   12 November 1867
   m. 12 November by G. W. Coleman, M. G.
   Reference: Marriage Book G Page 23

WALKER, Wesley to Elvira Crisp   25 August 1842
   m. 25 August by Dickerson Morris
   Reference: Marriage Book C Page 61

WALKER, William to Polly Shield
   m. 26 January 1832
   Reference: Oregon Donation Land Claim
   Number 471, Roseburg Land Office

WALKER, William R. to Amanda C. Wolff   20 June 1849
   m. 21 June by A. F. Shannon, M. G.
   Reference: Marriage Book D Page 15

WALL - see WALLS

WALLACE, S. A. to Harriet Maxwell   12 March 1855
   Reference: Marriage Book D Page 96

WALLACE - see also WALLIS

WALLEN, John to Emily Dillon   12 June 1843
   m. 12 June by Elisha Hays, J. P.
   Reference: Marriage Book C Page 79

WALLEN, R. S. to Martha Ann Combs   28 December 1867
   Reference: Marriage Book G Page 25

WALLER, Thos. B. to Mary D. Goforth   1 June 1864
   m. 2 June by Thos. B. Waller, M. G.
   Reference: Marriage Book F Page 3

WALLIN, Stephen to Sarah Bishop   10 March 1842
   m. 12 March 1843 /sic/ by John Jenkins, J.P.
   Reference: Marriage Book C Page 55

WALLIS, J. B. to Martha M. Pettette   28 July 1866
   m. 13 August by Hamilton Pearce, J. P.
   Reference: Marriage Book F Page 45

WALLIS, John E. to Katharine J. Maxwell   27 September 1853
   m. 28 September by J. Cunningham, M. G.
   Reference: Marriage Book D Page 71

WALLIS, Thos. J. to Nancy E. Helems   23 December 1865
   m. 26 December by Joseph Janway, M. G.
   Reference: Marriage Book F Page 34

WALLIS, W. N. to Mary Jane Munrow   2 February 1867
   m. 2 February by J. Janwary, M. G.
   Reference: Marriage Book G Page 10

WALLS (WALL), M. to Eliza Baker   19 June 1839
   m. June by C. W. Rice, J. P.
   Reference: Marriage Book C Page 18;
   Marriage Book C Page 20

WALSH, Columbus E. to Miss Frances Doss   24 March 1847
   Reference: Marriage Book C Page 154

WALSH, James L. to Sarah Ann Thompson   24 June 1868
   m. 25 June by F. A. Dixon, J. P.
   Reference: Marriage Book G Page 29

WALSH, Thomas B. to Martha C. Newton   4 January 1865
   m. 5 Janaury by E. Newton, M. G.
   Reference: Marriage Book F Page 13

WALSH, Thos. B. to Amanda C. Bingham   24 December 1867
   m. 26 December by P. M. Long, J. P.
   Reference: Marriage Book G Page 25

WALSH, W. J. to Sarah E. Swafford   11 July 1864
   m. 14 July by James Parkison, J. P.
   Reference: Marriage Book F Page 4

WALTON, John to Lucina Irwin   15 August 1856
   m. 22 August by R. A. Giddens, M. G.
   Reference: Marriage Book D Page 112

WAMAC, R. B. to Miss O. A. Thompson   2 January 1868
   m. 9 January by W. J. Russell, M. G.
   Reference: Marriage Book G Page 25

WAMMACK, Elijah P. to Lucina Marler   15 August 1865
   m. 16 August by S. W. Royston, J. P.
   Reference: Marriage Book F Page 24

WAN, Emsly to Mrs. Mary White   29 May 1845
   m. 29 May by Heil Buttram, M. G.
   Reference: Marriage Book C Page 121

WARD, Avery to Nancy Moore   26 April 1853
   m. 28 April by A. John, M. G.
   Reference: Marriage Book D Page 65

WARD, C. H. to Miss Jerusha Paris   14 February 1855
   m. 14 February by James C. Carlock, J. P.
   Reference: Marriage Book D Page 94

WARD, Daniel to Elizabeth McNabb   3 November 1847
   m. 4 November by R. A. McAdoo, J. P.
   Reference: Marriage Book C Page 162

WARD, David to Jane Marlow   29 February 1839
   Reference: Marriage Book C Page 15

WARD, Duke to Susannah Moon   23 February 1853
   m. 24 February by A. John, M. G.
   Reference: Marriage Book D Page 64

WARD, Henry Price to Mary McNabb   19 March 1851
   m. 20 March by Nathaniel Barnett, M. G.
   Reference: Marriage Book D Page 39

WARD, Leven A. to Charity Salle   8 August 1839
   m. 8 August by A. Slover, M. G.
   Reference: Marriage Book C Page 21

WARD, Lorenzo Dow to Nancy Jane Maynor   1 March 1847
   m. by M. C. Atchley, Minister
   Reference: Marriage Book C Page 153

WARDE, Duke to Martha Ware   5 April 1859
   m. 7 April by J. Whitesides, M. G.
   Reference: Marriage Book D Page 159

WARE, Jesse A. to Margaret Long   24 January 1842
   Reference: Marriage Book C Page 52

WARE, John to Sarah J. Alaway   10 January 1868
   m. 10 January by P. W. Long, J. P.
   Reference: Marriage Book G Page 26

WARE, John A. to Catharine J. Smith   15 October 1845
   m. 15 October by Samuel Snoddy, J. P.
   Reference: Marriage Book C Page 128

WARE, Joseph R. to Martha Ann Cobbs   23 July 1846
   Reference: Marriage Book C Page 140

WARE, William J. to Anna Cauldwell   20 September 1849
   m. 20 September by Robert Gregory, M. G.
   Reference: Marriage Book D Page 19

WARE - see also WEAR, WEIR

WARFORD, William J. to Harriett E. Dyer   29 July 1870
   m. 4 August by William Thompson, M. G.
   Reference: Marriage Book G Page 63

WARREN, Robert to N. C. Bogart   4 July 1866
   m. 4 July by Wallas W. Tharps, M. G.
   Reference: Marriage Book F Page 43

WASHAM, John W. to Mary C. Grayson   11 December 1858
   m. 12 December by R. Reynolds, J. P.
   Reference: Marriage Book D Page 153

WASHBURN, Henry to Nancy Murry   25 November 1870
   m. 25 Novemeber by Jno Scarborough, J. P.
   Reference: Marriage Book G Page 69

WASHBURNE, Henry to Louisa Constant   6 December 1864
   m. 6 December by W. C. Owen, J. P.
   Reference: Marriage Book F Page 11

WASSAM, John to Margaret Turner   30 July 1855
   Reference: Marriage Book D Page 101

WASSOM, Jacob to Sarah Jane Berry   13 September 1852
   m. 16 September by H. Small, J. P.
   Reference: Marriage Book D Page 56

WASSON, Benjamin to Lydia Tallant   1 August 1853
   m. 1 August by G. W. Kirksey, J. P.
   Reference: Marriage Book D Page 68

WASSON, Benjamin T. to Mary J. Bryant   7 June 1845
   m. 10 June by William Rucker, J. P.
   Reference: Marriage Book C Page 121

WASSON, E. T. to Miss Matta Lowery   25 February 1857
   m. 26 February by Geo. A. Caldwell, M. G.
   Reference: Marriage Book D Page 124

WASSON, Hamilton L. to Rachail M. Rucker   7 January 1847
   m. 7 January by William Rucker, J. P.
   Reference: Marriage Book C Page 150

WASSON, Henry to Mary Garrison   11 August 1842
   m. 12 August by G. W. Wallis, J. P.
   Reference: Marriage Book C Page 60

WASSON, John to Margaret Hughs   8 October 1839
    m. 10 October by Joseph Minze, J. P.
    Reference: Marriage Book C Page 24

WASSON, William to Jane Bedford   13 December 1845
    m. 21 December by W. Rucker, J. P.
    Reference: Marriage Book C Page 130

WATEN, W. W. to Maryann Grogan   11 July 1868
    m. 12 July by J. H. Magill, J. P.
    Reference: Marriage Book G Page 29

WATERS - see also WATTERS

WATKINS - see also WADKINS

WATSON, A. J. to Martha Hicks   13 July 1864
    m. 20 July by S. M. Haun, M. G.
    Reference: Marriage Book F Page 5

WATSON, David to Delila Atkinson   29 May 1853
    m. 29 May by J. W. Cox, J. P.
    Reference: Marriage Book D Page 66

WATSON, George to Nancy Bond   2 January 1839
    m. 3 January by A. Barb, J. P.
    Reference: Marriage Book C Page 12

WATTENBARGER, Annias to Miss Ameline McKeehen   24 September 1851
    m. 25 September by H. B. Brandon, M. G.
    Reference: Marriage Book D Page 43

WATTENBARGER, Christopher to Jane Buttram   3 May 1854
    Reference: Marriage Book D Page 83

WATTENBARGER, Jacob to Louisa Thomas   21 February 1849
    m. 22 February by T. B. Waller, M. G.
    Reference: Marriage Book D Page 12

WATTENBARGER, Levi to Jincey A. Stiles   8 May 1868
    m. 7 June by Goerge W. Morton, J. P.   or
    Reference: Marriage Book G Page 29;   6 June 1868
    Marriage Book G Page 32

WATTENBARGER, Peter to Nancy A. Buttram   7 March 1865
    m. 7 March by Heil Buttram, M. G.
    Reference: Marriage Book F Page 16

WATTENBARGER, Thomas to Sarah Ann McWhen   25 July 1851
    m. 31 July by Hiel Buttram, M. G.
    Reference: Marriage Book D Page 41

WATTERS, Bennett to Minierva Brannock   13 October 1842
    m. 13 October by C. W. Rice, J. P.
    Reference: Marriage Book C Page 65

WAUGH, F. W. to Miss T. S. M. Dixon   23 February 1862
    m. 23 February by A. D. Brient, J. P.
    Reference: Marriage Book E Page 4

WAUGH, William K. to Katharine Colville   30 July 1840
    Reference: Marriage Book C Page 30

WEAR, J. N. to Miss E. Cate   15 May 1856
    m. 15 May by Robert Gregory, M. G.
    Reference: Marriage Book D Page 109

WEAR (WEIR), Joseph C. to Salley Colville   15 January 1846
    m. 15 January by William McKamy, J. P.
    Reference: Marriage Book C Page 132

WEARE, Merit R. to Sarah Jane Pearce   23 January 1839
    Reference: Marriage Book C Page 13

WEARE - see also WARE, WEIR

WEATHERLY, W. H. to Eliza Jane Cook   25 February 1856
    m. 24 /sic7 February by Morgan Miller, J. P.
    Reference: Marriage Book D Page 108

WEATHERLY, Washington Y. to Emily J. Brannock   23 November 1841
    Reference: Marriage Book C Page 49

WEATHERLY, William to Rachel McAlister   15 July 1839
    m. 18 July by William J. Witcher, M. G.
    Reference: Marriage Book C Page 21

WEATHERLY, Woodson to Elizabeth Hanks   4 March 1841
    Reference: Marriage Book C Page 39

WEATHERLY - see also WETHERLY

WEATHERS, William to Caroline Orr   29 May 1865
    m. 7 June by T. R. Bradshaw, M. G.
    Reference: Marriage Book F Page 18

WEAVER, Alfred G. to Elizabeth Harris   19 June 1839
    m. 20 June by Hamilton Bradford, J. P.
    Reference: Marriage Book C Page 18

WEAVER, George W. to Julia Ann W. Walker   25 August 1854
    m. 28 August by Jas. Parkison, J. P.
    Reference: Marriage Book D Page 86

WEBB, H. to Miss P. A. Beasley   17 June 1856
    m. 19 June by Joseph Neil, J. P.
    Reference: Marriage Book D Page 11

WEBB, Hiram to Susannah Roe   22 April 1850
    m. 22 April by Thomas B. Waller, M. G.
    Reference: Marriage Book D Page 27

WEBB, John to Elizabeth Moses   16 April 1844
    m. 18 April by J. H. Benton, J. P.
    Reference: Marriage Book C Page 101

WEBB, Lewis to Nancy A. Wattenbarger   9 November 1864
    m. 10 November by Dan Carpenter, M. G.
    Reference: Marriage Book F Page 10

WEBB, William to Caroline Beasley   10 July 1856
    m. 10 July by Joseph Neel, J. P.
    Reference: Marriage Book D Page 111

WEBB, William to Martha Pearman   21 December 1865
    m. 21 December by J. H. Magill, J. P.
    Reference: Marriage Book F Page 33

WEDDOWS, Jabez to Mary Ann Ford   18 August 1842
    m. 18 August by L. R. Morrison, V. D. M.
    Reference: Marriage Book C Page 61

WEDDOWS - see also WIDOWS

WEEKS, David to Isabell Clark
    m. 9 November by John Jenkins, J. P.
    Reference: Marriage Book C Page 147
                                      9 November 1846

WEEKS, Hiram to Nancy Ann Helms
    m. 3 August by John Scarbrough, J. P.
    Reference: Marriage Book C Page 158
                                        2 August 1847

WEEKS - see also WEAKS

WEIR, David to Margaret Stuart
    m. 3 January /sic7 by William Walker
    Reference: Marriage Book D Page 37
                                    23 January 1851

WEIR, James to Sarah Bradford
    m. 3 March by L. W. Crouch, M. G.
    Reference: Marriage Book G Page 28
                                22 February 1868

WEIR, John to Martha Bonner
    Reference: Marriage Book D Page 72
                                4 October 1853

WEIR, Thomas J. to Gemimy C. Bonner
    m. 4 December by L. W. Crouch, M. G.
    Reference: Marriage Book G Page 24
                                4 December 1867

WEIR - see also WARE, WEAR

WELCKER, Benjamin F. to Sarah E. Reagan
    m. 17 January by J. Sewell, Minister
    Reference: Marriage Book C Page 71
                                17 January 1843

WELLEN, Berryman to Miss Arvazine Allison
    m. 21 January by William F. Forrest, M. G.
    Reference: Marriage Book D Page 47
                              16 January 1852

WELLS, Benjamin to Tathamany Prather
    m. 16 June by Robert Frazier, M. G.
    Reference: Marriage Book C Page 58
                              16 June 1842

WELLS, Robert H. to Sally L. Carlock
    m. 4 March by C. Long, M. G.
    Reference: Marriage Book E Page 14
                              3 March 1864

WELLS, William to Angeline Perry
    m. 9 January by C. Cate, J. P.
    Reference: Marriage Book F Page 35
                              9 January 1866

WEST, Archibald to Julia Swaffer
    m. by J. Jenkins, J. P.
    Reference: Marriage Book D Page 51
                              13 April 1852

WEST, Francis M. to Susan Kitchen
    Reference: Marriage Book D Page 92
                              7 December 1854

WEST, James H. to Elisabeth Bond
    m. 21 January by Samuel Wilson, J. P.
    Reference: Marriage Book C Page 150
                              9 January 1847

WEST, Samuel T. to Betsie J. Pierce
    m. 6 February by W. G. Horton, J. P.
    Reference: Marriage Book G Page 27
                            5 February 1868

WEST, Thos. P. to Margaret McClelan
    m. 24 March by N. B. McNabb
    Reference: Marriage Book E Page 16
                            23 March 1864

WEST, William to Mary Coggins
    Reference: Marriage Book F Page 21
                              14 July 1865

WHALEY, C. W. to Miss Becksey Filyaw   1 June 1846
    Reference: Marriage Book C Page 139

WHALEY, Ira to Sarah A. Rogers   28 June 1856
    m. 29 June by H. C. Cook, M. G.
    Reference: Marriage Book D Page 111

WHALEY, John S. to Mary E. Prince   4 March 1870
    Reference: Marriage Book G Page 59

WHALEY, Joseph L. to Sarah L. Huddleston   1 June 1846
    m. 1 June by M. C. Atchley, Minister
    Reference: Marriage Book C Page 139

WHALEY, Thomas F. to Mary A. Howel   22 March 1849
    m. 5 April by A. F. Shannon, M. G.
    Reference: Marriage Book D Page 13

WHELSELLE, P. K. to Miss N. F. Swinney   4 April 1856
    m. 4 Arpil by M. A. Cass, M. G.
    Reference: Marriage Book D Page 109

WHITE, Daniel to Maranda Fox   24 December 1844
    Reference: Marriage Book C Page 115

WHITE, Eadon to Nancy M. Dickey   24 October 1870
    Reference: Marriage Book G Page 68

WHITE, Edmund to Lucy Ellen Rothwell   24 February 1855
    m. 1 March by H. M. Roberts, J. P.
    Reference: Marriage Book D Page 95

WHITE, Elisha to Usler Cloud   2 March 1840
    m. 2 March by Moses A. Cass
    Reference: Marriage Book C Page 28

WHITE, Huston to Margret Tompson   3 October 1866
    m. 4 October by A. D. Briant, J. P.
    Reference: Marriage Book G Page 1

WHITE, James to Hariet McCall   31 December 1864
    m. 2 January by D. W. Beaver, M. G.
    Reference: Marriage Book F Page 13

WHITE, James M. to Mary A. Dennis   7 October 1843
    m. 8 October by J. H. Benton, J. P.
    Reference: Marriage Book C Page 86

WHITE, Jesse to Jemima Elliott   3 September 1840
    m. 3 September by Moses A. Cass, J. P.
    Reference: Marriage Book C Page 31

WHITE, Jesse to Eliza Casteel   10 April 1865
    m. 11 April by Elihu Kelly, J. P.
    Reference: Marriage Book F Page 17

WHITE, John to Mary McCarroll   11 May 1846
    m. 11 May by M. A. Cass, J. P.
    Reference: Marriage Book C Page 138

WHITE, John to Mary Loyd   22 July 1855
    m. 29 July by L. R. Hurst, J. P.
    Reference: Marriage Book D Page 104

WHITE, John H. to Jane Madden   29 January 1856
    m. 2 February by M. R. Wear, J. P.
    Reference: Marriage Book D Page 107

WHITE, Thos. R. to Mary Lamar   1 April 1858
    m. 1 April by H. M. Roberts, J. P.
    Reference: Marriage Book D Page 138

WHITE, William to Eliza Jane Daugherty   12 December 1845
    m. 14 December by Robert Mansel, M. G.
    Reference: Marriage Book C Page 130

WHITE, William to Ataline Cauldwell   29 February 1848
    m. 2 March by Tapley Gregory, J. P.
    Reference: Marriage Book C Page 168;
    W. P. A.

WHITE, William J. to Susan C. Hamilton   29 September 1864
    m. 2 October by Elihu Kelly, J. P.
    Reference: Marriage Book F Page 8

WHITECOTTON - see COTTON

WHITESIDE, W. F. to Miss C. L. Hamilton   27 September 1867
    m. 29 September by S. M. Thomas, J. P.
    Reference: Marriage Book G Page 21

WHITLOCK, William to Eliza Smith   26 August 1858
    Reference: Marriage Book D Page 145

WHITSIDES, Jas. T. to Margaret C. Harless   24 December 1857
    m. 24 December by Joseph Neil, J. P.
    Reference: Marriage Book D Page 133

WHITTEN, George to Louiza J. Lassiter   28 March 1856
    m. 28 March by J. Ziglar, J. P.
    Reference: Marriage Book D Page 109

WHITTON, S. D. to Manervy E. Gilly   18 August 1866
    m. 18 August by L. W. Crouch
    Reference: Marriage Book F Page 45

WIDOWS, Isaac to Anna Parsons   7 November 1849
    m. 8 November by Tapley Gregory, J. P.
    Reference: Marriage Book D Page 21

WIDOWS - see also WEDDOWS

WIGENTON, John to Elizabeth Lawson   1 October 1838
    m. 1 October by William Jones, M. G.
    Reference: Marriage Book C Page 8

WIGHT - see MIGHT

WILES, Alex to Rebecka McKeean   18 December 1829
    Alfred Thomasson, Security
    Reference: W. P. A.

WILHITE, Joseph to Elizabeth Walker   9 October 1841
    m. 14 October by L. L. Ball, J. P.
    Reference: Marriage Book C Page 48

WILKENS, Charles T. to Mary A. Kirkpatrick   21 July 1851
    Reference: Marriage Book D Page 41

WILKEY, Cicero C. to Mrs. Mary Ann Johnson   12 October 1870
    m. 12 October by J. M. Miller, M. G.
    Reference: Marriage Book G Page 67

WILKEY, William to Becky Ann McKee   24 June 1867
    m. 24 June by W. Beaver, M. G.
    Reference: Marriage Book G Page 16

WILKINSON, Elias to Easter Dearmon   2 March 1842
    m. 2 March by M. A. Cass, J. P.
    Reference: Marriage Book C Page 54

WILKISON, Lawson H. to Miss Frances Calhoun   19 April 1842
    Reference: Marriage Book C Page 56

WILLIAMS, A. J. to Miss M. S. Cate   16 January 1869
    m. 17 January by G. M. Hutsell, M. G.
    Reference: Marriage Book G Page 42

WILLIAMS, Calvin to Elizabeth Sherrill   13 October 1842
    m. 13 October by John Gaston, M. G.
    Reference: Marriage Book C P ge 65

WILLIAMS, E. to Miss C. C. Cooper   1 September 1864
    m. 1 September by Charles Cate, J. P.
    Reference: Marriage Book F Page 6

WILLIAMS, E. W. to Elizabeth Ann Ellis   20 March 1852
    m. 21 March by Robert Gregory, M. G.
    Reference: Marriage Book D Page 49

WILLIAMS, Eligah to Mary E. Cooper   28 May 1858
    m. 3 June by C. R. Hoyl, M. G.
    Reference: Marriage Book D Page 141

WILLIAMS, Elisha Z. to Amanda B. Ellis   5 April 1852
    m. 8 April by Robert Gregory, M. G.
    Reference: Marriage Book D Page 51

WILLIAMS, Frederick S. to Mary Barnet   11 March 1829
    Saml. A. Ewing, Security
    Reference: W. P. A.

WILLIAMS, Granville to Margaret Hamilton   5 November 1856
    m. 5 November by Hiel Buttram, M. G.
    Reference: Marriage Book D Page 118

WILLIAMS, Henry to Jane Edens   15 May 1841
    m. 20 May by M. C. Hawk, M. G.
    Reference: Marriage Book C Page 42

WILLIAMS, Henry to Elizabeth Nichols   12 May 1842
    m. 15 May by M. C. Hawk, Minister M. E. Church
    Reference: Marriage Book C Page 58

WILLIAMS, Henry G. to Nancy C. Gibson   10 June 1865
    m. 11 June by P. M. Long, J. P.
    Reference: Marriage Book F Page 19

WILLIAMS, J. H. to Miss Darcus Murry   1 December 1857
    m. 2 December by Joseph Gibson, J. P.
    Reference: Marriage Book D Page 132

WILLIAMS, J. W. D. to Florence T. Stowe   13 March 1869
    m. 18 March by Jacob Brillhart, M. G.
    Reference: Marriage Book G Page 45

WILLIAMS, James to Jinny Bunch   12 November 1846
    m. 12 November by M. C. Atchley, Minister
    Reference: Marriage Book C Page 147

WILLIAMS, John E. to Louisa Jane Hail   18 November 1847
    m. 18 November by William F. Forrest, M. G.
    Reference: Marriage Book C Page 162

WILLIAMS, Madison to Mary E. Clark   22 August 1843
    m. 22 August by J. W. Barnett, J. P.
    Reference: Marriage Book C Page 84

WILLIAMS, Noah to Mary Champlin   8 November 1845
    m. 8 November by A. Slover, M. G.
    Reference: Marriage Book C Page 129

WILLIAMS, Thomas to Maranda Randolph   26 July 1841
    m. 27 July by Rees Jones, Minister
    Reference: Marriage Book C Page 43

WILLIAMS, William H. to Amanda C. Dethero   4 February 1849
    Reference: Marriage Book D Page 12

WILLIAMSON, Martin B. to Margaret Ledford   11 August 1865
    Reference: Marriage Book F Page 23

WILLIMS, John G. to Nancy E. Bishop   22 September 1869
    m. 24 September by E. Z. Williams, J. P.
    Reference: Marriage Book G Page 51

WILLIS, F. M. to Miss H. Chambers   17 December 1869
    m. 20 December by S. M. Thomas, J. P.
    Reference: Marriage Book G Page 55

WILLIS, John to Elizabeth Hale   9 October 1852
    m. 10 October by James Bonner, J. P.
    Reference: Marriage Book D Page 58

WILLIS, William H. to Martha Hail   24 January 1851
    m. 26 January by William Walker
    Reference: Marriage Book D Page 37

WILLIS, William V. to Lucinda Newton   16 July 1839
    m. 18 July by Edward Newton, M. G.
    Reference: Marriage Book C Page 21

WILLIS - see also WILLES

WILLSON, James G. to Martha Canslor   20 December 1847
    m. 20 December by Samuel Wilson, J. P.
    Reference: Marriage Book C Page 163

WILSON, Armstead H. to Nancy Ann Sharrelt   20 December 1847
    m. 6 November 1851 by William C. Daily, M. G.
    Reference: Marriage Book D Page 45

WILSON, David A. to Amandy M. Burk   8 October 1846
    m. 8 October by M. D. Anderson, J. P.
    Reference: Marriage Book C Page 144

WILSON, David M. to Nancy L. Underdown   19 August 1856
    m. 21 August by M. A. Cass, M. G.
    Reference: Marriage Book D Page 113

WILSON, F. M. to Nancy J. Roland   29 September 1864
    m. 29 September by E. Z. Williams, J. P.
    Reference: Marriage Book F Page 8

WILSON, Franklin to Sarah B. Marcum   20 September 1842
    m. 20 September by M. D. Anderson, J. P.
    Reference: Marriage Book C Page 62

WILSON, George W. to Mary Glace   16 February 1852
    Reference: Marriage Book D Page 48

WILSON, Isaac M. to Eliza E. Newman   6 August 1851
    m. 7 August by Robert Gregory, M. G.
    Reference: Marriage Book D Page 42

WILSON, J. F. to Miss Francis J. Barnette   6 December 1856
    Reference: Marriage Book D Page 120

WILSON, J _____ y, to Lucy Newman   16 April 1867
    m. 21 April by E. Z. Williams, J. P.
    Reference: Marriage Book G Page 13

WILSON, Jackson C. to Sarah Martin   10 July 1848
    m. 11 July by W. W. Haymes, Acting J. P.
    Reference: Marriage Book D Page 3

WILSON, James to Mrs. Barbara Marcum   3 February 1844
    m. 4 February by John Gaston, M. G.
    Reference: Marriage Book C Page 97

WILSON, James E. to Nancy Gallant   5 January 1854
    m. 6 January by D. W. Beaver, M. G.
    Reference: Marriage Book D Page 77

WILSON, James M. to Delany Triplett   9 March 1843
    m. 9 March by Moses Swinney, Esq.
    Reference: Marriage Book C Page 76

WILSON, James W. to Catharine Shamble   1 August 1828
    C. G. Murrell, Security
    Reference: W. P. A.

WILSON, John to Lucinda Lawson   5 December 1827
    m. 6 December by Daniel Newman, J. P.
    Reference: W. P. A.

WILSON, John E. T. to Jane M. Richerson   14 December 1848
    m. 14 December by Urial Johnston, J. P.
    Reference: Marriage Book D Page 9

WILSON, John H. to Malindy Wilson   27 August 1867
    Reference: Marriage Book G Page 19

WILSON, Joshua B. to Nancy Miller   5 May 1851
    m. 6 May by M. A. Cass, M. G.
    Reference: Marriage Book D Page 40

WILSON, Patrick W. to Mary C. Barnett   14 February 1850
    m. 15 February by Thomas T. Russell, M. G.
    Reference: Marriage Book D Page 25

WILSON, Percival C. to Letitia S. Atlee   12 June 1865
    m. 13 June by Jno. F. Spence, M. G.
    Reference: Marriage Book F Page 19

WILSON, Raphael to Rebecca C. Ferrel   29 March 1858
    m. 1 April by D. W. Beaver, M. G.
    Reference: Marriage Book D Page 138

WILSON, S. P. to Miss N. P. Howard   6 January 1870
    m. 6 January by J. C. Barb, M. G.
    Reference: Marriage Book G Page 58

WILSON, Wilburn to Louisa Thompson   7 January 1851
    Reference: Marriage Book D Page 36

WILSON, William to Sidney A. Roberts   4 September 1845
    m. 4 September by William Rucker, J. P.
    Reference: Marriage Book C Page 126

WILSON, William M. to Paralee Marton   25 February 1869
    m. 28 February by Calvin Denton, M. G.
    Reference: Marriage Book G Page 44

WILSON, Zeake to Mary C. Letner   17 December 1868
    Reference: Marriage Book G Page 41

WIMBERLY, Jacob to Elizabeth Gray   1 December 1842
    m. 1 December by C. Sanders, M. G.
    Reference: Marriage Book C Page 68

WINGOE, W. H. to Miss R. C. Eadan   10 September 1866
    m. 12 September by Elias Gibson, M. G.
    Reference: Marriage Book F Page 46

WINSCH (WINCHER), John Karl to Mrs. Rebecca Fisher   11 September 1846
    m. 11 November by A. Slover, M. G.
    Reference: Marriage Book C Page 147;
    McMinn Chancery Case Number 59

WITT, Hezekiah to Martha M. Stephens   10 October 1864
    m. 16 October by Richard Spurling, M. G.
    Reference: Marriage Book F Page 8

WITT, James H. to Parthaney Kirksey   26 January 1830
    Rutherford Witt, Security
    Reference: W. P. A.

WITT, Rufus to Margaret Jane West   19 January 1848
    m. 20 January by Reuben Faulkner, J. P.
    Reference: Marriage Book C Page 166

WITT, Silas to Emaline Blankenship   24 February 1855
    m. 15 /sic7 February by John Douglass, M. G.
    Reference: Marriage Book D Page 95

WITTE, William C. to Mary J. Heran   20 September 1855
    m. 20 September by Geo. A. Caldwell, M. G.
    Reference: Marriage Book D Page 102

WOFFORD - see WARFORD

WOLF, Charles to Nancy E. Madden   19 January 1856
    m. 20 January by H. M. Roberts, J. P.
    Reference: Marriage Book D Page 107

WOLFF, Joseph to Dorcas Trimm   2 January 1843
    m. 2 January by G. W. Wallace, J. P.
    Reference: Marriage Book C Page 70

WOMACK, Daniel to Mary Benson   20 February 1846
    m. 20 February by R. A. McAdoo, J. P.
    Reference: Marriage Book C Page 134

WOMACK, Daniel to Serrepta McNutt   26 June 1868
    m. 26 June by G. M. Hutsell, J. P.
    Reference: Marriage Book G Page 33

WOMACK, Jacob to Catherine Beavers   21 February 1849
    m. 21 February by Tapley Gregory, J. P.
    Reference: Marriage Book D Page 12

WOMACK, James to Martha Gee   26 June 1869
    m. 21 /sic7 June by G. M. Hutsell, J. P.
    Reference: Marriage Book G Page 47

WOMACK, William to Ailsey Mynatt   6 February 1854
    m. 7 February by A. John, M. G.
    Reference: Marriage Book D Page 79

WOMACK - see also ROMACK, WAMAC, WAMACK, WAMMACK

WOOD, James E. to Lavisa Marrs   26 December 1866
    Reference: Marriage Book G Page 7

WOOD, John to Martha Wilson   4 March 1841
    m. 5 March by John Rogers, J. P.
    Reference: Marriage Book C Page 38

WOOD, John to Mary Wattenbarger   29 January 1868
    m. 30 January by Stephen Sharits, J. P.
    Reference: Marriage Book G Page 27

WOOD, John H. to Sarrah E. Stallcup   27 December 1858
    m. 30 December by S. M. Haun, M. G.
    Reference: Marriage Book D Page 154

WOOD, Richmond to Lize Ann Burges   16 January 1869
    m. 17 January by G. W. Morton, J. P.
    Reference: Marriage Book G Page 42

WOODDALL (WOODALL), William to Eliza Hetterbrand   17 October 1846
    (Hetterbran)
    m. 18 October by J. C. Weir, J. P.
    Reference: Marriage Book C Page 145

WOODEY, John to Nancy Shelton   22 July 1858
    m. 22 July by D. W. Beavers, M. G.
    Reference: Marriage Book D Page 143

WOODS, Andrew to Harritt Fuqueway   6 November 1856
    m. 6 November by William H. Ballew, J. P.
    Reference: Marriage Book D Page 118

WOODS, Clemont to Rebecca Harmon   2 August 1838
    m. 2 August by William Dotson, J. P.
    Reference: Marriage Book C Page 5

WOODS, Johnson to Rebecah Fowler   23 February 1842
    m. 23 February by John Jenkins, J. P.
    Reference: Marriage Book C Page 53

WOODWARD, A. to Mary L. Sullins   22 October 1838
    Reference: Marriage Book C Page 9

WOOLSEY, John to Margaret Ellis   13 August 1859
    m. 15 August by J. M. Gibson, J. P.
    Reference: Marriage Book E Page 2

WOOTEN, John R. to Ann Walker   27 October 1838
    m. 30 October by John Heniger, M. G.
    Reference: Marriage Book C Page 9

WORKMAN, John M. to Martha Ann Workman   1 January 1846
    m. 1 January by M. C. Hawk
    Reference: Marriage Book C Page 131

WORKMAN, Samuel to Mrs. Arrena Wolf   12 November 1855
    m. 13 November by O. M. Liner, J. P.
    Reference: Marriage Book D Page 104;
    McMinn Chancery Case Number 320

WORKMAN, Saml., Jr. to Mrs. Mary I. Johnson   20 December 1867
    Lon Blizard, Security
    m. 24 December by L. W. Crouch, M. G.
    Reference: County Archives; Marriage
    Book G Page 24; McMinn Chancery Case
    Number 129

WORLEY, John H. to Virginia F. Thornton   17 April 1851
    m. 17 April by Thomas T. Russell, M. G.
    Reference: Marriage Book D Page 40

WORLEY, William to Sarah Shook   16 January 1839
    m. 17 January by G. W. Mayo, J. P.
    Reference: Marriage Book C Page 13

WORLEY, William P. to Mary C. Slaughter   10 October 1865
    m. 11 October by Gilmore Randolph, M. G.
    Reference: Marriage Book F Page 28

WORTHY, Thomas to Mahaly Boards   22 February 1848
    Reference: Marriage Book C Page 168
    (Note: The page for returns on this
    license is missing)

WORTHY, Thomas to Mary McMahan   9 November 1848
    m. 9 November by William Walker, J. P.
    Reference: Marriage Book D Page 7

WRIGHT, Alex. to Martha Ann Wright   7 May 1870
    m. 8 May by C. C. Witt, J. P.
    Reference: Marriage Book G Page 60

WRIGHT, Andrew to Elizabeth Justice   30 April 1870
    m. 1 May by C. C. Witt, J. P.
    Reference: Marriage Book G Page 60

WRIGHT, Isaac G. to Dorcas C. Smith   28 April 1841
    m. 30 April by Jonathan Thomas, J. P.
    Reference: Marriage Book C Page 41

WRIGHT, James C. to Mary Beavers   19 May 1840
    m. 19 May by John Tate, M. G.
    Reference: Marriage Book C Page 29

WRIGHT, John H. to Sarah Ann Crittenden (Crittenan)   2 October 1848
    m. 2 October by Samuel Snoddy, J. P.
    Reference: Marriage Book D Page 5

WRIGHT, John M. to Milly Rivers   1 August 1846
    m. 9 August by R. A. McAdoo, J. P.
    Reference: Marriage Book C Page 141

WRIGHT, Robert to Vira Shill (Shell)   1 January 1841
    m. 5 January by Joseph Minzs, J. P.
    Reference: Marriage Book C Page 35

WRIGHT, Thmas B. to Iraanah Cruse   4 December 1850
    m. 5 December by J. C. Bryant, J. P.
    Reference: Marriage Book D Page 35

WRIGHT, William R. to Lucy Moon   6 April 1844
    m. 7 April by Tapley Gregory, J. P.
    Reference: Marriage Book C Page 100

WRIGHT, Willis to Mahala Newton   23 December 1846
    m. 29 December by B. K. Stewart, M. G.
    "In the presence of Sarah Walker and others"
    Reference: Marriage Book C Page 150

WRIGHT - see also RIGHT

WYATT, Charles to Mary Maxwell   26 June 1864
    Reference: Marriage Book F Page 4

WYATT, William to Mary Pike   28 March 1842
    Joseph Thomas, Security
    m. 28 March by J. H. Benton, J. P.
    Reference: Marriage Book C Page 56;
    County Archives

WYATT - see also WIATE, WIATT

WYRICK, O. F. to Jane Grisham   3 July 1844
    m. 4 July by Tapley Gregory, J. P.
    Reference: Marriage Book C Page 103

WYRICK, William to Nancy Renfro   18 April 1844
    m. 18 April by T. S. Rice, J. P.
    Reference: Marriage Book C Page 101

YEARWOOD, J. M. to Miss C. V. Netherland   3 November 1859
    m. 3 November by James Forrest, J. P.
    Reference: Marriage Book E Page 10

YEARWOOD, James M. to Susan R. Lowry   20 November 1855
    m. 20 November by Thos. R. Bradshaw, M. G.
    Reference: Marriage Book D Page 104

YODLE, Joseph to Sarah A. Sharits   22 July 1856
    m. 22 July by Geo. A. Caldwell, M. G.
    Reference: Marriage Book D Page 111

YOKUM, F. L. to Miss F. L. Henderson   27 November 1841
    m. 31 /sic/ November by James Sewell, Minister
    Reference: Marriage Book C Page 49

YONG, John H. to Miss E. J. Barnett   18 November 1845
    m. 27 November by Robert Gregory, M. G.
    Reference: Marriage Book C Page 129

YORK, John J. to Matilda Lutrell   27 August 1843
    Reference: Marriage Book C Page 84;
    County Archives

YORK, Uriah L. to Mary M. Deadrick   27 September 1858
    m. 28 September by George A. Caldwell, M. G.
    Reference: Marriage Book D Page 147

YOUNG, Jerrimiah to Rosanah Blanton   19 July 1847
    m. 21 July by Tapley Gregory, J. P.
    Reference: Marriage Book C Page 157

YOUNG, John to Mrs. Sarah Blevins   1 December 1849
    m. 1 December by R. A. McAdoo, J. P.
    Reference: Marriage Book D Page 22

YOUNG, Thomas L. to Rebecca W. Gammon   6 May 1845
    m. 6 May by O. F. Cunningham, M. G.
    Reference: Marriage Book C Page 120

YOUNG, William to Sidney Swinford   29 May 1856
    Reference: Marriage Book D Page 110

YOUNG, William F. to Nancy Ann Bolton   31 July 1847
    m. 22 August by J. W. Barnett, J. P.
    Reference: Marriage Book C Page 158

YOUNT, Daniel to Betsey Shepheard   21 December 1825
    John L. O. Falvey, Security
    m. 21 December by James McKamy, J. P.
    Reference: County Archives

YOUNT, John to Sarah K. Fry   20 January 1848
    m. 20 January by Rev. Edwin A. Atlee
    Reference: Marriage Book C Page 166

ZEIGLER, Benj. T. to Susan Mansell   26 December 1838
    Reference: Marriage Book C Page 11

ZEIGLER, Jacob to C. MCmillian   3 January 1858
    m. 3 January by J. B. Haney, J. P.
    Reference: Marriage Book D Page 154

ZEIGLER, Jacob to Amabelle Gibbory   23 May 1860
    m. 23 May by T. J. Pope, M. G.
    Reference: Marriage Book E Page 16

ZEIGLER, Michael to Malinda Mansell   6 February 1838
    m. 8 February by Robt. Mansell, M. G.
    Reference: Marriage Book C Page 1

ZEIGLER, Tubeller to Miss Francis J. Mansel   31 March 1852
    m. 31 March by Nathaniel Barnett, M. G.
    Reference: Marriage Book D Page 50

ZIEGLER, Joram R. to Catharine Yount   2 August 1853
    m. 4 August by C. P. Vandyke
    Reference: Marriage Book D Page 68

ZIEGLER, William B. to Louisa C. Holland   12 December 1866
    m. 13 December by D. Carpenter, M. G.
    Reference: Marriage Book G Page 6

ZIGLER, Joseph A. to Mary Ann Cate   22 December 1845
    m. 23 December by William Rucker, J. P.
    Reference: Marriage Book C Page 130

INDEX

Compiled by

Ella E. Lee Sheffield

A--, James 77
ABBOT, Polly 150
ACRE, Eliza E. 10
ADAMS, Elizabeth 48
   William C. L. 41
ADORE, Mary J. 71
   Rebecca E. 71
ADDISON, Elizabeth 67
ADY, Mary E. 43
AERINGTON, Louisa 59
AHA, Mary Sweeney 202
AIKEN, Catharine 95
AILEY, Fanny 115
AKIN, Sarah 126
AKINS, Thomas 180
ALAWAY, Sarah J. 221
ALEXANDER, G. W. 57
   Hamilton L. 130
   Saliva 60
ALLAWAY, Mary A. 120
ALLEN, Amanda 55
   Byrum 179
   Rev. Edwin A. 131
   Emmie 194
   Harriett S. 54
   James 13
   Jane 62
   Jonathan 42
   Mary 4, 146
   Mrs. Penelope J. 216
ALLISON, Arvazine 224
   James 59
   Rebecca M. 155
   Scynthia C. 156
AMARINE, Henery 167
   Isham 14
AMOS, Drucilla 40
   Elizabeth 181
   Martha 53
   Susan 41
AMURIN, Elizabeth 95
ANDERSON, Amanda 36
   Amandia 69
   Caroline 180
   Isaac 174
   Isabella 132
   Joseph 21
   Louisa E. C. 126
   M. D. 10, 26, 46, 47,
      76, 77, 89, 91, 93,
      94, 97, 127, 139,
      154, 158, 165, 190,
      191, 205, 228
   Mary Ann 1, 57, 204
ANDREWS, Matildy 72
ARIC, Marget A. 62
ARMSTRONG, A. J. 39
   Amanda J. 162
   Elizabeth 148
   Jane 105
   Katharine 149
   Louisa 9
   Malinda J. 198
   Margret 44
   Matilda 14
   Penelope 83
   Polly 43
   Sally 49
   Sarah A. 201
   Wm. 17
   Wm. B. 74
ARNEL, Sarah 136
ARNELL, Sarah 136
ARNWINE, Mahala 73
   Martha 58, 78
   Nancy 73

ARNWINE (cont.)
   Vinila 182
ASHLEY, Mrs. Mary 74
   Mary Ann 102
ASKINS, Visa 199
ASTON, S. W. 209
ATCHLEY, M. C. 44, 66,
      188, 196, 199, 220,
      225, 227
   Prissilla 27
   Sarah 144
ATCHLY, P. M. 103
ATKENS, J. 143
ATKIN, Rev. George 83
ATKINS, I. 46
   J. 12, 48, 52, 124
   Jas. 165
ATKINSON, Delila 222
   Frances 185
   J. 217
   James 216
   Malinda 66
   Nancy 162
   Parilee 82
   Vilenia W. 113
ATLEE, Amelia V. 45
   Edward 88
   Edwin A. 43, 71, 234
   Jane E. 48
   Letitia S. 229
   Mary P. 5
   Sarah Elizabeth 124
ATLEY, Catharine L. 116
AVANS, F. M. 88, 181
   Mary E. 207
AVENS, Marthy L. 200
AVERY, Rev. Jared R. 110
AVINS, F. M. 30
AXLEY, Rev. James 29
AYRES, David B. 212
   Omey 132
   Solina 212
AYTES, Sallie 72
B--, Elizabeth 193
BAB, J. C. 93
BACKLEY, J. M. 142
BAILEY, Adilla 7
   Jane 103, 155
   Nancy 191
BAILY, Rev. Mr. -- 214
BAINE, Malinda 155
BAKER, Catharine 168
   Catharine J. 41
   Celinda 3
   Eliza 219
   Emaline 132
   James 17, 36, 77,
      101, 114, 117, 138,
      142, 148, 149, 174,
      184, 200, 203, 206,
      208
   Jane 27, 100, 195
   Mary 19, 105
   Mary A. 14
   Maryann 3
   Mary F. 64
   Mary P. 36
   Sarah Louisa 23
BALDWILL, Rachel 59
BALDWIN, Henry 117, 177,
      189
   Susan E. 182
BALES, Artemesy 112
   Daniel 12
   James 184
   M. E. 195

BALES (cont.)
   Mary Jane 35
   Sarah C. 36
BALFOUR, Elizabeth R. 156
   Sarah C. 132
BALL, Eliza 215
   Mrs. Hudah 160
   L. L. 30, 78, 82, 113,
      162, 169, 179, 208,
      217, 226
   M. A. H. 129
   Martha 114
   Mary Ann 197
   Sarah 93, 192
   Sarah J. 7
BALLARD, Elizabeth 30
BALLERD, William H. 206
BALLEW, A. J. 105
   Texanna L. 73
   W. H. 34, 47, 75, 84,
      116, 133, 176
   Wm. H. 3, 5, 8, 19,
      27, 49, 52, 61, 73,
      86, 93, 94, 99, 115,
      138, 140, 147, 148,
      164, 178, 184, 191,
      199, 215, 231
BARB, A. 27, 29, 31, 36,
      50, 53, 66, 71, 84,
      88, 93, 109, 115,
      135, 138, 140, 145,
      160, 162, 222
   J. C. 48, 81, 93, 113,
      127, 130, 149, 175,
      229
   Rachel 113
   Sarah E. 16
BARBE, J. C. 74, 169
BARCLAY, Elihu S. 40
BARDEN, David 45
BARK, L. 16
BARKER, Algeline 18
   Catharine A. 215
   Elizabeth N. 125
   J. S. 78
   Jane 143
   Keziah L. 197
   Lamira Ann 147
   Margaret Ann 8
   Susan 22, 59
   Thursa A. 144
BARKLEY, A. H. 48
BARKSDALE, Elizabeth 181
BARLOW, Malinda 171
BARNET, Mary 69, 227
   Nathaniel 155
BARNETT, Barbara 162
   J. C. 75
   J. W. 21, 62, 71, 88,
      89, 228, 233
   Jas. 55, 111, 141
   John W. 79, 138, 182
   Margaret E. 27
   Mary C. 229
   Mary E. 59
   Mary O. 161
   Nancy A. 16
   Nancy L. 14
   Nat. 46, 47, 78, 96,
      104, 113, 138, 140,
      187, 209, 220, 234
   Thuney 22
   W. C. 27, 119
   Wm. C. 5
BARNETTE, Francis J. 229
BARNES, Abraham 9

235

BARNES (cont.)
Letty 24
BARNS, Margaret 128
BARTER, Thos. W. 147
William W. 147
BARTON, Miss M. M. 70
BASINGER, Miss K. H. 164
BATES, Margaret Young 183
Mary 214
BATSON, Betsey 188
BAYLESS, Louisa 6
Sarah Jane 64
BAYSINGER, Mary L. 23
BEAN, Sarah J. 147
BEARD, Mary 117
Sarah E. 10
Welcome 117
BEASLEY, Caroline 223
Miss P. A. 223
BEATY, Jane 129
BEAVER, D. 129
D. W. 7, 13, 18, 68,
69, 72, 73, 80, 82,
85, 102, 120, 155,
170, 173, 192, 197,
207
David W. 16, 35, 50,
61, 73, 100, 196,
199, 214
Lewis 25
Mary E. 31
Matilda 25
Sarah C. 60
W. 226
BEAVERS, Ann Eliza 11
Catherine 230
D. W. 103, 225, 229,
231
David W. 80
Joysey 142
Mary 232
BEBIBIN, Nancy 84
BECK, Mary Darkes 87
Rody 186
BECKET, Miss -- 191
Mary B. 124
BECKETT, Saprina 47
BEDFORD, Catherine 61
Elisabeth 61
Jane 222
Mary 67
Mira 82
Sarah 8
Susan 158
BEENE, Sarah E. 131
BEEVER, Mahaly 112
BELCHER, Elizabeth 147
BELDING, John 118
BELL, Mary 195
Matilda 163
BENCH, Avy E. 11
BENNETT, Rachel 25
Sarah Jane 127
BENSON, Martha 176
Mary 230
Sallie A. 46
Tobitha 196
BENTON, Abigale 7
Elijah 179
Elizabeth A. 49
Elmira 39
Hannah 10
J. H. 3, 18, 43, 48,
70, 71, 80, 83, 85,
100, 101, 115, 117,
172, 173, 177, 179,
190, 193, 215, 223,
225, 232
Jane 178
Martha 126
Mary Elvira 33
Melissa 130
Olevia 164

BENTON (cont.)
Rebecca 9
Sarah J. 65
BERRY, Sarah Jane 221
BESTER, Rev. D. P. 129
BEVERS, D. W. 35
BICKNELL, Sarah 99
Winney 189
BIGGS, Charity 32
BIGHAM, Miss M. L. 172
Matilda 163
Nancy Ann Lunna 163
BILLINGS, Jos. 218
BILLINGSLEY, Emelia 124
Joseph 124
BILLINGSLY, L. D. 190
Sally 10
BINGHAM, Amanda C. 220
Celia 114
BIRD, Elvira 56
BISHOP, Nancy E. 228
Hannah 166
J. M. 128
Mary A. 177
Nancy A. 177
Ruth 129
Sarah 219
Sylvester 16
BLACK, Betsy 62
Elizabeth Ann 163
Nancy M. 2
R. A. 5, 48, 116,
BLACKBURN, Eliza 141
J. M. 12, 145
Malinda E. 60
Susan A. 35
BLANKENSHIP, Emaline 230
BLACKWELL, Angeline 209
Anna 120
Caroline 51
Hellen E. 19
Mary 120
Narcissa C. 78
Silvester 81
BLAIN, B. C. 61
B. E. 47, 56, 117,
129, 155, 189
C. E. 168
BLAIR, James 159
BLANKENSHIP, Elizabeth
142
Malinda C. 3
Mary 53
BLANKINSHIP, Calaway 118
Elizabeth Jane 127
Martha 142
BLANSHIPP, Mary 104
BLANTON, John A. 6
Rosanah 233
BLEDSOE, Amy 81
Mahala 80
BLEVINS, Elizabet 93
Frances E. 155
Ruth J. 99
Mrs. Sarah 233
Wilson 93
BLIZARD, Lou 130, 231
BLIZSARD, Sallie 29
BLOOM, E. P. 3, 6, 7, 12,
17, 31, 141, 159
G. M. 19, 40, 72, 102,
116, 145, 146, 161
BOARDS, Mahaly 232
BODWELL, Martha J. 217
BOGARD, Elizabeth F. 29
BOGART, Mary L. 177
N. C. 221
Solomon 167
BOLAN, M. 171
BOLDEN, Sidna 22
BOLDING, Amanda 55
Matilda C. 12
Obadiah 51, 81

BOLDING (cont.)
Obediah 40
BOLEN, Marinda 157
BOLIN, Jane 125
BOLING, Tabitha 114
BOLTON, Nancy Ann 233
BOMAN, Elizabeth 65
BOND, Elisabeth 224
Elizabeth 148, 164
Nancy 222
Polly 47
Rachel 174
Rosanna 109
BONNER, Dianner 110
Elizabeth 81
Gemimy C. 224
James 23, 41, 132,
166, 192, 228
Margaret 102
Martha 224
Mary 20
Paralee 189
Sarah 218
Sarah B. 121
BOOKER, Peggy 86
BOOKOUT, Elizabeth 199
John A. 15
Martha 134
BOON, Elizabeth 137
Mary C. 59
Sarah 25, 94
Vashti 141
BOONE, Jennie 185
BORDEN, Janettie 67
BORING, Carline 151
BORLISON, Melinda J. 65
BORNER, Jennie 185
BOTTOMS, Elizabeth 39
BOWERMAN, David 12
Nancy L. C. 153
Sarah 193
BOWLING, Amanda 55
BOWMAN, Geo. 67, 102, 165
R. P. 82
BOWREN, Lony 104
BOYD, Cora 116, 130
George 12
Lucinda 13
Miss M. C. 44
BRACKET, Nancy A. 59
BRADEN, Elizabeth 76
R. F. 7
BRADFORD, Hamilton 46,
191, 223
Henry 77, 210
Mary G. 42
Mary J. 35
Sarah 224
BRADLEY, Nancy E. 189
BRADLY, Nancy Ann 104
BRADOCK, A. H. 188
BRADSHAW, T. K. 194
T. R. 38, 78, 93, 104,
223
T. W. 137
Thos. R. 233
BRALAN, Bery H. B. 218
BRANDON, Ann E. 192
H. 108, 133
H. B. 222
Hiram H. 101
Mira 10
BRANHAM, Jane 140
Patsey 78
BRANNOCK, Emily J. 223
Minierva 222
BRANUM, Elvira 211
BRAZEAL, Sarah 38
BRAZELTON, Julia A. 104
William 104, 134
BREAZEALE, J. W. M. 110
BREDEN, Zilpha 170
BREEDEN, Talitha 157

BREEDLOVE, Sarah Ann 18
BREWER, John H. 5, 156
  L. 92
  Lewis 8, 90
  Lucinda N. 192
  P. W. 147
BRIANT, A. D. 1, 7, 32,
  35, 52, 69, 71, 79,
  80, 95, 111, 128,
  131, 193, 195, 225
  Hannah 71
  Martha 214
  Millie B. 40
  Mollie B. 40
BRIDGES, Frances E. 30
  Isabella S. 30
  J. L. 106
  Miss J. S. 95
  James S. 95
  Lois A. 111
  Martha W. H. 217
  Mary D. 29
  Mary M. 173
BRIENT, A. D. 186, 222
BRILLHARD, Jacob 32
BRILLHART, Jacob 28, 119,
  143, 227
BRITT, Laura 150
BROCK, Anna 205
  Artilessa 5
  Miss C. C. 140
  Caroline 150
  Catharine 77
  D. H. 189
  Mrs. Eliza 110
  Eliza Jane 66
  H. J. 80, 84, 123,
    152, 177, 211
  Hester E. 195
  Joel 188
  L. 211
  Lawrence 19, 152
  Malinda 162
  Martha 133
  Mary A. 114
  Mary E. 170
  Matilda 135
  Sarah 195
  Sarah A. 209
  Susan 127
BROOKMAN, Jane G. 82
BROOKNER, Angis 67
BROOKS, A. F. 64
  A. T. 16, 92
BROOKSHIRE, Ann 205
  Mary 20, 171
  Katherine 72
BROOSHIRE, Rebecca C. 21
BROWDER, Celia 105
  Ciley 105
  Debora 186
  Miss E. S. 67
  Luvann 83
  Martha 28
  Mary E. 216
  Sarah R. 62
BROWER, Talitha 14
BROWN, Ann Eliza 24
  C. 21
  Mrs. Eliza 65
  Elizabeth 37
  Elizabeth A. 190
  Mrs. Hester Ann 22
  John H. 216
  Joseph 23
  Josephine 66
  Miss M. E. 65
  Mrs. Martha 88
  Mary 98
  Mary A. 184
  Mary J. 21
  Nancy 132
  Nancy Ann 189

BROWN (cont.)
  Nannie E. 204
  Rutilda 208
  Sarah 34
  Sarah C. 147
  Sarah L. 56
  Thos. 158
  Virginia Lane 116
BRUMIT, Jon F. 179
  Telitha E. 84
BRUMMUT, Mary Ann 140
BRUNER, John 84
  John H. 83
BRUNNER, Jno. H. 184
BRYAN, Elizabeth E. 93
  J. C. 46, 208
  Jas. C. 22, 28, 42,
    65, 136, 145, 183
  Nancy A. 107
  Nancy M. 98
BRYANT, A. D. 1, 4, 52,
  192
  Elizabeth Jane 70
  Esther C. 163
  J. C. 42, 232
  Loduska 115
  Mary J. 221
BRYENT, A. D. 75
BUCK, Mary E. 65
BUCKNER, Rev. B. 42
  Rev. Danil 29
  Elizabeth A. 158
  James R. 216
  Miram 121
  Rufus 25
BULLARD, Jacob 121
  Patsy 121
BULLINGTON, Martha 96
BUMBRAUGH, J. B. 32
BRUMIT, Telitha E. 84
BUNCH, Adaline 144
  Caty 11
  Eliza 73, 215
  Jane E. 164
  Jinny 227
  Margaret 67
  Paul 180
  Rosamond 10
  Urlinia 194
BURGER, Lidia 159
BURGES, Lize Ann 231
BURK, Amandy M. 228
  Manervy J. 211
  Mrs. Margart 191, 215
  Marthee 189
  Mary A. 184
BURKE, H. H. 175
BURKS, Sela 190
BURN, W. L. 198
BURNET, Elizabeth 156
  Martin 132
  Nancy Ann 154
BURNETT, Eliza Jane 106
  James S. 107
  Margaret L. 59
  Martha J. 139
  Mary P. 196
  Sarah 173
  Sarah M. 126
BURN, Mrs. Martha 23
  W. L. 9
BURNS, Emaline 187
  Mary Ann 157
  Sarah 43
  Wm. 38, 83, 90, 94,
    95, 101, 117, 131,
    133, 143, 157, 203
  William L. 198
BUSTER, Manurvy 187
BUTLER, Amanda 98
  Elizabeth 85, 169
  Margaret 92
  Nacy M. 4

BUTRAM, Nancy 195
BUTTRAM, Degenira 70
  Elihu E. 187
  Heil 17, 27, 28, 33,
    56, 101, 147, 195,
    220, 222
  Hial 72
  Hiel 11, 13, 14, 67,
    70, 97, 99, 103,
    107, 112, 132, 136,
    149, 166, 176, 179,
    192, 195, 202, 222,
    227
  Hile 31, 100, 195, 200
  Jane 194, 222
  Julia 187
  Lurana 192
  Malissa 70
  Margaret 187
  Mary A. 13
  Mary C. 70
  Mollie C. 102
  Nancy A. 222
  Permelia 71
  Sarah 70
  Sarah E. 176
  Sophrona 147
  Vincy 33
BUTTREM, Hiel 131
CABE, Sarah A. 11
CADE, Sarah J. 111
CAGLE, Peggy 14
CALDWELL, G. A. 98, 143
  George A. 9, 19, 21,
    26, 29, 40, 43, 46,
    51, 52, 58, 60, 68,
    86, 105, 126, 137,
    154, 155, 156, 160,
    161, 162, 163, 168,
    176, 186, 216, 221,
    230, 233
  Geo. A1 108, 109
  Lucinda 47
  Mahala H. 8
CALHOUN, Frances 227
CALLAHAN, Phany 18
CALLOWAY, L. E. 142
  Malinda J. 65
  Sallie L. 60
CAMEL, Lizzie 111
CAMERON, W. O. 16
CAMP, John 181
  Sarah 7
  Thos. 28, 129
CAMPBELL, Miss C. R. 186
  Catharine 180
  Charlotte R. 132
  Elizabeth 181, 211
  Louisa J. 42
  Margaret L. 86
  Mary Eleanor 130
  Mary L. 135
  Matthew 139
  Penelope Smith 216
  Thomas J. 3
CANNADY, Mary Ann 136
CANNON, Charlotty 181
  Elizabeth 193
  Jane 58, 180
  Mary Jane 58
  Nancy 56
  Polly 77
CANRON, Sarah M. 133
CANSLOR, Martha 228
CANTRELL, Alice E. 183
  Atalina 99
  Clementine 155
  D. 3, 15, 78, 98, 103,
    105, 119, 125, 137,
    173, 197
  David 3, 158
  E. 111
  F. M. 185

237

CANTRELL (cont.)
Lucinda 119
Malinda 123
Mary 149
Nancy 185
Nancy M. 143
Sarah Ann 196
CARDEN, Mrs. Jane 193
CARDWELL, N. A. 135
CAREY, Nancy 107
CARLISLE, D. B. 190
CARLOCK, A. 7, 8, 185,
186
Asahil 42
E. W. 158
J. C. 15, 43, 59, 68,
95, 118, 121, 152,
159, 160, 16-. 182,
185, 186, 216
Jas. C. 68, 123, 220
Nancy J. 210
Sally L. 224
CARNEY, Frances 38
Sarah 47, 63
CARPENTER, D. 1, 6, 27,
31, 33, 38, 40, 45,
48, 60, 77, 82, 101,
111, 114, 118, 134,
136, 167, 176, 178,
179, 192, 195, 202,
234
Dan 6, 32, 41, 59, 81,
83, 101, 105, 106,
111, 118, 138, 147,
158, 182, 195, 203,
217, 223
Daniel 217
M. D. 119
CARR, Frances N. 173
CARRIGHT, Sarah 93
CARROLL, Miss C. E. 190
Evaline 118
Elizabeth 68
Mary 22
Nancy 187
CARSON, James 99
Sarah E. 164
CARTER, Adaline Amanda 26
Catherine 1
Eliza 146
Elizabeth J. 179
Francis T. 79
Hiley 194
James 180
Kezia 185
Lewis 27
Martha M. 80
Mary 13, 16
Polina 79
Susan 143
Susan A. 77
CARTNEY, Jas. M. 186
CARTRIGHT, Elizabeth Jane
147
CARVER, Mary A. 207
Nancy J. 12
CASADA, Phebe 91
CASE, Daniel E. 7
CASEY, A. 125
Miss M. E. 70
Susanah 59
CASH, Louisa 191
Lucinda 175
Susan 61
CASS, B. E. 19, 66, 102,
129, 157, 188, 211
Benj. E. 75, 103
E. B. 32, 83
Ellen 187
J. A. 213
J. W. 35
James A. 5
M. A. 21, 26, 28, 31,

CASS (cont.)
M. A. (cont.) 38, 50,
59, 63, 65, 66, 90,
98, 103, 109, 124,
138, 147, 167, 172,
177, 184, 203, 206,
208, 211, 212, 225,
227, 228, 229
Marthey Jane 120
Moses A. 12, 15, 31,
52, 75, 85, 114,
125, 165, 225
Nancy C. 32
Sallie L. 218
CASSADA, Calista 189
CASSADAY, Rachel 190
CASSIDY, Phebe 123
CASST, Louize 210
CASTEEL, Edmond 40
Eliza 225
Elizabeth 138
Elvira 114
Margaret 138
Milvena 176
Rebecky P. 176
Sarah 138
Sarah A. 66
CASTELL, Barney 20
Elizabeth J. 22
Elvery 17
CASTELLER, Alfred 13
CASTRELL, Alice H. 18
CATE, C. 54, 90, 97, 110,
144, 175, 216, 224
Charles 24, 74, 94,
115, 146, 189, 227
Miss E. 222
Easter C. 2
Eliza 101
Eliza Ann 48
Ellen S. 218
Francis 176
G. H. 134
Harriet 154
Jane 118, 191
John 22
L. H. 137, 180
Miss M. S. 227
Magdalena 36
Mahala 99
Maldonethy 184
Manday 41
Martha A. 110
Mary 96, 152, 204
Mary Ann 218, 234
Mary L. 24
Mattie E. 133
Melissa Jane 112
Permelia E. 179
Polly 96
R. C. 44
Rebecca 61
Rebecca M. 144
Robert E. 24
S. H. 36, 134, 215
Sallie 23
Sarah 83, 208
Sarah E. 191
Tenness 190
Thos. J. 194
Virginia 53
W. H. 65, 152
W. M. 72
William 86
Wm. H. 87, 96, 141
CATES, Lydia N. 200
Menada 167
CAULDWELL, Anna 221
Ataline 226
Elizabeth 176
CAVES, Manda 26
Wm. 38
CAVET, Malinda 138

CAYWOOD, Mary Ann 11
CEARL, Edy 67
CECIL, Elizabeth 96
Sarah 92
CENTER, Lousian 113
Pertina 99
CHAMBERS, Miss H. 228
Mc Connell 203
Susan 158
CHAMPLIN, Mary 228
CHANCY, Margaret 82
CHANLEY, Mary Emaline 67
CHAPMAN, Nancy 137
W. 105, 155
Wilson 6, 44, 57, 59,
71, 99, 116, 141,
159, 165, 174, 175,
184, 189, 198, 203
CHAPMON, Maiden 213
Wilson 213
CHAVIS, Margaret 62
CHESNUT, Mary Ann 216
CHESNUTT, I. R. 39, 98,
100, 170
Raleigh 197
CHILDERS, Catharine 78
Narcissah C. 94
Sarah Matilda 191
Surrepta C. 215
CHINN, Mrs. Sarah A. 73
CHRISTIAN, Eliza 95
James 95
CICILL, Mary 72
CLARK, Dorothy 198
Isabell 224
Lotty Ann 26
Miss M. E. 13
Mary E. 228
Nancy 181
Sarah 52
Sarah A. 122
CLEAGE, Sarah E. 77
CLEMENSON, Mary Ann 159
CLEMENTSON, Sarah Jane 11
CLEMMONS, Sarah 204
CLINE, Caroline 141
Margaret 121
Nancy A. T. 140
Sinthy Morris 135
CLOUD, Elizabeth 152
Patsy 152
Polly 20
Sarah 20
Usler 225
COATES, Mary E. 132
COATNEY, Salina J. 171
COATS, Aby 204
Catharine 178
Miss E. A. 215
Lucianah 90
Margaret 178
Martha 64
Mary S. 139
Mrs. Nancy 168
Sarah A. 39
COBB, A. 80
Angeline 12
Elizabeth 68
J. B. 125, 198
Joseph 33
Margret 122
R. A. 53
COBBS, D. A. 85, 97, 192
J. P. 193
Joseph 33, 142
Juliet C. 175
Martha Ann 221
Mrs. Mary 11
Mary Elizabeth 143
Nancy 77
Penelope 80
COCHRAN, Mary E. 9
Robert 6, 34, 47, 76,

COCHRAN (cont.)
  Robert (cont.) 93, 94,
    100, 115, 121, 141,
    169, 170, 172, 198
COE, Elizabeth 35
COFER, Elizabeth 205
  Nancy 81
COFFEE, Delilah T. 20
  James 140
  Judieth C. 16
  Miss M. A. 80
  Sarah F. 127
COFFEY, Henrietta 128
  P. F. 196
COFMAN, A. N. 203
  Lucy 156
COGGHILL, Mary L. 68
COGGINS, Mary 224
COLBOCK, Nancy 217
COLDWELL, Eliza 63
  Miss M. M. 14
COLE, Margret J. 161
  Mary 71
  Sarah 195
COLEIR, Eliza 197
COLEMAN, Ann E. 188
  G. M. 49, 194
  G. W. 8, 35, 123, 125,
    219
  Harriet C. 98
COLLIER, Jane 12
  Miss M. J. 128
  Mary Ann 160
  Sarah 71
  Susan 71
COLLINS, Eliza A. 101
  Margaret 54
  Maria 99
  Nancy 92
COLMAN, G. W. 87, 172
COLONINGER, Miss N. J.
    113
COLVELL, Nancy J. 47
COLVILLE, Betsey 22
  George 22
  Katharine 222
  Salley 223
COLWELL, Marthy 91
COMBS, Louisa M. 67
  Martha Ann 219
  Mary J. 74
CONNER, Mary T. 200
  Peggy 119
  Polly 204
CONSTANT, Louisa 221
COOK, Eliza E. 213
  Eliza Jane 223
  Elizabeth 4, 82
  H. C. 8, 29, 56, 59,
    77, 99, 108, 120,
    225
  Jane 103
  Mary 52
  Mary E. 112
  Mrs. Sarah 104
COOKE, Derendy 170
  Mrs. Eliza 27
  H. C. 49, 77, 112, 124,
    186
  Margret 31
  Margaret A. 31
  Melvina 117
  Miss S. M. 99
  Susan 38
COOKSTEN, Sarah 74
COOLEY, Lidia 44
  Martha 115
COOPER, Miss C. C. 227
  Miss D. A. 49
  Miss E. J. 129
  Elmira 59
  Hiram 198
  Lucinda 23

COOPER (cont.)
  Mary E. 227
  Mary V. 41
  Nancy 163
  Sarah E. 37
  W. H. 116, 196
COPELAND, Elizabeth 89
  Elizabeth Ann 157
  Emily 174
CORBET, W. A. 204
COTTON, Eliza White 218
COUCH, -- 45
  Elizabeth 34
  Mary 55
  Sarah 42
COUPEPPER, Joel 79
COURTNEY, Charlotte R.
    145
  J. 71
  J. M. 145
  John 55, 66, 101, 124,
    166
COWAN, Andrew 107
  Robert 164
  William S. 118
COWDEN, Martha 148
COWIN, Ellen 97
COX, A. F. 102, 190
  Arista 92
  Eliza 124
  Elizabeth 89
  G. W. 132
  J. W. 125, 142, 157,
    169, 187, 201, 260,
    206, 222
  Jane 119
  Louisa E. 103
  Marthey E. 198
  Mary M. 15
  Susan 81
  W. D. 103
COXEY, Almira 202
  R. 68
CRABTREE, Anis 144
  Elizabeth 34
  Percilia 156
  Thomas 7
CRAIG, Mary 58
  Wm. 58
CRAIGE, Milly 133
CRAWFORD, Amanda 91
  Andrew 64, 161
  Cornelia 42
  Ellen 84
  Malissa B. 1
  Martha A. 217
  Matilda 30
  Matilda A. 11
  Susan 46
  W. H. 54
CRAYN, Amanda 210
CREASMAN, Nancy 85
CREASMAN, Sarah 89
CREGORY, Charlotte A. 191
CREWMAN, Rebecca 48
CREWS, Elizabeth 34
  Harriet M. 109
  Nancy 215
  Miss S. J. 193
CRISMAN, Elizabeth 85
CRISP, Elvira 219
  Nancy Manerva 34
  Susannah 80
CRITTENAN, Sarah Ann 232
CRITTENDEN, Josephine 133
  Louiza Jane 124
  Nancy 145
  Sarah Ann 232
CRITTENDON, Mary J. 205
CROCKET, Becky E. 131
  Eliza J. 63
  Rebecca 31
CROCKETT, Elvira 40

CROCKETT (cont.)
  Josephine A. 216
  Mary E. 185
  Sarah J. 211
CROMWELL, John B. 48
CROSS, Mahala 168
  Mary E. 97
CROUCH, L. W. 1, 17, 20,
    82, 88, 92, 102,
    116, 121, 123, 135,
    150, 151, 158, 181,
    185, 195, 216, 218,
    224, 226, 231
  Sarah 90
CROUGH, L. W. 72
CROW, Benjamin S. 206
  C. C. 84
  Catherine 201
  Sarah M. 2
  Susan 67
CRUMLEY, C. C. 28
CRUSE, Iraahah 232
CRUTCHFIELD, Mary Jane 127
  Thomas 127
CRY, Polly 176
  Sarah 178
CRYSOCK, Frederick 62
CULBERSON, Louisa E. 43
  LLPEPER, Miss S. E. 197
  LPEPER, Joel 39, 124
  LPEPER, Joel 16, 56,
    92, 118, 126, 129,
    187, 188, 207, 215
  Mariah J. 172
  Mary A. 4
CULTAN, Anna 9
CULTON, Ursula 100
CUNINGHAM, Amanda 166
  J. 140
  Jane 94
  Malinda 133
  Thos. W. 193
CUNNINGHAM, Charity 136
  D. B. 61, 88, 208
  Ellen Luvine 30
  J. 5, 19, 56, 64, 109,
    113, 126, 127, 147,
    198, 219
  M. W. 47, 80, 108, 112
  Mary Ann 133
  Nancy 148
  O. F. 91, 109, 233
  Sallie A. 168
  Sarah D. 57
  W. G. E. 196
  W. M. 26
CUNNUNGHAM, D. B. 16
CURD, Evaline 45
CURRY, Frances L. 125
CURTIS, Miss C. M. 56
  Nancy 81
DAILY, W. C. 22, 24, 68,
    74, 85, 127, 142,
    204
  Wm. C. 40, 168, 218,
    228
DAKE, Sarah C. 177
DARLIN, Millie 97
DAUGHERTY, Cathrine 15
  Eliza Jane 226
  Letty 26
  Mary 177
DAULS, Miss Bar-- 16
DAUNY, Nancy 137
DAVID, Frances 54
DAVIS, Anna L. 82
  Cassa 149
  Eliza Ann 153
  Elizabeth 51, 85
  Hariet E. 192
  Henry M. 147
  John 15, 90, 103, 134,
    135, 153, 157

DAVIS (cont.)
Jucilla 208
Lizzie 69
Miss M. S. T. 51
Malinda 153
Martha R. 123
Mary 92
Mary C. 210
Pemela 7
Rachel 50
Rebecah 15
Rebecca 83, 214
Rebeccah 35
Rebecky 61
Safira 208
Sallie 181
Sarah 12
W. A. 103
DAWNY, Susan M. 116
DAY, Mary J. 155
DEADERICK, Eliza Ann 216
Penelope Smith 216
William H. 216
DEADRICK, Margaretta
Amanda 19
Mary M. 233
DEAN, Charlotte Craven
218
Mary Ann 107
Polly Ann 42
DEARIN, Larinda 173
DEARMON, Easter 227
Eliza 196
DEARMOND, Sarah 16
DEATIN, Sarah O. 133
DEATON, Ellin H. 130
Malinda 164
DEAVERS, Reuben 18
DECKER, Dorcas Ann 157
DELDAY, Anna Caroline 157
DEMPSEY, Eliza 1
DENNIS, Delily E. 137
Jane 121
L. A. 121
Lizzie 65
Mary 53
Mary A. 225
Nancy 53
Mrs. Virginia 4
DENNISS, Rachel E. 37
DENTON, C. 10
Calvin 13, 14, 49, 70,
93, 99, 155, 175,
183, 186, 194, 204,
213, 230
Martha A. 43
Miss S. E. 201
DERRICK, Elizabeth M. 6
Iwanona 47
Mary 31
Mary E. 175
Sally C. 50
Sarah 31
Susan 17
Susan M. 65
DERTHEROW, Nancy 76
DESHAM, Margarette 50
DETHERAGE, Rebecca 106
DETHERO, Amanda C. 228
DETHERROW, Sarah Ann 131
DETHRO, Lorene 51
DETHROE, Mary Elizabeth
172
DEWITT, Sarah I. 13
DICKARD, Emily E. 116
DICKERSON, Mary C. 26
DICKEY, Nancy M. 225
DICKSON, Isabella 43
Polly Ann 185
DILLAN, Joseph A. 72
DILLBECK, Mary E. 167
DILLEAN, Rhue H. 126
DILLON, Emily 219

DILLON (cont.)
Sarah E. 106
DITMORE, Eliza 171
Mary 103
DIVINE, Jemima 186
DIXON, Earl 58
Eliza J. C. 175
Elizabeth 127
Elizabeth C. 199
F. A. 40, 42, 55, 145,
146, 189, 202, 207,
220
John J. 199
Maggie A. 186
Mary 112
Mary A. 106
Miram 142
Nancy L. 64
O. R. 136
Sarah E. 182
Susan S. 210
Miss T. S. M. 222
Willer M. 148
DOAN, Rachel A. 201
DOBBINS, Sarah 156
DOBBS, Eva 157
Jarusha 33
Manila 146
Polly Zenny 172
DOBKINS, Rebecca 18
Wm. 18
DOCKERY, Sarah 56
DODD, James M. 202
DODSON, Angeline 87
Miss E. E. 100
Elijah 191
Eliza Jane 38
Elizabeth 105, 160
Elizabeth Ann 179
Francis 203
H. M. 123
Henry M. 156
Jesse 47, 197
John 57
Katharine 154
L. 142
L. B. 202
Lou D. 174
Miss M. L. 15
Margaret P. 173
Martha 167
Mary Jane 175
Nancy W. 141
Rebecca K. 159
Rhoda 197
Salena 84
Sarah W. 41
Wm. 22, 58
DOGAN, W. H. H. 93
DOLAN, Jane 81
DOLEN, Margaret 24
DOOLEY, Nancy E. 171
DOPHERTY, Sarah M. 103
DORHERTY, Nancy 96
Serena 2
DORSEY, Dimmon 55
Martha 79
Nancy 73, 133
Sarah D. 46
DOSS, Charity Temple 13
Frances 219
Mary 30
DOTHERROE, Ataline 50
DOTSON, Jane 56
William 33, 35, 60,
70, 231
DOUGHERTY, Charlotte 74
Julian 159
Sarah 17
DOUGLAS, Julia A. 35
Sarah 175
DOUGLASS, E. C. 183
Elizabeth Jane 10

DOUGLASS (cont.)
Hiram 37
J. 99, 194
Jas. 18, 69, 88, 106,
120, 144, 198, 209,
213
John 9, 230
Mary 32, 43
Mrs. Susan 22
DOVER, Elizia 209
DRAKE, S. F. 76
Williametta M. 76
DUCKETT, Elizabeth 114
DUCKWORTH, Hopy 213
Martha J. 104
Mary 61
Waitslell 201
DUFF, Emma R. 7
Harriate 146
Mahala 213
Mary E. 149
DUGAN, A. L. 4, 14, 64,
96, 114, 172, 202,
213
Leantine 148
Margret N. 29
Mariah 78
Matildy Elizabeth 184
Robert 148
DUGGAN, Mary Ann 211
W. H. H. 113, 178
DUGGER, Mary E. 47
DUGIN, A. L. 100
DULY, Debara A. 66
DUNLAP, E. N. 39
DUNN, Joseph 149
Martha 24
Texas 158
DURHAM, Matilda 165
DUKE, Juliet 173
DY, Artimelia 185
DYE, Betsey 62
Judy 60
Margrt A. 90
DYER, Cealey Ann 77
Eliza 19
Eveline 192
Harriett E. 221
Nancy 199
Sarah Elizabeth 165
EADAN, Miss R. C. 230
EADEN, Martha J. 177
EADENS, Margaret Elizabeth
150
EAKIN, Elizabeth J. 35
EARLY, A. P. 105
EATEN, Matilda 91
EATON, Mrs. Jane 75
Luisa 135
Margaret Elizabeth 150
Martha J. 177
Mary C. 84
EDDINGTON, Eliza Jane 44
EDEN, Clarinda 1
EDENS, Jane 227
EDGEMON, Sarah 103
EDGMON, Margaret 142
EDINGTON, Miss A. C. 77
EDMISSONS, Samuel 120
EDMONSON, Eliza 52
J. 187
EDWARDS, Eliza 114
Mary E. 107
Nancy 137
ELBERT, Mary N. 36
ELDER, Mary W. 53
Nancy 205
Susan H. 150
Susannah H. 150
Wm. R. 39, 59, 140,
154, 161
ELDRIDGE, Mollie T. 16
Susan 108

ELIOT, J. J. 212
    Sarah Jane 168
ELIOTT, Elisabeth 141
ELKINS, Mary C. 30
ELLIOT, Elizabeth 36
ELLIOTT, Elizabeth A. 177
    J. J. 15, 20, 50, 54
    Jemima 225
    Letty 110
    M. K. 9
    Margaret E. 91
    Nancy 177, 182
    Nancy J. 165
ELLIS, Amanda B. 227
    Angeline 101
    Dicy 118
    Elizabeth Ann 227
    Manada 146
    Manerva 190
    Margaret 231
    Nancy Jane 70
    Samantha 47
    Sarah Jane 205
ELLISON, Barbay 66
    James 35
    Jane 112
ELLISTON, Susana 170
ELMORE, Josephine 143
ELSSLY, Catharine 163
EMERSON, Carel 64
    Caroline 216
    Nancy 104
EMERY, Caroline 41
    Elizabeth 121
EMLEY, Selia 208
EMMERROSON, Mary 124
EMMERSON, Delila 87
    Delily 111
    Miss M. E. 159
    Mrs. Sarah E. 177
EMORY, Harriet 42
ENSMINGER, Kate 98
    Mary 162
    Nancy M. 182
    Sarah E. 200
    Virginia A. 57
EPERSON, Kate 94
EPPERSON, J. W. 172
    Rebecca C. 57
ERECKSON, W. 179
    Wm. 65, 205
ERICKSON, Clarinda A. 157
ERIXON, Wm. 51
ERKERSON, Allamarinda 66
ERRICKSON, Harriet 37
    Miss P. 205
ERSKIN, Eliza 214
    Nancy 144
ERVIN, Keziah 177
    Mary M. 130
ERWIN, Arminda C. 21
    Catharine 65
    Joseph 28
    Malinda J. 10
    Mary Jane 83
ESMON, Margaret 198
ETTER, Mary Ann 75
EVANS, Elizabeth 62
    J. 114
    Lucinda 162
    Nancy J. 49
EVERTON, Ann 7
    Miss E. R. 203
    Hannah R. 26
EWING, Saml. A. 227
F---R, Sarah Ann 140
FAIN, Elizabeth I. 113
    Jane 43
    John 113
FAIR, Edny 146
    Elizabeth 38
FAIRBANKS, Mary 93
    Nancy 60

FAIRLL, Elizabeth J. 177
FALKNER, Nancy 118
    Reuben 124
FALVEY, John L. O. 233
FANE, Adaline 103
FARMER, John 142
    Margaret A. 81
    Mary 40
    Sarah 3
FARRIS, Isbell 196
FAULKNER, Ann 60
    Nancy 117
    Reuben 106, 121, 124,
        126, 230
FEILDS, Rebeckah Jane 149
FENNY, Mary 68
FERGURSON, Miss S. H. 68
FERGUSON, Ede 161
    Sarah J. 143
FERREL, Rebecca C. 229
FERRELL, Martha C. 127
    Rachel L. 62
FERRYMAN, Miss W. R. 73
FETZL, L. M. 155
FIELD, Nancy 198
FIELDS, Elizabeth 57
    Lucinda 56
    Malinda 139
    Mary 13, 148
FILIO, Mary J. 37
FILLPOTS, Elizabeth Ja
    50
FILPOT, Nancy J. 194
FILYAW, Becksey 225
FIRESTONE, David 60
    Elizabeth 60
    Mary 77
    Mary A. 12
    Permelia 163
    Prussia 141
    Sarah A. 169
    Tilathea Q. 18
FISHER, Adareus 81
    Ann T. 136
    H. C. 197
    Margaret 45
    Martha A. 134
    Mrs. Rebecca 230
    Reuhamy 169
    Virginia 85
FITCH, Mary E. 192
    Rody A. 69
    Theby 192
FITE, Ester E. 65
FITZGERALD, A. 153
    Esther S. 119
    James T. 172
    Levi 4, 66, 103, 151,
        187
    Mary C. 151
    Sarah E. 103
FLATFORD, Elizabeth 8
FLEMING, Elizabeth 72
    Mrs. Jane 193
    Mrs. Mary 171
    Texas A. 46
FLINN, Eliza 129
FLOYD, Lucy Ann 138
FORD, Martha J. 89
    Mary Ann 223
    Micajah M. 144
    Rinda 89
    Thos. J. 153
FORE, Augustine P. 100
    J. W. L. 144
    Sarah 110
FOREST, James 37, 105
    Sarah C. 127
    W. F. 49, 57, 162, 176
    Wm. F. 38, 124, 156,
        210
FORESTER, Miss M. R. 34
    Melvina 193

FORGEY, Mrs. Mary 129
    Nancy E. 152
FORGIE, Sarah Jane 90
FORGUSON, Ann 38
FORGY, Sarah 49
FORISTER, Lydiann 152
FORREST, James 9, 176,
        233
    Rachel C. 57
    W. F. 31, 51, 55, 64,
        69, 71, 115, 129,
        139, 141, 158, 159,
        199, 213, 216
    Wm. 25
    Wm. F. 22, 57, 174,
        224, 227
FOSTER, Caroline 39
    Elizabeth 39, 204
    Elizabeth Ann 28
    Elja Elizabeth 86
    John 58
    Lucinda 170
    Malinda 63
    Manervy Jane 140
    Mary Ann 28
    Mary R. 153
    Sarah 39
    Sarah J. 28
    Simion M. 77
OSTERP, Margret 82
FOWLER, Mary 61
    Rebecah 231
FOX, Maranda 225
    Mary 187, 214
    Nancy 186
    Rebecca 78
FRADY, Margaret E. 7
FRANCE, Mrs. Martha Shook
        16
FRANK, Matilda N. 195
    Sarah J. 132
FRANKLIN, Catherine 43
    Leucy Ann 95
    Lucy F. 218
    Martha Jane 10
    Martha S. 203
FRAZIER, B. 53
    Nancy 166
    Permelia 164
    Rebeckah 105
    Robert 21, 45, 73, 95,
        180, 224
FREEMAN, Miss S. A. 201
    Mrs. Sureptha 181
FRENCH, J. S. M. 14
FRISBY, Julia A. 86
FRIZZELL, Martha J. 28
FRY, Anna Jane 131
    Eliza Ann 57
    Miss M. E. 203
    Marthey E. 97
    Nancy 173
    Sarah Q. 97
    Sarah K. 234
    Sidney Jane 108
FRYAR, J. R. 73, 149
FRYOR, J. R. 194
FULKS, Nancy 94
FUQUA, Louisa A. 81
FUQUEWAY, Harritt 231
FURGERSON, Martha E. 38
FYFFE, Elizabeth Jane 197
FYKE, Ann 149
GADLEY, C. 49
GAGE, Nancy 58
    Sarah 188
GALION, Elizabeth 162
GALLAHAR, G. M. 202
GALLAHER, Mary Ann 201
GALLANT, Mary 188
    Nancy 229
    Thomas 73
GALLION, Elizabeth 162

241

GAMBLE, Louisa Minerva
52
P. L. 27
Rebecca A. 185
Miss S. M. 75
GAMMON, Rebecca W. 233
GANDD, Miss M. A. 211
GARLAND, Eliza 184
Elisabeth C. 119
GARRELT, Mary M. 36
GARRISON, I. S. 79, 122,
131, 135, 198
Isah 72
Jane 72
Mary 221
GASTON, Elizabeth 34
J. C. 44, 70, 176
John 5, 14, 191, 227,
229
John C. 26
Thomas 63
GAUT, Manerva 208
GAULT, Mary 174
William 174
GEDDENS, R. A. 84
GEE, Elisha 190
John 47
Martha 230
GENTERY, Z. F. 188
GENTRY, Nancy 132
GEORGE, Mary E. 29
Nancy 22
P. H. 150
William C. C. C. 214
GERALD, A. F. 79
GERALDS, Hiram 74
GERRELD, A. F. 74
GETTYS, Ann M. 68
Eliza J. 19
Margaret D. 19
W. 9, 194
GIBBORY, Amabelle 234
GIBBS, Emily 26
Martha J. 66
GIBONEY, Jane 69
GIBSON, Miss A. A. 92
Mrs. Barbara B. 47
E. P. 76
Elias 230
Elizabeth 54
J. M. 15, 231
J. W. 82, 87, 91, 148
Mrs. Jane 120
Joseph 26, 115, 227
Joseph W. 37
M. R. 75, 84
Malinda C. 70
Margret 207
Matthew R. 168
Mary Ann 195
Nancy C. 227
Naomy 192
Sallie A. 14
GIDDENS, R. A. 74, 220
GIDENS, R. A. 175
GIGG, Manday J. 110
GILBERT, Edmon 207
Deliia 30
Eliza C. 9
J. W. 32, 35, 48, 125,
166, 168
John W. 26
Magga 196
Mary Ann 160
GILBREATH, Sarah J. 44
GILES, John 213
Lurany S. 213
GILLENWATER, E. E. 28
GILLEY, Catharine 34
GILLY, Elisa A. 89
Manervy E. 226
GIPSON, Miss M. J. 108
GIVENS, Caroline 88

GIVENS (cont.)
Elisa 71
Martha A. 13
Sarah 88
GIVINS, Mahaly 151
GLACE, Mary 228
GLAIZE, Elizabeth 154
GLASS, Caroline 208
Elizabeth 118
GLAZE, Emeline 48
Lucinda 144
Permelia 8
GODARD, Harret C. 5
Jane M. 137
Mary Ann 205
GODBEY, C. 9
GODDARD, Elizabeth C. 120
GODSEY, D. L. 218
GOFORTH, Mary D. 219
N. B. 32, 39, 43, 45,
57, 63, 94, 155
GOINS, Elizabeth A. 171
Nancy Ann 202
GOLD, Rebecca 187
COLLAHON, C. P. 21
Elizabeth 162
GOLLORAH, Caroline 88
GOLTONNEY, Sely 1
GONCE, Abraham 137
GOODE, Eliza 199
Lucinda 182
Meldridge 3
GOODWIN, Barbary 192
Catharine 174
GOODWINE, Louisa 214
GOOLEY, Elizabeth 53
GORDEN, Nancy 33
GORE, Ann R. 192
Nancy 121
GORLLEY, Crocket 120
GOSS, Elizabeth 70
Mary 149
GOSSETT, Mrs. Malinda 163
GOULDY, William S. 185
GRADEY, Mrs. Margret 144
GRADY, Eliza Ann 42
Mary 23
GRAHAM, Mrs. Ann 50
GRANT, Mrs. Lodicy 39
GRAVES, Elizabeth 196
Lucinda 196
Mrs. Margaret A. 49
Nancy 82, 133
Sarah 64
Sarah E. 14
Vilana 189
GRAY, Elizabeth 230
Mrs. Milly 124
GRAYSON, Mary C. 221
Sarah Ann 160
GREEN, B. F. 141
Deielea 118
Miss E. J. 195
Easter 46
Miss Elmy 118
J. L. 193
Jane 178
Jno. P. 107, 114
Leticia 137
Mrs. Lorenah 111
Miss M. T. 207
Malinda 53, 109
Mandy 146
Margaret T. 107
Martha 8
Martha A. 106
Parthena 49
GREENE, Catharine L. 90
Mary O. 162
GREENS, John P. 66
GREENWAY, Harriet E. 141
Sarahann 139
GREENWOOD, Lucy 141

GREGG, Anna 13
Mabel 170
Sarah 90
GREGORY, Mrs. Elenor 26
Elizabeth 183
Malissa A. 130
Martha 88
Mary 36
Matilda 212
Mivinda 183
Robert 2, 9, 12, 16,
23, 25, 28, 37, 41,
47, 55, 58, 64, 68,
73, 76, 91, 116,
119, 123, 132, 139,
145, 148, 149, 155,
161, 174, 175, 176,
178, 190, 191, 195,
204, 205, 221, 222,
227, 229, 233
Sarah 66
Sue V. 93
T. 165
Tapley 2, 53, 60, 80,
103, 178, 190, 194,
206, 210, 214, 226,
230, 232, 233
Taply 14
GREGRY, James 82
GENNELL, Margaret 90
GRESHAM, James 176
GRIFFIN, Mahale 206
Salenia C. 76
GRIFFITH, Clarissa 52
John N. 140
Margaret 13
GRIFFITTS, Francis 60
Margaret 83
GRIGERON, James 15
GRIGG, Mrs. E. A. 206
Eunice 169
GRIGSBY, Elizabeth 41
Margaret Ann 57
Mary 24
Rebecca 153
GRILLS, Mary E. 115
GRISHAM, Elizabeth 113,
131
Ellen 164
Jane 232
Jesse 83
Mary Jane 28
Polly 67
Ruthey Ann 36
Thos. 26
William T. 17
GROGAN, Diletha 185
Fany 66
Maryann 222
GRUBB, Elizabeth Ann 49
Margaret 74
Mary 73
GRUBBS, Mary E. 6
GUFFEY, Clarissa E. 126
Cloe 179
Elizabeth C. 28
Francis J. 46
Sarah A. 196
GUFFY, Susan 180
GUINN, Nancy 29
GULLENWATER, E. E. 70
GULLIAGE, Sarah Ann 24
GULLIDGE, Mary E. 70
GUNTER, Susanah 2
GUTHERY, Catharine 173
Judith A. 184
GUTHREY, Elizabeth 173
Thomas 201
GUTHRIE, Elizabeth 113
GUTHRY, Martha 200
HACKLER, Catharine 55
Katharine 101
Martha M. 53

HACKLER (cont.)
  Sarah 72
  Susanah 46
HADEN, Huldah H. 187
HAFLEY, W. C. 93
HAGGARD, Mrs. Isophene 64
  Jane 34
  Mrs. Josephine 64
  N. H. 162, 163, 164
HAIL, Louisa Jane 227
  Martha 228
  Serenah 209
HALE, Miss C. P. 89
  Elizabeth 228
  M. J. 187
  Martha L. 51
  Miss S. H. 200
  Thos. 128
HALL, Catharine 149
HAM--, May E. 144
HAMBRICK, Celia 61
  Emaline 122
  Lucinda 165
  Narcissa 102
  Thena 112
HAMBRIGHT, Benj. 195
  Denize 187
  Malissa 63
  Nancy 172
  Sarah M. 12
HAMELTON, Amanda 23
HAMELTREE, Nancy Jane 191
HAMES, Delily 89
HAMILTON, Miss C. L. 226
  J. W. 24
  Jas. 143
  Joseph 8, 32, 87, 143
  Julia A. 109
  Margaret 227
  Martha J. 167
  Mary 25
  Mary E. E. 115
  Miss N. C. 149
  Penelope Smith 216
  Susan C. 226
HAMMER, Elizabeth 44
HAMMONDS, Mary E. 49
HAMMONTREE, Mary 205
HAMOND, R. T. 74
HAMPTON, Elizabeth 207
  Lewis 177
  Louisa 197
  Lucinda 56
  Nancy 40
  Nearva 195
  Rebecca 145
  Sarah Ann 119
HAMRICK, Olivia 140
HANCE, Margarit A. 203
HANDLEY, Mary P. 70
HANEY, Anna 16
  C. 105
  Eliza Jane 143
  H. 151
  I. B. 165
  J. B. 234
  Manervia 159
  Mary B. 174
  Matilda 173
  Nancy 88, 165
HANKS, Catherine 42
  Elizabeth 223
  Elizabeth W. 129
  Johnathan 79
  Mrs. M. A. W. 62
  Martha 205
HANNAH, Jane 79
HARDEN, Louisa 64
  Talitha 79
HARDIN, Martha 115
  Mary J. 37
  Peggy 54
HARDY, Anna 15

HARDY (cont.)
  Martha 1
  Mary 179
  Susan 57
HAREN, A. 1
HARKRIDER, Mary 60
  Sarrah 203
HARLESS, Elza J. 24
  Lurena E. 102
  Margaret C. 226
  Minerva C. 193
HARMON, Elinera 204
  Elizabeth 20
  Marthia L. 151
  Mary 1
  Orinda 79
  Rebecca 231
HARMOND, Sarah 9
HARRELL, John 143
HARRIS, A. N. 6
  Elizabeth 223
  Frances E. 23
  Lucinda 70, 185
  Minerva 33
  Nancy Ann 2
  Zeporah 71
HARRISON, N. 57
  Nathan 154
HARROD, Lucy 162
HART, Elizabeth 147
HARTE, Polly 164
HARTLY, Marinda 156
HATFORD, Elizabeth 8
HAUN, A. 42, 180
  S. M. 68, 135, 222, 231
HAWK, M. A. 18
  M. C. 1, 21, 59, 62, 78, 80, 117, 135, 181, 183, 192, 196, 199, 203, 210, 213, 227, 231
  Madison C. 191
  Nancy 166
  Wm. C. 17
HAWKINS, Jane 45
  Mary 25, 26
HAWKS, Mary E. 175
HAWN, A. 39, 101
HAYES, Adaline 6
  L. L. 168
  Martha 97
  Sarah 91
  W. T. 181
HAYMES, Elizabeth J. 113
  Nancy 46
  Sarah 135
  W. W. 55, 183, 229
  William W. 63, 81
HAYNES, Emily 142
  Martha 153
HAYNIE, Ann A. 10
  Susan 116
HAYS, Elisha 70, 92, 219
  John 144
  Marjara 212
  Martha 32
  Mary Ann 166
HAZE, Mary 149
HEARALD, Martha A. 92
HEAD, Martha Ann 33
HEARD, Glaphrey 42
  Mrs. Nancy 111
HEATH, John S. 91
HECK, Elizabeth 198
  Rachel A. C. 79
HEDRICK, Lidy 83
HEINGER, John 231
HELEMS, Nancy E. 219
HELLUMS, Anna 166
  Rebecca 55
HELMS, John J. 70
  Martha 189

HELMS (cont.)
  Martha Jane 32
  Nancy Ann 224
  Rebecca 182
  Zelpha 201
HELUMS, Sarah J. 170
HELVY, Ann 178
HEMPHILL, John 93
  Margarett 10
HENDERSON, Miss E. J. 233
  Elizabeth 99
  Emaline 119
  James 2
  Jas. M. 166
  Margret 123
  Martha 67
  Mary 6, 49
  Robert 63
  Mrs. S. B. 57
HENDLY, Edmond R. 10
HENDRIX, G. W. 69
  Geo. W. 212
HENEGAR, William T. 108
HENINGAR, William T. 108
HENLEY, Frances 178
  J. D. 141
  James D. 61
HENLY, J. D. 144, 176
HENRY, Margaret 80
  Sally 207
  Vinsant 180
HENSON, Elizabeth 139
HERALD, Elizabeth 21
  Francis 203
  Patsey 140
HERAN, Mary J. 230
HERON, Will B. 121
HERRELL, Lydia 139
HERRING, Catharine 189
HERROLD, Miss J. E. 207
HESTER, Nancy A. C. 125
HETTERBRAND, Eliza 231
HIBBERTS, Martha M. 20
HICKEL, Mrs. Parthena 153
HICKEY, Nancy Emelina 7
  R. M. 81, 102, 214
  Rufus M. 99
  W. E. 11
HICKMAN, Elizabeth Jane 140
  P. M. M. 140
HICKOX, Lemira Jane 112
HICKS, Elizabeth 143
  G. M. 207
  Hannah 138
  Matilda 22
  Martha 222
  Ursley 120
HIGDON, Amanda 46
  May 84
  Nancy 154
HIGGENS, J. A. 58
HIGGINS, Mary A. 120
HILL, Absolom 12
  Elizabeth 100, 217
  Lucinda 67
  Nancy 216
  Miss S. L. 26
  Sarah J. 166
  Stephen 15, 23, 44, 45, 62, 85, 89, 109, 110, 142, 151, 192, 194
HILLIARD, Jane 166
HINKLE, Catharine 51
HISS, Margaret C. 106
HIX, Elizabeth 4
  Margaret 98
  Mary C. 195
  Merody 83
HOBACK, Addie C. 33
  Dorthula 7
  Eliza L. 148

HOBACK (cont.)
  Susan 40
HOGAN, Sarah 10
  Wm. 10, 181
HOGE, Julia 70
HOLLAND, G. S. 202
  Hugh P. 153
  Louisa C. 234
  Sarah 155
  W. H. 131
HOLLIS, Miss A. J. 17
HOLMES, Margaret 212
HOLSE, Nancy A. 98
HOLT, Irby 113
  Serena J. 114
HOOD, Margaret A. 80
HOOZIER, Amanda 126
HOPE, Margaret 109
  Nancy M. 167
HOPKINGS, Kizzie 111
HORD, Mrs. Elizabeth 17
HORN, Rev. George 17
HORNSBY, James H. 7, 197
HORTON, Anna 28
  Elizabeth A. 178
  Mahala 89
  Mary 37
  W. G. 16, 36, 179, 209,
    224
  Wm. G. 17, 170
HOUER, F. M. 37
HOUNSELL, Susan 214
HOUNSHELL, Nancy Ann 73
HOUSELY, Ann 167
HOUSLEY, Mary 3
HOUSLY, Tabitha 167
HOUSTON, Mrs. Marye Ann 202
HOWARD, Cale 74
  Francis J. 82
  Mary 90, 190
  Mary E. 105
  Miss N. P. 229
  Nancy 213
  Nancy L. 142
  Susannah 18
  William H. 16
HOWEL, Mary A. 225
HOWELL, James M. 3
  Nancy A. E. 56
HOYL, C. R. 3, 6, 20, 30,
    37, 38, 41, 43, 44,
    47, 49, 59, 60, 83,
    84, 94, 96, 110,
    112, 114, 125, 160,
    162, 163, 170, 181,
    184, 185, 190, 196,
    197, 210, 227
  John 86, 95, 107, 139,
    151, 208
  Mary C. 174
  Mary J. 39
  Narcissa 143
  Susan C. 99
  Susan E. 109
  T. 159
  T. L. 5, 8, 41, 49, 67,
    77, 81, 90, 105,
    121, 125, 143, 155,
    159
  T. L. 187
  Thomas 13
  Thos. L. 142. 154
HOYLE, C. R. 21, 23
  Thos. L. 22
HOYT, Sarah Cornelia 216
HUCKABY, Anna 70
HUDDLESTON, Sarah L. 225
HUDELSTEN, Martha 192
HUDGENS, Mrs. Elizabeth 7
HUDGINS, Sarah 24
HUDSON, B. F. 201
HUFFAKER, J. N. S. 69
HUFFER, Cyntha A. 79

HUGES, Mrs. F. J. 176
HUGGINS, Eliza J. 200
HUGHES, Amy A. 152
  Miss C. M. 148
  Mrs. F. J. 176
  Lucy 117
  Malissa Jane 184
  Martha C. 117
  Susan A. D. 3
HUGHS, Elzira 163
  Lucy 117
  Margaret 222
  Mrs. Sarah J. 136
HUMPHREYS, Mira 185
HUMPHREY, Abigail 40
  Crata 40
HUMPHREYS, Sarah 5
HUNK, Susan 218
HUNT, Catharine 158
  Elizabeth 108, 213
  Judith 113
  Mary Ann 99
  Phebe 212
  Rebecca 135
  Sarah 136
HUNTER, Mary J. S. 212
HURST, Elijah 29, 40, 81,
    182
  Jemima 40
  Mary T. 75
  Sarah Ann 29
HURT, Betsy Jane 33
HUSE, Katharine 152
HUST, L. R. 163, 225
HUTSELL, Miss C. V. 78
  Ellen 142
  Erthula 183
  G. M. 4, 41, 68, 96,
    100, 128, 146, 227,
    230
  George M. 107, 145
  Miss M. E. 75
  Miss N. E. 125
  Sam 75
HUTSON, Sarah Jane 162
HYDEN, J. A. 36, 202, 208
  J. Albert 54, 72, 87,
    95
  Miss M. E. 28
HYDERS, J. A. 140
HYMAN, Henry 181
ICKES, Zoe L. 53
IGOU, Mrs. Eliza J. 117
INGRAM, H. 29, 34
  Hiram 11, 31, 32, 75,
    144, 161, 170, 175
  Mrs. Sarah A. 135
IRELAND, Roady 119
IRVIN, Amanda 88
  Martha 86
IRWIN, Lucina 220
ISBELL, Benjamin 40, 91,
    127
  Francis D. 100
  Miss J. M. 135
  Miss M. A. 135
  Mary L. 88
  Nancy M. 214
  Sarah Elizabeth 73
ISHAM, Mahala 37
  Rody 84
IVANS, Eliza Jane 183
  J. 217
  Martha 54
IVINS, Emma C. 86
  Mollie 51
IVY, Mary 13
JACK, Andrew 103
  Caroline 66
  Emeline 19
  J. 2, 15, 20, 26, 27,
    33, 37, 59, 79, 90,
    110, 126, 138, 139,

JACK (cont.)
  J. (cont.) 147, 152,
    165, 172, 203, 209,
    211
  John 19, 103, 140, 204
  Louisy 206
  Mahaly 74
  Martha 41
JACKSON, Clarrissa 126
  John 80
  Martha 78
  Marthy C. 28
  Mary 111
  Pegyann 58
  Sarah A. 48
  Sarah C. 135
  Susan 146
JAMERSON, David F. 39,
    140, 198
JAMES, Malinda 3
JAMESON, David F. 46, 148
  Mary J. 69
JAMISON, David F. 30, 63,
    70, 79, 143, 161,
    167, 190
  Elizabeth 25
  Evaline T. 108
JANWARY, J. 219
JANEWAY, J. 14, 85, 128,
    133, 207, 215, 218
  Jos. 6, 211, 219
  Looney 104
JANWAY, J. 161
JARNAGAN, Bynum 44
  Sarah L. 61
JARNAGIN, Amanda M. 199
  Bynum 31, 45
  Martha 43
  Mary E. 205
  Milton P. 73
JARNIGAN, Bynum 45
  Sarah J. 196
JEMISON, Elizabeth 25
  Elza 168
  Rebecca E. 129
JENKINS, Mrs. Elizia 49
  J. 22, 51, 76, 77,
    131, 134, 153, 197,
    224
  John 1, 10, 13, 16,
    17, 18, 43, 45, 46,
    51, 54, 75, 89, 95,
    99, 120, 153, 156,
    163, 166, 169, 175,
    181, 193, 195, 197,
    201, 206, 219, 224,
    231
  Mary Jane 159
JIMERSON, Nancy B. 68
JINKINS, John 40
JOHENS, Miss F. C. 28
JOHN, A. 25, 67, 68, 104,
    135, 139, 178, 183,
    186, 220, 230
  Andrew 188
  B. A. 46
  Lydia 201
  Mary 87
  Rebecca R. N. 201
  Robert 182
JOHNS, Lydia H. 176
  Parthena J. 65
JOHNSON, Mrs. Eliza J. 6
  Elizabeth 96
  Hattie 98
  Huson 76
  Hutson 76
  Jane 96
  Lecy 168
  Louisa I. 38
  Lucinda J. 28
  Mrs. Malvina 160
  Mrs. Mary Ann 226

JOHNSON (cont.)
  Mrs. Mary I. 231
  Maryann J. F. 168
  Mollie J. 104
  Nancy 20
  Miss P. C. 182
  Perlina 137
  Rebecca 59
  Sarah 180
  Susan 96, 157
  Tennessee 107
  Uriel 120, 157, 206
  Wm. B. 19
JOHNSTON, Mrs. Elizabeth
  A. 133
  Elizabeth J. 154
  Mary S. 189
  Uriah 46, 72, 180,
    213
  Urial 229
  Uriel 104
JOINES, Elizabeth 204
JONES, Ann 129
  Delila E. 167
  Mrs. Eveline 206
  Leathy 206
  Martha 211, 218
  Martha C. 112
  Mary Ann 34, 73
  Mary E. 100, 151
  Mary J. 151
  Miss N. E. 128
  Nancy 4
  Reece 123, 171, 228
  Sarah E. 155
  Susan M. 76
  William 108, 194, 226
  William R. 23
JORDAN, Mary Jane 83
  S. H. 27, 191
  Saml. H. 43
JORDON, Marenda L. 181
  Samuel H. 185
JOURDIN, Sarah S. 204
JOYCE, Margrate L. 12
JUREL, Eliza 97
KAHILL, Margaret C. 56
KANTZ, Margaret E. 175
  Mary A. 44
KEATON, Tempy 177
KEELING, Margaret 109
KEETEN, Viney 41
KEETON, Caroline 157
  Emeline 157
  Matilda 108
  Sally 180
KEGGAL, Celie 210
KEIKER, Martha A. 155
KEITH, Elizabeth D. 11
  Louisa J. 183
  Mrs. Martha C. 149
  Sarah M. 17
  Wm. F. 11
KELLEY, Angeline 57
  Elihu 15, 20, 26, 29,
    36, 41, 50, 55, 60,
    74, 111, 168, 170,
    177, 188, 206
  J. M. 36, 160
KELLY, Daniel 1
  Elihu 2, 3, 25, 63,
    107, 111, 140, 141,
    210, 211, 225, 226
  Eliza 15
  Emelin 63
  J. M. 9, 91
  William 111
KEMP, Roselvirn 168
KENNEDY, Elizabeth J. 158
  Louisa J. 112
  Nancy M. 177
KEY, John 17, 117, 200
KIBLE, Nancy 166

KIKINS, John G. 202
KILE, Mary 121
KILLINGSWORTH, Elizabeth
  A. 113
  Nancy 60
KIMBROUGH, A. E. 12
  J. B. 41, 54, 70, 122,
    154
  John 194
  Sallie L. 94
  Sarah J. 204
  Susan C. 3
KINCHELO, Ferebe Ann 113
  Louisa 42
  Phereby A. 113
  Polly 150
KINCHELOW, Julia A. 117
  Mahala 217
KINCHLOW, Gemima 84
KINDER, Mary Ann 105
  Nancy 17
  Peter 17
KING, E. W. 200
  Elizabeth 195
  Elizabeth A. 35
  Jas. M. 134
  John 216
  Martha 108
  Mary 194
  Mary C. 196
  Nellie I. 217
KINMAN, Wesley 176
KINSER, A. 69, 136, 157
  Caroline 180
  Elizabeth 42
  J. A. 79
KINSHELO, Nancy 76
KINSOR, Louisa 25
KINZALOW, Elmira 204
KIPPS, Mary 89
KIRBY, H. M. 140
KIRD, Eliza 156
KIRKEY, A. J. 126
KIRKPATRICK, Amelia 158
  Caroline 69
  Margaret Emaline 127
  Mary A. 226
KIRKSEY, A. J. 11, 47, 94,
    118, 125, 185, 193
  E. F. 170
  G. W. 31, 56, 90,
    125, 161, 204, 221
  George W. 187, 198
  J. J. 178
  Parthaney 230
KITCHEN, Rebecca Ann 106
  Susan 224
KIZER, Emeline 110
KNIGHT, Mary A. 211
KNOX, Elizabeth 101
  Lidia Lucindy 50
  Pheby E. 195
  Susanah 52
LACY, Ester 142
  Rebeckah 138
LAFFERTY, Mary A. E. 20
LAFFORTY, Eliza 117
LAMAR, Hannah 196
  Mary 226
  Sarah L. 90
LAMARE, Rachel 90
LAMBERT, Addie 204
  Cathrin 180
  J. M. 19
LANB, Mary 146
LAND, Eliza J. 27
  Elizabeth A. 45
  Nancy Jane 19
LANDERS, Luke 119
  M. A. F. 18
  Martha E. 110
  Sarah E. 188
LANDS, Ruth 158

LANE, Elizabeth 32
  Fanney S. 18
  Mandy 200
  Russell 78, 86, 96,
    106, 107, 109, 131,
    167, 190, 192, 199,
    201
  Sallie E. 53
  Sarahann 190
  Sidney Ann 182
LARGE, Nancy Jane 132
LARGENT, Susan 211
  Susanah 166
LARGIN, Lucinda 60
LARREW, Keziah 188
LARRIMORE, Emaline 82
LASATER, Sarah E. 32
  William 133
LASETER, Mary 41
  Sarah Jane 203
LASITER, Nancy A. 135
LASSITER, Louiza J. 226
LATHAN, Miss C. A. 161
LATTIMORE, Caroline 41
  Orlenia 113
  Rachel 169
  Susan C. 143
LAUFTUS, Mary Ann 87
LAUGHMILLER, Hannah E. 110
LAWSON, Abner 65
  Caldena 194
  Carneth 77
  Charlotte 182
  Elizabeth 226
  Jane 33
  Letty 46
  Louisa 31
  Louvicy 202
  Lucinda 191, 229
  Martha 147, 213
  Mary Ann 100
  Matilda 63
  Polly A. 141
  Sarah 72, 138
  Sarah M. 165
  Savanah 198
  Scyntha 6
LAYS, Elizabeth 85
LEA, Ann Elizabeth 8
  Luke 8
LEAMAR, Mahaly 200
LEAMON, Sarah 124
LEDBETTER, Mary C. 89
LEDFORD, Margaret 228
LEE, Elizabeth 191, 174
  J. B. 94
  Marthia 72
  Mary E. 9
  P. N. 95, 98
  Susan 119
  W. C. 182
  Wm. C. 78, 96, 114,
    131, 154, 204
  William G. 216
  Miss Z. L. 43
  Zilpha 38
LEED, Edward 128
LEMARE, Mahaly 200
LEMMON, Eliza Jane 197
LEMMONS, Lieu Anna 51
  Nancy 28
  Miss P. M. 49
LEMONS, Mary Jane 88
LETNER, Margaret J. 68
  Mary C. 230
LEWIS, Eliza 81
  Emely 96
  Mrs. Giminey 150
  Mary 180
  Mary A. 8
  Patience 32
  Sarah 80
  Scyntha 24

LEWIS (cont.)
Mrs. Susannah 148
LIDE, Jennette V. 44
Lizzie 122
O. H. 196
Miss S. G. 140
LIGHT, Mary 167
LILE, Elisabeth 186
Martha Jane 39
LILES, Jemima 131
Martha 172
LILINS, Martha A. 202
LILLARD, Cinthia Ann 82
J. W. 105
Mary L. 118
LINER, E. C. 141
J. W. 145
Jane 150
Nancy E. 124
O. M. 13, 24, 39, 40,
70, 93, 124, 152,
170, 174, 183, 201,
207, 231
Phebe J. 200
LINOR, Clarrinda 33
LIPSCOMB, Caroline L. 199
Margaret T. 149
Spotswood 199
LITTLE, Polly 165
LOCK, Martha D. 57
LOCKE, Jesse 138
LOCKMILLER, John 178
LOGAN, Eglinetin 198
Elizabeth 120
Huldy 22
Marthy 161
Mrs. Mary Ann 28
Telitha 125
LONG, C. 8, 12, 22, 35,
37, 73, 98, 112,
115, 162, 168, 193,
224
Carroll 105, 162
Casander 59
Elizabeth 124, 152
Elizabeth H. 125
Jane 86
John 35
Lidia 64
Lourena 66
Lusey 37
Miss M. A. 94
Margaret 221
Martha 130
Mary 97, 134
Nancy 79
Nancy H. 110
P. M. 4, 34, 47, 76,
98, 104, 120, 133,
163, 172, 187, 202,
220, 221, 227
Ruth 79
Thomas 124
W. R. 18
Wm. R. 4, 172, 215
William T. 123
LONLEY, James 152
LOUDERMILK, Malinda 113
LOUGHMILLER, Angeline 87
Darcus E. 5
Elizabeth A. 186
Mary Jane 185
LOVE, Elizabeth 109
Elizabeth J. 8
M. 173
Miss M. J. 85
Major John 111
Mary 100
Mary Adaline 111
Mary E. 192
Miss S. C. 102
Samuel 100
T. B. 4, 18, 70, 90,

LOVE (cont.)
T. B. (cont.) 96, 164,
165, 169, 197, 209,
213, 214
LOWER, Caroline 33
Elizabeth 152
George W. 139
Zany 138
LOWERS, Katherine 125
LOWERY, Miss A. E. 137
Harriet M. 43
Mary L. 216
Matta 221
Virginia M. 163
LOWREY, John D. 127
LOWRY, Eliza J. 66
Francis E. 68
J. C. 104
Jane H. 200
Marry 23
Mary Jane 126
Nancy J. 53
Nancy L. 165
Purmilia 85
Susan R. 233
T. J. 126
Thomas J. 27
William 174
William, Jr. 127
LOYD, Jane 10
Mary 225
LUMPKIN, Col. -- 127
LUSK, Elizabeth M. 120
F. M. 134
Martha 176
LUTRELL, Matilda 233
LUTTRELL, C. A. 125
Matilda 108
LYLE, Catharine C. 121
Clarrissa Jane 166
J. D. 48, 72
LYONS, John 216
Jona. 14
Jonathan 62
MABS, Martha E. 218
MADDEN, Jane 225
Nancy E. 230
MADDIN, Elizabeth 178
MADDUX, Margaret 85
MADISON, Martha 35
MADOX, Rachel 62
MADUX, Caroline 29
MAGEER, Myran 210
MAGILL, Amanda E. 54
Miss H. M. 48
J. H. 50, 62, 89, 222,
223
MAHAN, Mary 153
MAHERY, Mrs. F. O. 116,
130
MAKAMY, Wm. 21
MALOAN, Sarah 88
MALONE, Hetty 36
Mrs. Jincy 206
Mary A. 182
Mary Ann 36
Sarah 31
MANCELL, Robert 132
MANDAGRIFF, Eliza 138
MANELL, W. B. 167
MANERY, Adeline 126
Maranda J. 31
Martha 172
MANIS, Miss A. J. 56
G. S. 148
Miss M. A. 131
Matilda J. 138
Sarah Ann 44
MANKER, J. J. 5
MANN, J. L. 60
J. W. 19, 28, 57
MANNERY, Mary 55
Rheda 19

MANREY, Sarah 114
MANSEL, Francis J. 234
Martha 65
Robert 226
MANSELL, Elizabeth 65,
109
Malinda 234
Robert 42, 48, 160,
234
Susan 234
Susanah 178
W. B. 121
MANUS, Easter 169
MAPLES, Dicy 107
Elizabeth J. 145
Hannah 64
Martha M. 37
Mary Ann 63
Sarah 139
W. H. 121
Wm. 37
MARCH, Lucindy 132
MARCUM, Mrs. Barbara 229
Eliza J. 154
Nancy L. 55
Sarah B. 228
MARLER, George 151
Lucina 220
Marion 217
MARLOW, Jane 220
MARNOE, Elizabeth Jane 131
MARR, Mary C. 116
MARRS, Lavisa 231
MARSHAL, Miss L. L. 40
MARSHALL, Rheny 98
MARSHMAN, A. 49, 109, 140,
157, 171, 187
MARTIN, Caroline 47
Catharine 206
Eliza G. 152
J. H. 29
Joanna 118
Joseph H. 217
Lucindy 217
Margaret Rebecca 4
Rachel 182
Sarah 229
MARTON, Mary Jane 123
Paralee 230
MASHBURN, Miss H. M. 170
MASINGALE, J. C. 210
MASSEY, Judith 25
MASSINGALE, H. L. 152
MASSINGELL, Celia 15
MASSONGALE, Eve 209
MASTIN, Sarah A. 169
Susan N. 109
MASTON, George W. 186
MATHEWS, A. A. 181, 189
Rachel 53
Sarah 2
MATHEYS, Joannah 127
MATHIES, A. A. 146
MATHIS, A. A. 183
A. J. 6, 147, 149,
162, 179
Archibald A. 131
MATLOCK, Elizabeth 120
Jane 188
Miss M. E. 122
Martha 163
Nancy Jane 188
Nancy P. 162
Sarah 76
Sarah Jane 22
MATTHEWS, Jane 139
Mary Ann 132
Miss N. T. 35
MATTOCKS, Jane 29
MAXFIELD, Eliza C. 202
MAXWELL, A. 16
Elizabeth 171
Harriet 219

246

MAXWELL (cont.)
Katharine J. 219
Mary 232
Nancy 76
MAYABB, Margaret 108
MAYFIELD, Miss E. F. 76
Elizabeth 96
Emma 184
Huldah 207
Lue 75
Mrs. Nancy C. 180
MAYNOR, Nancy Jane 220
Rachel 116
MAYO, G. W. 232
George W. 2, 10, 208
Martha K. 150
MAYRIOD, Sarah 4
MC ADOO, Judiah 29
Martha 115
R. A. 7, 10, 12, 14,
29, 37, 61, 67, 81,
85, 86, 98, 102,
114, 135, 146, 147,
149, 156, 157, 170,
173, 177, 183, 190,
191, 212, 220, 230,
232, 233
Richard A. 25, 51, 53,
89, 131, 210
MC AFFEY, Louiza E. 6
MC ALISTER, Rachel 223
MC ALPIN, R. 167
MC AMIS, Nancy J. 34
MC AMY, William 34, 76,
187, 211
MC ANNALLY, Rev. Charles
175
MC ATCHLEY, -- 81
MC BROOM, Marthy A. 87
MC CAFERY, Mary Jane 160
MC CALL, Catharine 125
Hariet 225
Judah 125
Margaret 129
Nancy 206
MC CALLAN, J. B. 62
MC CALLEY, Margaret 30
MC CALLIA, Rebecca
Elizabeth 183
MC CALLIE, Ellen M. 1
Mrs. Mary 56
MC CALLON, J. B. 211
MC CALLUM, Mary Ann 106
MC CALLY, Nancy 74
MC CAMMON, Elizabeth A. 51
Mary J. 104
MC CAMPBELL, Rev. John
113, 134
MC CAMY, Wm. 76, 207
MC CAN, Catharine 15
MC CANCE, Melissa 75
MC CANN, Marha E. 211
Martha E. 74
MC CARIEL, Eliza 37
MC CARROLL, Hetty 208
Mary 225
MC CARTNEY, John 89
Sarah A. E. 173
MC CARTY, Elizabeth Jane
43
Jane D. 130
Martha E. 199
Mary Isabilla 107
MC CASLIN, Miss S. M. 108
MC CLARY, Robert 218
Robert W. 4, 195, 218
MC CLATCHEY, M. M. 130
MC CLATCHY, A. P. 82
Elizabeth M. 127
MC CLELAN, Margaret 224
MC CLORG, John 170
MC CLUEN, Sarah 83
MC CLUNG, Chas. 11

MC COG, John 170
MC COLLUM, Catharine 69
Margaret 80
Sarah 13
MC CONNELL, Mary 106
MC COY, Daniel 210
J. N. 148
MC CRARY, Fanny 27
Marthey 114
Nancy 84
Miss S. A. 23
Serelsey 36
MC CRAY, Franky L. 27
MC CROSKEY, James S. 131
Sarah A. 183
MC CROSKY, Mrs. Isaphena
M. 85
MC CUISTION, Robert 131
MC CULHANY, Elizabeth 52
MC CULLY, Elizabeth 145
Jane 215
Mira 107
Nancy 146
Sarah C. 131
MC DONALD, Louvicy 106
Virginia 183
William 109
MC DONELL, Polly 182
MC DOUGALD, Katharine
MC DOWEL, Malinda 167
MC ELHANEY, Ellen M. 140
Mary 147
MC ELRATH, Mrs. E. L. 61
Elin F. 152
Susan C. 92
MC ELWEE, Ann 32
Jane 72
MC FALLS, Narcissa 163
MC FARLAND, Melissa 50
MC FARLING, Mary 69
MC GAUGHEY, Hattia A. 72
John 18, 44, 112, 194
Rebecca A. 155
J. 11, 12
John 6, 126, 139, 164,
166, 214
Margaret J. 98
MC GHEHAN, Adaline 217
MC GHEHEE, Malinda 200
MC GINTY, John 132
John M. 132
Martha Katharine 9
MC GONEGAL, Floyd 80, 137
MC GONIGAL, F. 41, 71,
206
MC GOSS, Lucindy 9
MC GREW, Mary E. 61
Serena 209
MC GRUE, Mary E. 61
MC GUGHEY, Hattia A. 72
MC GUIRE, Mrs. Letitia M.
133
Letty 146
Mary 47
Nancy 128
Sarah 52
MC INTURFF, Mary Ann 188
Serena Caroline 136
MC KAMY, Elizabeth J. 57
James 48, 67, 233
W. 133
William 9, 20, 21, 30,
51, 78, 123, 130,
145, 163, 167, 171,
174, 179, 189, 205,
211, 217, 223
MC KEE, Becky Ann 226
MC KEEAN, Rebecka 226
MC KEEHAN, Nancy 101
MC KEEHEN, Ameline 222
Elizabeth 101
Margaret M. 32

MC KEHAN, Lydia 159
Martha M. 14
MC KEHEN, Amy A. 101
MC KENZIE, Christian P. 11
Darcus 101
Elizabeth A. 21
Mary Jane 218
MC KICHIN, Matildey 153
MC KINEY, Rachel V. 25
MC KINNEY, Nancy E. 144
MC KINNY, Martin 8
MC KINSEY, Miss E. A. 197
Miss M. A. 123
Margaret 74
MC KNIGHT, Miss L. A. 111
Wm. 55
Wm. L. 39
William S. 189
MC LANE, Victory 162
MC LEMORE, Young L. 202
MC MA CAUTS, Mary L. 186
MC MAHAN, -- 232
Molly C. 94
MC MILLAN, Narcessa 36
MC MILLIAN, C. 234
MC MILLIN, J. -- 77
J. W. 29, 62
MC MILLON, Jane 52
MC MINN, Alzira 31
Chresada 159
Nancy G. 214
Mrs. Savilla 181
MC NABB, Elizabeth 157,
220
Miss M. E. 103
Maranda 15
Mary 220
N. B. 224
Rhoda T. 178
MC NATT, Mary 69
MC NELLY, Isabella 124
MC NUTT, Serrepta 230
MC PHAIL, D. 118
Daniel 3, 13, 30, 35,
46, 62, 63, 85, 86,
111, 117, 135, 155,
157, 172, 177, 178,
180, 192
Nancy M. 11
MC PHERSON, Elizabeth 154,
172
Isabella M. 172
MC REYNOLDS, D. 148
Sarah A. 73
MC ROBERTS, Margaret 67
MC ROY, Curtus 136
MC SPADDEN, Rev. J. 156
Jane 108
Nancy Jane 156
MC SPADDIN, Mary E. 102
MC SPADEN, Joseph 218
MC WHEN, Sarah Ann 222
MEE, Mrs. Susan 18
MEEK, John B. 19
MEGHEE, Susan J. 38
MEIGS, Mrs. Elizabeth 29
Grace S. 29
Theresa C. 167
MELTAN, Martha A. 190
MELTON, Ailcy 206
Arme Jane 206
Darcus 4
Edy 65
Elizabeth 8, 187
J. H. 50
J. M. 46, 143
Jas. H. 46, 128, 144
Julia N. 9
Lucinda 134
M. K. 9
Mahala 213
Malinda 210
Mandy 78

MELTON (cont.)
  Margret 78
  Milla 38
  Rebecca 5
  Sarah 43
  Sarah C. 204
  Sarah E. 141
  Susan 134
  Susannah 144
MELVIN, Elizabeth 5
MEREDITH, Jincy 138
MESERMAN, Thos. 145
METCALF, G. C. 146
METCALFE, Amelia 135
  G. C. 44, 200
MICHAIL, Elizabeth L. 129
MIDDLETON, Rebecca 63
MIDELTON, Francis 154
MIERS, Marinda 171
  Rhoda 171
  Rody 171
MIGHT, Mariah 82
MILER, D. L. 183
MILL--, Morgan 97
MILLARD, Eliza S. 161
  G. W. 160
MILLER, Armenia 116
  E. C. 184
  E. L. 16, 23, 39, 67,
    70, 75, 85, 89,
    102, 118, 125, 128,
    136, 137, 163, 167,
    168, 178, 193, 200,
    201, 203, 207
  E. S. 33
  Elizabeth 89
  G. M. 13
  Hassie Lock 170
  Isaac 189
  J. M. 40, 44, 46, 49,
    65, 66, 77, 84, 97,
    111, 115, 122, 124,
    128, 129, 130, 135,
    137, 181, 226
  J. W. 33, 45, 92, 132,
    153
  James 206
  James A. 189
  Mrs. Jemima 171
  John 5, 189
  Joseph 146
  Katharine 165
  L. B. 158
  Lillith Lock 213
  Lydia E. 96
  M. 103
  Miss M. E. 109
  Margarett 210
  Mary 138
  Mary A. 68, 146
  Mary Ann 44
  Morgan 14, 24, 48, 56,
    65, 83, 87, 89, 92,
    110, 131, 143, 144,
    159, 209, 210, 223
  Miss N. R. 117
  Nancy 179, 229
  Nancy C. 48
  Parallee C. 116
  Sarah Ann 47
  Susan 156
  Tennie 36
MILLION, Elizabeth 180
MILLIRS, J. W. 91
MILLSAPS, Isabella 128
  Lidia 81
MINS, Margaret 89
MINTEN, E. L. 136
MINTON, Anna 86
MINZE, Joseph 222
MINZES, Joseph 33, 146,
  172
MINZS, Joseph 232
MIRERS, Rhoda 171

MIRERS (cont.)
  Rody 171
MIRES, Margaret 160
  Peggy Salina 215
  Rhoda 171
  Rody 171
MITCHAEL, Sarah 134
MITCHEL, Salie H. 52
MITCHELL, Currinda 124
  Mrs. Hazy 32
  Julia A. 149
  Lavista 24
  Laura A. 121
MIZE, Miss E. M. 121
  Margaret C. 94
  Rebecca Jane 21
MIZELL, Eveline 201
MO---, J. W. 212
MONROE, Catharine 56
  George 188, 200
  Lizer 117
  Louisa 117
  Margaret 136
  Mrs. Mina 116
  Surmintha P. 203
MONTGOMERY, Elizabeth A.
  67
  Rev. J. F. 111
MOON, Lucy 232
  Susannah 220
MOORE, Caroline 201
  Christen 151
  Elizabeth 140
  George W. 124
  J. N. 101
  Jno. M. 29
  Jno. N. 1, 66, 134,
    141, 183, 197
  Jno. W. 123
  Malissa 190
  Mary 208, 212
  Mary E. 180, 194
  Nancy 220
  Narcissa 104
  Miss R. E. 69
  R. J. 39, 171
  Sarah 106, 139
  Sarah Ann 12
  Sarah B. 86
  Sophia 54
MORE, George W. 124
MORELAND, Peggy 80
  Thomas 86
MORGAN, C. A. 181
  Cherokee A. 181
  Delila 108
  Eliza 219
  G. W. 181
  James 150
  Keziah A. 218
  Keziah J. 28
  Lydia 146
  Mary 19
  O. S. 152
  Rebecca 200
  S. S. 150
  Samuel K. 151
  Sarah E. 108
MORISON, A. D. 192
  L. 58
MORRIS, D. 196
  Dialtha 16
  Dickerson 219
  Eliza 156
  Elizabeth 51, 141
  John 215
  Malvina 93
  Mariah J. 99
  Martha 169
  Martha J. 197
MORRISON, L. R. 3, 11,
  30, 43, 44, 53,
  57, 68, 73, 80,

MORRISON (cont.)
  L. R. (cont.) 110,
    111, 127, 129, 135,
    149, 154, 158, 166,
    173, 174, 187, 194,
    212, 223
  Miss S. A. 122
  Sarah 93
  W. H. 5
MORROW, Mary J. 193
  Sarah Ann 12
MORTON, G. W. 7, 64, 136,
    210, 231
  George W. 112, 115,
    201, 212, 215, 222
MOSES, Elizabeth 223
MOSS, Claressa 14
  Jane 160
  Nancy E. 66
  Quintina 116
  Rebecca 209
  Sarah M. 44
MOUNTCASTLE, G. E. 45
MOYERS, John 178
MULKEY, Louisa 81
  Reminda 159
MUNROW, Elisa B. 133
  Mary Jane 219
MINSEY, T. K. 209
IRPHEY, Saml. 80
URPHY, Celia 180, 217
MURRAY, Mary 171
  Sally 186
MURRELL, C. G. 229
MURRILL, Emily L. 105
MURRY, Darcus 227
  Gilbert 171
  Martha 28
  Nancy 221
  Stacia 134
MYERS, Elizabeth C. 69
  Elvira 69
  Martha E. 152
  Mary J. 65
  Sydney Ann 155
MYNATT, Ailsey 230
  C. W. 136
  Levesta 136
MYRES, Lethey L. 2
  Sarah F. 202
NACION, Nancy 20
NAILE, Nancy M. 198
NANCE, Jennett 114
  Julian 89
  Mary Ann 21
NAPIER, Nancy 58
NATION, Elizabeth 63
NATIONS, Nancy 90
  Rachel 165
NEAL, A. B. 189
  Katharine S. 45
  Maggie S. 76
  W. W. 44, 218
NEEL, Joseph 51, 223
  Sarah E. 69
NEIL, Joseph 11, 24, 27,
    53, 106, 111, 148,
    164, 192, 223, 226
  Mary A. E. 169
NEILL, Elizabeth 17
NELSON, M. C. 15
  Minerva J. 34
  Nancy H. 110
  Rev. Thomas H. 207
  W. A. 3, 10, 11, 12,
    18, 20, 40, 65,
    86, 110, 114, 157,
    158, 164
NETHERLAND, Miss C. V. 233
  Virginia W. 93
NEWBURY, Dorcas 5
NEWCUM, Eliza 157
NEWKIRK, Elizabeth Ann 71

248

NEWKIRK (cont.)
Nancy 43
NEWLAND, Sarah Ann 182
NEWMAN, Ailsey M. 57
Daniel 229
Eliza 172
Eliza E. 229
Elizabeth 58
Emily C. 112
Hetta S. 210
Laura S. 58, 161
Lucy 229
Mahala Jane 123
Margret 3
Margaret S. 169
Maria C. 20
Marthy A. 14
Mary 54
Nancy A. 212
Rebecca 6, 58
Rebecca Ann 110
Rebecca J. 111
Sarah 100
Sarah E. 55
Sarah F. 49
Sarah J. 91
Mrs. Susannah 170
W. H. 29, 202
W. M. 6
Wm. 14, 34, 42, 57,
  128, 155, 182, 200
Wm. H. 25, 165, 190
NEWMON, Mary S. 139
NEWLAND, Mary 21
NEWTON, Arrena 149
Caroline 214
E. 2, 49, 59, 89, 220
Ed 156
Edward 64, 82, 84, 137,
  228
Lucinda 228
Mahala 232
Malinda L. 209
Martha C. 220
Neddy 133
Polly 83
Rebeca E. 123
Miss S. E. 159
Sarah 57
William 33, 35, 83,
  122, 123, 155, 181,
  190, 200, 213
NICELEY, Anna 166
NICHELS, Elizabeth 206
NICKELSON, Marthy Jane
  150
NIEL, A. B. 166
NOEL, Tilitha 203
NORMAN, Nancy 141
NORRIS, Susan 164
NORV---, George James 98
NORVELL, Martha J. 142
NORVILLE, Eliza Jane 94
NORWOOD, J. W. 69
Thoams W. 78, 205, 217
NUCKLES, B. F. 204
B. Floyd 214
Floyd 153
O'DANIEL, Mary 186
ODOM, Caliona 113
OFFICER, Nancy 6
OGLE, Fany 28
OLIVER, Elizabeth A. 175
ONLEY, Martha 112
ONLY, Mary E. 11
ORICK, Martha 95
ORR, Caroline 223
Delila 199
Nancy 217
Rachel 209
ORRICK, Scyntha 215
ORTEN, Susan 153
ORTON, Emelin 209

ORTON (cont.)
Mary 46
OTTER, Sallie 89
OVERBY, Elizabeth 36
OVERTON, John W. 181
OWEN, C. L. 157
Harriate 32
Martha 184
Mary 94, 196
Mary J. 25
Simanthia 168
W. C. 41, 81, 138,
  182, 221
Wm. C. 2, 24, 32, 36,
  43, 53, 71, 83
OWENS, Eliza 8, 212
Elizabeth 142
Elizabeth A. 64
Elizia 145
Harriet 179
Hayney 157
Martha 3
Nancy 86
Miss S. E. 25
Virginia 19
W. C. 65, 94, 138,
  180, 199
OWINS, Haney 81
PAIN, Elizabeth E. 46
Martin 16
PAINE, M. 46, 69, 209
PANGLE, Margaret 88
PARDON, Catharine 62
PARIS, Elvy 105
Jerusha 220
Mary W. 95
Sarah 216
PARK, James 11
PARKE, Sarah A. 195
PARKENSON, James 11
PARKER, Catharine 111
Louiza C. 92
PARKERSON, James 10, 23,
  66, 104, 109, 130,
  134, 171, 193, 195
PARKINSON, Mrs. Julia
  Ann 112
James 4, 13, 65, 86,
  159, 214, 217, 220,
  223
Nancy 174
Polly 29
PARKS, Elizabeth J. 8
Martha 77
PARMLY, May Jane 142
PARR, Vina 188
PARRIS, Lucinda 161
PARSHALL, Elizabeth 183
Dr. J. 183
PARSONA, Anna 226
Nancy 157
Sarah 212
PARTIN, Miss T. J. 115
PATRICK, Hillery 99, 150
PATTERSON, Caroline 75
Elizabeth 121
M. E. 186
Polly 107
Sarah J. 89
PATTON, J. M. 133
Jane O. 87
Mary A. 158
PATTY, Amanda E. 6
Mrs. Edith 47
Elizabeth 58
Martha 9
Mrs. Mary J. 41
R. W. 34, 110, 123,
  136
Sarah F. J. 60
Sarah M. 128
Susan J. 68
Susan T. 59

PAYN, Mary 99
PAYNE, Josephine 80
Uriah 50, 68, 79, 94,
  113, 152, 160, 169,
  170, 185, 206
PEAK, Fansina 82
Fransina 82
PEAL, E. G. 11
PEARCE, Abigail A. 210
H. 178
Hamelton 61
Hamilton 219
John L. 168
Louisa E. 185
Lucinda 7
Miss M. F. 84
Martha A. 1
Minerva 64
Nancy 164
Sarah 12
Sarah Jane 223
PEARMAN, Eliza 106
Martha 223
Susanah 203
PEARSCE, Hamilton 109
PEARSON, Abel 69, 127,
  132
Eliza 148
Gazilda 126
Louisa 54
Mary J. 100
Mathew J. 126
Nancy 63
Sherwood W. 116
Thos. P. 193
PECK, Laura Jane 75
PEELER, Joseph 75, 110,
  147
Margaret S. E. 193
PELLER, Joseph 9, 28, 143
PENDERGRASS, J. C. 36,
  159
PENNINGTON, F. M. 71
L. C. 24
PEOPLES, Caroline 186
James 170
PERRIN, Lucinda 190
PERRY, Angeline 224
Mary 2, 170
Rebeca A. 45
PERRYMAN, Elizabeth 130
PERTILEO, Emaline 58
PESTERFIELD, Elizabeth A.
  198
PETERS, Barzilla 147
Delila 6
Eliza 84
John 18
N. G. 152
Phebe S. 164
Susan 151
PETTETTE, Martha M. 219
PETTITT, Elizabeth C. 178
PETTY, J. S. 26, 142
PEW, Rebecca 26
Amanda 58
PHILIPS, Juliann 218
Louisa 114
M. L. 169, 204
Mariah 175
S. 5, 92, 184, 208,
  210
S. J. 32
S. V. 7
PHILLIPS, M. L. 83
Martha 16
PICKEL, James H. 118
PICKENS, Marry E. 29
Martha 213
Nancy 51
Sarah J. 125
PICKINS, Rebecca 154
PICRING, Mahala J. 14

249

PIERCE, Amanda 141
  Betsie J. 224
  David 130
  Eliza J. 15
  JOana 211
  Joriah 137
  Mary A. 214
  Mary Ann 130
PIKE, Eliza M. 89
  Lile 43
  Mary 233
PILGRIM, Miss M. E. 206
PINION, Hiley 215
  Nancy 208
PLANK, Nancy 104
PLEASANT, T. J. 150
POE, Jane 143
  Mariah 97
POPE, Fielding 9, 170
  T. J. 98, 234
PORTER, Amanda 48
  Ann A. 131
  Eliza 25
  Elizabeth Catharine
    27
  Harriet 214
  Jane 2
  John H. 36
  Jno. T. 107
  Lusena J. 58
  Miss M. J. 137
  Mary D. 189
  Mary F. 216
  Milla Ann 160
  Narcissa 85
  Robert W. 2
  W. 200
  William W. 189
POTTER, Adeline 151
  Sarah 150
POWER, Artie E. 126
POWERS, Malinda 121
  Sarah S. 167
PRATHER, Arminda 105
  Sarah Ann 105
  Tathamany 224
PRESLEY, Mary 23
PRESLY, Lucinda 106
  Mrs. Nancy 106
PRESNELL, Elias 203
PRESSELY, Harriate 151
PRESSNELL, Phebe L. 106
PRESSWOOD, C. M. 163
PRESTWOOD, Mary 177
PRESWOOD, Evvie M. 63
PREWIT, Caroline 52
PRICE, Henry 43, 50, 63,
    71, 86, 91, 93, 107,
    130, 135
  Jane 120
  John 6
  Marha 27
PRICHARD, Martha C. 207
  Nancy J. 2
PRIDE, William E. 187
PRIGMORE, Miss H. 162
  Miss L. G. 197
  Ruth K. 32
PRINCE, Catharine 27
  Mary E. 225
PROFFIT, Rebecca 206
PROPHET, B. A. 27, 116
  Jane 83
  Martha J. 129
  R. A. 99, 160
PRUET, Hezekiah 173
PUGH, Eliza 172
  Evaline 78
  J. F. 83, 105
  Mary 25
  Mathursa 177
  Mrs. Nancy 132
  Mrs. Sarah 196

PURKINS, Rebecca 123
PUTNAM, Rev. C. 95
QUALLS, Miss A. J. 210
  S. A. 7
QUEENER, Elizabeth 118
  Susan E. 50, 169
R---, S. W. 176
RABAY, Nancy A. 214
RABOURN, Eliza J. 20
  Joseph 103
  Sarah 137
RABURN, Lucinda 15
RACKET, Isabell 196
RAGAN, Elizabeth 98
  Peter 98
RAINS, Amanda 40
RAMSEY, Ann Amelia 207
  Edmund 153
  Rev. S. G. 207
  William B. A. 119
RAMY, Elizabeth 209
RANDELL, Jane 208
RANDOLPH, Clarissa 64
  E. G. 51
  E. H. 6
  Elihu H. 106, 171
  G. 170
  Gilmore 171, 195, ???
  Harriet E. 50
  Malessa 55
  Maranda 228
  Robert 26, 68, 171,
    178, 180
  Sarah 117
  Sarah E. 138
RAPER, Rebecca 8
RATLEDGE, Clara 49
RAY, Eliza 102
  F. S. 116
  Melvina 174
RAYBURN, Elizabeth A. 176
READ, Mary 177
REAGAN, J. H. 191, 194
  James H. 194
  Julia 125
  Sarah E. 224
REATHERFORD, Adaline 152
  Margaritt 184
  Silday M. 184
REATHFORD, Sarah Jane 164
REDFEARN, Emeline 131
REED, Elizabeth 169
  Loretta 6
  Martha 1, 99
  Mary 112
  Nancy 210
  Tempy L. 209
REEDER, Frank K. 104
REESE, Sarah 88
REGAN, Francis E. 174
REGGINS, Hily 165
REID, Ann 217
  Jane 158
RENEAU, Louisa 155
  Susan 135
  Winney 100
RENFRO, C. W. 71
  Nancy 233
RENFROW, Elizabeth 37
RENOE, Louisa C. 163
RENTFRO, G. W. 25, 59
  Geo. W. 59
  Manda M. 23
  Misouri 71
RENTFRON, G. W. 35
RENTFROW, Ellen 87
REW, Mandy 74
REYNOLDS, Catharine 214
  Elin V. 36
  Eliza Ann 13
  Elizabeth 41, 63
  Emaline 119
  Green L. 13, 31, 54,

REYNOLDS (cont.)
  Green L. (cont.) 74,
    79, 121, 145, 155,
    160, 174, 201
  H. C. 65
  Hannah 30
  Humphrey 197
  John 187
  Lucy J. 78
  Molley 176
  Pelina 161
  R. 18, 22, 23, 185,
    199, 211, 221
  Rebecca 174
  Robert 8, 10, 12, 21,
    79, 171
  T. J. 174, 186
  W. C. 129
RHEA, Mary 189
  Nancy 15
RHOM, Henery 101
  Mahala 101
RICE, C. W. 60, 88, 106,
    13, 148, 160, 219,
    222
  Charles W. 113
  Elizabeth 91
  H. 25
  H. M. 142
  Henry 188
  Mrs. Indanah P. 103
  James H. 188
  Larorah L. 136
  Laura L. 136
  Miss M. W. 204
  Martha 143
  Nancy 171
  Nancy P. 158
  Susan 63
  T. S. 7, 38, 39, 42,
    102, 106, 107, 146,
    150, 201, 215, 232
  Tandy S. 106
RICHARD, Adaline 105
RICHARDS, Cinthia Malissa
    86
  Eliza 189
  Jane 72
RICHARDSON, Rebecky A. 58
  Robert A. 207
  Tabitha Ann 180
RICHERSON, Jane M. 229
  Julia A. 32
RICHEY, Elizabeth 208
RIDDLE, Ann 50
  Emeline 56
  Julia 102
  Martha 56
  Mary 35
  Sally C. 103
RIDER, Miss C. M. 94
  Caroline 186
  Mary 75
RIGGINS, Ann E. 100
  Elizabeth J. 26
  Hiley 166
RIGGS, Mrs. Amanda J. 86
  Martha E. 50
  Nancy 50
  Rhoda 55
  Sallie A. 54
  Sarah 31
  Sarah Ann 35
RIGHT, Mary E. 104
  Suzanah J. 23
  Tempy A. 119
RILY, Sarah Katharine 44
RIPLEY, Thomas C. 11
RITCHARDSON, Robert 165
RITCHEY, Cynthia E. 205
  Mrs. Sarah 164
RIVERS, Mary Ann 96
  Milly 232

ROADS, Mary E. 11
ROARK, Nancy 1
ROBBERTS, Sarahan 53
ROBERSON, A. C. 18
ROBERTS, Carolene 203
   Caroline 203
   Catharine 86
   E. M. 88
   Edmund 26
   Elizabeth 199
   Elizabeth H. 156
   H. 139
   H. M. 37, 47, 48, 53,
     54, 66, 81, 85,
     121, 146, 152, 178,
     199, 225, 226, 230
   James 199
   Mrs. Jennie 18
   John 190
   Lois 137
   Mary 139
   Mary E. 216
   Sidney A. 229
   Syphey 93
   Sythuy 93
   Tenesse 26
ROBERTSON, Catharine 39
   Glapha Ann 97
   Joseph 133
   Milton 179
ROBESON, A. C. 104
   A. S. 34
   Ann 199
   Emeline 77
   Jane 19
   Margaret 193
   William 179
ROBINETT, Hugh 217
   May C. 85
ROBINSON, John 49
   John J. 214
   Joseph 132
   Mary 44
   Nancy A. 84
ROBISON, A. C. 59, 91,
     105, 168
   Elvira 14
   Jane 19, 61, 93
   John J. 38, 98
   Malinda 189
   Mary Ann 97, 171
   Mary C. 91
   Nancy 147
   Susan A. 209
   Synthy 154
ROBSON, A. C. 196
RODDAN, Miss N. J. 84
RODDEN, Eliza Jane 30
   Elizabeth 204
   Hariet R. 185
   Sarah Emeline 121
RODGERS, Mary J. 194
ROE, Easter 101
   Susannah 223
ROGERS, Caroline 159
   Miss E. E. 171
   Eliza J. P. 144
   Elizabeth 187
   John 153, 205, 208, 231
   Leona A. 23
   Margret 104
   Mary 19
   Mary D. 155
   Mildred 197
   Nancy 55
   Nancy L. 46
   Sarah A. 225
   Thos. 17, 39, 128, 164
   Thomas J., Jr. 181
ROGES, Joseph M. 181
ROGGERS, Catherine 30
ROLAND, Katharine 212
   Mary J. 93

ROLAND (cont.)
   Nancy J. 228
ROLLING, Elijah 182
ROLLINGS, Martha J. 196
ROLLINS, Mary 114
ROLLS, J. A. 149
ROMACK, Margaret 150
ROMINES, Mrs. J. 179
   Jane 80
ROSE, Caroline 41
   D. 100
   Mrs. Francis 11
   Mary M. 167
   Mattie 109
   Susan A. 59
   Z. 8, 30, 36, 56, 132,
     153, 199
   Zachariah 138
ROSS, Elizabeth 117
   Lewis 153
   Mattie W. 126
   Minerva 153
ROTHWELL, Jane 27
   Lucy Ellen 225
   Miss M. C. 73
   Salley J. 205
ROWAN, Keziah 88
   Miss M. M. 160
   R. C. 127
ROWLES, Miss M. L. 130
   J. A. 87, 92
ROWLEY, E. 51, 54, 76,
     134, 186, 206
   Erastus 86
   Eugenie E. 76
ROYSTON, S. W. 20, 65,
     87, 90, 137, 147,
     166, 220
RUCKER, Nancy E. 208
   Polly 24
   Miss M. M. 101
   Mary C. 98
   Milly 83
   Rachail M. 221
   Sarah C. 26
   W. 61, 222
   Wm. 16, 28, 34, 36,
     42, 51, 136, 143,
     156, 205, 221, 229,
     234
RUDD, Elizabeth J. 176
   Henrietta 99
   John 142
   Mahala 27
   Margaret A. 108
   Martha 75
   Mary 80
   Mary Ann 170
   Nancy 194
   Permelia 78
   Sarah Jane 143
   Sophrona 75
RUE, Caroline 15
   Mary Jane 139
   Rebeca Ann 172
RUETHURFORD, Alpha 71
RUNNELZ, Sarah 35
RUNNION, Nancy E. 201
RUNYANS, Mary M. 208
RUSH, Malinda 202
   Syrus 202
RUSSEL, J. S. 2
   Thomas J. 151
RUSSELL, Mrs. Ada L. 43
   Elizabeth 60, 102
   J. S. 7, 20, 37, 40,
     41, 43, 45, 49, 54,
     56, 59, 61, 67, 72,
     81, 82, 106, 126,
     133, 149, 167, 168,
     174, 182, 184, 210,
     216
   James L. 130

RUSSELL (cont.)
   Jane 43
   Miss L. C. 36
   Mrs. Lucinda 92
   Martha L. 174
   T. J. 52, 180, 194,
     203, 204
   T. T. 10, 31, 97, 160,
     174
   Thos. 25, 96, 166, 176
   Thomas J. 43, 107, 120
   Thomas L. 211
   Thomas T. 22, 64, 87,
     185, 204, 229, 232
   Taylor 128
   W. J. 220
   W. T. 47
RUTHERFORD, Elizabeth A.
     158
   Fanny E. 125
   Lydia Ann 96
   Mary J. 63
   Sarah 56
RUTLEDGE, Elizabeth 8
RYAN, Isaac N. 147
ST. JOHN, Catharine 155
   Mary E. 51
   Rebeckah O. 19
SALLE, Charity 220
SALLEE, Amanda M. 9
   Caroline 27
   Eliza 99
   Margaret 49
SALYER, T. T. 81
SAMS, Sarah Ann 187
SANDERS, C. 4, 32, 33, 55,
     114, 116, 132, 152,
     154, 162, 165, 230
   Elizabeth 21, 114
   Mary Jane 20
   Miss N. J. 95
SATTEFIELD, Eliza 67
SAUNDERS, Catharine 172
SAWTELL, E. N. 115, 148
SAXTEN, Edna 209
SAXTON, Mary M. 74
SCARBOROUGH, J. 128
   J. M. 209
   M. J. 1
SCARBROUGH, Ellen 155
   J. H. 141
   J. M. 61
   J. N. 162
   James 55, 130
   John 120, 171, 172,
     212
   John 221, 224
   M. G. 208
SCOTT, Mrs. Elizabeth 23
   Robert 41
SCRUGGS, John 9, 10, 17,
     30, 36, 43, 48, 49,
     58, 66, 86, 93, 94,
     95, 127, 142, 162,
     171, 174, 175, 176,
     183, 184, 204
SEAHORN, Mary 134
SEAY, Jane 85
   Nancey 17
SECREST, Nancy Malinda 170
SEHORN, Elizabeth 64
   Mat A. 165
   Nora 5
SEIVILS, Polly Ann 166
SELLARS, Harriett L. 215
SELLERS, Martha M. 31
   Martha T. 173
   Sarah J. 56
   Sintha 108
SENTER, B. 103
   Elizabeth K. 175
   James 120
   Luzireene 45

SENTER (cont.)
  Matilda 164
  Polly 41
  Sarah 92
  Stephen W. 175
  Susan 87
SESRETT, Sarah Jane 66
SEVIL, James 107
SEWELL, J. 108, 224
  James 77, 120, 140,
    156, 185, 187, 192,
    198, 205
  Robert 75
  Thomas 165
  Robert 163
SHADDEN, Mrs. Mary E. 99
SHAMBLAIN, Sarah 16
SHAMBLE, Catharine 229
SHAMBLIN, Mrs. Jane 79
  William 7, 26, 62,
    104, 112, 119, 120
  William M. 189
SHAMLEE, Miss N. A. 41
SHANNO, A. F. 218, 219,
  225
SHANNON, A. F. 191
  Jane 94
SHANON, A. F. 75
SHARETS, Mary 109
  S. 57, 67, 158, 212
  Stephen 137, 188
SHARETTS, Stephen 7, 215
SHARITES, Sarah S. 202
SHARITS, Mary J. 136
  S. 82, 97, 131, 153
  Sarah A. 233
  Stephen 15, 100, 152,
    231
SHARITTS, Stephen 69
SHARP, Eliza E. 117
  Elizabeth 170, 192
  Martin 89
SHARRELT, Nancy Ann 228
SHARRETS, S. 8
  Stephen 209
SHARRTTS, S. 190
SHAW, Mary Ann 45
SHEARER, Elmira A. 146
SHELL, Francis E. 50
  Luamey 2
  Nannie 134
  Rebeckah 84
  Sarah 136
  Sarah L. 75
  Vira 232
SHELTON, A. J. 35, 88, 92,
    135, 197
  Anna 39
  Catharine 192
  Elizabeth 80
  Eveline 4
  James W. 133
  Jane 90
  John 132
  Lucinda 210
  Malinda 140
  Mary 154
  Nancy 132, 231
  Polly 86
SHEPHEARD, Betsey 233
SHERMAN, Malinda 70
SHERRILL, Elizabeth 227
SHIELD, Polly 219
SHIELDS, Margaret 48
  Rebecca Jane 153
SHILL, Vira 232
SHIPLEY, Eliza 212
  Elizabeth 199
  Mary 12
  Nancy A. 7
  Sarah E. 218
SHOEMAKER, Calvin 205
  Reuhama 22

SHOOK, Ann 191
  Eliza 183
  Elizabeth 202
  Hetty 91
  Lucy 210
  Margaret 17
  Martha 71
  Mary 191
  Sarah 232
  William 204
SHUEMAKE, Mary Ann 151
SHUGART, Sarah A. 46
SHULTS, Elizabeth A. 156
  Emma J. 141
  G. 136
  Mary Ann 133
  Sarah S. 27
SHULTZ, Granville 193
SHUMAKER, Nancy 124
SHUMATE, Martha J. 110
SIBSTS, William 134
SIMMONDS, Eliza Ann 175
SIMONS, Mary 59
SIMPSON, Anna 98
  Margart 148
  Mary 34
SIVELS, Miss A. 95
SIVIL, Abigale 21
SIVILS, Lurana 151
  Mary Ann 77, 91
  Polly 192
  Rebecca 38
SIVLEY, Abigale 80
SLACK, Mary D. 184
  Sallie F. 106
SLAUGHTER, John D. 113
  Mary C. 232
  Melissa E. 55
  Rebecca 113
  Sallie M. 51
SLIGAR, Isabelah 128
SLIGER, Mrs. Mary 97
SLOOP, Caroline 160
  H. M. 1, 55, 63, 71,
    75, 97, 131, 160,
    177
  Juletta 97
  Malvina 107
SLOVER, A. 10, 22, 27,
    43, 44, 48, 58, 63,
    67, 69, 79, 82, 88,
    91, 97, 99, 105,
    108, 127, 135, 150,
    184, 186, 198, 200,
    203, 214, 218, 220,
    228, 230
  Rev. Abraham 98
  John F. 14, 141
SMALL, A. G. 2, 22, 24,
    118
  Elizabeth 126
  Emaline 22
  H. 221
  Jane 148
  Mary S. 111
  Thos. H. 32, 57, 126,
    147, 196
SMALLWOOD, Partheny 116
SMART, Isaac 80
  John B. 78, 167
  Nancy 78
SMEDLEY, Abner B. 196
  Elizabeth E. 101
SMELSER, Leah 123
SMITH, B. T. 161
  C. D. 21, 179
  Caleb 214
  Catharine J. 221
  Dorcas C. 232
  E. A. 119
  Mrs. Eglentine 68
  Eliza 42, 199, 226
  Elizabeth 57, 148

SMITH (cont.)
  Elizabeth D. 122
  Elizabeth Jane 144
  Emeline 127
  Hannah E. 186
  Hariet 19
  Harriet A. Delia 137
  Harriet W. 83
  James 57, 69, 199
  James T. 61, 89
  Jane B. 5, 156
  Julian 115
  Leah 161
  Lettice W. 214
  Louisa 104
  Louisa J. 35
  Mrs. Louisa P. 3
  M. A. 5, 9
  Miss M. F. 136
  Malinda 165
  Manerva 5
  Manerva J. 198
  Margaret 86, 164
  Margaret Ann 167
  Martha 23, 145
  Martha C. E. 34
  Mary 100, 145, 165
  Mary A. 168
  Mary Ann 16, 79
  Mary B. 109
  Mary Elizabeth 140
  Mary M. 156
  Mary M. M. 174
  Mary T. 218
  Matilda C. 205
  Nancy 39, 140
  Nancy B. 127
  Nancy Jane 17
  Nancy M. 69
  Rachel 206
  Rebecca C. 95
  Russell H. 81
  Salina J. 101
  Sarah 48, 57, 89
  Sarah A. 54
  Sarah E. 180
  Silas 16
  Susan E. 68
  Tennessee 115
  W. L. 14
SNEAD, Robert 103, 135,
    136, 153
SNEED, Robert 96
SNEEDE, Liddy A. 128
SNIDER, Heriet A. 90
  M. Caroline 118
  Mary 85
  Moses 200
  Mrs. Sarah E. 179
SNODDY, Isbell 90
  Mary J. 153
  Nancy 198
  Samuel 4, 27, 85, 144,
    147, 182, 185, 197,
    202, 213, 221, 232
  Sarah C. 153
SNODGRASS, Eleanor 82
  Elizabeth 138
SNOOK, Mary Ann 39
SNOW, Dolly 30
SOUTH, Lea--- E. 160
SOUTHARD, Elizabeth 201
  Emeline 131
  Jackabena 148
  M. 1, 52, 89, 93, 179,
    201
SOUTHERLING, Avalene 157
SOWELL, Mary 99
SPARKS, Celia D. 7
SPEARES, John 79
SPEARMAN, Mary 179
  Sarah 51
  Susan 9

252

SPEARS, J. M. 76
  John 19, 60, 77
SPENCE, J. F. 76
  Jno. F. 200, 229
SPENCER, John 78
SPHERSON, W. H. 166
SPOFFORD, S. A. 58
SPRADLIN, Amanda 97
  J. L. 202
SPRADLING, Amanda 195
  J. L. 101
SPURLING, Richard 230
STAINER, Elizabeth 185
  Polly 150
STALIONS, Martha 142
STALLCUP, Miss M. E. 153
  Mary H. 40
  Sarrah E. 231
STAMPER, Jas. N. 102
  John N. 33, 82, 192,
    207
STANDEFER, G. W. 182
  Miss M. E. 42
STANDIFER, Elizabeth 165
  Martha L. 162
STANDLEY, George W. 201
STANNER, Coonrod 23
STANSBERRY, Elizabeth 79
  Mrs. Jane 184
  Louisa 54
  Martha A. 101
STANSBURY, Mrs. Elizabeth
    55
  Elizabeth Jane 147
  Esther J. 31
  Sarah Ann 95
STANTON, Abigail S. 59
  Miss E. C. G. 115
  Lewis 117, 203
  Phebe E. 195
  William M. 117
STAPLES, Luzany F. 191
STAPP, Sarah Ann 167
STARR, Nancy 118
STAWK, Amanda C. 17
STEAD, Lucinda 127
STEED, Bettie 98
  Justice 24, 96
  Justis 148, 106, 201
  Justus 11, 42, 95, 99,
    106, 136
  Mary 40
  Matilda 168
  Mildred 86
  Nancy L. 99
  Nancy M. 102
  Miss P. C. 98
  Sarah T. 168
STEPHENS, Margaret A. 30
  Martha M. 230
  Polly 125
  Thomas 204
STEPHENSON, Anna 218
  Arminda 37
  Mrs. Catharine 130
  Elizabeth 11
  John C. 192
  Martha 189
  Rachel 2
  Miss S. B. 94
  Sarah 51
  Susanah 25
  Synthia 147
  W. H. 7, 9, 43, 70, 94,
    108, 164
  Wm. H. 68
STEPP, Mary J. 184
STERNS, Mary C. 42
STEPHESON, W. H. 12
STEWART, B. K. 232
  Mary 96
  Wm. 65, 139
STILES, Jincey A. 222

STONE, Carline 71
  Sarah 136
STOUT, Ann 20
STOWE, Florence T. 227
STRAIN, Martha J. 145
STRATTON, Miss E. 78
  Louvina 163
STRINGFIELD, J. K. 125,
    136
STRUHTON, Jenney 4
STRUTON, Jinny 4
STRUTTEN, Darcus E. 121
STRUTTON, Rhoda 52
STUART, Margaret 224
STUBBLEFIELD, Mary Ann 88
STUDDARD, Elizabeth 55,
    206
  Martha T. 194
  Mary A. 115
  Nancy 76
SUGART, Mary J. 112
SULINS, Timothy 75
SULIVAN, Margaret 64
SULLENS, Hazy 32
  Nathan 32
  T. 2
SULLINS, Mary L. 231
  Morris C. 21
  Rebecca L. 57
  T. 32, 57, 62, 66,
    189
  Timothy 175
SURTMAN, Jane 95
SUTHARD, Miss M. M. 154
SUTHERLAND, Sarah M. 96
SWAFFER, Elizabeth M. 39
  Julia 224
  Martha C. 55
SWAFFORD, A. 20, 30, 49,
    55, 56, 58, 76,
    144, 145, 184
  Alfird 49
  Alfred 58
  Catherin 207
  Mary 40
  Nancy 39, 76
  Sarah 207
  Sarah E. 220
  Sarah J. 39
  Thos. L. 207
SWAFORD, Lucinda 197
SWAGGERTY, Malinda 3
SWATZELL, Elizabeth 52
SWEENEY, Moses 102
SWEENY, Moses 80, 105,
    211
SWENNEY, M. 61
  Maryann F. 94
SWENNY, Moses 61
SWENY, Moses 107, 162
SWINFORD, Charity 27
  Mariah 38
  Polly 21
  Sidney 233
SWINNEY, Moses 229
  Miss N. F. 225
SWISHER, Anney E. 158
  J. G. 43, 61, 76
SWISHIR, J. 179
TABER, Patience 36
TABOR, Polly 200
TALENT, Cathirin 178
  Fanny A. 128
  Narcissa 123
TALIAFERRO, C. 86
TALLANT, Lydia 221
TALLENT, Emeline 176
TALLY, Margaret 161
TALY, Mandee 72
TANNER, Mary Ann T. 55
TATE, John 2, 22, 23, 104,
    113, 159, 165, 197,
    202, 207, 232

TATE (cont.)
  Robert 197
  Sarah 48
TAYLOR, Catharine 200
  Elizabeth 5, 38
  L. V. 48
  Larkin 183
  Larkins 1, 97, 158
  Susan 18
TEADFORD, R. E. 33
TEAGUE, Julia A. 168
  Sarah 154, 207
  Sarah A. 107
TEDFORD, Rev. James 8
  Ralph E. 3, 173
TEMPLETON, A. 37, 40, 41
  Carline 91
  Emily 159
  Lear Jane 6
  Martha A. 2
  Matilda 45
TEMPLTON, Eve 215
TENNEY, Elizabeth Jane
    105
  Rebecca 100
TERRY, Isabella 193
  Joab H. 130
  Mary 190
  Miss P. T. 175
  Sarah Ann 103
THALCH, Eliza 38
THARPS, Wallas W. 221
THERMAN, Malindy 87
THOM, S. M. 38
THOMAS, Angeline 4
  Anna 10
  Caroline 158
  J. 27, 37, 79
  James 168
  Joana 168
  Johnathan 162, 172, 202
  Jonathan 4, 6, 13, 16,
    41, 42, 45, 63, 68,
    84, 86, 98, 101,
    118, 137, 147, 153,
    168, 182, 191, 217,
    232
  Joseph 233
  Louisa 222
  Margret 142
  Maryan 5
  S. M. 4, 11, 15, 38,
    44, 58, 78, 87, 97,
    99, 113, 144, 151,
    159, 164, 169, 173,
    180, 196, 210, 226,
    228
THOMASSON, Alfred 226
THOMPSON, Amy 63
  C. S. 181
  Miss D. A. 188
  Eliza Ann 44
  J. W. 24
  James B. 211
  Jane 76
  Jemimah 77
  Louisa 229
  Miss M. A. E. 112
  Malvina 20
  Martha L. 212
  Mary 29, 86
  Mary Ann 22
  Nancy 2
  Nancy A. 128
  Nancy J. 45
  Miss O. A. 220
  Rachel 181, 216
  Rebecca 53
  Miss S. C. 41, 61
  Sarah 64, 198
  Sarah Ann 220
  Sarah J. 181, 198
  Miss V. K. 110

253

THOMPSON (cont.)
W. H. C. 181
Wm. 1, 17, 23, 35, 52,
56, 59, 97, 102,
113, 137, 155, 167,
169, 192, 215, 221
William H. C. 165
THORNHILL, Rachel M. 38
THORNTON, Mary 48
Mildred A. 71
Mirah 10
Sarah A. 9
Virginia F. 232
THORPE, W. W. 29, 177
THORP, Wallace W. 75
THURMAN, John 200
Nancy 69
TINNELL, Melinda 116
TINSLEY, Lucinda 93
TIRA, Juliann 212
TOMMY, Theressa 193
TOMPKINS, Libbie J. 46
TOMPSON, Lousinda Jane 85
Margret 225
TOMSON, Elizabeth 22
TORBALT, Rachel 69
TORBERT, Miss A. E. 145
TORBET, Martha 204
TORBETT, Miss E. S. 145
Mary Ann 147
TOWNSEND, Lotty 190
Jennie 72
Nancy A. 92
Polly Ann 107
TOWNSLY, Annaliza 104
TREADWAY, Mrs. Adaline
143
TREW, Caroline 194
Eliza 169
Mary Ann 213
Miss N. E. 81
TRIM, Emeline C. 71
Eviline C. 212
Narcissa 151
Phebe R. 65
TRIMM, Dorcas 230
TRIPLET, Luvecy 97
Mary 110
Nancy 21
TRIPLETT, Angeline 194
Delany 229
Eliza A. 83
Elsy 202
Jane 114
Martha A. 216
Mary 162
Milly 93
Sinthey C. 213
TROTH, James J. 127
TROUT, Katharine 201
Mary E. 197
TUCKER, Eliza 143
TUELL, Jno. R. 149
TUNEL, Miss J. A. 21
TUNNEL, Elizabeth 110
TUNNELL, Esther C. 179
Margaret N. 102
Nancy J. 51
TUNULL, Nancy M. 61
TURK, Elizabeth 137
Mrs. Gincy 59
Laura Ann 190
Sarah Jane 131
TURNER, Corrie 48
Dialpha 1
Emaline 53
James 214
Margaret 221
Sarah J. 131
TURNMEIR, Evanna 218
TURNMILES, Sarah 160
TURNMIRE, Margaret 188
UNDERDOWN, Jane M. 208

UNDERDOWN (cont.)
Nancy L. 228
UNDERWOOD, Elizabeth 128
Mrs. Martha 115
URSERRY, Letty 114
URY, Mary Jane 109
VALE, Elizabeth 197
VANCE, A. 27
VANDERPORL, Elizabeth 203
VANDIKE, C. P. 216
VANDYKE, C. P. 124, 234
Penelope S. 40
VAN DYKE, Thos. J. 216
VANSANT, Ezekiel 151
VARNEL, Rhoda 213
VARNELL, Mary E. 48
VARNER, Margaret E. 87
VAUGHAN, Elizabeth 50
Florantha 60
J. L. 83
John M. 74
Sarah W. E. 31
VAUGHN, Nancy E. 31
Nancy J. 115
Sarah 139
VERNOM, Mahala 78
VERSHA, Nancy 59
VINCEN, Catharine 172
VINCENT, Jane 163
Nancy 147
VINSANT, Henry 180
VINSON, Jane C. 146
Margaret 217
Martha 3
VINZANT, M. E. 54
Margaret 151
WADE, S. W. 119
Mrs. Sarah J. 101
WADKINS, Rachael 103
WAIDE, Eliza 88
Louisa 17
WAKEFIELD, Thos. 3
WALERMAN, J. 29
WALIS, G. W. 70
WALKER, Adaline 144
Ann 231
Bhaney 102
Caroline 116
Catharine 92
Elizabeth 20, 226
Elizabeth G. 42
J. V. 108
James 150
Jane 102
Jesse 151
John 22, 25, 149, 156,
183, 217
Jno., Jr. 2
Julia Ann W. 223
Katherine 179
Malinda 44
Mary 151
Milner Frances 102
Narcissa 187
Rebecca 166
Miss S. A. 75
Sarah 232
Sarah A. 82
W. R. 150
William 11, 21, 45, 80,
108, 112, 166, 190,
196, 202, 218, 224,
228, 232
William R. 20, 28, 37,
69, 117, 150, 205,
216, 219
WALLACE, Rev. Benj. 199
G. W. 44, 73, 149,
230
James A. 87
Jane 213
Mary Ann 96
WALLEN, Nancy 198

WALLEN (cont.)
Sarah A. 187
Thos. B. 210
WALLER, J. B. 147
L. B. 6, 63, 158
T. B. 4, 62, 90, 222
Thos. B. 100, 115,
219, 223
WALLIN, Letticia 181
Polly Ann 49
Rebecca 77
WALLING, Sarah 58
WALLIS, Eleanor J. 154
G. 56
G. W. 15, 18, 56, 57,
71, 106, 118, 138,
143, 148, 151, 156,
157, 188, 221
Geo. W. 185
J. F. 128
Julie Ann 109
Mary J. 211
WALSH, A. R. 211
Thursey C. 34
W. J. 74, 187
William 143
WALTON, Mrs. Elizabeth 4
Polly T. 213
!AMACK, Mary J. 149
AMMACK, Nancy A. 90
Jemima 199
WARD, B. L. 193
Celia 46
Charlotta 52
Duke 140
Ezekiel 62, 92
Henry P. 139, 140, 150
Martha Jane 138
Mary L. 161
William 129
WARDE, Mrs. Elisey 134
WARE, Clementine 118
Eliza T. C. 172
Elizabeth Ann 83
Ellen C. 62
Jesse A. 123
Miss M. E. 13
M. R. 12, 78, 141, 157,
218
Martha 220
Mary 45
Miss S. I. 45
Sarah Jane 2
William J. 178
WARREN, Wm. A. 18
WASHAM, Mary 161
Sarah 4
WASSAN, Lydia C. 126
WASSOM, Mariam 205
Mary 15
Orpha 161
Pharibe 135
WASSON, -- 183
Jane T. 51
Martha 188
Nancy 188
WATERS, Nancy 160
WATKINS, Mary C. 5
WATSON, Miss B. A. 208
Catharine 120
James M. 176
Jane 142
WATTENBARGER, Jenira 176
Louisa 217
Luesie 33
Margaret A. 136
Martha J. 111
Mary 231
Maryan 210
Nancy A. 223
Nancy Jane 192
Sarah 27
Sarah W. 97

254

WATTS, W. R. 14
WATZ, Bartheny 56
WEAKS, Jane 70
WEAR, Rev. David 111
  Eliza Jane 209
  Elizabeth A. 42
  Jane M. 135
  M. R. 24, 25, 101, 137,
    151, 180, 218, 225
  Martha 17
  Marthy C. 158
  Mary 173
  Maxey E. 116
  Nancy 71
WEATHERLY, Judy E. 123
  Mary 23
  Sarah 185
WEATHERS, George 117
WEATHERY, Patsy 159
WEAVERS, Polly 77
WEB, Miss M. E. 44
WEBB, Elizabeth 139
  Katherine 8
  Mary E. 169
WEIR, George 209
  J. C. 231
  Jo C. 21, 32, 39
  Mary A. 129
  Syvilla 135
WELCH, Serbriney Vandary
  211
WELLER, Thomas B. 50, 53,
  154
WELLS, Arminda 170
  Arvizena 134
  Dianah 123
  Jane 68
  Julia Amanda 152
  Mary J. 32
  Rebecca 152
  Sarah E. 199
  Texana 219
WESSENGTON, Mary 191
WEST, Miss E. S. 45
  Elizabeth 107
  Mrs. Hannah 202
  Margaret 105
  Margaret Jane 230
  Mary 215
  Mary Jane 80
  Mary S. 9
  Polly 215
  Samuel B. 22, 72
WESTON, Martha 189
WETHERLY, Eveline 125
  Julian 185
WETTEN, L. 163
WHALES, Martha 122
WHALEY, Malinda 158
  Sarah 119
WHEELER, Margaret 159
  Saml. 54
  Sarah 141
WHETSEL, Peter K. 132
WHETSELL, Angelina 75
  Lucy 21
  Michael 75
WHITAKER, George E. 23
WHITE, Clarinda A. 153
  Miss E. L. 32
  Elizabeth 3, 167
  Rev. Gideon S. 104
  Lucinda 190
  Mrs. Mary 62, 220
  Mary L. 103
  May L. 157
  Narcessa 12
  Sarah J. 63
  Thos. R. 140
WHITESIDE, J. 150, 151,
  220
WHITSIDES, Jacob 186
WHITTEN, Marinda 97

WHITTEN (cont.)
  Polly 132
WIATE, Miss H. J. 159
WIATT, Elizabeth Ann 72
WIGGINS, J. A. 5
  J. W. 161
WILKA, Mrs. Clearinda 55
WILKINS, Elizabeth J. 118
  John 84
WILKY, Sarah A. 8
WILLES, Sarah Jane 169
  Thoams B. 96
WILLETT, Thomas G. 164
WILLHIGHT, Mary Jane 95
WILLHITE, Cintha P. 66
WILLIAMS, Amy 42
  Armena 18
  Barbary 93
  E. Z. 8, 15, 26, 51,
    55, 64, 78, 93, 94,
    110, 134, 139, 142,
    144, 160, 163, 164,
    173, 177, 191, 196,
    205, 208, 212, 215,
    228, 229
  Eliza J. 113
  Emily Jane 210
  G. C. 110
  James 199
  Jane 118
  Malisy A. 4
  Martha J. 118
  Mary E. 160
  Mattie E. 16
  Sarah 87
  Sarah Ann 66
  Talitha Q. 24
  Z. 78
WILLIS, Sarah 25
  Thomas B. 54
WILLSON, Eliza C. 47
  Joshua 146
WILSON, A. H. 5
  A. R. 21, 142, 163
  Catharine J. 26, 115
  Clarinda 128
  Clarissa 134
  David M. 76
  Dialtha R. 163
  Dicey 74
  Dicy 49
  Miss Effee N. 206
  Eliza 79
  Mrs. Elizabeth 115
  Emaline 1
  Francis Jane 200
  H. P. 101, 180
  Hugh P. 132
  J. A. 47, 218
  Jane 146
  John S. 48, 187
  Joseph 119
  Josephine 27
  Joshua 146
  Leander 10, 72, 92,
    96
  Lemyra 206
  M. L. 202
  Malindy 229
  Margaret A. 26
  Margaret E. 100, 188
  Martha 145, 231
  Martha C. 207
  Martha J. 205
  Mary 81, 124, 145
  Mary Ann 182
  Mary L. 156
  Mattie F. 130
  Nancy 198
  Nancy A. 169
  Mrs. Nancy J. 116
  Miss R. J. 91
  Sally 78

WILSON (cont.)
  Saml. 9, 30, 56, 63,
    82, 83, 85, 88, 89,
    108, 132, 138, 143,
    148, 156, 199, 224,
    228
  Sarah 73, 81
  Sarah H. 98
  Sarah Jane 1
  Sophrona Adaline 145
  Wm. G. 13, 14, 71,
    167, 195
WIMPY, J. 129, 212
WINGO, A. J. 24
  Jane C. 11
WINGWOOD, Jane 61
WINTERS, Nancy A. 198
WISEMAN, Darcas 3
WITCHER, W. 35, 163
  William J. 223
WITT, C. C. 150, 232
  Margaret A. 179
  Martha 48
  Mrs. Mary 62
  Mrs. Mary J. 5
  Nancy J. 24
  Sarah J. 37
WITTE, Thoams 173
WITTEN, Thos. 192
WOLF, Mrs. Arrena 231
  Mary 37
WOLFF, Amanda C. 219
  Elizabeth 84
  Martha 145
WOLFFE, Martha 217
WOMAC, J. A. 90, 168
  James A. 213
WOMACK, Gemima 37
  Jacob 115
  Jacob M. 25
  Mary 74, 178
  Morning E. 181
  Narcissa 54
  Polly Ann 154
  Mrs. Prudence 6
  Sarah 54
WOOD, Mary 31
  Matilda 12
  Permelia E. 33
  Rev. William 119
WOODALL, Dellily 94
  Matilda 120
WOODEN, Sarah M. 159
WOODS, Elizabeth J. 92
  Kiziah 208
  Mary S. 83
  Matilda 138
  Sally 58
  Samuel W. 66
WOODY, Eliza Ann 194
  Elizabeth 52
  Nancy M. 52
  Sally 199
  Sarah 88
WORDEN, Eliza 95
WORKMAN, J. M. 24
  Martha Ann 231
  Sarah E. 163
WORLEY, Matilda 45
WORLY, Elizabeth 111
WRAY, Sarah 42, 117
WRIGHT, C. J. 65, 106,
  135
  Elizabeth 191
  Hannah G. 86
  Martha Ann 232
  Nancy 13
  Thomas B. 200
WYATT, Catherine 14
  Eliza 60
  Syrrefita 216
WYETT, Nancy Ann 211
  Rebecky 82

WYRICK, Katharine 174
    Margaret 89
YANCY, Winny 8
YEAROUT, Samuel L. 208
YEARWOOD, Mrs. Cordelia V.
        86
    Nancy 107
    Sarah D. 97
YERWOOD, Martha J. 86
YONCE, Mary 25
    Nancy L. 211
YOST, George 30
YOUNG, Bendience 14
    Charlotte 62
    Jane 44
    Margaret 173
    Martha C. 5
    Nancy 100
    Nancy A. 51
YOUNT, Catharine 234
    Louisa Jane 215
    Mary M. C. K. 216

YOURY, Mary Jane 109
ZEAGLER, Rebeca 91
ZEIGLER, Miss C. M. 184
    Miss D. E. 101
    J. A. 53, 84
    M. 74
    Martha 183
ZIEGLER, Catharine 124
    Joseph A. 26
ZIGLAR, J. 226
    J. A. 217
    Jas. 184
ZIGLER, J. A. 38
    James A. 37, 61
    Joseph 114
---, Eliza A. 50
---, Elizabeth B. 193

256

www.ingramcontent.com/pod-product-compliance
Lightning Source LLC
Chambersburg PA
CBHW072100020426
42334CB00017B/1584